Masters of Repetition

Poetry, Culture, and Work in Thomson, Wordsworth, Shelley, and Emerson

Lisa M. Steinman

St. Martin's Press
New York

ISBN 0-312-21141-4

Library of Congress Cataloging-in-Publication Data to be found at the Library of
Congress

Permissions

Macmillan Press Ltd. has granted permission to reprint a revised form of Lisa
Steinman's chapter, "These Common Woes: Repetition and Conversation in the
Work of Percy Bysshe Shelley" from Blank (ed): *The New Shelley.*

Modern Language Association has granted permission to reprint a revised form of
Lisa Steinman's essay, "'A Power Friendly Virtue': On Teaching 'The Ruined Cot-
tage'" *Approaches to Teaching Wordsworth's Poetry,* pages 100–103.

Northeastern University has granted permission to reprint a revised form of Lisa
Steinman's essay, "From *Alastor* to *The Triumph of Life:* Shelley on Nature and
Source of Linguistic Pleasure," which appeared in its earlier form in *Romanticism
Past and Present 7* (1983): 23–26.

Internal design and typesetting by Letra Libre

First published: March, 1998
10   9   8   7   6   5   4   3   2   1

. . . Perhaps,
The man-hero is not the exceptional monster,
But he that of repetition is most master.

—Wallace Stevens, "Notes toward a Supreme Fiction"

A Poet only to myself, to men
Useless . . .

—William Wordsworth, Prelude 10.199–200

Nor would I be a Poet—
It's finer—own the Ear—
Enamored—impotent—content—
The License to revere,

—Emily Dickinson, No. 505

Publication—is the Auction
Of the Mind of Man—

—Emily Dickinson, No. 709

Contents

Preface

When I first began this project I thought of it as analogous to the short film feature, "Bambi Meets Godzilla," only my version was "Poetry Meets the Modern Age." In both literary and academic circles these days, there is much talk about how infrequently poetry is read or taught, and I was interested in how poetry first came to be seen as a marginal genre. As I continued my study, however, it became clear to me that poetry, unlike Bambi, was not so easily crushed and that my book, unlike the film, would get past the opening credits as I was forced to think more deeply about what came to constitute British and Anglo-American poetry after it entered the world of mass markets, mass audiences, and modern print culture. While I do not offer my study as a master narrative, nor wish to prescribe any particular canon or school of poetry by my choice of poets, I do think that what I have to say is widely relevant, not least in trying to document how the relationship between poetry and history is complex, rooted in local detail and thus different in different circumstances. Indeed, I would like to think my study might be of use to contemporary poets who continue to struggle with ways of defining why poetry matters. As my final chapter suggests, the details of what is valued in poetry and how poems might matter in more than literary history will change in different cultural contexts, but the answers to questions about poetry's aesthetic or political value will not be forged in isolation . . . nor will they be easy answers. And I would suggest that many of the problematic aspects of poetry remain constant, including the fact that most people who sit down to write poetry want not simply to change the world or to change their readers; they want to be poets, however that subject position is locally defined.

My narrative then, like poetry itself, looks at both history and literary history. In part my story is about the deeply intertextual nature of poetry in its materiality—about how literary tradition itself is a cultural entity and thus about how what individual writers since the early eighteenth century could hear or imagine as poetry was (and is) transmitted culturally. This is why I concentrate on writers whose work had a widespread impact on their peers or on the next generation of poets. I have chosen to focus on Thomson,

Wordsworth, Shelley, and Emerson because these writers allow me to trace clearly the formation of their sense of poetry in relationship to one another's work. However, my story is not just about poetic tradition, but also about the reconfigurations of traditional tropes and discourses in different historical periods, about the interaction of history and literary history, which is why the writers I discuss are also those who had political ambitions for their poetry and so were deeply, overtly self-conscious about readerly interventions—that is, about what it meant not just to position themselves as poets, but also to place poems in public circulation. I argue that at least from the early eighteenth century—as the sociology of literature, of print culture, and of readers changed—the various contexts in which poems live (literary, historical, and in historically located readers) have not rested easily together. This is not, on my argument, a problem to be solved so much as a fact that is too often ignored or repressed, a fact that, once acknowledged, makes reading and writing poems both more vexed and more interesting than might otherwise be the case.

Over the course of this study I've incurred debts to many people and institutions without whose support this book would not have been written. I would like to thank The Rockefeller Foundation; The National Endowment for the Humanities; Howard and Jean Vollum, for a Vollum Award; and Reed College, both for financial support and for the chance to work with some impressive students who helped forge and refine much of my thinking for this book. Portions of this book first appeared, in earlier versions, in the following journals or books, which I would like to thank for permission to reprint: *ELH; Romanticism Past & Present; Approaches to Teaching Wordsworth* (New York: Modern Language Association); and *The New Shelley*, ed. Kim Blank (New York and London: Macmillan). Many individuals provided me with ideas, encouragement, and inspiration, from those with whom I first studied the poets I discuss here—including Susan Morgan, who first introduced me to and taught me to think about Shelley's work; Neil Hertz; and Reeve Parker—to those generous with their time later on: William Ray, Kate Nicholson, William Galperin, Julie Ellison, John Michael, Vernon Shetley, Catherine Labio, Michael Foley, John Marshall, and Christopher Newfield, among others. Jim Shugrue deserves a special acknowledgment for his stubborn, sustaining belief in the power of poetry and his willingness to listen endlessly but not passively even to half-formed ideas about poetry. I suspect it is obvious that I have not followed all the good advice I was offered and that what faults remain here are my own.

Introduction

Their human names, have into phantoms passed
Of texture midway between life and books

—Prelude 3.580–81

Many critics have discussed how definitions of poetry and poetic imagination shifted between the eighteenth and early nineteenth centuries in England.[1] Others, though fewer, note the continuity of romantic and eighteenth-century poetry.[2] These views need not be mutually exclusive, however. In this study, I examine in particular ideas of poetic power, looking at the responses of four influential eighteenth- and nineteenth-century writers to the problems posed on the one hand by inherited literary models and on the other hand by contemporary cultural changes. I discuss Thomson's career, Wordsworth's writings from 1790 to 1815, and selections from Shelley's as well as Emerson's writings because they so clearly show all four writers' overt concern about how they might connect poetry with contemporary public or political issues even as the modern world was changing the very definitions of the words "public" and "political." I also chose the particular poets and texts I discuss here because they allow me to trace something like a game of literary "gossip," in which Thomson's echoes of Milton and the classics are reechoed by Wordsworth, who in turn sets the terms of a dialogue variously confronted and entered by both Shelley and Emerson.

This dialogue between generations of poets was complicated by changing views of past literature, including an emerging consciousness of the literary past as an institution. It was not just the appearance of a literary canon that posed a challenge to poets in this period, however. There was also the rise of a new class of readers, whose tastes were fostered by the periodicals and, later, novels of the day and who swelled the subscription lists that mark the shift from private patronage toward a new, mass dissemination of literature.

The whole structure by which poets were read and supported was not the same structure within which past readers and poets had worked. The problem was not simply how to matter in a public setting; there were changes in what counted as public and who constituted the public. Poets faced the question of how to place their work within a tradition of literary power, while at the same time trying to envision their writing as a form of productive and effective public action in a world that was rapidly redefining both literary tradition and concepts such as *action, public,* and *power.*

The "anxiety of influence" I explore thus is not primarily a Bloomian anxiety about individual predecessors but rather an anxiety occasioned by cultural changes, including the new consciousness of poetic tradition as an increasingly fixed cultural entity, and so as a closed structure.[3] I hope to offer both new insights on specific writers and a way of approaching poetry and poetics that focuses on writers' attempts to ground poetic vision and the power of the self in literary history and, at the same time, to claim poetry's power in the present, that is, in history proper.

What poets mean when they refer to poetry's power is not self-evident. While definitions of poetic power shifted as cultural conditions changed, all four of the poets on whom this study focuses attempted to align poetry with what they called power, variously defined as literary seductiveness or as moral, rhetorical, or political authority. James Thomson, for instance, looked back to earlier poets and called for a contemporary poet "of equal power," in part defining such poets as those having the ability to move readers with theological or moral insights drawn from some higher "Parent-Power."[4] At the same time, Thomson linked poetic power with political power, even as he implicitly betrayed a fear that to be like earlier poets of higher vision might entail resting outside what his culture considered active, effective power.

More explicitly than Thomson, and partly in response to him, William Wordsworth, in his first writings, re-envisioned poetry as a form of direct political action, capable of influencing legislative reforms, as well as possessing a more internalized "power to virtue friendly."[5] While Wordsworth later retreated from his early representations of poetry's ability to affect public policy directly, he nonetheless continued to focus on questions of how poetry might be defined in a way that grounded poetic power in larger, extraliterary structures. Both Wordsworth's early optimism and his later retreat were confronted in Percy Bysshe Shelley's defense of poets as *unacknowledged* legislators serving an *inner* "power," a power Shelley linked with imaginative desire and defined as the force behind both poetic and political action.[6] Finally, the British poets' attempts to define poetry's power in the context both of the literary tradition they inherited and the larger culture in which they wrote influenced American writers. Ralph

Waldo Emerson, for example, who often cited Wordsworth's poetry as a model of literary seductiveness, felt as Shelley did that the older poet had too constricted a notion of what poets could accomplish in the larger, more culturally valued world of public action. Emerson concludes a late journal entry with the statement that his "quarrel with poets [Wordsworth in particular] is that they do not believe in their own poetry," specifically, that they do not connect their poetic images with "history natural & civil."[7] The question the four writers in this study pose is whether poetry has a social or political role, and what that role might be. As I will argue, although none of these poets finally offered a wholly compelling account of how to reconcile traditional representations of literary power with more contemporary definitions of power as rhetorical, moral, or political effectiveness, their poetry was nonetheless fueled by their resistance to the separation of writing from cultural definitions of public action.

Let me illustrate with Thomson's *The Seasons,* by way of John Berryman's ode to Thomson in which Berryman worries that to follow Thomson involves losing "his place (in the book) and each thing that/ever he valued. He'll lose his minstrelsy."[8] A study of Thomson suggests Berryman is right to call attention to the relationship between displacement and loss of poetic power in Thomson's writing: although the early preface to "Winter," for example, invokes an uneasy marriage of divine and natural inspiration, Thomson's claim to enter the company of those who have been so inspired is accompanied by a tacit recognition that he does not have access to the authority he desires.

Thomson's doubts about his own authority can be seen in the often commented upon abrupt shifts of scene in his poetry, which present a series of falls into self-consciousness about the derivative nature of his poetic vision. The passage from "Summer" describing the speaker's discomfort under the glaring sun (l. 432 ff.) is exemplary. Thomson's speaker projects a dreaming figure under a tree, by means of which he envisions a pastoral landscape, including a further sleeping figure—a Spenserian "monarch-swain" (l. 494). The two reclining figures are both naturalized (though literary) emblems of virtue and of the act of poetic projection from which they arise. Yet from this point in the poem, Thomson's poetic subject—both in the sense of the thematic concerns of the poem and in the sense of the implied controlling poetic consciousness—gets out of hand; the grammar of the passage, like the cattle and horse described in it, runs amok, and the images become insistently and self-consciously Miltonic. The reverie is then suddenly terminated (l. 516) and replaced by a vision (reported in the past tense) of former poets conversing with angels in an Edenic landscape. Thomson's vision is not of Eden but of others whose inspiration was more direct and less problematic than his own; his visions are presented in language authorized by earlier literature, not by divine inspiration nor by the natural world he claims merely to describe, and still less by the present—commercial and industrial—world that elsewhere Thomson views in typically Augustan terms as a corruption of the past.

Thomson also, however, aligns poetic power with political power, explicitly in *The Seasons* and *The Castle of Indolence* in his praises of British military might and his suggestion that poets might help forge a public consensus that would serve the national interest, implicitly in his suggestions throughout his writings that gentlemanly (and poetic) country retirement produces those with the political vision and wisdom the nation requires to exercise its strength effectively. At the same time, Thomson further (and confusedly) implies that country seats may place statesmen and poets outside of the increasingly urban centers of political decision making. Moreover, he warns that expansive power, while necessary for poetry as traditionally defined, may be dangerous in the public forum. Given contemporary definitions of active power and inherited representations of poetic vision, as well as his view of literary tradition as a closed structure, Thomson is unable in the long run to locate a source of present poetic power. Indeed, his poems are constituted of his struggle, even his failure, to define the unique source and end of his poetic inspiration.

I begin my study, then, with a close reading of Thomson's "Summer" as well as with some attention to the whole of *The Seasons,* "Liberty," and *The Castle of Indolence.* Also, in passing, I offer readings of the work of other writers from Finch to Collins in order to trace how changes in the readership and distribution of poetic texts and in the configuration of political power in England rendered traditional images of poetic power problematic for Thomson and his contemporaries, who became increasingly self-conscious about the nature, if not the source, of their inability to represent the contemporary usefulness of their activity while still sounding to themselves like poets.

In my second chapter, I discuss the eighteenth-century roots of Wordsworth's poetry, arguing in particular that the dreaming figure in retirement with which the 1799 version of *The Ruined Cottage* opens is the central image behind Wordsworth's poem and is a conscious repetition of earlier poems, most specifically Thomson's "Summer." More explicitly than Thomson, Wordsworth makes his repetition of the past and his related fictionalization of the self an enabling force in his poem. Like Thomson, Wordsworth is concerned with perception, with the limits of physical vision, with poetic vision, and with human community. However, the first full text of *The Ruined Cottage* begins with a quotation from Burns emphasizing that Wordsworth will not strain to hear angelic voices. As "A Letter to a Friend of Robert Burns" suggests, the strategy attributed to Burns is what allows

Wordsworth to revise "Summer," avoiding the earlier poet's felt loss of poetic authority: "Burns avail[s] himself of his own character and situation in society, to construct out of them a poetic self . . . for the purpose of . . . recommending his opinions, and giving point to his sentiments."[9] Wordsworth here correlates moral authority with the construction of a poetic self. Moreover, the complex narrative structure of Wordsworth's poem shifts readers away from the image of the poet as solitary seer to the image of the poet as storyteller, one whose stories are passed on to others to retell. In this way the poem readdresses the problem of the source and ends of poetic power, as Wordsworth redefines power, and in particular poetry's "power to virtue friendly." In other words, Wordsworth explores poetic power in the terms set for him by predecessors such as Thomson but ultimately uses his characters to redefine, by humanizing, the issues that plagued Thomson; Wordsworth's poet figure's claim to power in the present rejects "idle dream[ing]" (l. 231), the activity of the reclining Thomsonian dreamer; the power claimed ultimately, if uneasily, resides in the activity of storytelling. Wordsworth thereby inverts Thomson's self-conscious gaze and shows that claiming the power to narrate one's self (or to create the self in a fiction) is a form of authority, a way of turning a closed past into presence and opening—in the telling of the poem—a place where people can dwell, temporarily.

The Ruined Cottage, by insisting on the presence of narration, claims the minstrelsy Thomson felt he could not find. At the same time, though, Wordsworth wants to claim more for the power of poetry than his narrative sustains: he insists that poetry has moral power, and yet his poet-figure is unable to help the woman whose story he tells; the comfort and human community projected are felt only as human history is told and retold, forging a bond between the poet, the narrator who retells the poet's story, and the reader who is implicitly invited to make the story his or her own. The power Wordsworth claims is marked as a pure creation of words in the same world of words in which Thomson felt lost. Ironically, then, *The Ruined Cottage* reinscribes Thomson in a tradition and here, perhaps, makes most convincing its claim for poetic power over the past even as it underlines the radical gap between what it would claim and what it can claim.

I conclude the second chapter with an examination of the degree to which Wordsworth's views had changed by 1814 when he published *The Excursion.* As the historian E. P. Thompson has pointed out, discussing the situation in England in the late nineties, Wordsworth's early claims for poetic power were made in the face of growing disillusionment with the political world, and yet Wordsworth maintained an insistence on poetry's power in more than literary history insofar as *The Ruined Cottage* is a text against war.[10] Thompson's argument, that Wordsworth later defaulted in rewriting his poem as *The Excursion,* has been countered by critics such as William

Galperin who argue that *The Excursion*'s revisions mark Wordsworth's explicit and modern realization that the gap between self and community, inspiration and real power, is not easily bridged.[11] This latter argument depends, however, on reading *The Ruined Cottage* as more purely romantic and less problematic than I argue it is. If the earlier poem already, though tacitly, underlines the provisional and performative nature of the power it claims, then *The Excursion* represents neither a new tough-mindedness nor a default but Wordsworth's reiteration of his own past vision, an activity also evident in other work done between 1791 and 1804 as Wordsworth confronted a rapidly changing world. *The Excursion* is an attempt to foreclose further repetitions; however, *The Ruined Cottage* similarly insists on the adequacy—and a blindness to the provisionality—of the poem's power. As Thomson already illustrates, it is difficult to write with a clear-sighted foreknowledge of the limits of the poetic enterprise.

My third chapter argues that Shelley's critique of Wordsworth may best allow readers to see the problems involved in the dynamic described above, as Shelley marks yet more explicitly the tension between the sources, the claims for, and the necessarily frustrated ends (in practical terms) of poetic work. As *The Ruined Cottage* replaces Thomson's dreaming swain with Wordsworth's projected poet-storyteller, so poems from Shelley's *Alastor* volume address and revise Wordsworth's work in *The Excursion* (repeating Wordsworth's own revisions of *The Ruined Cottage* and of Thomson). Shelley's readings of Gothic novels (and of their readership) also informed his theories on the power of lyric as opposed to the power of narrative. Presenting a tale told by an unreliable narrator, "Alastor," in particular, calls into question whether story-telling per se affords the kind of power to affect readers or listeners Wordsworth tried to claim for it. Shelley suggests instead that poetic desire is for some pure, untroubled communion with others and, ultimately, for an embodiment of the source of desire, which entails a spiral of self-consciousness leading to a place where words fail, as described in Shelley's "Essay on Life." And yet the failure to pursue the course of such desire curtails language and its potential to effect change even more abruptly, as when in Shelley's last poem, "The Triumph of Life," Rousseau quenches his thirst prematurely and has his thoughts "[t]rampled . . . into the dust of death" (l. 388).[12]

In 1815, this dust, this dryness, a function of abandoning the search for origins and originality as well as for human community, is Shelley's diagnosis of Wordsworth's ailment, using Wordsworth's own pronouncements on those "whose hearts are dry as summer dust" to condemn the "dull" older poet, who had first seemed to Shelley to embody the ideal of the engaged poet and to offer the possibility of a poetic community. Yet, just as "The Triumph of Life" balances itself between heaven and hell, blinding itself to the true end of imaginative desire already traced in "Alastor," so too "Alastor" reenacts, most explicitly in its framing structure, the uncertainties and self-narration that already inform *The Ruined Cottage;* in this process "Alastor" provides the most self-conscious of claims for poetic power, while at the same time suggesting the futility of inscribing anything that might reliably be termed a unique poetic self. Many of Shelley's poems also make clear, however, that to reenact this futile quest, even for Thomson, is to allow poetry. As Wallace Stevens writes in "Notes toward a Supreme Fiction," it may be that the poet "is not the exceptional . . . /But he that of repetition is most master."[13]

As I argue in the final chapter, repetitions of the past (even one's own past) and the narration of the self as a source of power are common, if double-edged, responses to the powerlessness felt by modern poets; these strategies for empowerment are not limited to English poetry. Despite the arguments of critics who maintain that American and English romanticism cannot be compared, I suggest that the perceived inadequacy of language when addressing the present and an overwhelming vision of past power reappear in American literature.[14] Indeed, Milton, Thomson, and Wordsworth were part of the poetic heritage of American writers; most significantly, Thomson's poem was a favorite of men such as Thomas Jefferson (who carried a copy of *The Seasons* in his pocket). America imported English commonplaces about poetic power, commonplaces that rested even more uneasily in America than in England. Thomson's poem in particular bespoke, if unclearly, a relationship between poets and practical men. American poets' admiration (and repression) of practical power, seen as the prerogative of earlier generations, presented them with the same problems that in a different guise are at the center of much eighteenth- and nineteenth-century English poetry; namely, the problem of how to ground poetic vision and the power of the poet in some larger, preexisting structure while still defending poetic work as a form of present, productive labor.

Following his own prescription, and given his place in American literature, Emerson can be taken as a representative American romantic. He had access not only to an Americanized Thomson, but also to Wordsworth's response to Thomson. Like both Wordsworth and Shelley, Emerson had an acute awareness of how novels posed the challenge of incorporating social facts into literature. Like Shelley, Emerson was also aware of a changing readership for poetry. Without denying that American writers faced some unique problems or that American literary predecessors are as important as English predecessors for later American writers, my discussion of Emerson shows how American writing shares with contemporary English writing the need to ground poetic vision in a larger, authorizing structure; the difficulty of finding such a structure without being subsumed by it; and the obsession with the relationship between poetic and practical power even while associating dreaming with poetic integrity.[15] Emerson's "search after power" and his turn to the narration of the self are variations on the repeated turn to the presence of narrative in order to reclaim power and to insert the self into what Diderot calls "the great scroll of history."[16] Shelley's and Emerson's common structural solutions to the problems posed by inherited models of poetic power coupled with common feelings of present powerlessness support later views of Emerson as "a sort of Yankee Shelley" (1897).[17]

I hope that the interpretations I offer suggest that how (and why and which) past literary works are brought into any present culture will change over time as well as differ from culture to culture. I make no claim here to have found an exclusive, let alone a global or universal, paradigm, although I do propose that all modern poetry could profitably be considered as looking both to a literary past and to an historical present.[18] At the same time, I am aware of how my attempts to understand poems in terms of both literary history and their authors' lived historical experiences necessarily retrace—at the same time that they reveal the lacunae within—the narratives provided by the writers with whom I am in dialogue. In other words, these are the writers by whom my own ear has in part been trained, and my interest in how the public role of poetry has been described in the past is tacitly a contemporary interest, my own act of looking back, from the context of the late twentieth century.

Chapter I ▩

Milton's Evening Ear: Displacement and Loss of Minstrelsy in the Work of James Thomson (1700–1748)

The Man . . . who Learns or Acquires all he Knows from Others, Must be full of Contradictions.

—Blake's *"Notes to Reynolds's* Discourses"

Past Voices and Present Visions in *The Seasons*

As the critic Alan Dugald McKillop argues, an "age must give an artist a sufficient occasion, a program by which to work, or at least, to put it in the lowest terms, a pretext."[1] The eighteenth century posed problems for its artists, and especially its poets, in part because it was an age in which the literary program was being rethought and in which, as I shall argue, there were numerous, often conflicting, programs by which to work.[2] This chapter, which begins with a close reading of a passage from "Summer" by James Thomson, explores the pressures that informed and shaped the work of one of the most widely read poets of the eighteenth century, the period when Britain entered what historians call the modern age. In particular, I hope to show how specific historically located changes made it difficult for Thomson to describe convincingly the function and nature of poetry especially given that he inherited ideas and voices from poets who wrote in quite different cultural contexts, yet whose work allowed him to hear his own voice as poetry. I am thus also interested in how the *topoi* that marked high poetry—or poetic power—for someone like Thomson were refigured in light of changes in literary production and readership, as well as in light of socioeconomic change in Britain. My argument focuses on how Thomson struggled to redefine poetry's role and status on two fronts; he engaged both current events and a newly solidified literary tradition in which he hoped to place himself, even as the world in and for which he wrote seemed to have changed the criteria for literary achievement.

Thomson himself, in his 1726 preface to "Winter," suggests that the measure of poetry had been set by earlier writers, and that he hopes to find a contemporary poetry "of equal power." The use of the word "power," as I trace it in this book, is slippery. In 1726, Thomson is most obviously using the word to describe literary prowess and the ability of literature to move and impress its readers. Yet Thomson's descriptions of the sources of poetic power often conflate the literary with not only the theological and moral, but also with the political, as when he identifies the "Queen of [British] Arts" as a source of "Liberty" and proposes that the muse authorizes not only poetry but also "wealth," "Property," and military power ("Summer," ll. 1442–70). On the one hand, this conflation is one of the sites of Thomson's anxiety over the fact that contemporary literary power did not seem to him to result in or be informed by the kind of political influence he thought characterized earlier poetry.[3] On the other hand, Thomson drew on contemporary political discourse and, indeed, partly for this reason became in his turn a figure of effective power as well as of literary fame for future writers, some of whom would view Thomson much as Thomson himself viewed figures such as Milton and Spenser.

Thomson's poetry is in fact a pastiche of borrowings from literary and extraliterary texts, most often from Virgil and Milton, although his contemporaries do not seem to have found his use of verbal echoes problematic.[4] On the contrary, reviews from the twenties and thirties suggest that contemporary critics found Thomson obscure rather than derivative, while supporters praised his originality.[5] By 1753, Joseph Warton, in the dedication of his edition of Virgil to Sir George Lyttelton, wrote that after the Roman poet "every succeeding painter of rural beauty (except THOMSON in his *Seasons*) hath copied his images from [Virgil], without ever looking abroad upon the face of nature themselves [*sic*]. And thus a set of hereditary objects has been continued from one poet to another."[6] Warton's diplomacy admittedly takes into account Lyttelton's friendship with Thomson (who had died only a few years earlier), but the view is widely echoed, as in John Aiken's 1778 essay, often printed and bound with *The Seasons,* in which Aiken explicitly exempts Thomson when writing that the "scarcity of originals . . . is universally acknowledged and lamented, and the present race of poets are thought particularly chargeable with this defect."[7]

Nonetheless, a close reading of the first third of "Summer"—especially the twelve verse paragraphs (ll. 432–606) often singled out as exemplifying the poetic strain that marked *The Seasons* as sublime to later readers— suggests that Thomson was acutely aware of his own echoes of earlier poets.[8] Such a reading can show how Thomson internalized Milton's poetry in particular, and suggest how his contemporaries could hear such echoes and still understand Thomson's poetry as nonderivative. Before reading specific passages in detail, however, I want to comment briefly on the genre—and ambitions—of the poem as a whole.

In 1778 Aiken characterized "Summer" as "a season which . . . does not admit of any strongly-marked gradations, [so that Thomson] has comprised the whole of his description within the limits of a single day, pursuing the course of the sun from its rising to its setting. A Summer's day is, in reality, a just model of the entire season."[9] As Aiken intimates, both *The Seasons* and, by synecdoche, "Summer" were read as epic in scope and unity of theme—perhaps, to draw on Addison's contemporary definition of epic, even in greatness of theme.[10] Moreover, eighteenth-century critics consistently used Miltonic epic as a kind of touchstone. For example, Samuel Johnson felt called upon to announce that Thomson's "blank verse is no more the blank verse of Milton or of any other poet than the rhymes of Prior are the rhymes of Cowley."[11] In other words, Johnson saw that the poem would call Milton to mind even as he rejected the comparison. Similarly, Swift wrote of *The Seasons*, "I am not over-fond of them, because they are all Description, and nothing is doing, whereas *Milton* engages me in Actions of the highest Importance."[12] In short, from the time of the poem's publication even readers who decided the question negatively were moved to consider whether or not *The Seasons* could be read in light of *Paradise Lost*.

Such references to Miltonic epic suggest that *Paradise Lost* functioned as a measure of high seriousness and poetic accomplishment, especially for longer poems.[13] Internally, there are also obvious ways in which Thomson's poem is a kind of displaced epic.[14] "Summer" first proclaims its relationship to English epic and romance when it opens with an announcement of its proposed subject followed by a traditional invocation to the muse, notably to a highly selective and solitary Miltonic or Spenserian muse (foreshadowing William Collins's Fancy, who, in "Ode on the Poetical Character," to "few the godlike gift assigns/To gird their blessed prophetic loins,/And gaze her visions wild, and feel unmixed her flame!" [ll. 20–22][15]). Thomson writes, "Come, Inspiration! from thy hermit-seat,/By mortal seldom found: may fancy dare,/From thy fixed serious eye and raptured glance/Shot on surrounding Heaven, to steal one look/*Creative of the poet, every power/Exalting* to an ecstasy of soul" (ll. 15–20, emphasis added). Thus Thomson announces his daring, his aspiration to equal Milton in poetic power.

The 1744 and 1746 editions of the poem then move to a dedication to its patron, followed by a "reflection on the motion of the heavenly bodies," followed in turn by a description of the dawn, morning, and noontime activities of a rural village, with some brief digressions, including one on insect life and on microscopic creatures (ll. 236–351).[16] A first reading of this section of the poem suggests that Swift was right; the passage falls short of the "ecstasy of soul" originally invoked, although Thomson ends his description of rural Britain's "simple scene" (l. 423) by insisting that British power (including the political power that "hangs o'er Gallia's humbled coast" [l. 430]) is based on the agrarian economy he portrays.

Yet Thomson also inserts a second invocation, to nature, within his description of dawn. The passage appears as a digression, given that his prefatory argument does not emphasize the second invocation in which Thomson cautions that his theme, and even his poetic flights, will be closer to the ground than Milton's. The invocations and the digression on British power have in common that they notify the reader of the contemporary importance of the pastoral scenes described. That is, the digressions self-consciously acknowledge that readers such as Swift, trained by Milton, will wonder what "is doing."[17] Aiken suggests as much when he reads the digression on insects as Thomson's successful attempt "to enliven the silent and drooping scenes" of the season's monotony.[18] Finding many of the digressions on moral subjects "more abrupt and unartful," Aiken further suggests that Thomson does not always convincingly link his statements of moral purpose to the poetry in which they are embedded.[19] At least the digressions just mentioned, then, mark the need to provide a moral and intellectual rationale for readers who could not otherwise be counted on to see how Thomson's project was both relevant to contemporary British life *and* aligned with Milton.

Thomson's apparent need to pause in order to define and defend his project suggests that the poem is not simply attempting to impose familiar poetic pastoral landscapes, traditionally affiliated with Whig and Country party politics, on a changed contemporary reality.[20] Indeed in "Summer" Thomson reveals his own and his readers' sense that his poem is not easily identified as a familiar poetic gesture derived from Miltonic epic, even though poetry such as Milton's set the terms by which poetry was seen to insert itself within the canon of literary greatness in the present. In short, the issue is not simply how the traditional tropes of landscape description might rest uneasily with political "reality," but also how to place contemporary writing within a tradition of literary power, while trying at the same time to envision poetry as a form of productive and effective public action in the present.[21]

To pursue the example of Thomson's second invocation, the immediate impetus is provided by a description of the sun; Thomson asks "may I sing of thee?" (l. 96) and then presents a personified sun, "Parent of Seasons" (l. 113). The invocation proper begins with the following: "How shall I then attempt to sing of Him/Who, Light Himself, in uncreated light/Invested deep, swells awfully retired?" (ll. 175–77). Finally, the poet concludes that he need not directly sing of God, since the book of Nature already proclaims divine power:

> To me be Nature's volume broad displayed;
> And to peruse its all-instructing page,
> Or, haply catching inspiration thence,
> Some easy passage, raptured, to translate,
> My sole delight; as through the falling glooms
> Pensive I stray, or with the rising dawn
> On fancy's eagle-wing excursive soar.
> (ll. 192–98)

Thomson's flight is not the Miltonic gesture that the first invocation might have suggested: first, Thomson's "rapture" or "inspiration" has already been defined in the body of the poem, as in these lines, as the translation of "easy passages," rather than the pursuit of things "unattempted yet in Prose or Rhyme" (*Paradise Lost*, I. l. 16); second, while Milton defines his ambitions vertically, rejecting any "middle flight" (I. l. 14), Thomson specifically defines his flight as "excursive," which is to say a short, pleasurable outing, or varied and digressive. While "excursive" can also carry connotations of "going beyond fixed bounds," it suggests here a horizontal rather than a vertical sweep. Most startlingly, Thomson echoes—and establishes his distance from—Milton's invocation to light, which opens the third book of *Paradise Lost:* "Hail, holy Light, offspring of Heav'n first-born . . . May I express thee unblam'd?" Thomson repeats Milton's question: "How shall I then attempt to sing of Him?" (l. 175), and Thomson's answer is both an invocation of and an answer to Milton.

The earlier poet writes of blindness in his invocation: "Thus with the Year/*Seasons return, but not to me* returns/Day, or the sweet approach of Ev'n or Morn,/Or sight of vernal bloom, or Summer's Rose,/Or flocks, or herds" (ll. 40–44, emphasis added). Finally, Milton invokes a higher light, hoping to "*see and tell/Of things invisible* to mortal sight" (ll. 54–55, emphasis added). Thomson insists he can see and write of just what Milton could not attempt: the seasons. Yet it is clear that at the same time Thomson thus insists on the importance and originality of his poetry of the eye, his ear is still attuned to his predecessor, in whose line he purposefully places his own work.

All echoes of past poetry in "Summer" are not so obviously purposeful. As Cowper writes, advising a friend in 1782 to educate a son by having the boy memorize Milton, "The sooner the ear is formed . . . the better."[22] Thomson's ear was similarly formed, and his education probably accounts for the subtler echoes of earlier poets in passages like the digression on insects. Yet the way in which echoes are used also clearly places the poem in dialogue with the English tradition. The passage on insects, which Thomson expanded in 1744 by transferring over thirty lines from "Spring," describes various insects seen and heard: "Nor undelightful is the ceaseless hum/To him who muses through the woods at noon" (ll. 282–83). The passage added in 1744 comments on microscopic life—that which is invisible—and the digression ends with praise to God for the *limits* of vision, with a final note on how, like insects in winter, the men who "pass/An idle summer life" will be stricken "from the book of life" (ll. 346–47; 351). The poem then returns to its description of a rural day with a new verse paragraph that opens, "Now *swarms* the village o'er the jovial mead" (l. 352, emphasis added). The entire digression again announces "Summer" as a poetry of the eye and—in a way that plays defiantly against Milton's lines on seeing what is "invisible to mortal sight"—claims there is virtue in avoiding what is invisible to the eye.

The image of the swarming village, which presents Thomson's rustics as if they were insects, further suggests a distanced perspective, from on high, of the village. The shift in perspective coupled with the emphasis on the limits of physical vision also echoes earlier poetry. Milton uses a similarly distancing image of beings as insects in his simile describing the council in Hell in the first book of *Paradise Lost:*

> . . . As Bees
> In spring time, when the Sun with *Taurus* rides,
> Pour forth their populous youth about the Hive
> In clusters; they among the fresh dews and flowers
> Fly to and fro, or on the smoothed Plank,
> The suburb of thir Straw-built Citadel,
> New rubb'd with Balm, expatiate . . .
>   * * *
> . . . they but now who seem'd
> In bigness to surpass Earth's Giant Sons,
> Now less than smallest Dwarfs, in narrow room
> Throng numberless, like that Pygmean Race
> Beyond the *Indian* Mount, or Faery Elves,
> Whose midnight Revels, by a Forest side
> Or Fountain some belated Peasant sees,
> Or dreams he sees . . .
> (ll. 768–84)

The belated peasant not only links Milton's image of the insectlike fallen angels with rural life (and superstition) but also raises questions about the reliability of the human eye cast on nature, as Milton suggests his figure may only dream what he sees. Thomson's swarming village, like Milton's, has its roots in classical poetry, but as he writes later in "Summer": "Is not each great, each amiable muse/Of classic ages in [Britain's] Milton met?" (ll. 1567–68).

Spenser is also mentioned in "Summer," and Spenser too seems to lurk behind Thomson's digression on insects. The first book of the *Fairie Queene* again links rustics and insects in an heroic simile describing the Red Crosse Knight's battle with Error and her brood:

> As gentle Shepheard in sweete even-tide,
>   When ruddy Phoebus gins to welke in west,
>   High on an hill, his flocke to vewen wide,
>   Markes which do byte their hasty supper best;
>   A cloud of combrous gnattes do him molest,
>   All striving to infixe their feeble stings,
>   That from their noyance he no where can rest,
>   But with his clownish hands their tender wings
> He brusheth off, and oft doth mar their murmurings.
> (Book I, Canto i, stanza 23)

For Spenser, as for Milton, the simile reduces his poetic subject (the knight is compared to a rustic clown). Spenser thus both advises the reader that the knight has underestimated his enemy and, from a larger vantage point, again like Milton, places unaided human effort in proper perspective. Like Thomson's bird's-eye and apparently diminishing view of rural existence, which is his central subject in "Summer," Spenser's simile emphasizes the doubleness of the world's order. Both Spenser and Milton, then, like Thomson in some ways, underline the limits of human vision. But while their allegories are unified by their views of how the book of nature cannot be read without grace, Thomson's warning is simply that humans should not presume "aught was formed/In vain" (ll. 319–20). Thomson assumes what *is* seen is purposeful, without asking whether the act of seeing is itself problematic, even as he adopts Milton and Spenser's shifts of perspective, a strategy that, as used by both earlier poets, potentially undercuts his project by calling into question whether human readings of nature are reliable.

Thomson's apparent unconcern with the problematic nature of his vision is not simply a sign that such questions did not arise for him. In fact, "Summer" does implicitly address the issue of vision or sight raised by the poem's echoes and revisions of Milton and Spenser. First, for Thomson, the invisible that defines the limits of vision is deliberately a far more physical reality than either Milton's or Spenser's, a point reinforced when the passage on microbes was moved from "Spring" (the season in which Milton originally set his insects) to "Summer" to exemplify and expand Thomson's passage on physical vision (ll. 287–317). Second, when "Summer" shifts back to its primary subject, namely a rural village in summer, it seems to belittle that subject, apparently claiming by analogy that rustics, like the insects mentioned one line earlier, will not be written into "the book." As if to counter this, however, within two verse paragraphs Thomson has again interrupted his description to insist that his subject *is* important, not *sub speciae aeternitatis* in a Spenserian or Miltonic vein, but historically—precisely in "the book of life"—and in British political history. The transitions in "Summer" thus carefully place the poem in dialogue with voices from the past as the poem moves from its Miltonic invocation of light, with light redefined as part of the physical world, through a short passage on village life, to the digression on insects, which also echoes Milton, but which argues for accepting the limits of physical vision and proposes a link between a poetry of the eye and the basis of contemporary political power in Britain. The image of insects, as I have argued, infects the following two verse paragraphs on village life, prompting Thomson to return abruptly to a final and more overt defense of the importance of his subject.

Speaking of microscopic life, Thomson also writes that what escapes the unaided "*eye* of man" serves to protect the race from being "stunned with *noise*" (ll. 313, 317, emphases added). If human vision is unreliable, as Milton and Spenser imply in the passages Thomson echoes, Thomson follows Locke and counters that the limits he accepts serve a purpose. However, his shift from the visual to the aural is telling: only a kind of deliberate blindness to the way his literary allusions might affect his text can protect the poet from being overwhelmed ("stunned with noise") by his predecessors, against whom he nonetheless measures the sound and scope of his own poetry. Such "noise," then, defines *poetic* power for those whose ears were trained by Milton, but—on Thomson's own account—to concentrate on such aural resonance is to occlude the eye and so to risk being left without anything to say to contemporary British readers.

Thomson inhabited a world that had changed since Milton's day, and, whatever Thomson's intentions, the reviewers made clear that his audience often found more sound than meaning in his most Miltonic passages. Johnson—who praised Thomson's natural descriptions—nonetheless thought he included too many passages that might "be charged with filling the ear more than the mind."[23] By 1750, Voltaire would praise Thomson for not being the kind of poet "just above a fidler [*sic*], who amuses our ears,"[24] but in Britain, particularly in the twenties, many saw—or rather heard— Thomson precisely as a poet who a-mused the ears; although Thomson's critics did not say so, the muse in question was often Milton.

Two letters from Thomson to friend and fellow poet David Mallet, written just after the first appearance of "Winter" and while Thomson was working on "Summer," are relevant here. In the first, responding to criticisms of his poem, Thomson writes how a poet "might make a glorious Apostrophe to the drooping Genius of Britain—have Shakespear, and Milton, in [his] Eye, and invite to the Pursuit of genuine Poetry," without moving the British public, who showed contempt for poetry.[25] The second letter (which also discusses Thomson's work on "Summer") praises Mallet's "Sublimity" as being like Milton's in the following lines from Mallet's *Excursion,* published in 1728: "Or to the Cypress-Grove, at Twilight, shun'd/By passing Swains"; Thomson praises Mallet's "meritorious Theft" in another line and approvingly comments that in his friend's poem "more is meant than meets the Ear."[26]

The last comment picks up the language of Thomson's critics and emphasizes that Thomson was not content in meeting only the ears of his readers. Yet it is also clear that *Thomson's* ears, as well as his eyes, are full of Milton, as his image of apostrophizing the "drooping Genius of Britain" echoes both "Lycidas" and his own apostrophe to *"Lycidas,* the Friend" in the first published version of "Winter" (l. 298). The images from Mallet that Thomson praises—the twilight groves, the swains who recall Milton's swain and whose superstitions allowed Mallet's readers a sympathetic frisson of horror—are literary images; here, and by praising Mallet for literary theft, Thomson raises the question of what he means when he praises poems in which there is "more than meets the ear." The phrase indicates that "genuine Poetry" fills the mind as well as the ear. But the phrase also comes from Milton's "Il Penseroso," in which Milton's speaker sits by his lamp "at midnight hour" and reads "great Bards" who in "sage and solemn tunes have sung,/Of Tourneys and of Trophies hung,/Of Forests, and enchantments drear,/Where *more is meant than meets the ear*" (ll. 85; 116–20, emphasis added).[27] In "Il Penseroso" Milton is describing allegorical poetry, specifically the "tunes" of poets such as Spenser, whose narratives meant more than met the ear not simply by having meaning, but also by virtue of being allegorical.

Milton himself, assuming his "dread voice" in "Lycidas," introduced an allegory on the corruption of the church. Misreading Milton, Johnson found the poem not only lacking music and genuine emotion, which is to say failing in sensibility, but also "unskilful" and even "indecent."[28] In particular, Johnson's misreading of "Lycidas" as an untoward mixture of the sacred and the profane (rather than as a figuring of the sacred by the profane) may stem from a slightly changed understanding of allegory, which in the eighteenth century most often was identified with personification, as in Thomson's *The Castle of Indolence.*[29] Milton's "meaning," in any event, was not always clear to eighteenth-century readers. Indeed, echoing the reviewers' responses to Thomson, Cowper took issue with Johnson's criticisms of "Lycidas," not by proposing a more convincing reading of the poem's meaning, but instead by writing that Johnson had "no ear for poetical numbers"; Cowper considered Milton's later work in the same vein: "Was there ever any thing so delightful as the music of the Paradise Lost? It is like that of a fine organ."[30] In Cowper's letter, the image is of church music, or music in the service of higher things, but Cowper still defends Milton primarily on the grounds that he appeals to the ear.

Such judgments propose a curious regress. Thomson wants "more" than meets the ear. Yet the "more" to which Thomson refers is less the doubleness of allegory and more a kind of chronological layering, a layering of Milton's language in particular, referring to a passage in which Milton in turn refers his readers back to Spenser. It appears that what underlies Thomson's references to Miltonic or Spenserian allegory is more the sense of high music— of past literary power—than any literal meaning; when Thomson says he wants to invoke more than mere music, he means that he wants to invoke the music of past poets, who were themselves looking back on their predecessors. Similarly, the poetic power of some of Thomson's passages depends in part on a figuration of the poetic self in the act of looking back (to Milton, who himself looks to a genius of the shore). Thomson's poetic self, as well as his music, is thus constituted in part of a tissue of repetitions from past poetry.

Thomson's apology for poetry—the "Preface" first published with the second edition of "Winter"—reveals the complexity of his self-consciousness about his poetic predecessors. In the "Preface" Thomson argues, again emphasizing the aural, that to slight poetry is to declare "against what has charmed the *listening* world from Moses down to Milton" (emphasis added).[31] Not only is it significant that the line ends with Milton, but it is also clear, when he begins his ancestry with Moses, that Thomson views poetry as a high moral music.[32] Claiming Nature as the muse of his poetry of the eye, Thomson then proves unable to locate himself in the line of sublime poets whose music he admires; he invokes an uneasy marriage of divine and natural inspiration, yet his claim that by describing Nature he might enter the company of those who write "the peculiar language of heaven" *and* "awake . . . moral sentiment" is accompanied by an underlying recognition that he may be confirmed as a poet neither by the power of sight nor by the power of higher music.[33]

In "Summer," this anxiety is enacted and given precision as the poetic voice whose self-proclaimed muse is "parental Nature" (l. 577) attempts to claim the force of sublimity and turns out to be composed of past utterances, already written by Milton and Spenser. Again, the poetic voice claimed is mediated by the past, which is viewed as a closed book. Finally, Thomson's most "airy vision" (l. 585) is self-consciously of poet-prophets who had "higher powers" (l. 584), powers Thomson cannot claim for his own, but

against which he measures his own achievement. The passage that intro-
duces this vision—a passage often illustrated in eighteenth- and nineteenth-
century editions of *The Seasons*—helps underscore Thomson's self-conscious
relationship to past poetry:[34]

'Tis raging noon; and, vertical, the sun
Darts on the head direct his forceful rays.
* * *
In vain the sight dejected to the ground
Stoops for relief; . . .
* * *
. . . the cleaving fields
And slippery lawn an arid hue disclose,
Blast fancy's blooms, and wither even the soul.
* * *
. . . In vain I sigh,
And restless turn, and look around for night:
* * *
Thrice happy he, who on the sunless side
Of a romantic mountain, forest-crowned,
Beneath the whole collected shade reclines;
Or in the gelid caverns,
* * *
Emblem instructive of the virtuous man,
* * *
Welcome, ye shades! ye bowery thickets, hail!
* * *
Delicious is your shelter to the soul
As to the hunted hart the sallying spring
Or stream full-flowing, . . .
* * *
Cool through the nerves your pleasing comfort glides;
The heart beats glad; the fresh-expanded eye
and ear resume their watch; . . .
* * *
Rural confusion! On the grassy bank
Some ruminating lie, while others stand
Half in the flood and, often bending, sip
The circling surface. In the middle droops
The strong laborious ox, of honest front,
Which incomposed he shakes; and from his sides
The troublous insects lashes with his tail,
Returning still. Amid his subjects safe
Slumbers the monarch-swain, his careless arm
Thrown round his head . . .

* * *

Light fly his slumbers, if perchance a flight
Of angry gad-flies fasten on the herd,
That startling scatters from the shallow brook
In search of lavish stream. Tossing the foam,
They scorn the keeper's voice, and scour the plain
* * *
Oft in this season too, the horse, provoked,
While his big sinews full of spirits swell,
Trembling with vigour, in the heat of blood
Springs the high fence,
* * *
. . . quenchless his thirst,
* * *
Still let me pierce into the midnight depth
Of yonder grove, . . .
* * *
. . . all is awful listening gloom around.
These are the haunts of meditation these
The scenes where ancient bards the inspiring breath
Ecstatic felt, and, from this world retired,
Conversed with angels and immortal forms[.]
(from ll. 432–525)

   While the status of the first sheltered landscape in this passage is uncertain, the most obvious way of understanding the progress of the poem seems to be the following: the speaker (and the use of the first person singular outside of the poem's didactic digressions is unusual) moves from direct confrontation with the world—that is, from the physical vision, which the poem as a whole defends but which here is said to blast "fancy's blooms"—to a more oblique meditation on the emblem of the virtuous man whose temperance is figured in a classical landscape of retreat. The landscape that follows is then an idealized and literary interior world, where fancy does operate and where, the speaker argues, both eye and ear are renewed. What the reader "sees" in the poem, then, is less a poetry of physical vision than a poetry of thought, in that by the time the first sheltered landscape is described, readers are witnessing not a moralized landscape so much as a landscaped meditation.

   One way in which the poem signals the fact that it is not describing a literal landscape is by its use of a Miltonic rhetorical device, the nonexclusive "or," which marks the scene both as literary and as a series of entertained ideas. For example, the happy man is *either* on the shaded side of a mountain *or* in a cavern; the shade he welcomes is to the soul as a sallying spring *or* a full-flowing stream is to a hunted deer, just as Milton's fallen angels are like insects, then like pygmies *or* fairies that a belated peasant sees *or* dreams he sees. Thomson's image of a herd troubled by insects may also owe something to Spenser's and Milton's peasants with their insects. Similarly, the Virgilian image of the reclining figure in the shade, which leads to the imagined pastoral landscape with its reclining figure of the sleeping shepherd, is related to Milton's dreaming peasant (just as Collins's later image of Milton himself is of a reclining figure lying in the shade of "fancied glades" in "Ode on the Poetical Character").

In "Summer" Thomson says that the slumbering monarch-swain sleeps amid "his subjects safe." Yet Thomson's poetic subject—both in the sense of the thematic concerns of the poem and in the sense of the implied controlling poetic consciousness—does not seem so safe. More like a nightmare than an illustration of harnessed energy, the meditation gets out of control; indeed, more aptly, the grammar runs amok. Not only is it unclear whether the swain or his herds are safe, but the reader is told that the shepherd is alert lest "*perchance* a flight/Of angry gad-flies" descend.[35] While the flies are introduced conditionally, within two lines the guarded-against anarchy has as much presence in the poem as did the controlling calm: the herds "scorn the keeper's voice, and scour the plain."

From this point, images of rebellion and of desire, rather than of control, become the central emblems of the season, found in the herd's unruly quest for a "lavish stream" and in the horse's fence-leaping and "quenchless" thirst. The passage, then, contains what Thomson's contemporaries identified as the sublime. Specifically, Thomson was called sublime (though it was not always meant as a compliment) because of his "music." The *British Journal,* which mentioned Thomson's "Excellence in the Sublime-obscure," identified his style as one "which, without fettering Words with Sense or Meaning, makes a sonorous rumbling Noise";[36] similarly, Johnson, as already mentioned, charged Thomson with certain overly exuberant passages that emphasized music at the expense of meaning. In part, such criticism seems to respond to Thomson's use of blank verse, a Miltonic form Thomson himself theoretically associated with "harmony," but which in passages like the one in question is linked less with the calm, harmonized passions initially attributed to the poet in retirement and more with the sublime, or visionary passion in a Gothic setting, marked by exclamations, the piling up of nouns and epithets, as well as by the use of participles and active verbs.[37]

In light of these earmarks of the sublime, several displacements can be seen. First, the way in which the grammar, like the horse, overleaps bounds is most obviously and most self-consciously the poet and poem becoming the sublime that is drawn. The highly charged language of the poem is marked as sublime not only because of its "music," however, but also because of its echoes of Milton's Satan, who,

> At one slight bound *high overleap'd* all bound
> Of Hill or highest Wall, and sheer within [Eden]
> Lights on his feet. As when a prowling Wolf,
> Whom hunger drives to seek new haunt for prey,
> Watching where *Shepherds* pen thir Flocks at eve,
> In hurdl'd Cotes *amid the field secure,*
> *Leaps o'er the fence* with ease into the Fold
> (IV. ll. 181–87; emphasis added)

The lines underscored above are closely echoed in Thomson's passage on his shepherd sleeping "Amid his subjects safe" before the horse springs "the high fence, and, o'er the field . . . /Darts." Moreover, the image of Satan overleaping bounds was well-known, singled out by Addison in his 1712 *Spectator* paper on *Paradise Lost.*[38]

Thomson's speaker ultimately breaks sharply with what began as a description of a sheltered grove—a "shelter to the soul" (l. 472)—with its Miltonic or Spenserian swain and directly addresses the earlier poets who have informed his language and his images. The section begins with a description of a darker yet more lofty setting: "the haunts of meditation . . . where ancient bards the inspiring breath/Ecstatic felt." It is tempting to read Thomson's pastoral anarchy as a loss of poetic control—a projection of the self that has gotten out of hand—and so to read in the rejection of this anarchy a sudden self-consciousness of poetic presumption as the poet confronts his use of Miltonic and Satanic echoes. The pastoral is rejected, broken off with the line, "Still let me pierce into the midnight depth." Further, the process of envisioning the swain's landscape seems to be linked by associative logic with the ensuing awareness that the direct inspiration of earlier poets is no longer available. However, the brisk, impatient way in which the voice casts off various emblems of its own activity (from meditating man to monarch-swain to Satanic horse) might also suggest that the swain's landscape is rejected not as presumption but because it does not go far enough ("Still let me pierce"). In either case, the voice whose first meditative landscape both is and is about poetic projection terminates the reverie because the self-projection, attempting a type of sublimity, turns out to have been written by Milton and Spenser and so is unable to claim the unmediated vision attributed to earlier poets whose private visions could serve public "offices" and rouse patriotism (ll. 531–37). Thomson's shifts of scene, then, mark a series of falls into self-consciousness about the nature of his poetic vision, described in language authorized not by divine inspiration nor by the natural and political worlds he claims to describe and address, but by his literary predecessors. Even the last attempt at vision in the passage from "Summer," above, announces its secondary status: "these/The scenes where ancient bards the inspired

breath/Ecstatic *felt*, and, from this world retired,/*Conversed* with angels."
Feeling inspired, conversing with angels, are activities firmly in the past
tense. Thus again the visionary scene Thomson claims is populated by
others—by past poets—just as earlier the poetic self was constructed out of
past utterances.

Yet Thomson wanted not only to find a project that might be called his
own, but at the same time to place his poetry within the canon of earlier writ-
ers. Thomson's ancient bards, he writes, fill his ear—explicitly not the physi-
cal ear, but "the abstracted ear/Of fancy" (ll. 543–44). Thomson's
predecessors are made to say, "'Be not of us afraid,/Poor kindred man! thy
fellow-creatures, we/From the same Parent-Power our beings drew'"
(544–46). They continue, "'Then fear not us; but with *responsive* song, . . .
Of Nature sing with us'" (552, 555, emphasis added); to hear angelic voices,
they add, is "'A privilege bestow'd by us alone/On contemplation, or the hal-
low'd ear/Of poet swelling to seraphic strain'" (561–63). It is again significant
that Thomson's syntax seems to present his poetry about nature as respond-
ing not to nature but to the earlier poets whose voices he here describes as fill-
ing his ear and offering him kinship in their select company. His vision is still
not of Eden but of others whose inspiration was more direct and less prob-
lematic than his own, which is mediated by theirs (as *they*, not the angelic
voices which they heard, now bestow the privilege of poetic insight).

This vision ends, finally, in terms suggesting again how Thomson fore-
shadowed and informed later eighteenth-century poets such as Collins
whose anxiety over their own poetic project was even more explicit. Thom-
son writes,

> Thus up the mount, in airy vision rapt,
> I stray, regardless whither; till the sound
> Of a near fall of water every sense
> Wakes from the charm of thought: swift-shrinking back,
> I check my steps and view the broken scene.
>
> Smooth to the shelving brink the copious flood
>   * * *
> Dashed in a cloud of foam, it sends aloft
> A hoary mist and forms a ceaseless shower
> (ll. 585–90; 597–98)

The "near fall" that sends Thomson back to the physical world of the senses
is as much another near fall into self-consciousness as a literal cascade, espe-
cially in light of the way the passage picks up echoes of Thomson's descrip-
tion of Spenser (who, "like a copious river, poured his song" [l. 1574]) and
Milton's description of the consequences of the fall, after which Adam and

Eve, heralded by cherubim compared with "Ev'ning Mist," see the world "all before them" as they proceed down a cliff with "wand'ring steps" (XII. ll. 629, 646, 639, 648). In Milton, having the world, complete with mist, spread out before Adam and Eve is a sign of their banishment from Eden. Collins's "Ode on the Poetical Character" almost seems a gloss on Thomson's veiled image of his banishment from the Eden of previous writers: Collins makes explicit that his cliff is from Milton's Eden, and that his age, in which literary tradition is viewed as a closed structure, has "curtained [an echo of Thomson's and Milton's mists] close[d] such scenes."

Less explicitly, Thomson descends from his cliff (l. 607) with an image of birds who "Responsive, force an interrupted strain [while]/The stock-dove only through the forest coos" (ll. 614–15). The image of the birds as "responsive" echoes the visionary bards' invitation to modern poets to sing of nature with "responsive" song; the dove, the only bird whose strain is neither forced nor interrupted, echoes Milton's image of original creation in the first book of *Paradise Lost* in which Milton invokes the spirit that created the world and "Dovelike satst brooding on the vast Abyss" (l. 21). In sum, the movement of "Summer" is a seemingly endless regress in the attempt to find an immediate, present source of poetry that will nonetheless place the poem within the tradition of high poetry. Continuously, Thomson's visions (of self in the dreaming figures, of poetic power in the Edenic glade, of expulsion and return to natural description or physical sight) are presented in the language of earlier literature. In this way, Thomson ultimately presents his most visionary landscapes as secondary, that is, as not representing unmediated inspiration. Nor are they original description, either of the natural world or of the present commercial and industrial world that Thomson said he wanted to address but alternately viewed as unpoetic (though civilized) or as a corruption of the past. Ironically, when Thomson turns at last from his "broken scene," he attempts to leave the closed haunts of earlier bards and return to a poetry of the eye with a digression on the torrid zone, as if there he might find a landscape untouched, "where, retired/From little scenes of art, great Nature dwells/In awful solitude, and naught is seen/But the wild herds that own no master's stall" (ll. 701–4). Such herds may not "own" the earlier masters of poetry, but Thomson's "torrid zone" does: Milton has Michael preside over the expulsion from Eden with a sword "Fierce as a Comet; which with torrid heat,/And vapor as the *Libyan* Air adust" (ll. 634–35). The suggestion is that all parts of the contemporary world, out of and for which Thomson hoped to write a poetry equal in effect to that of the past poetry he invokes, have been marked as fallen or secondary by earlier poets in at least two ways. First, to be heard as great poetry, Thomson's language most often echoes his predecessors'; second, within the terms of Miltonic epic, all physically present or historically located landscapes are postlapsarian.

The Present Task of the Poet

The above reading of "Summer" suggests that even as Thomson sought a modern *subject matter* of importance in the historical and empirical realm (the realm of the eye and of public discourse), he heard the *language* or music associated with poetic power as the province of earlier (and given Thomson's Whig views, less enlightened) writers with whom he tried to rank himself. The language that in Milton was the voice of private inspiration still marked high poetry but also seemed obscure or suspect in the present.

Contemporary examples from other writers of this uneasy relationship between the eye and the ear are illuminating here. Throughout the century there are frequent links proposed between poetic originality and a poetry of the eye or of "real" experience. For instance, Thomas Warton, in *The History of English Poetry* (begun in 1774), examines Gawain (Gavin) Douglas's description of spring in one of his prologues to the *Aeneid* and praises the "effusion of a mind *not overlaid by the descriptions of other poets*, but operating . . . on such objects as *really* occured" (emphasis added).[39] A decade later, William Cowper proudly wrote of his poem *The Task;* "My descriptions are all from nature. Not one of them second-handed. My delineations of the heart are from my own experience. Not one of them borrowed from books."[40] A 1709 *Tatler,* however, was already making fun of pseudo-historical accuracy or exhaustive empirical description by printing parodic verses containing "a Description of the Morning; . . . of the Morning in Town; nay, of the Morning at this End of the Town."[41] Here the humor depends on the reader's acknowledgment that the contemporary historical world is not necessarily poetic (perhaps just because it is not "overlaid by the descriptions of other poets").

In a related vein, despite his ability to suggest elsewhere that poets needed only to look around them to find an unsullied vision, Joseph Warton concluded in *The Adventurer* in 1753 that imitations were an "invincible necessity and the nature of things," adding that "the first copier [i.e., in that all poets are copiers of nature] may be, perhaps, entitled to the praise of priority; but a succeeding one ought not certainly to be condemned for plagiarism."[42] Yet again a few months later, Warton insisted that the mind should "follow truth instead of authority."[43] Warton, in other words, wavers between condemnation of those who write using only the "set of hereditary objects" handed down to them and apparent acceptance of the idea that nothing new of poetic interest could be written. Thomson is then not atypical in his confused conception of poetry's relationship to both the present and the past, a past that itself appeared to define poetry as both unmediated vision ("truth") and as traditionally handed-down speech (which it thus mediated and authorized).[44]

In the 1726 preface to "Winter," Thomson asks that "poetry once more be restored to her ancient truth and purity," adding that it would take a poet "of equal power and beneficence"—equal to earlier poets, that is—to renew the contemporary "wintry world of letters."[45] Thomson's impassioned plea for the regeneration of poetry, a plea he appended to his own poetic efforts, marks his ambitions. Yet he also clearly worries that poetry cannot do well in modern times; his characterization of the world of contemporary literature as lesser and "wintry," when his own poem is entitled "Winter," suggests again his particular uncertainty about his own ability to place himself in the canon of poets he sees as having literary power.

Such uncertainty over how poetry could be original within the world of eighteenth-century Britain stems in part from the availability of earlier texts and the beginnings of literary history as a discipline. As Raymond Williams has pointed out, the very meaning of the word "literature" changed in the eighteenth century.[46] The word once meant simply what was written; only after what might be called the institutionalization of a canon did people recognize the literary in the modern sense as a distinct entity. Various publications helped to focus attention on the poetic tradition and to solidify a poetic canon. Addison's 1712 *Spectator* papers on *Paradise Lost* were perhaps the most influential writings, followed by, to cite a few examples, John Hughes's 1715 edition of Spenser, Thomas Blackwell's 1735 *Enquiry into the Life and Writings of Homer,* Bishop Robert Lowth's 1753 volume on Hebrew poetry (first presented as a lecture in 1741), Joseph Warton's 1753 edition of Virgil, his brother Thomas's 1754 work on Spenser, and Johnson's *Lives,* which appeared between 1779 and 1781.[47] Further, the end of the century saw a spate of revivals (and forgeries) of earlier primitive British writers. And by 1774, Thomas Warton had begun his three volume *History of English Poetry,* the first ancestor of our poetry anthologies and surprisingly close to such modern volumes as the *Oxford Anthology of English Literature* in its fashioning of the English canon.

Knowledge of literature as an institution seemed to banish contemporary writers from inclusion in such a structure. To cite Thomas Warton on medieval literature: "when books began to grow fashionable, and the reputation of learning conferred the highest honour, poets became ambitious of being thought scholars; and sacrificed their native powers of invention."[48] In other words, native invention or imagination diminishes as knowledge—in particular the knowledge of what has already been written—increases. Joseph Warton also noted that in no nation, "after criticism has been much studied, and the rules of writing established, has any very extraordinary work ever appeared."[49] And in "Of Eloquence," as well as in his essays on refinement and on progress, David Hume wrote that modern good sense led to inferior eloquence; to many, knowledge and rhetorical power seemed incompatible.[50] In short, the past was for the first time represented in print as a fait accompli, a closed structure the shape of which was already fixed and from which contemporary writers could feel excluded. In the face of a virtual flood of books recuperating the past, the eagerness with which primitive writers were read and the nostalgia with which unwritten poetry was regarded is not surprising.[51] While other factors clearly influenced Thomas Gray's "The Bard" or his image of a "mute inglorious Milton" in "Elegy Written in a Country Churchyard," the vision of poets who did not burden their heirs with writing and who themselves were not readers owes something to the century's feeling of being overwhelmed by, and excluded from, a literary canon. The same might be said of Thomson's image of "The Harp of Aeolus" in the celebratory "An Ode on Aeolus's Harp" and in the 1748 *The Castle of Indolence,* in which he describes a "certain music, never known before,/ . . . /Full easily obtained" (I, XL).[52] Thomson's seems to be the first use of this now-familiar image; indeed, he felt the need to add a footnote insisting that the instrument was not a figment of his imagination. In both texts, Thomson's image emphasizes the ear, or a music (not a text) obtained directly from nature without any straining after originality. Most important, his use of the image in *The Castle of Indolence* suggests the harp is an emblem of a *false* ideal of ease and unself-consciousness to which poets of his day could not in good faith aspire.

Sir Philip Sidney could write in the first sonnet of "Astrophel and Stella" that "Invention, Nature's child, fled stepdame Study's blows;/And others' feet . . . seemed but strangers in [his] way"; that is, that he needed to ignore earlier writers and "look in [his] heart" to write (a pose that itself looks back to the classics). Thomson's placement of the wind harp in his Castle of Indolence suggests he did not think modern poets *could* any longer write without study and effort. In part, as I have tried to suggest, changes in the conception and canonization of literary accomplishment, for the first time seen as a closed structure, inform Thomson's nostalgia for an original poetic music, a poetry of the ear, for which he could not find an adequate contemporary equivalent. In other words, such music—defined in terms of syntax, meter, and image—marked what Thomson could hear as powerful poetry, despite contemporary appeals to unmediated experience or unvarnished sight and despite Thomson's own association between a poetry of the eye and political power in eighteenth-century Britain. Such mixed allegiances obviously complicated ideas about precisely what modern poetry offered its contemporary readers and about the poet's public role.

The Poetic Self in Retirement

Certainly Thomson did propose ideas about what his descriptive poetry offered readers, ideas that were influential. For instance, when Cowper claimed in 1784 that his descriptions were to "recommend rural ease and leisure, as friendly to the cause of piety and virtue," he echoed Thomson, who had written in the 1746 version of "Autumn" that he "meditate[d] the book/Of Nature, ever open, aiming thence/Warm from the heart to learn the moral song" (ll. 670–72).[53] Thomson insists the salient characteristic of the book of nature is its openness, a gesture that tacitly underlines the closed nature of other canons. More explicitly, Thomson draws on Shaftesbury's speculations and eighteenth-century deism in his reference.[54] "A Hymn on the Seasons," which concluded the first complete (1730) edition of the poem, repeats this insistence that "the varied God" (l. 2) as well as moral lessons can be read from nature. Thus descriptive poetry is given a moral justification.

The justification is one Thomson's friends and contemporaries found familiar. For example, Thomas Rundle, writing to Mrs. Barbara Sandys in March of 1729 to inform her that he has entered her as a subscriber to *The Seasons,* observes that Thomson is a moral poet who "employs his muse to make virtue agreeable," adding that in the poem "Nature and its explainer, and its author are . . . joined to the praises of the Great Creator." Yet Rundle then explains that Thomson's poem is enjoyable because the poet "now and then inserts a digression of a short story, which relieves from the uniformity of the prospect, and seems as figures in the works of that sort of painters, to give life and action to what is in itself merely inanimate."[55] By 1778, John Aiken writes as if Thomson's digressions contain the poem's moral lessons, concluding of the poem that "its *business* is to describe, and the occupation of its *leisure* to teach."[56] The two responses are not identical: Aiken places the poem's moral lessons outside Thomson's readings of the book of nature and outside the central "business" of the poem. Rundle's earlier comment more uncritically accepts the idea that Thomson's natural description has a moral purpose; however, his note on the need for narrative digressions to animate the same landscapes he has just characterized as leading to the praise of God reveals a tension between deistic pieties and Rundle's actual taste.[57] In both cases, what interested these readers was not what, according to their commonplaces, was important or morally instructive about the poetry. As Thomas Warton wrote, explicitly assuming a rift between what instructed and what excited the public: "people [have always] loved better to be pleased than instructed."[58]

Thomson's own language similarly fosters confusion over the sources and ends of poetry's "moral song." He most often grounds his early poetic practice in some version of deism, with appeals to the natural sublime, drawing on overlapping if not always consistent images of the structure of the world.[59] Yet his descriptions of nature uneasily merge description and thought, which is to say external observation and internal meditation.[60] For instance, in a letter dated 27 October 1730, Thomson describes a poet as someone who "in some rural retirement, by his own intellectual fire and candle as well as natural, may cultivate the muses, inlarge [*sic*] his internal views, harmonize his passions, and let his heart hear the voice of peace and nature."[61] Although placing poetry in a rural setting, Thomson's comments on what occurs in such a setting give equal weight to self or sensibility ("intellectual fire and candle") and to nature. If anything, the structure of the sentence gives priority to inner "fire" as that which cultivates the muses. Moreover, the effects cultivated are largely internal: enlarging the imagination, harmonizing the passions, and letting the heart hear (rather than, say, letting the eyes see). Implicitly, nature's voice is "out there" to hear, and the setting is also pastoral. But Thomson seems primarily concerned with internal expansion, inner fire, and emotional response. He focuses on the psychological effects possible in such a setting. Indeed, it is not clear what the relationship is between the rural setting and the self's reveries, or how important the natural element is in Thomson's conception of the poetic self.

Similar questions are raised by other of Thomson's comments. For example, writing about one of David Mallet's poems in a letter of August 1726, Thomson praises a line of Mallet's in which fancy "Posts over Regions, like the darted Beam," commenting that "a good Imagination is pleased with this Image of itself."[62] Again, poetic activity includes natural observation (the fancy "posts over regions"). But the imagination is imaged as casting its own light-beam, like the "candle" in the 1730 letter. Further, what excites Thomson in Mallet's poem is the image of self, or rather of imagination; the emphasis once more is not on what is seen, not even on steady observation, but on the darting beam of the imagination in action. In a 1743 letter, in fact, albeit one pleading a special cause, namely that Elizabeth Young should marry him, Thomson argues that he does not need a country seat but could settle anywhere because the "Mind is it's [*sic*] own Place, the genuine Source of it's [*sic*] own Happiness."[63] The echo—which again underlines Thomson's blurred double allegiance to originality and to inscription within a tradition—is of Milton's Satan, who in Book I of *Paradise Lost* bids farewell to the "happy Fields" of heaven and claims he brings a "mind not to be chang'd by Place or Time./The mind is its own place, and in itself/Can make a Heav'n of Hell, a Hell of Heav'n" (ll. 249; 253–55).

This Satanic pose is a special case in Thomson's writings and has as much to do with his sense that Elizabeth Young, one way or another, would banish him from paradise as with any proto-Romantic poetics asserting the mind's autonomy; still—to invoke biography and psychology for a moment longer—by all accounts Elizabeth Young's "banishment" of Thomson was specifically related to his poetic profession, so that his declaration of the mind's power and the irrelevance of the external world is made by a man who is conscious of himself as both poet and suitor. And although it would be surprising, even in the most visionary poets of the forties, to find assertions of the autonomy of the individual imagination, Thomson's poetry, like his letters, nonetheless testifies to an attraction to the expansion of self—an expansiveness later clearly associated with the sublime—and a turn toward the self, a turn that emphasizes how the poetic imagination is less and less able to find an adequate external object for its feelings.[64]

In the lines from "Autumn" quoted earlier, Thomson identifies both external nature and his own heart as the source of poetry. The 1746 edition of the poem, in fact, substituted "[w]arm from the heart" for the 1730–1738 phrase "Heart-taught," the earlier phrase an even stronger image of inner authority. At the same time, theories of the sublime, drawing in part on recent translations of Longinus, did propose a relationship between external views and inner expansiveness that may have informed Thomson's double focus, although the majority of Thomson's poetic landscapes tend toward the picturesque of landscape gardening rather than drawing on set pieces of the sublime; in any event—drawing also on the concept of the association of ideas—meditation and description could in the eighteenth century go together.[65] It is in this sense that Thomson presumably understood his own descriptions of inspiration, as in his 1725 letter to William Cranstoun in which he places "Contemplation" and "the genius of [a] place" in apposition and claims that this mixture of self and place "prompts each swelling awfull thought."[66] Even so, there are unacknowledged tensions in the way Thomson varies the sources and ends he claims for his poetry; he refers his readers at times to the divine order evident in nature as described in his poems, at times to a somewhat more problematic and literary nature, at still other times to the individual creative consciousness (in the associations made by the speaker of the poem), and through that consciousness to higher spheres of "light ineffable" and "expressive Silence" (ll. 117–18).[67]

Not only does Thomson invoke an uneasy mixture of external and internal inspiration as the source (and guarantee) of his poetry, but the very status of the external and internal worlds—the status of nature and of the self—increasingly posed problems for the eighteenth century. I have already raised questions about the nature of Thomson's poetically "observed" landscapes. Thomson's contemporaries also explicitly raised the question of what constituted the observing self and in particular the poetic self. To quote from Hume's *A Treatise of Human Nature,* written in the later thirties, almost at the same time as Thomson's "Liberty," "[the] identity, which we ascribe to the mind of man, is only a fictitious one"; Hume also wrote that personal identity, the "soul," can only be known as an inconceivably rapid succession of perceptions.[68] Even earlier, and with far more public press, Locke had raised questions about the nature of the self and about what the observing self could know of the external world.[69]

Such philosophical statements were part of a mid-century fascination with individual psychology.[70] This movement, with its theological implications, was addressed by eighteenth-century religious writers from William Law to John Wesley and also was evidenced in the growing attraction to a poetry of sensibility, including an emphasis on the visionary or psychological, which in turn required new assessments of poetic power and led to attempts to ground poetic truth in felt authenticity or the self.[71] The new interest in psychology was also accompanied by a mid-century defection to the sublime or Pindaric ode; the genre was glossed by followers of Shaftesbury as well as by readings of Longinus and was seen as giving a picture of the poet's inner harmony on the one hand and of a mental or spiritual expansiveness on the other hand.[72] The ode was characterized by its verbal energy (an image of the poetic imagination in action) and by its use of landscapes (alps, ravines, and vast expanses) that were associated with the natural sublime and seen as expanding the observing self.[73] Gray's ode on poetic power, "The Bard," for example, proclaims the poet's power as much by its form and its rhetorical energy as by its story. (Gray looks back to the reign of Edward I as a time when bards were dangerous enough to be persecuted. With the advantage of historical hindsight, he allows his bard to foresee—and, by implication, call forth—Edward's end). Gray also fills the poem with images of the natural sublime; the bard at the end of the poem plunges "to endless night" off a mountaintop into a roaring stream after announcing, with a somewhat peculiar cry of triumph, "To triumph, and to die, are mine." In part following speculations on poetry and the sympathetic imagination, Gray identified his bard with himself; but skepticism over exactly what kind of self such visionary odes revealed was voiced by Gray's contemporary, Johnson, who wrote that Gray's poem "forsakes the probable" and concluded that he did not "see that ['The Bard'] promotes any truth, moral or political."[74] For Johnson, "The Bard" was too eccentric, too much a creation of an individual psychology, to contain any general psychological truth, let alone other kinds of truth.

Unlike Johnson, Thomson did not discuss his reaction to the century's growing philosophical and literary interest in individual psychology in any detail. In general, it seems that he tried to resist the dislocation of communal identity often associated with mid-century trends (ideological, psychological, economic, and political).[75] That is, the direction of Thomson's poetic development can be seen as diametrically opposed to the direction in which younger writers were moving. Poems like "Liberty" or *The Castle of Indolence* do not edge away from history or the external world toward the visionary or the purely psychological but rather treat public and historical questions more explicitly and at greater length than the issues that are addressed in Thomson's earlier work. Yet Thomson's later work is concerned with the problem of how to insert the individual self into both literal and literary history. And if in his later work Thomson's poetic self is more often located in a public setting and is less overtly self-conscious than that of Collins, Young, or Akenside, the very move to a public setting is a sign that Thomson questioned the meaning or value of the solitary poet in nature. Such questioning is not simply implied by the way Thomson wavers in his appeals to deistic views of nature even as he suggests that the (unstable) poetic self might find inspiration without any natural setting. Descriptions of solitary natural settings—the pieties of deism notwithstanding—also raised other problems about which Thomson was explicit (if ambivalent), as is especially evident in his defenses of the public role of the poet and the public ends of poetry in his day.

The first (1726) version of "Winter" places the poet in a twilight "Retreat/A rural, shelter'd, solitary, Scene" where he can "hold high Converse with the mighty Dead" (ll. 255–56; 259). In 1730, the setting of "the private virtues" is specifically identified as these "shades and plains along the smoothest stream/Of rural life" (ll. 601–3). Such passages link private virtue with retirement, the setting in which Thomson most often envisions not only virtue but visionary power. To take another example, ten years after first writing "Winter" Thomson provided a similar scene in "Liberty," which assembles a group of England's "native genii" (IV. l. 479), including "Sincerity" and "Thoughtful Power, apart"—that is, as solitary figures— near which "Retirement, pointing to the shade,/And Independence stood—the generous pair/That [prefer the] simple life, the quiet-whispering grove" (IV. l. 517ff.). The poem also notes that Independence, when forced into a "public scene" (IV. l. 535), maintains his virtue because he was nurtured by the solitude of groves and shade. Thomson characterized his personal experience in similar terms. A letter of 13 June 1926 written to David Mallet praises one of Mallet's poems: "How wild you sing, while I, here [in London], warble like a City-Linnet, in a Cage."[76] And a late (1748) letter to William Paterson claims "Retirement, and Nature, are more and more my Passion every Day."[77]

However, Thomson's attraction to solitary contemplation in rural landscapes is in tension with his insistence that poetry should serve the public and operate in a public forum. The preface to "Winter" exhorts poetry to take as her subject that which is "useful."[78] The poem itself marks rural life and the shaded landscapes of retirement as the places where poets can learn the presumably useful "private virtues," in direct opposition to the "public haunt" of the city where the "sons of riot flow/Down the loose stream of false enchanted joy/To swift destruction."[79] Yet the private muse is also allied with "Historic truth" (in a late addition, this becomes an "historic muse"); the muse then allows poets to "inhale," or be inspired by, "that ray/Of purest heaven, which lights the *public* soul/Of patriots and of heroes" (ll. 587; 594–97, emphasis added). Similarly, in the 1730–1738 editions of "Liberty" Thomson insists that the arts are of most use when they serve as handmaidens to "public virtue" (II. l. 365).

Eighteenth-century ideas of solitude commonly assume that solitary poetic musings include a social dimension; solipsism and subjectivity were viewed with distaste.[80] It is then not surprising that Thomson suggests the historic muse can visit solitary poets, although the result is often what Geoffrey Hartman has called "visionary history."[81] In "Winter," for example, Thomson's "converse" with the dead is exemplified by a brief catalogue—a progress piece—listing historic figures from ancient Athens to modern Great Britain. However, the revisions of *The Seasons,* like poems such as "Britannia" and "Liberty," written while *The Seasons* was being revised, show a growing concern with poetry's treatment of the public sphere, as Thomson turned to more historically located and public subjects. In short, even when setting the poet in retirement Thomson maintains an insistence on poetry's role in society. But he also betrays some clear anxiety about whether poetry can best play its role when the retired poet spends his time describing solitary contemplation or rural retreat. That is, Thomson was as aware of a possible rift between his simple scenes and his political morals as he was of a rift between the rural settings that he claimed gave rise to useful contemplative knowledge (the knowledge of a country gentleman) and the urban settings that he acknowledged the possessors of knowledge had to enter in order to take any sort of effective action.[82]

That the pastoral, contemplative model of poetry seemed to involve shirking public responsibility, leaving poetry without a clear rationale, helps explain why Thomson increasingly, if with ambivalence, turned from rural landscapes toward more historical and political subjects. His mistrust of rural contemplation is clearest in his last poem, *The Castle of Indolence,* in which Indolence, the poem's villain, lures men to an illusory paradise described in terms that might have served as Thomson's description of his own project in *The Seasons:* "Amid the groves you may indulge the muse,/Or tend the blooms, and deck the vernal year" (I. XVIII. ll. 3–4). Contemporary critics have noted that Thomson invests a good deal of imaginative energy in (and writes some of his best poetry about) what in *The Castle of Indolence* he claims is a vice, namely the retreat to rural description.[83] The Reverend Thomas Morell made a similar point as early as 1742, when he wrote a poem urging Thomson to complete *The Castle of Indolence.* Morell playfully suggests that Thomson has been seduced by his own descriptions of leisure and rural retreat, but he also implies that such descriptions yield Thomson's most powerful poetry; Morell wrote to Thomson, "And lulled with thine own enchanting Lays/[Thou] Didst lie adown; entranced in *the Bow'r,/The which thyself didst make, the Gathering of thy Pow'r*" (emphasis added).[84] If Morell is right, then when Thomson is most powerful as a poet, he is by his own lights courting indolence, and at risk of shirking public engagement.

Thomson's ambivalence about figuring poetry's retreat to a calm, contemplative world can be illuminated by looking at the work of another poet from the early eighteenth century whose work helps to define further problems associated with the trope of the poet in retirement. Anne Finch, Countess of Winchilsea, confronted what it meant to be outside the sphere of political power both as a woman and as someone who, with her husband, was forced into retirement with James II's fall in 1688. It may be significant, too, that Finch's place of retirement was Kent, a traditional setting for poems of retreat going back to Wyatt's "Mine Own John Poins" (of the 1530s), which concludes by embracing retirement in "Kent and Christendom,/Among the Muses." Finch's "A Nocturnal Reverie," published just after her return from exile in 1713, is in any case a night piece, a poem of shade and meditative retreat.[85] It opens,

> In such a night, when every louder wind
> Is to its distant cavern safe confined;
> And only gentle zephyr fans his wings,
> And lonely Philomel, still waking, sings;
>   * * *
> In such a night, . . .
>   * * *
> When darkened groves their softest shadows wear,

The poem then ends, describing the "short-lived jubilee" of night creatures:

> Which but endures while tyrant man does sleep:
> When a sedate content the spirit feels,
> And no fierce light disturbs, whilst it reveals;
> But silent musings urge the mind to seek
> Something, too high for syllables to speak;
> Till the free soul to a composedness charmed,
> Finding the elements of rage disarmed,
> O'er all below a solemn quiet grown,
> Joys in the inferior world, and thinks it like her own:
> In such a night . . .

The overt argument of "A Nocturnal Reverie" prefigures Thomson's claims about some of the descriptive passages in *The Seasons*. The poet in shaded retirement is beyond the cares of daily life (commercial, political, or passional), so that the soul is harmonized and sees itself in calm, rural nature. However, beginning with the refrain ("In such a night") taken from *The Merchant of Venice* (Act V, Scene 1), Finch's poem contains also a counterargument. Shakespeare's play, of course, is appropriately echoed in a poem that contemplates the desires and tyrannies of the sociopolitical world from a higher plane. But the dialogue alluded to is more precisely a battle of wits that focuses on the question of gender and of the spheres appropriate to men and women, as well as on whether night is or is not a romantic setting. "In such a night," then, locates Finch's readers not only in an English countryside viewed after sunset, and not only in such a landscape viewed through the generic lens of the poetic night piece, but also in a night full of the themes of Shakespeare's play. The echo, in short, raises the question of Finch's role as a woman writing poetry, and of whether, like Jessica in Shakespeare's play, Finch can define on her own terms the setting in which she finds herself. When Philomel is then mentioned in the fourth line of the poem, the reader is invited to think both of the nightingale as the bird that standardly sings at such times in such poems *and* of the myth of Philomel. The myth is about the rape of Philomel, after which her tongue is cut out; the bird sings sweetly as recompense for being rendered speechless. After such an opening, it is difficult to read the end of the poem without asking whether "tyrant man" is not gender-specific and without asking as well what it means to have "the elements of rage disarmed" or the soul tricked, as it were, into enjoying an "inferior world."

It is difficult to pinpoint how far Finch meant her counterargument to be taken. In the poem, "the inferior world" of nature—clearly a rural world—is set against the world of the soul, not obviously against the world of political power. The end of the poem also seems at first reading a genuine celebration of retreat. Yet Shakespeare's Jessica ends the dialogue in blank verse to which Finch alludes, "I would out-night you, did nobody come;/But, hark! I hear the footing of a man" (V. i. ll. 23–24). That is, the female speaker's attempt is to define the night in her own way and specifically to define it less romantically than her male counterpart. The approach—or the poetic feet—of a man foils her, however. Placed in such a light, it is difficult not to read Finch's poem also as a protest *against* retirement, which disarms the disenfranchised poet, depriving her of speech and leaving her only with a lesser, though lovely, music.

Thomson's view of the dangers of retirement is less explicitly linked with gender, and he was not literally banished from the spheres of political power as Finch was (although he did spend time as part of the Opposition).[86] Still, his letters suggest that he felt poets as a group were left on the margins, and in his work there is a double vision similar to that in Finch's poem whereby retirement is both the setting for a high poetic flight *and* a sign of poetry's retreat from the realms of more publicly exercised and effective power. John Aiken's 1778 essay justly notes that in *The Seasons* Thomson contrasts retirement with "the turbulent agitations of ambition and avarice."[87] Thomson himself wrote in his preface to "Winter" that poets have always "been passionately fond of retirement, and solitude. . . . [F]ar from the little busy world, they were at leisure, to meditate, and sing the Works of Nature." Placing themselves in retirement, however, poets also place themselves outside the very forum ("the little busy world") on which Thomson wanted to have an impact.

Thomson also shows other, if more submerged, tensions in his attempt to reconcile the qualities he associates with contemplative retirement with his insistence on the poet's public responsibilities. He presents Liberty's arrival in Britain, for example, as the dawning of the sun that brings civilization (and art) by dispelling vice and tyranny. In "Liberty," vice and tyranny are characterized by images of shade, fog, dusk, and darkness (IV. ll. 589–96). Yet these appear to be the same "fogs" (of what Thomas Warton called "ignorance and superstition") often seen as having nurtured earlier poets; specifically, the images of shade and dusk are Thomson's characteristic images, still used in the revisions of *The Seasons* written in the same year that "Liberty" was written, of the rural retirement in which poetry (and in particular Thomson's own poetry) is said to thrive.[88] In part I of "Liberty," the poet does ask Liberty to be the sole patron of poetry's muse (a sign of the new, more public-minded foundations on which poetry is to be set), but he still characterizes this muse as follows: "*narrow* life her lot, and *private shade*" (I. l. 351, emphasis added). At the very least, Thomson maintains a view of the sources of poetic power that rests uncomfortably in the public setting on which he also comes to insist, with the result that poetic virtue is often difficult to distinguish from public vice in his characterizations.

Along similar lines, in *The Castle of Indolence* Indolence asks, "what is virtue but repose of mind?/A pure ethereal calm that knows no storm . . . /Above those passions that this world deform" (I. XVI. ll. 1–2; 4). The public virtues for which such calm is rejected are extolled by Liberty: "That godlike passion! which, the bounds of self/Divinely bursting, the whole public takes/Into the heart, enlarged, and burning high/With the mixed ardour of unnumbered selves" ("Liberty," III. ll. 107–10). Although Thomson was not consistent in his characterization of calm as the sole mood of the solitary poet, the pose is nonetheless one he commonly invoked, usually without the condemnation implied by giving the speech to Indolence. "Summer," for instance, celebrates the calm of "Thrice happy he, who . . . [is]/Emblem instructive of the virtuous man,/Who keeps his tempered mind serene and pure,/And every passion aptly harmonized" (ll. 458;

465–67). A letter of 27 October 1730 repeats the image: "Happy he! who can . . . in some rural retirement . . . cultivate the muses . . . [and] harmonize his passions."[89] Again, the virtues Thomson urges in the public forum and those he celebrates as conducive to (or exemplified in) high poetry are not easily reconciled.

Moreover, even the ardor Thomson alternately proposed as the emotion poetry should rouse was a quality his century also often found problematic.[90] In the passage from "Liberty" quoted above, for example, passion is carefully qualified as unselfish and publicly shared. Similarly, in the same poem, when Thomson describes the British subject (in particular he is talking of a fellow Scot) as fired "with a restless, an impatient flame,/That leads him raptured where ambition calls," he quickly has Liberty add that the flame of ambition must be unselfish: on "virtue can alone my kingdom stand,/On *public* virtue" (V. ll. 75–76, 93–94, emphasis added). Especially at the beginning of the eighteenth century, there was concern with gathering social or public agreement, with preserving the social fabric, and so with avoiding the eccentric, including appeals to a God or a muse too inclined to promote private enthusiasm.[91] Thomson's 1727 "Britannia," for example, contains an exhortation to Englishmen to "ardent rise" and to cherish "*unexpensive* power,/*Undangerous* to the public" (ll. 186, 205–6; emphasis added). The awareness of the costs and dangers of other kinds of ardor is clear. In the same vein, in "Liberty" Thomson looks back with dismay at the English wars when "no unity, no nerve/Combined the loose disjointed public," pointedly warning that a "nation once *inflamed*/(Chief, should the breath of factious fury blow,/With the *wild* rage of mad *enthusiast swelled*)/Not easy cools again. From breast to breast,/From eye to eye, the *kindling passions* mix/In heightened *blaze*" (IV. ll. 837–38, 1034–39, emphasis added). The images, then, of private enthusiasm—wildness, passion, heat or fire, and swelling or expansiveness—mark what can be dangerous unless specifically practiced as a public gesture. In light of cultural suspicions of private enthusiasm—associated with political turmoil and religious strife in the first portion of the century, and later ambiguously associated with an emergent ideology of sensibility—Thomson's attraction to the view that contemplative poetry soothes the passions may be related to his suspicions of private ardor and his inchoate critique of liberal philosophy. Yet he finds that contemplative calm does not seem to count, in his day, as poetic power; thus, Thomson equates poetry's power with the rousing of *public* passion.

At the same time, Thomson does not abandon traditional images of the solitary poet indulging in something suspiciously close to private enthusiasm. In the 1726 "Winter," for example, Thomson pleads for a nocturnal "soaring Soul" and invokes

> *Silence!* thou lonely *Power!* the Door be thine:
> See, on the hallow'd Hour, that none intrude,
> Save *Lycidas* . . .
> (ll. 295–98)

This is the strain in Thomson—similar to the strain in the passage from "Summer" with which this chapter opens—that, as the critic Martin Price says, "helped prepare the way for the theories of the sublime," and which John Aiken, just under fifty years after the poem was first published, called "the sublimest . . . of its kind since the days of MILTON."[92] Such passages also suggest the diversity of Thomson's poetic models; he was a poet who not only wavered between visionary history or public spiritedness and disarming night music, but who had internalized a fiercer Miltonic music as well.[93] The passage above was preceded by a brief vision of classical law-givers, that is, of public figures meant to present a model (and moral) to contemporary readers. In short, Thomson's sublime strain does not always invoke calm Arcadian groves, nor avoid public issues, but rather can follow Milton's "dread voice" (a voice that provides an apocalyptic vision of a "two-handed engine at the door" in "Lycidas" [ll. 130–32], although Thomson's door is not the same as Milton's). Milton's "Lycidas" may be sung by an "uncouth Swain," but Milton also makes Lycidas the guardian of the British Isles ("the Genius of the shore" [ll. 186, 183]). Just so, Thomson looks to Milton for guidance in assuming a voice of poetic power and public importance.

Assuming a Miltonic stance does not entirely solve the problem of how to distinguish the poetic ardor of "lonely *Power*" from, on the one hand, dangerous private enthusiasm or, on the other hand, ineffective contemplation. Thomson takes care to distinguish divisive rapture from positive ambition or passions that soar "above the little selfish sphere/Of doubting *modern* life" ("Liberty," I. ll. 112–13, emphasis added). It is telling, however, that he describes such poetic flights as again leaving the poet outside (if above) the public sphere he wants to influence. Further, Thomson suggests that he finds the public life of his own era lacking both because it is "selfish" and because it is "little" and "doubting," without the soaring expansiveness that in literature was associated with sublimity and private enthusiasm—what Thomson in a letter described as "Poetry! . . . Fancy! Enthusiasm! Rapturous Terror!"—rather than with political exhortations about public virtue.[94] In the thirties, Thomson suggested that the communitarian society of classical Sparta had been able to merge public and private by rooting out the "treacherous self" ("Liberty," II. l. 129). But in Britain, at least by the forties, not only was the self treacherous, because unstable, it was also difficult to see how public and private could be merged in light of Thomson's associations between a Miltonic poetic power and the language of either retirement or private enthusiasm, neither of which in the second quarter of the eighteenth century granted poetry a public role.

The Poetic Self and Public Affairs

Thomson's emphasis on poetry as an active force in public affairs became greater and more self-conscious in the thirties and forties. "Liberty," for instance, is introduced as a hybrid, a "Poetical Vision" partaking of the traditional and more private higher dream vision, but also proposing an overtly historical subject. Thomson's own aspirations are sketched in part when, in Book II of the poem, he proposes as an ideal the world of Sparta, where the "public and the private grew the same" (II. l. 130). By the end of "Liberty," Thomson takes as his subject political power, wealth, and commerce. He characterizes these as signs of public well-being and yet insists they are not indicative of a truly healthy society unless accompanied by the arts: "Cursed by the muses! by the graces loathed!/Who deems beneath the public's high regard/These last enlivening touches of my [Liberty's] reign"; he adds that "these neglected, these recording arts,/Wealth rots, a nuisance; and, oblivious sunk,/That nation must another Carthage lie" (V. ll. 378–80; 386–88). The literal argument of these last lines is traditional: art confers future immortality. However, the larger argument goes beyond this to suggest that the arts are a visible sign of the height of civilization (the "last enlivening touches") without which a nation cannot be said to thrive, even in the present: nations require a publicly shared and respected art in order to be confirmed as thriving. The corollary of this argument is that poetry is useful because it serves the public by treating public issues, rousing ambition and exalting the mind (V. l. 396). Thomson thus proposes that poets should focus on public and historical subjects. Without the public record and celebration of poets, he argues most strongly in *The Castle of Indolence*, "Who then had toiled, rapacious men to tame?/Who in the public breach devoted stood,/And for his country's cause been prodigal of blood?" (II. LIII. ll. 7–9).

Thomson nonetheless had difficulty imagining the poet's place in his culture, a problem linked in part with his sense that, like the music of earlier poets, inherited tropes (for instance, of the poet in retirement or of poetic ardor) both defined poetic power and on various levels rested uneasily in eighteenth-century modern life. An extraliterary ambivalence about modern life itself (which most visibly informs Thomson's work after his later turn to public issues) also added to the confusion engendered by his relationship to past poetry. On one hand, Thomson's increasing emphasis on political and historic subjects responds to and participates in a larger national mood. The critic James Sambrook argues that, despite many social problems, English (Thomson would say British) self-confidence grew, "a reflection of a real economic strength . . . as much attributable to what has been called the 'financial revolution' as to the more famous agrarian and industrial revolutions."[95] Thomson seems to confirm this view of national self-confidence when he writes in a 1730 letter to George Dodington of the "solid magnificence of trade and sincere plenty . . . where industry and liberty mutually support and inspirit each other," adding a year later, in another letter to Dodington, that the "vital arts of life . . . depend on liberty, labour, and all-commanding trade."[96] Both letters describe Britain, although they were written during Thomson's trip abroad as companion to the son of the solicitor general, a trip that by and large reinforced his progressive perspective on his native Britain and that inspired "Liberty."[97]

On the other hand, Thomson also shared with many of his contemporaries a mistrust of the commerce and the bustle—indeed, the very success—of modern life. The same journey abroad gave rise to letters such as one to Lady Hertford in 1732, in which Thomson notes that the French, judging English tourists, must think England "a cold, dark, dull, dirty country, where there is nothing but money."[98] The note of dismay about the financial well-being of Britain is repeated in the poetry: in "Liberty," the fall of Greece is linked to commerce run amok (II. l. 408); luxury is characterized as the "rapacious, cruel, mean,/Mother of vice" (III. ll. 352–53); and Thomson's native country is warned, "Be no such horrid commerce, Britain, thine!" (IV. l. 920). By 1748, in *The Castle of Indolence,* Thomson has Britain rescued from a "sylvan life" by "Sir Industry," who institutes commerce, along with other modern practices. In fact, critics have suggested reading *The Castle of Indolence* as a parable of the eighteenth century's confidence in modern progress.[99] But in the poem, Sir Industry (seeing that "prime vigour" does not last) is forced to set off to rescue the individuals of his country for whom progress and commercial success have led to decadence, a state in which "every power [is] dissolved in luxury" (II. XVII–XX; XXIX; LXI). Such passages suggest that at some level Thomson mistrusted British success.

Thomson's mixture of progressivism and primitivism can be related to his ambivalence about modern Britain.[100] In "Liberty," for example, Thomson proclaims that political progress (associated with modern British liberty) fosters the arts: "Forced is the bloom of arts," he writes, "A false uncertain spring, when bounty gives, /Weak without me [Liberty], a transitory gleam" (V. ll. 529–31). Thomson implies that Liberty (and a true spring for the arts) has arrived in his country and century. Like many poets writing so-called progress pieces, he insists that art generally has progressed through the ages, its growth having culminated in modern Britain as it, following Liberty, westward "irrevocable rolled" ("Liberty," III. l. 326). Yet, as in his tale of Lavinia and Palemon included in the 1730 version of "Autumn," Thomson is also capable of describing the joys of primitive pastoral existence, joys "such as Arcadian song/Transmits from ancient uncorrupted times,/When tyrant custom had not shackled man,/But free to follow nature was the mode" (ll. 220–23). These lines about an earlier golden age unshackled by tyrant custom show that the tension between progressivism and primitivism applies to both political and literary thinking.

Thomson most often views the past with nostalgia when he is, as in his preface, musing on the conditions favorable to his own art. But he also at times mistrusts modern commercial success in itself, and he even betrays uncertainty about whether political progress is as obvious and straightforward as he sometimes insists. For example, Thomson's call for the British to protect liberty seems at odds with his view of the inevitability of liberty's progress; what role do individuals have to play if the march of liberty is, as Thomson says, "irrevocable"?[101] In the same way that Thomson had trouble seeing how he might be original and at the same time insert himself into the literary canon, so too everyone's ability to affect the course of events becomes problematic if the course of history is laid out like a great scroll (to quote Diderot's fatalist). Discussing Liberty's westward unrolling, Thomson specifically, and traditionally, uses the image of the sun, not a scroll. And yet the view of history as a text is also found in the poem; Thomson warns his countrymen to maintain public virtue, since without it life would become "A dull gazette!" (V. l. 268). His worry is that modern Britain will not get written into a permanent text but will rest on the level of journalism. Such gestures confirm Thomson's awareness of the imposing and seemingly already written structures of the past (literary and historical), an awareness that raised questions about how modern individuals could affect, let alone insert themselves in, such texts.[102]

To take another example, in *The Castle of Indolence* Thomson reiterates his view of poetry's public role: Sir Industry is accompanied on his rescue mission by a poet (II. XXXII–XXXIV). Significantly, however, the bard is "a little Druid wight" (XXXIII), a description that combines with the poem's Spenserian form and archaic diction to provide an image of past poetic power. It has been suggested that the Druidic bard was intended to represent Pope, a suggestion bolstered by Herbert E. Cory's early argument on the neoclassical roots of Thomson's view of Spenser.[103] But the Druidic poet who accompanies Sir Industry is drawn most immediately from Milton's "Lycidas" (l. 53) with its pastoral strains. That is, although the image is not restricted to a single source, Thomson's Druid seems to look back beyond Pope to a Miltonic power that was pastoral as well as publicly and politically engaged (just as in "Liberty" Thomson's blank verse rests on Milton's definition of his metrics as an "ancient liberty recover'd . . . from the . . . bondage of Riming").[104] Thomson also draws on the common association of ancient

British political virtues with primitive Druids.[105] In both cases, Thomson looks back to poets who lived in a more agrarian society for his model of poetry that has the power to affect the public sphere.

It is an irony of history that by the time William Collins wrote his "Ode Occasioned by the Death of Mr. Thomson," Thomson himself had not only become a Druid, but "Meek Nature's child," effortlessly playing an Aeolian harp, like one of the individuals who is captured by Indolence in Thomson's poem.[106] In his allegory, Thomson tries to imagine an older model of poetic power at work in a modern and increasingly commercial society, a society of which he had mixed views and in which neither contemplation nor poetic ease could be clearly defended as socially or nationally useful. From Collins's perspective, however, Thomson's pastoral images eclipse his image of the poet operating in a public forum. Collins thus retrospectively confirms Thomson's own fear that the poetry of his age could not carry weight in a public setting. In *The Castle of Indolence* Thomson's voice seems to be heard most clearly in the first lines of stanza twenty-three in canto two (an aside to the reader that breaks the narrative, following the description of Sir Industry's establishment of modern Britain): discussing the role of the arts, Thomson writes, "But now, alas! we live too late in time:/Our patrons now even grudge that little claim [of poets to please their readers]." Allegorically, and in traditional terms, the poem announces that poets are to serve Industry in rallying modern Britain. But speaking in the first person, Thomson worries that contemporary poetry cannot even engage individual readers, let alone inspire the public.

If historical changes as well as the desire to insert his own work within the newly identified institution of British literature made it difficult for Thomson to describe coherently the function and the proper subject of his poetry, these difficulties were exacerbated by the fact that he had (and could have had) no historical perspective on, and thus no vocabulary in which to analyze, the changes his culture was undergoing. Thomson's poetics were equally troubled by his implicit acceptance of his century's redefinition of effective or active power as something that did not encompass poetry, even as something essentially unpoetic. This view may be illustrated by looking at how the second (1789) edition of the *Biographia Britannica* identifies Captain Cook—whom James Sambrook offers as the representative man of his age—as a true genius: Cook, the entry reads, is a man not of "imagination merely, or that power of culling the flowers of fancy which poetry delights in; but an inventive mind; a mind full of resources; and which, by its own native vigour, can suggest noble objects of pursuit, and the most effectual methods of attaining them."[107] In *The Castle of Indolence* Thomson tries to define writing poetry as a form of action when he has his Druidic bard sing, "Who does not act is dead."[108] Yet elsewhere his writing shows that even for him poetry did not easily count as public action. In a 24 October 1730 letter to George Dodington, written just before going abroad, Thomson said, "But not to travel intirely [*sic*] like a Poet, I resolve not to neglect the more prosaic advantages of it; for it is no less my ambition to be capable of serving my country in an active than in a contemplative way."[109]

Milton, particularly the Milton of "Il Penseroso" and "L'Allegro," provided Thomson with the traditional view that poetry could celebrate equally both the active and the contemplative life. However, despite his interest in defining poetry as publicly useful, Thomson often identified true poetry with contemplation, solitude, or retreat, while he and his age defined action as something other than what "poetry delights in." To quote Thomson, it seemed that to be active was *not* to be "like a Poet." Conversely, to be like a poet—to follow in the footsteps of Shakespeare, Spenser, or Milton—seemed to entail (1) shirking public responsibility; (2) at times celebrating virtues that in a public forum would be unhealthy; (3) resting outside what the century counted as power; or, to return also to the opening argument of this chapter, (4) merely repeating past poets, thus being left without political *or* poetic power. In light of this, it is no wonder that Thomson's representations of the poet and his attempts to construct a poetic self are troubled.

Figuring the Economy of Poetic Production

Thomson's difficulty with envisioning the present power of the self—poetic or political—can be linked not only with his misgivings about the world of modern Britain and its place in the scrolls of history or literary history, but also with a change in the audience for poetry. The eighteenth century's "financial revolution" was accompanied by a high rate of geographical mobility (a large percentage of the population moved to or passed through an increasingly urban London) and by the replacement of more traditional social relationships with a "cash nexus."[110] Given that the very structures of public and private life were in flux, it is not surprising that Thomson and others had some problem deciding whether poetry's power was public or private, and what might be meant in either case. There is some argument over how abrupt or clear-cut social change was and when a change might be said to have occurred. Yet, to quote John Sitter on mid-century England, while it "is not self-evident that the social contract suddenly changed in this period, . . . it is clear that the literary contract did."[111]

Among other things, the period saw the rise of a new class of readers whose tastes were fostered by the periodicals and, later, novels of the day, and who swelled the subscription lists that mark the shift, especially for poets, from private patronage toward a new, mass dissemination of literature.[112] It is not certain just how clearly contemporary writers saw that their relationship to their readers *could* not have been the same as that of their predecessors. Thomson analyzed the problem in various ways. A 20 July 1725 letter to William Cranstoun reads, "As for Poetry, she is now a very Strumpet and so lost all her life, & Spirit, or rather a common Strumpet, passes herself upon the world for the chaste Heaven-born Virgin."[113] The complaint is that so-called poets are catering to public taste, an acknowledgment, though not acceptance, of the new general readership. The same stance is renewed in Thomson's lament to Aaron Hill a decade later: "I may . . . very well live to see all Poetry reduced to Magazine-Miscellanies . . . all Learning absorb'd into the Sink of hireling scurrilous News-Papers."[114]

The problem is more complex than such complaints allow, however. On the one hand, Thomson deplores public taste and implicitly shares with Johnson the idea that newspapers and magazines directed public attention to superficial and essentially private concerns.[115] In a 1736 letter, Thomson even blames what he calls the public's "Want of Taste" for the fact that British wealth "pour'd in upon this Nation by Commerce, [has] been lost again in . . . Luxury," allying lack of taste with the turn to "private Jobs, instead of public Works[.] To profitable, instead of fine Arts . . . to the whole venal System of modern Administration . . . centering all in Self."[116] On the other hand, Thomson's increasing insistence on "public Works" suggests that poetry should reach the same newly constituted public he mistrusts. Moreover, he apparently did not recognize that the idea of poetry reaching a large public audience was something that could not have been imagined without the presence of the very forums, such as newspapers, he disparaged. In other words, Thomson's comment on the "system of modern administration" is more to the point than his more usual focus on the decline of personal virtue in individuals. The whole structure by which poets were read and supported was not the same structure within which readers and poets of the past had worked.[117]

Thomson could say, as if his situation did not differ from that of earlier poets, that poets "have been long us'd to [there being a] truly-spiritual and almost only Emolument arising from their Works," but the comment is part of a bitter complaint about his modern public and in particular about his own lack of financial support.[118] Indeed, Thomson's railing in the same letter against the public's turn to private jobs over public works, to profit and to "Gain, instead of Glory," has an odd ring in the context of his own desire for payment.[119] What was perhaps not clear to him was that even if correct in his assessment of his modern audience's materialism, he nonetheless owed his own place in the literary world in part to the changes in taste and in economics he bemoaned. For at the same time that Thomson grappled unhappily with the effect on poetry of Britain's emergence as a modern commercial nation and identified his lack of support as due to the public's bad taste, he was admired by and did reach the new audiences, although they preferred the Thomson of *The Seasons,* or of what the *British Journal* called the "Sublime-obscure."[120]

Insofar as the reaction against a new taste (the taste to which Thomson appealed despite himself and which the *British Journal* disliked) was a defense of "the traditional values of a dominant cultural group," Thomson was also part of the new public that he both tried to reach and criticized.[121] Thomson's biography, like his poetry and poetics, shows how his descriptions of poetry and the poet's role are related both to his ambivalent respect for past literature and to the social and economic realities with which he lived. As a late eulogy by William Shenstone put it, Thomson "had nothing of the Gentleman in his person or address."[122] He was also a Presbyterian and a Scot, from a poor though genteel family, trying to make ends meet as a writer in urban London.[123] In an earlier era, someone like Thomson, coming to London from outside the mainstream of traditional English culture, might have gained a readership, at least if armed with the proper letters of introduction. But, especially given Thomson's relative lack of success as a dramatist, the readership would have been small and personalized. In his own day Thomson did have a series of patrons both private and public, the last during his brief tenure as secretary of the briefs and as surveyor general of the Leeward Islands. But he was read by the new class of readers, and he himself, especially in his later work, at least implicitly wanted to reach (and to be supported by) a large, public readership.

Indeed, the very retreat to the private (though not necessarily the materialistic) realm Thomson confronted and condemned in his later writings was what his audience enjoyed in his work. The curious fact is that the earlier poets on whose public standing (and by implication more publicly engaged writing) Thomson looks back with nostalgia wrote for a smaller, more personal—what we would call a more private—circle of readers, although it was a politically powerful circle. Thomson himself necessarily wrote for more of a mass—what we would call a more public—audience and for people whom he did not know. Paradoxically, the facelessness and uncertain character of this new audience made writing and reading seem like far less social or public activities to him.[124]

Furthermore, Thomson saw the lack of financial support for his poetry as a sign of how poetry was undervalued—rather than, for example, a sign of his own desire for profit—suggesting how fully he participated in a world where relationships were increasingly mediated by and measured in currency and where literature was becoming a commodity. Just as material exchange was mediated by currency—and currency exchange itself mediated in a debt economy—so too authorial productions were mediated by new forms of print distribution. The copyright law of 1709, rather than underlining the century's obsession with originality as one might first think, speaks more of how literature had become a booksellers' commodity. Literature did not truly reach a mass audience, by becoming available in cheap editions, until a court ruling against perpetual copyright in the 1774 case of *Donaldson* vs. *Beckett;* it is another—if later—sign of Thomson's appeal to a mass audience that the case was over an attempt to reissue *The Seasons.*[125]

Thomson may mark himself as a man of his century simply by having expected he could make a living because he was a poet; in any event, not coming from wealth, he knew firsthand, and complained about, how little cash went to poets.[126] Not only did Thomson apparently spend time in debtor's prison, but popular myth had it that his one romance was thwarted because the mother of the woman he loved did not consider marriage to a poet without a steady income a good financial risk.[127] There is a deep irony in reading about how, on Thomson's death—when he left a number of debts—his friend Thomas Birch, in two separate letters to other friends, analyzed Thomson's problem in the same terms of personal character that Thomson had used to characterize his audience: Thomson's plight, Birch wrote, was due to the poet's personal "excessive ill œconomy and luxury."[128] The problem, as I have suggested, was probably better analyzed in terms of a society in the throes of larger social, political, and economic changes.

Although Thomson was in many ways like the new readers of poetry on whom he depended and to whom he appealed, he was also probably, as his complaints suggest, more highly educated than many of the those who swelled the ranks of the new reading public. For example, it was only from the much-maligned periodicals that part of this new reading public knew of Addison's essays on *Paradise Lost* or heard, at least at second hand, of the aesthetic and philosophical speculations of Locke, Shaftesbury, Dennis, and others.[129] Still, if such readers desired the sensational, or seemed to have untraditional taste, they also aspired to gentility, and the press provided them both with a reading list and with the same terms of criticism used by their critics. Thomson's own use of the epithet "modern Goths" as a synonym for "barbarians," as well as his prophecy that the lack of good poets or readers revealed the approach of "a new Gothic Night," would have gained the genteel assent of many of the readers and writers about whom he voiced his complaints in much the same way that his poetic style allied him with those Addison had labeled "*Goths* in Poetry, who, like those in Architecture, not being able to come up to the beautiful Simplicity of the old *Greeks* and *Romans,* have endeavoured to supply its Place with all the Extravagances of an irregular Fancy."[130]

Joseph Mitchell wrote of the first edition of "Winter," which Thomson sent to him: "Beauties and faults so thick lye scattered here,/Those I could read, if these were not so near."[131] Responding to related criticisms, Thomson fumed about the failure of the British to accept genuine poetry, which he defined as that which gives rise to "Fancy! Enthusiasm! Rapturous Terror!"[132] The debate might be recast as a quarrel over whether poetry should or should not be—in Addison's definition of the term—"Gothic," or, alternately, whether the "Goths" were those who failed to appreciate the fancy that Thomson (deviating from Addison) allied with enthusiasm and rapture. In either case, despite his own stated dismay about the unaristocratic and barbarian readership that did not value poetry (or pay its poets sufficiently), Thomson in fact appealed to a taste that general readers—both "Goths" and those with a taste for the "Gothic"—increasingly shared, a taste finally associated less with the public uses Thomson tried to claim for poetry (as in "Liberty," which did not sell well), than with the poetic music he so uneasily echoed.[133] The changing conditions by which poetry was distributed and read helped foster rereadings of Thomson's work by contemporary and later readers who read him variously as a poet of sublime music, a poet of natural description, or (less frequently) a political poet. Ironically, the loss of a perceived communitarianism—a loss Thomson protested—authorized a more readerly "liberty."

Past, Present, and Future

Within Thomson's lifetime Collins would redefine not only Milton's but also Thomson's music. In his 1746 "Ode on the Poetical Character" (written twenty years after the first version of "Winter," but two years before Thomson died), Collins opens with a deliberate misreading of Spenser and closes with an image of Milton as all ear:

> I view that oak, the fancied glades among,
> By which as Milton lay, his evening ear,
> From many a cloud that dropped ethereal dew,
> Nigh sphered in heaven its native strains could hear:
> On which the ancient trump he reached was hung;
> (ll. 163–67)

Collins further rejects minor poetry such as Waller's for the greater "glory" of the Miltonic sublime. The picture of Milton as a reclining figure in his own Eden (that of *Paradise Lost*), where high music drips without effort into his "evening ear," prefigures Thomson's images in the 1748 *The Castle of Indolence* (I. XL) of the Edenic ease with which original music once was found. Thomson suggests that such ease and originality are no longer in good faith available, placing his Eden in the illusory kingdom of Indolence.

Collins similarly implies that the power and music of Milton are no longer available, yet he also says that his own attempt to take Milton as a guide is an attempt to claim Milton's "trump" and his Eden—that is, to rival his music and his originality.[134]

By the time Thomson died, Collins portrayed himself as haunted by both earlier poets: Thomson is described in the "Ode Occasioned by the Death of Mr. Thomson" in language borrowed not only from "Lycidas" but also from *The Castle of Indolence*. Thomson becomes for Collins a late "haunt[er of] the shore" (l. 13).[135] It is worth speculating, in light of the "Ode on the Poetical Character," about Collins's elegiac description of Thomson as "*Meek* Nature's child" (l. 36, emphasis added), that is, as perhaps closer to Waller than to either Collins's Milton or Thomson's own Miltonic stance. Perhaps, in the same way his misreading of Spenser in the "Ode on the Poetical Character" allows Collins his own, more psychological, allegory, Collins's domestication of Thomson is defensive. If so, there would be an irony in Collins's representation of Thomson as a guide who was simply a naive chronicler of the "year's best sweets," that is, of the rural settings of *The Seasons:* Thomson was at least as haunted as Collins by the ghosts of his literary past. The irony is doubled when Collins makes Thomson himself a haunting shade: Collins inserts the older poet into the literary canon in a way that Thomson wished to, but felt he could not, insert himself, and Collins then seals off the canon from the historical realm of the present, which Thomson increasingly wanted to affect, by envisioning Thomson in a "poet's sylvan grave" (l. 4).

Popular myth proclaimed that Thomson's father died while exorcising a ghost; Thomson himself tried not so much to exorcise as to reanimate the ghosts of his literary past, and neither he nor his poetry died in the attempt. His anxiety over whether his poetry of nature or of the sublime allowed him to claim poetic or political power helps explain Thomson's later turn to increasingly historical subject matter. Yet if Thomson was unable to give an account of present power that joined the poetic and the political, or the private and the public, nonetheless his poetry and especially *The Seasons* is successfully constituted of his struggle, even his failure, to define the unique source and end of his poetic work.

Indeed, I chose to discuss at length the long passage from "Summer" with which this chapter begins not only because it illustrates how past poetry informed Thomson's ear and the nature of the sublime strain in Thomson's work, but also because it is a passage that filled the ears of later poets: Collins, Cowper, and Wordsworth.[136] Collins already saw Thomson as one of the chorus of earlier and imposing bards. Cowper, in 1784, wrote of Milton and Thomson: "He that should write like either of them, would in my judgment deserve the name of a copyist, but not a poet."[137] In short, Thomson's repetitions of the past—repetitions that I have argued were some cause for anxiety in Thomson's work, viewed from the perspective of 1726 through 1748—quickly fostered another view of Thomson when he was read in retrospect as already written into literary history and ensconced in readers' ears.

Finally, even though Thomson insisted he wanted to affect a different, more historical realm, it is the future poets he influenced who inscribe Thomson's poetry in the books now read. Thomson's poetry, in fact, already enacts the way poetic tradition enters and is reformed (or deformed) by contemporary realities, the realities not only of the sociopolitical and economic worlds but also of literary production and reception. Since Thomson himself understood that poetry looked both backward and forward, it is not untoward to read Thomson in light of the later poets who gave him a place "in the book." And it is to just such a poet—William Wordsworth—that I turn in my next chapter.

Chapter II 🎴

A Power to Virtue Friendly:
The Art of Power and the
Power of Art in the Work
of William Wordsworth

I went by the field of the slothful, and by the vineyard of the man void of under-
standing and, lo! It was all grown over with thorns, and nettles covered the face
thereof, and the stonewall thereof was broken down. Then I saw and considered it
well: I looked upon it, and received instruction.

—*Proverbs,* 24: 30, from the title page of
William Cobbett's *The English Gardener*

Wordsworth Reading Thomson:
Poetic Fame and Poetic Tradition

The late eighteenth-century culture in which Wordsworth first began to
publish was not Thomson's, but Wordsworth's poetry, at least through 1815,
attempts to recast and reconcile the same oppositions that are found in
Thomson's work, specifically the oppositions between the literary and the
political, the ear and the eye, past and present, rural and urban, idleness and
labor. This is true in part because by the time Wordsworth began to write
poetic tradition had changed; Thomson's poetry had become part of the lit-
erary past by and against which the later poet measured his own ambitions.
By revising Thomson, Wordsworth repeated the relationship of Thomson to
his literary predecessors. As I will argue, Wordsworth self-consciously
claimed such revisions and repetitions as an enabling force, ultimately, by
1815, repeating and revising even his own earlier poetic self.

It is clear that by Wordsworth's day Thomson was firmly part of the English canon. Wordsworth's first overt reference to Thomson is in *An Evening Walk,* on which he began work in 1788–1789, but Wordsworth would have known Thomson's work well by the time he left school at Hawkshead in 1787.[1] Wordsworth referred to a wide range of Thomson's work later in his life. For example, in an 1829 letter he writes of once having hoped to publish a short life of Thomson as a preface to an edition of *The Seasons, The Castle of Indolence,* "Liberty," and a "few minor pieces"; he adds that "Thomson, Collins, and Dyer, had more poetic Imagination than any of their Contemporaries."[2] Similarly, in 1815 Wordsworth wrote that with few exceptions "the poetry of the period intervening between the publication of the Paradise Lost and the Seasons does not contain a single new image of external nature; and scarcely presents a familiar one from which it can be inferred that the eye of the Poet had been steadily fixed upon his object, much less that his feelings had urged him to work upon it in the spirit of genuine imagination."[3]

Despite his insistence that the poetic eye should view "external nature" rather than repeating past poetry, Wordsworth drew on literary tradition frequently. While Milton's importance to Wordsworth's work is perhaps most obvious, Wordsworth also absorbed much from Thomson's work and in particular from Thomson's early attempt to write a poetry of sight even while inserting himself within the Miltonic tradition.[4] Critic J. Douglas Kneale has discussed the "trope of collaboration" or "joint labouring" as a way to approach the literary (and especially the Miltonic) "underpresence" in the 1850 version of *The Prelude.*[5] Yet in the early 1790s, Milton and Thomson, rather than being simply co-laborers on whose work Wordsworth could draw, would most likely have reinforced Wordsworth's "instinctive humbleness,/Upheld even by the very name and thought/Of printed books and authorship."[6] While in his own day Thomson had anxieties about his place as a poet, from Wordsworth's perspective, especially before 1800, Thomson, like Milton, would have seemed more a figure to inspire awe than a co-laborer.[7] In short, Thomson would appear, as Coleridge put it in the *Biographia Literaria,* a born poet rather than someone who saw writing as work, let alone someone who himself saw ease of writing as a thing of the past.[8] Coleridge's famous comment on Thomson's status is described by Hazlitt: Coleridge found a dog-eared copy of *The Seasons* in a small wayside inn near Linton, and Hazlitt reports him as saying, "*That* is true fame."[9]

By 1819, in his dedication of "Peter Bell" to Robert Southey, Wordsworth would define fame not only as the ability to reach a broadly defined audience but also as the ability to insert one's self into a permanent canon: "pains have been taken . . . to make the production [of "Peter Bell"] less unworthy of a favorable reception; or, rather, to fit [the poem] for fill-ing *permanently* a station, however humble, in the Literature of our Coun-try. This has, indeed, been the aim of all my endeavours in Poetry, which . . . have been . . . laborious."[10] I will return to discuss the differences between early and later Wordsworth; here, I would note that despite the relative self-confidence of his 1819 remarks, throughout his life Wordsworth clearly was anxious about whether he might earn a place in "Literature" (with a capital "L"). Even more obviously, he worried about his own labor or productivity and his public reception within his own lifetime, as well as about whether literary permanence and public favor could coexist. The last issue is implicit in Wordsworth's note to the effect that he has tried to write so as to be well-received *or rather* to take his place in literary history.

In short, Wordsworth's concerns are a variation on Thomson's double ambition to matter in literary history and to have something to say to his contemporaries (although both literary history—now including Thomson—and contemporary society had changed between Thomson's day and Wordsworth's). As Raymond Williams pointed out almost half a century ago in a still valuable formulation, the late eighteenth and early nineteenth centuries saw both an acceleration of the changes already underway in Thomson's day and the evolution of new literary strategies in response to such changes, which included the changed contract between readers and writers as books entered an impersonal marketplace; the changed nature of the reading public; and an increased emphasis on specialized production, in-cluding artistic production.[11]

Wordsworth's anxieties over his own productivity are clear from his earli-est writings, as in his 23 November 1791 letter to William Matthews on how he fears he is "doomed to be an idler thro[ughou]t [his] whole life," or his 1794 letter, also addressed to Matthews, written just after the publication of both *An Evening Walk* and *Descriptive Sketches,* in which Wordsworth writes, "*I have been do*[*ing*] *nothing* and still continue to be doing nothing. What is to become of me I know not" (emphasis added).[12] Wordsworth's worries were in part linked to his need to support himself. Later the same year, Wordsworth reacted to the mixed reception of his first two books—which he says he had hoped would prove "that [he] could do something"—by say-ing of newer work, "I certainly should not publish it unless I hoped to de-rive from it some pecuniary recompence."[13] Such statements also underline Wordsworth's anxiety over whether writing might count as "doing" and his sense that payment might help mark an activity as true labor and success. The idea that poetry rarely counted as productive labor in late eighteenth-century England is obvious in Dorothy Wordsworth's 1791 description of her brother: "William has a great attachment to poetry . . . which is not the most likely thing to produce his advancement in the world."[14]

Contemporary reviews of Wordsworth's first two volumes must have ex-
acerbated his worries over his own "idleness." Both 1793 volumes were re-
viewed, for better and worse, as merely descriptive poems; *An Evening Walk*
was not only proposed as a simple traveler's companion, but—while various
reviewers singled out for attention one narrative passage in the poem, the
beggar's story (ll. 241–300)—critics tended to discredit descriptive poetry in
general.[15] Disparaging remarks about descriptive poetry were commonplace;
The European Magazine reprinted the following lines: "That which was
formed to captivate the eye,/The ear must coldly taste; description's
weak,/And the Muse falters in the vain attempt."[16] The *Monthly Review*
complained about more "descriptive poetry . . . Have we not yet enough?"[17]
In the same vein, if more sympathetically, the critic writing for the *Analytic
Review* expressed a desire for "a general thread of narrative to connect the
several descriptions, or of some episodical tale, to vary the impression."[18] Fi-
nally, the *Monthly Review*—in a way that must have reinforced Wordsworth's
anxieties about poetic labor—also included a complaint about the lack of
thought in poetry and proclaimed that "No man will ever be a poet, till his
mind be sufficiently powerful to sustain this *labor*" (emphasis added).[19]
Even more obviously than in Thomson's day, questions were being raised
about the function or usefulness of poetry and especially about whether po-
etry might be located somewhere other than in description or whether the
ear and eye might diverge.

Given both his personal anxieties about being idle and the critical re-
sponse to his first publications, Wordsworth's earliest concern with Thom-
sonian questions about the uses of poetic description and about poetic labor
are not necessarily a matter of direct influence. It is even unclear which
Thomson, or what part of Thomson's work, might have made an impression
on Wordsworth: the poet of natural description; the poet of interpolated sto-
ries and varied narratives; the poet whose eye was not sufficiently on "exter-
nal nature"; or, again, the poet whose language had helped form
Wordsworth's ear, a traditional voice of "poetical authority."[20] The *relation-
ship* between narrative and description may be part of what interested
Wordsworth in Thomson's poetry; the story of Celadon and Amelia in
"Summer" informs the purely descriptive passage following Thomson's story
in the same way that the story of the beggar and the swan (the passage con-
temporary reviewers found of most interest) in *An Evening Walk* informs the
description of waterfowl in a calm lake that follows Wordsworth's interpo-
lated narrative.[21] Yet Wordsworth's note to the 1793 edition of his poem that
refers his readers to Thomson's "Summer" does not appear near the story of
the beggar but rather marks a more descriptive passage on the sunset (ll.
173–74) under which Wordsworth wrote, "From Thomson: see Scott's Crit-
ical Essays," a reference to John Scott's 1785 discussion of Thomson in *Crit-*

ical Essays.[22] Indeed, the passage may serve as a correction of Thomson's descriptive poetry; Wordsworth would have read in Scott's book that Thomson was a poet whose descriptions were too literary, not sufficiently of the eye.[23] This is not to mention echoes found in other early Wordsworth pieces of Thomson's more public poetry in "Liberty" and "Britannia," nor allusions to Thomson's *The Castle of Indolence.*[24]

I raise the above issues to suggest that Wordsworth drew on different views of Thomson in different contexts and to set the stage for a more detailed examination of several strands I wish to trace in Wordsworth's work between 1793 and 1814, beginning with a return to the issue with which I opened this chapter, namely, how Thomson had become canonical and even had come to stand for poetic power by Wordsworth's day. Given Thomson's stature, it may seem surprising that in Wordsworth's "Essay, Supplementary to the Preface" he is described as a model poet not simply because of his writing (Wordsworth notes flaws in the writing, in fact) but because some of his best work was "the delight only of a few."[25] Wordsworth then discusses Collins, his poetry's lack of sales, and his poverty. The suggestion that the line of true poetry is marked by obscurity and need is reinforced in Wordsworth's praise of Collins's elegy for Thomson. Collins's elegy says that anyone who overlooks Thomson's grave will be cursed with lack of imagination and lack of joy. Wordsworth writes that had Collins himself in turn been elegized just after he died (that is, written into literary history posthumously), many would have inherited Collins's curse on those who fail to mourn the death of a true poet. What Wordsworth does not say is that Collins *was* elegized "by a surviving admirer," namely Wordsworth himself, who by 1798 had published "Remembrance of Collins Composed upon the Thames near Richmond," placing Collins's grave in the watery line established by Milton in "Lycidas," as well as by Collins's elegy for Thomson and, finally, by Wordsworth's elegy on Collins, for whom he "suspend[s]" an oar to find evening attended by calm, by a suspension of grief, and by "virtue's holiest Powers."[26]

In "Remembrance of Collins," the specular image of Collins's heart is "seen" in the calm water of the Thames, an image which recalls Wordsworth's image of the "uncertain heaven received/Into the bosom of the steady lake," composed in 1798.[27] Found in manuscript JJ of *The Prelude,* what became the Winander Boy passage is cast as autobiography; Wordsworth describes his own suspension ("I hung/Listening"), hearing echoes of his own voice until "the visible scene" of the lake containing the world enters his mind.[28] Both the Winander Boy passage and Collins's absorption into the Thames resemble what critic Alan Liu calls a "locodescriptive moment," referring to the way the beggar's story in *An Evening Walk* ends with an apparently abrupt transition to "sounds that mingle from afar,/Heard by calm lakes, as peeps the folding star"—the last image itself taken from Collins's "Ode to Evening."[29] Wordsworth's technique in *An Evening Walk* also recalls how Thomson's description in "Summer" of a youth gazing on an "inverted landscape" (reflected in a pool) appears just after the tragic story of Celadon and Amelia. There is a "subliminal element" in Thomson's reflecting pool—not simply because the preceding *narrative* informs the landscape, but also because it does so with a flourish of *literary* echoes, including an echo of Milton's Eve gazing into "the pool of Narcissus," with both narrative and verbal echoes buried, as it were, in visual description.[30] It is significant, then, that the figure of echo informs Wordsworth's 1798 Winander Boy passage, suggesting his growing self-consciousness about how poetic voice and literary echoes can inform natural description, as they do in the Thomsonian elegy for Collins completed the same year. The latter poem also shows how Wordsworth came tacitly (but clearly) to position himself within the English literary tradition while implying that canonization comes along with, even necessarily involves, a present lack of money and popular acclaim.[31]

Within the first decade and a half of the nineteenth century, Wordsworth's position became more secure than it was in 1798–1799, let alone in 1793. It seems odd that his willingness to assume that he could write himself only into some future (or past) book at the expense of present fame or financial security was most often voiced after the Wordsworths' financial and domestic situation became more or less secure. The growth of Wordsworth's family—he was married in 1802 and had his first child in 1803—offset to some degree the security that came with the settlement of a family legacy in 1802. It was not until 1813 that Wordsworth was granted an annual gift from Lord Lonsdale and became Distributor of Stamps for Westmorland and the Penrith District of Cumberland. Still, the growing self-confidence found in Wordsworth's stance after 1803 is evident, if peculiar. For instance, Wordsworth's 1808 letter to Richard Sharp aligns Wordsworth's own poor sales with the poor sales both of Collins's poems, especially in Collins's lifetime, and of "Milton's minor Poems . . . utterly neglected."[32] If Thomson looked back and saw earlier poets as more established (and so, by implication or projection, better paid, with more public support), Wordsworth seems gradually to have reversed the image, looking back to reimagine the canon into which he wanted to fit himself—a canon of "men of real power, who go before their age"—as marked by neglect, especially financial neglect but also by a lack of present effective public influence in the writers' own day; after 1803 or so, the "real power" Wordsworth imagines for poets is never present.[33] More precisely, throughout his life Wordsworth separates the power of poetry from present power of the sort that is marked by fame or financial security, although there was a brief period in the nineties—perhaps through 1803—when Wordsworth entertained the hope that poetry might effect social or political change and seemed less comfortable with the idea of trading present powerlessness for future fame.

It can be said that as Wordsworth's personal and poetic situation became more secure, he seemed more frequently to imagine his own place within the line of (impoverished, apparently ineffective) past poets, and—especially after 1813—he seemed less obsessed with whether his vocation was "work" or "idleness." Wordsworth's confidence, however, is less clear in his earliest letters. There especially, he often voiced a defensive reluctance to trust his work to a public audience and aligned financial pressures with vocational anxiety. For example, in a 1798 letter to James Tobin, Wordsworth wrote that there "is little need to advise me against publishing; it is a thing that I dread as much as death itself. This may serve as an example of the figure by rhetoricians called hyperbole, but privacy and quiet are my delight."[34] Similarly, in 1799 Wordsworth wrote two letters to Joseph Cottle, one proclaiming the poet's "aversion from publication . . . [such] that no motives whatever, nothing but pecuniary necessity, will . . . ever prevail upon me to commit myself to the press again," and a second complaining about Robert Southey's less than enthusiastic review of *Lyrical Ballads,* a review that Wordsworth says should not have been written since Southey "knew that I published those poems for money and money alone. [Southey] knew that money was of importance."[35] In other words, money and long-term literary merit may be incompatible; money forces poets—inappropriately—into the marketplace and dismayingly becomes the touchstone of what publicly counts as productive labor. After 1803 Wordsworth could propose a traditional association between posthumous literary immortality and present lack, as in his 1807 letter more approvingly quoting Southey on how reviewers "cannot *blast* our *laurels,* but they may *mildew* our *corn.*"[36] During his own years of highest financial and vocational anxiety, although he still linked entering the marketplace with financial need, Wordsworth less frequently invoked the authority of the past as precedent for his own situation. These years marked Wordsworth's struggle to redefine labor and to resist the idea that poets cannot be effective in the present. In this period especially, Thomson's poetry of the eye and his representations of poetic tradition and poetic labor helped to focus, for Wordsworth, the problem of what kind of power in the historical present might be claimed for poetry and what kind of work poets might be said to do.[37]

Historical Engagement and the Move
to Narrative in Early Wordsworth

Despite the locodescriptive nature of his earliest books, Wordsworth, like Thomson, clearly understood the problematic nature of writing a poetry of the eye, which offered present fact rather than traditional poetic tropes and yet in so doing could sound unpoetic and trivial. In this way, the genre of *An Evening Walk* and *Descriptive Sketches* posed for Wordsworth the question of how to write a poetry of the present without abandoning what was culturally understood to be poetic power as defined by the canon of British poetry. Even in these early writings, Wordsworth looked in two directions, to the landscapes and culture of his historical present and to the literary tradition. The very revision of Thomsonian description (by way of John Scott) in *An Evening Walk,* undertaken because Thomson seemed too literary, implies less an "eye on the object than on other poems," in this case, Thomson's poems.[38] Even the late Fenwick note on *An Evening Walk,* in which Wordsworth insists that the poem has "not an image in it which [he has] not observed," also (in retrospect) acknowledges his early "unwillingness to submit the poetic spirit to the chains of fact & real circumstance," thus suggesting that the factually based natural description of which the poem is apparently constituted is not the ground on which Wordsworth would ultimately rest his claim to poetic power.[39] Furthermore, even if Wordsworth in the early nineties had understood himself as simply correcting Thomson by moving toward a more honest poetry of the eye, critical reactions to *An Evening Walk* and *Descriptive Sketches* would have reraised the very questions that motivated much of Thomson's digressive logic, namely, whether a poetry of sight is more than the *Gentleman's Magazine*'s "companion of the traveller," or—to follow *The European Magazine*'s line—if the muse and the ear find the poetry of the eye "weak."

One Thomsonian portion of *An Evening Walk* that was revised and served as a starting point for other poems between 1793 and 1797–1798 is especially useful in tracing Wordsworth's developing answer to the question of what makes poetry powerful and what kind of a poetry of the eye might be defended. The story of the beggar (and swan) was singled out for praise by the reviews of the time and has more recently been associated with interpolated narrative in Thomsonian description. Wordsworth's story from *An Evening Walk* is related not only to Thomson's stories but also to Wordsworth's own story of the female vagrant in "Salisbury Plain" (later published as "The Female Vagrant" in the 1798 *Lyrical Ballads*). Wordsworth's revisions of his story are increasingly self-conscious in the way they deflect his readers' attention from description to narrative. While the use of narrative to enliven and inform description is Thomsonian, Wordsworth's apparent self-consciousness about the function of human stories is new. Moreover, his use of narrative, as well as the specific narratives invoked, transform Thomsonian poetic strategies in view of the contemporary context of the French Revolution. Not only had the implicit appeal to the "eye" of picturesque traditions become politicized between 1793 and 1798; the vagrants found in Wordsworth's tales had as well.[40]

Although vagrants were "part of an established literary tradition," by the early nineties there was an "increasing awareness of contradictions" between political analyses of vagrancy and paternalistic literary treatments of beggars.[41] Wordsworth's vagrants have indeed served as the locus of debates about the poet's precise political stance and about how informed his relationship to Painite radicalism was in the middle to late nineties.[42] Without denying the significance of such debates, I want here to note simply that the hope of affecting the contemporary world (embracing political and economic issues from the global to the personal) and the hope of literary immortality posed problems that Wordsworth addressed even before 1793, in his earliest questions about his own poetic labor. The political discourse surrounding the French Revolution (and the English response to that event) then shifted and focused the more literary and personal terms in which Wordsworth first (and last) posed questions about how poetry might affect the world. Because world politics of the period required Wordsworth to reframe his questions about what counted as useful labor, about how writing could affect the world, and about financial security, Wordsworth wrestled with the idea of poetry's engagement with the world most strenuously between 1793 and 1798. The poetry of this period directly and insistently addresses historical and political questions; moreover, up through at least 1798, Wordsworth entertained his most hopeful and optimistic ideas of how poets might not simply pass from obscurity in their lifetimes to posthumous immortality (as in his post-1803 letters), but how they might effect direct historical change.

Certainly, the creation of an historically engaged poetry seems the implied motive behind Wordsworth's relatively late 14 January 1801 letter to Charles James Fox, the liberal statesman, in which Wordsworth enclosed two poems ("Michael" and "The Brothers"):

> I hope, whatever effect they [the poems] may have upon you, you will at least be able to perceive that they may excite profitable sympathies in many kind and good hearts, and may in some small degree enlarge our feelings of reverence for our species, and our knowledge of human nature, by shewing that our best qualities are possessed by men whom we are too apt to consider, not with reference to the points in which they resemble us, but to those in which they manifestly differ from us. I thought . . . that the two poems might cooperate, however feebly, with the illustrious efforts which you have made to stem this and other evils with which the country is labouring.[43]

The 1801 letter to Fox recalls Wordsworth's 1795 letter to Francis Wrangham, a friend, describing a version of the Salisbury Plain poems as poetry whose "object is partly to expose the vices of the penal law and the calamities of war as they affect individuals."[44] The later letter has a far more detailed, and paternalistic, view of the uses of poetry, which it sees as arousing compassion in those in power, while the earlier letter simply describes poetry as akin to what we now might call investigative reporting with a human interest slant.[45] Both letters, however, imagine poetry as potentially affecting the society in which it is written and as doing so by telling individuals' stories, that is, by using narrative.

The particular narrative Wordsworth mentions to Wrangham is almost certainly the female vagrant's story, related to the story of the beggar in *An Evening Walk* and to the interpolated narratives of Thomson's *The Seasons*. The story underwent significant changes between its first reincarnation in the 1793–1794 "Salisbury Plain," its elaboration and revision in the 1795–1799 "Adventures on Salisbury Plain," and its extraction for publication as "The Female Vagrant" in *Lyrical Ballads*. The first revision I will examine was written during the summer in which Wordsworth voiced his response to war between France and Britain in *A Letter to the Bishop of Llandaff*.

Although Wordsworth was affected by the changing climate in England (away from sympathy for France) after 1793, the letter to Wrangham, like the more detailed *A Letter to the Bishop of Llandaff* and the documentary roots of the narrative itself, suggests that in both 1793 and 1795 Wordsworth was sharply critical of contemporary British politics and society.[46] Wordsworth also wrote to his friend William Matthews in 1794, "I am of that odious class of men called democrats," adding in a slightly later letter,

> I disapprove of monarchical and aristocratical governments, however modified. Hereditary distinctions and privileged orders of every species I think must necessarily counteract the progress of human improvement: hence it follows that I am not amongst the admirers of the British constitution . . . [although] I recoil from the bare idea of a revolution.[47]

In short, the uses to which Wordsworth first dedicated his narrative seem newly politicized (compared, say, to the related narrative in *An Evening Walk*); it is worth examining Wordsworth's fleshing out of the set piece beggar's story to see how his revisions are linked to his prose statements on the political import of his narratives.[48]

Introduced early in the poem (l. 138), the female vagrant eventually tells her own story in "Salisbury Plain" (ll. 226–394).[49] Although the story is similar to that of the female beggar in *An Evening Walk*, the woman in "Salisbury Plain" is given her own, first-person narrative. Stripped of ornament, the story is of an idyllic pastoral existence, broken when the woman's father has his fishing rights taken away. The woman then marries her childhood sweetheart, who takes in both daughter and father (and who has himself had to leave the land to make a living) until unemployment (a passing reference to looms suggests the husband has become a weaver) pressures the man to enlist to fight the American war, which kills the husband and three children. The vagrant finally describes her journey home and—briefly—her three years as a wanderer in England. Although the description of the woman's early life conflates freeholders and customary tenants and contains no detailed portraits of labor or war, the bulk of the story is devoted to evoking the general causes of the speaker's poverty and displacement.[50] The vagrant's story, in turn, is framed by the Gothic description of a night on Salisbury Plain, which introduces a male vagrant to whom the female vagrant tells her tale. Also, although the internal audience is insisted upon (as the female vagrant's tale is interrupted by daybreak, readers are reminded of the male vagrant's presence by being told that both characters pause to watch), a more didactic voice takes over by stanza forty-seven—"Adieu ye friendless hope-forsaken pair!" (l. 415)—concluding with a diatribe advocating justice, peace, and reason.

Several significant aspects of the story change in the next revisions. First, Wordsworth complicates the narrative frame stories; second, the didactic authorial voice that delivers the ending moral is replaced by the completion of one of the frame stories (as the sailor-murderer, though not the story, is left hanging); and, finally, the end of the female vagrant's story is recast. In "Salisbury Plain" the woman ends, "'Oh! tell me whither [I go], for no earthly friend/Have I, no house in prospect but the tomb.'/She ceased" (ll. 392–94). A Miltonic description of the city at sunrise follows.[51] In the later "Adventures on Salisbury Plain," the story ends, "'Oh! tell me whither—for no earthly friend/Have I.'—She ceased, *and weeping turned away,/As if because her tale was at an end/She wept;—because she had no more to say/Of that perpetual weight which on her spirit lay*" (ll. 554–58, emphasis added). All three changes insist on the poem *as* narrative and as testimony to social and political ills.

In the revised ending of the poem, Wordsworth's changes emphasize that his character's story is a sufficient vehicle for his moral, a moral that originally appears as an authorial comment in much the same way Thomson's didactic points appear in "Summer." For example, Thomson's statement that pastoral existence forms the backbone of British political power ("A simple scene! yet hence Britannia sees/Her solid grandeur rise" [ll. 423–34]) is simply juxtaposed with a description of a rural village. While Wordsworth's strategy in "Salisbury Plain" is thus Thomsonian, his moral in all versions of his tale is not Thomson's. Rather than celebrating British thunder hanging over France (as Thomson does just after the lines from "Summer" cited above), Wordsworth is criticizing Britain's declaration of war with France, although his poem is set during the 1770s and the war with America, and focuses most generally on the "calamities of war as they affect individuals" (to refer again to the 1795 letter to Wrangham).[52]

Considering further the moral weight of the narrative, it might also be said that Wordsworth's poem places little emphasis on the social or human agents that cause the destruction of his female vagrant: "Then rose a mansion proud our woods among," his character says, describing the displacement of her father in "Adventures on Salisbury Plain," almost as if the mansion were an organic, if malignant, growth.[53] In the earliest version, the dislocation is described even more passively: "My father's substance fell into decay./Oppression trampled on his tresses grey:/His little range of water *was denied* (emphasis added).[54] Similarly, "the noisy drum" and barely specified economic hardships metonymically substitute for the national depression and war as the forces that strip the woman and her family of hope.[55] This does not, however, mark Wordsworth's tragic tale as a repression of political realities or a sentimental plea for sympathy akin to Thomson's tale of a lightning-struck lover ("Summer," ll. 1168–222). First, at no time during the period from 1793 to 1795 did the political implications of Wordsworth's tale need to be spelled out; the poem clearly uses "the idiom of contemporary anti-war protest" and focuses on the "reality of social injustice."[56] Second, to have suggested (as both Wordsworth's 1795 letter and his tale suggested) that laws and war adversely affect individuals, and that even the most powerless—for instance, female vagrants—have inner lives, histories, and (implicitly) rights, was to place one's self within a camp that included most prominently Paine, who in his 1776 introductory remarks to *Common Sense* wrote that "declaring war against the natural rights of all mankind . . . is the concern of every man to whom nature hath given the power of feeling."[57]

Indeed, it may not be coincidence that Thomson's moral rhetoric in "Summer," and especially his glorification of British yeomen and British power, are brought to mind by the original closing of "Salisbury Plain." Paine provides a precedent for using a Thomsonian rhetoric of liberty against itself, citing lines from "Liberty" on the title page of *Common Sense:* "Man knows no master save creating heaven,/Or those whom choice and common good ordain." The appeal against tyranny and for reason or common sense—"common" having become a far more politically freighted word in Paine (as in *Lyrical Ballads*)—is taken from Thomson's description of how the British were taught by the Druids to despise fear and live without tyranny:

> Man knows no master save creating heaven,
> Or such as choice and *common* good ordain.

This general *sense,* with which the nations I
Promiscuous fire, in Britons burned intense,
Of future times prophetic.
(emphasis added)[58]

Thomson's "future" is eighteenth-century Britain; Paine's is America; he appropriates Thomson and parallels images such as James Barry's 1776 etching and aquatint "The Phoenix or The Resurrection of Freedom," which shows liberty dead in Britain and fleeing to be reborn in America.[59] Wordsworth's setting for "Salisbury Plain"—with its remnants of Druidic "Superstition" and its own prophetic voice—similarly overturns Thomson's definition of the British legacy by appropriating Thomson's eighteenth-century Whig rhetoric to make a contemporary political statement.[60]

The most startling revisions of the story of the female vagrant in "Adventures on Salisbury Plain" involve Wordsworth's increasing self-consciousness about tale-telling or narrative. That is, not only is the moral weight of the poem shifted from polemic statement to story or plot, but Wordsworth foregrounds the act of storytelling, first, in the complex framing that calls the reader's attention to the acts of telling and hearing stories and, second, in the increased emphasis on the importance of the vagrant's active role as storyteller: "As if because her tale was at end/She wept." In "Adventures on Salisbury Plain," the female vagrant's tale-telling is represented as a form of present power at the loss of which she not only weeps but disappears from the poem. All versions of the poem from 1793 to 1798 also underline the woman's role in presenting her own narrative as she "her artless story told."

There may be a form of ventriloquism involved in Wordsworth's act of giving voice to the vagrant; ironically, the insistence that the story is "artless"—meaning natural, uncrafted, and also guileless—if anything reveals Wordsworth's "artfulness." His readers hear a story cast in Spenserian stanzas (anything but artlessly uncrafted), and the plot, as Wordsworth says in the letter to Wrangham, does have designs on its audience (and so is artful in the sense of having an ulterior motive). In other words, in the Salisbury Plain poems and "The Female Vagrant" Wordsworth was rethinking questions about both where his own powers as a poet lay (that is, his claim to artful writing or to a place in the British literary tradition) and the power of literature, its art in a more general sense, to affect its contemporary audience.[61] The rise of the novel, with its emphasis on storytelling and its popularity, certainly informs Wordsworth's concern with how to reach a contemporary audience. However, Wordsworth most centrally wants to test the power of his own craft or art against what he calls the violence, or "the *art, of power*" in an early 1795 letter to Matthews on political power (emphasis added).[62] The Salisbury Plain poems and "The Female Vagrant" might almost be thought of as samplers of narrative strategies—Thomsonian, Gothic, sensationalist, political, and allegorical—that test the capacity of poetry to resist sensationalism while remaining relevant.[63] Finally, we can trace in such samplings how Wordsworth turned from a poetry of the eye to a poetry of the ear—but increasingly neither to the high prophetic strains of Thomsonian civic poetry, nor of Spenser and Milton, but rather to the more intimate ear and voice of public discourse, that is, of speech as a form of testimony.

Put another way, Wordsworth's problem might be seen as analogous to Thomson's: how to be a poet and to engage the world in which he lived. However, the transformation of the female beggar into the female vagrant reveals an astonishing catalogue of different textual strategies for addressing this problem; Wordsworth attempts social commentary in a variety of forms as he moves from the disembodied and traditional voice of public poetry that ends "Salisbury Plain" to the narrative voice that ends "Adventures on Salisbury Plain" to the woman speaking in the *Lyrical Ballads.* In both the Salisbury Plain poems the narrative is embedded in a frame that sets testimonial against nationalist primitivism (embodied in the Druidic setting associated with the Gothic and with traditional poetic and political, even anthropological, discourse), which allows Wordsworth implicitly to invert the eighteenth-century progress poem.[64] In this context, the use of the Spenserian stanza in all three later versions might be seen as another example of the uneasy mixture of present relevance and poetic tradition.

If intertextuality is defined as the discursive space of a culture or cultures, then Wordsworth's diverse textual strategies explore what can be said in which discursive spaces. Furthermore, if the embodiment of Wordsworth's tale in "The Female Vagrant" poses its own problems of suppression, that is, of ventriloquism and allegorizing, Wordsworth's experiments with another version of the same story in *The Ruined Cottage,* written in 1797–1799 even as he was working on "Adventures on Salisbury Plain" and "The Female Vagrant," show his awareness of the difficulties raised by his turn to narrative, that is, his attempt to be artful both literarily and politically.[65]

Storytellers, Dreaming Men, and Twilight Shade: Action and Retirement

Before looking in detail at *The Ruined Cottage,* I would like briefly to note two other, related, issues. The first is Wordsworth's increasing self-consciousness about the uses and potential abuses of narration, or a *contemporary* poetry of the ear, which is matched by an equal self-consciousness about the problematic nature of appeals to sight, or observation. Again, if the story of the beggar from *An Evening Walk* uses a Thomsonian strategy of allowing narrative and literary echoes to invest apparently neutral description with emotional and aural power (a process figured in the Winander Boy passage's representation of echo become reflection), the Salisbury Plain poems and "The Female Vagrant" unmask this Thomsonian strategy by showing *how* place becomes associated with story. Typically Wordsworthian "spots"—the cliff over the Derwent, the "hereditary nook" from which the family is ousted—take on meaning as part of an unfolding story associated with a particular speaker affected by larger sociopolitical forces. In the process, Wordsworth's descriptive passages attempt not only to change cultural icons but also to demystify their production.

The second issue I wish to discuss is Wordsworth's exploration of the uses of description, which can be seen by turning to another Thomsonian passage from *An Evening Walk* in which Wordsworth describes a "twilight shade" found at high noon (EW, p. 34, ll. 53–84). Wordsworth's notes direct readers to think of unmediated, physical vision: "The reader, who has made the tour of this country, will recognize, in this description, the features which characterize the lower waterfall in the gardens of Rydale."[66] Readers of poetry, however, have recognized other features here, such as the passage's debts to travel literature as well as to the picturesque tradition in literature and in the visual arts.[67] Especially as the muted noon landscape reappears in *The Ruined Cottage* and is brought together with the narrative strategies Wordsworth was also exploring between 1793 and 1799, the trope is most obviously taken from "Summer" (in which it figures both the insistence on physical sight and, ultimately, Thomson's inability to merge his poetry of the eye with what his ear heard as traditional poetic music).[68] There is of course an irony in Wordsworth's first masked uses of a passage that in Thomson was already part of an insistence on a present poetry of the eye, as Wordsworth equally insists on observation without acknowledging (perhaps without being aware of) how mediated his vision is. However, by 1797–1799, as he was writing *The Ruined Cottage,* Wordsworth clearly seems to be exploring and criticizing the sources of his earlier descriptive manner.

Critics have suggested many sources for *The Ruined Cottage.*[69] Thomson's poem is sometimes mentioned as a source of Wordsworth's poetry, but usually only in passing or to dismiss the resemblance as superficial.[70] The resemblance, however, is striking if one compares the lines from Thomson discussed in chapter one to the beginning of *The Ruined Cottage.* Thomson's lines are as follows:

> 'Tis raging noon; and, vertical, the sun
> Darts on the head direct his forceful rays.
> * * *
> In vain the sight dejected to the ground

Stoops for relief;
* * *
. . . In vain I sigh,
* * *
Thrice happy he, who on the sunless side
Of a romantic mountain, forest-crowned,
Beneath the whole collected shade reclines;

Here is Wordsworth's opening to *The Ruined Cottage:*

'Twas summer and the sun was mounted high.
* * *
. . . far as the sight
Could reach those many shadows lay in spots
* * *
Pleasant to him who . . .
Extends his careless limbs beside the root
Of some huge oak whose aged branches make
A twilight of their own, a dewy shade
Where the wren warbles while the dreaming man [looks out]
* * *
Other lot was mine.
(ll. 1, 6–7, 10–14, 18)

Both poets are concerned with perception, with the limits of physical vision, and, most strikingly, with poetic vision. Moreover, Wordsworth purposefully begins with a description, apparently unrelated to the story that follows, of Thomson's reclining figure in retirement; as in *The Seasons,* the figure is clearly imagined, an *emblem* of the poet in nature. The critic Annabel Patterson argues that Wordsworth's dreamer—the otherwise "gratuitous figure"—must be drawn from Tityrus, from Virgil's *Eclogues,* a figure of what Patterson calls "soft pastoral" which is associated with, among other things, ease, reflection, and an obliviousness to civic engagement, against which Wordsworth sets a harder "labor theory of poetic value."[71] Yet despite his first-hand knowledge of Virgil, whose work he translated, Wordsworth understood Virgil as filtered through Milton and Thomson: in a late (1824) letter to Lord Lonsdale, for instance, Wordsworth connected Virgil's verse in the *Aeneid* and the *Georgics* with Milton's blank verse.[72] In 1803, Wordsworth also insisted in a letter to De Quincey that poets must pay attention to "the great names of past times, *and above all to those of our own Country*" (emphasis added).[73] Although by 1842 Wordsworth dismissed Thomson's use of blank verse (written "before his ear was formed"), the admiration for *The Seasons* he voiced earlier suggests that Thomson, as well as

Virgil and Milton, informed Wordsworth's ear in 1798–1799.[74] Wordsworth also described Virgil's as a poetry of the eye, and the most prominent British poet of the eye in Wordsworth's own early writings was Thomson, whose work Wordsworth would certainly have seen as drawing on Virgil's within a British context.[75] Finally, Wordsworth looked to Thomson's formulation of the contrast between the "careless" meditative solitude of the natural world (echoing the "careless limbs" of *The Ruined Cottage*'s dreaming man) and the urban, civic world; a (1806) letter to Lady Beaumont cites Thomson's 1725 "Hymn on Solitude": "I just may cast my careless eyes/Where London's spiry turrets rise,/Think of its crimes, its cares, its pain/Then shield me in the woods again."[76] By 1806, Wordsworth could cite Thomson on solitude, echoing the language in which the dreaming man of 1798–1799 is described, in apparent support of a thoroughly aestheticized and distanced view of civic concerns. However, the Thomsonian dreaming figure in poetic solitude is far from disengaged landscape architecture in 1798–1799.

The issues of the uses of sight and of poetic labor or idleness raised by Wordsworth's Thomsonian figure in rural retirement can be connected in a detailed way with Wordsworth's personal situation. In 1794, even as he was working on the Salisbury Plain poems, Wordsworth was still writing of his desire to be in town—"cataracts and mountains . . . are good occasional society, but they will not do for constant companions"—although the same letter linked the countryside around Keswick with poetry and linked poetry, in turn, with leisure.[77] From February through August 1795, Wordsworth stayed in London, where he associated with the radical Godwin circle, before himself retiring to the country (from 1795 through 1798).[78] In *The Ruined Cottage,* then, Wordsworth's image of a leisured figure in country retirement is a personal, a political, and a literary emblem on which the poem as whole comments (and which it dismantles). The figure allowed Wordsworth to defend his own retreat from the civic, politically engaged community of London to the countryside that seemed a traditional emblem of poetic accomplishment, possibly at the expense of such community. His defense entails redefining retreat not as disengagement or idleness, but as the site of writerly labor, disengaged only from the urban marketplace.[79]

In *The Ruined Cottage,* the opening Thomsonian figure of the dreaming man in retirement is deliberately contrasted with both the narrator's struggle and Armytage's more active "ease."[80] Throughout the poem, Wordsworth uses his major characters to redefine the issues that had plagued Thomson. More explicitly than Thomson, Wordsworth makes his repetition of the past and his related fictionalization of the self an enabling force in his poem; his poet figure's claim to power in the present rejects "idle dream[ing]" (l. 231),

the activity of the reclining Thomsonian dreamer; the power claimed ulti-
mately, if uneasily, resides in the present act of storytelling. Explicitly re-
placing Thomson's emblematic poet-figure with a figure, Armytage, who
actively tells a story of earthly human suffering, *The Ruined Cottage* can also
insist on the moral authority of the poet by humanizing his insights, em-
bedding them within a narrative and a narrator.

Wordsworth's first full (1798) text of *The Ruined Cottage* is prefaced by
a quotation emphasizing his rejection of the higher music Thomson at-
tempted; Wordsworth writes that he will not strain to hear angelic voices
but rather rest content with a muse in "homely" dress: "Give me a spark of
nature's fire,/Tis the best learning I desire."[81] The passage is from Burns,
another Scot Wordsworth admired; as "A Letter to a Friend of Robert
Burns" suggests, the strategy he attributes to Burns is what allows him to
revise the locodescriptive manner of "Summer," avoiding the earlier poem's
loss of poetic authority: "Burns avail[s] himself of his own *character and sit-
uation in society, to construct out of them a poetic self,—introduced as a dra-
matic personage*—for the purpose of inspiriting his incidents, *diversifying his
pictures,* recommending his opinions, and giving point to his sentiments"
(emphasis added).[82]

Wordsworth's rationale echoes the calls for narrative to enliven descrip-
tion found in critical responses to descriptive poetry from *The Seasons* to *An
Evening Walk,* but it again suggests further motives for a turn from Thom-
sonian rationales for the use of description. Specifically, Wordsworth corre-
lates moral authority with the construction of a poetic self out of
psychological and sociological (that is, neither divine nor literary) sources.
Moreover, in *The Ruined Cottage* he goes on to include a story of human suf-
fering and to suggest that poetry helps call forth human sympathy. Finally,
though, it is the performative act of storytelling (by the writer and for the
reader who implicitly will become in turn a storyteller) that is the source and
the end of poetry's power.[83]

Explicitly, the poem claims moral power is a necessary quality of true po-
etry. Armytage opens the second part of the poem claiming that a "power to
virtue friendly" (l. 229) must inform his narrative: without such power his
storytelling would be "a wantonness" (l. 221). The "pedlar" in manuscript A
is already apologizing: "You will forgive me Sir/I feel I play the truant with
my tale."[84] The storyteller's power first seems to lie in his ability to move his
audience to virtuous acts, although the power Armytage ultimately claims is
that of storytelling. This can be seen in part in the way the complex narra-
tive structure of Wordsworth's poem, on which his revisions through March
of 1798 placed increasing emphasis, shifts the reader from an image of the
poet as one who sees to an image of the poet as storyteller.[85] Moreover, at
the same time, the content of Armytage's story, the inclusion of a narrator

who listens to his story, and ultimately even Wordsworth's insistence on the performative power of narration problematize the moral authority claimed for poetry. I want to consider, first, the contents of the story and especially its ambiguous lessons on the uses of the poetic eye and on nature's role in promoting virtue.

The Ruined Cottage most immediately invites comparisons between Margaret (a more personalized version of the female vagrant) and Armytage. Margaret's response to the losses nature and society have visited on her is diametrically opposed to the acceptance of loss Armytage preaches and seems to exemplify.[86] Yet, paradoxically, Margaret's inflexibility is related to the power of her imagination and to her refusal to accept what the natural world can offer her: "About the fields I wander, knowing this/Only, that what I seek I cannot find" (ll. 350–51). Margaret's fixed gaze as well as her restlessness marks her as a Wordsworthian figure of imagination: the reader last hears of her with her eye "busy in the distance, shaping things" (l. 456).[87]

Armytage's eye also shapes things: "I see around me here/Things which you cannot see" (ll. 67–68). However, when the narrator contrasts the "secret spirit of humanity" with nature's "oblivious tendencies" (ll. 503–4), Armytage chastises the narrator for reading the "forms of things with an unworthy eye" (l. 511). In short, there appear to be proper and improper uses of the eye. Armytage implies elsewhere, too, that he knows how to read nature properly; he insists his reports of Margaret, for instance, are drawn in part from a reading of the landscape (another example of Wordsworth's use of "narrativized landscapes" and an even more explicit representation than in "The Female Vagrant" of how description and narrative are connected). Armytage further claims to draw comfort from nature, as his first and last readings of landscapes illustrate. But the line between the proper and improper uses of the eye or of imaginative vision is not as clear-cut as first appears.[88] It is difficult to avoid asking whether the comfort Armytage finds is either natural, virtuous, or convincing. Certainly, his communion with Margaret's spring is a peculiar one: he says that he and the spring waters "*seemed* to feel/One sadness" (ll. 83–84, emphasis added) and then says that for them "a bond/Of brotherhood is broken" (ll. 84–85); they no longer minister to "human comfort" (l. 88).

The shared sadness, it appears, is over the fact that nature does *not* minister to humanity. As when the "blighting seasons" (l. 134) help lead to Margaret's loss, or as when Wordsworth writes of those whose "place knew them not" (l. 144), nature and man do not seem to have an easy relationship. Rather, nature seems to offer Armytage emblems of its own inadequacy.[89] It may even be suggested that nature's lesson is not to care. On the most literal level, this is the problem that those reading the poem for the first time generally point out: Armytage does not stay and help Margaret;

his later moralizing is thus unconvincing.[90] This is in part a function of the most disconcerting aspect of Armytage's apparent lesson: what he learns from nature is to be detached, to have no home, which presumably accounts for the end of the 1799 poem in which the two travelers move on to an inn, a mere "evening resting-place" (l. 538). Since early Wordsworth uses cottages as emblems of peace, love, and hope, the very title of *The Ruined Cottage* calls into question whether the natural world can be the comfort or home to man Armytage seems to suggest it is.[91]

Armytage is not simply allowed to exemplify his questionably achieved calm, however. The narrative distance provided by the poet-narrator comments on Armytage's position in the poem. First, the narrator allows Armytage to reveal that his calm is far from easy. Armytage ends the first part of the poem with a series of questions, usually taken as cautionary, similar to the warning sounded against impotent grief toward the end of the poem:

> Why should a tear be in an old man's eye?
> Why should we thus with an untoward mind
> And in the weakness of humanity
> From natural wisdom turn our hearts away,
> To natural comfort shut our eyes and ears,
> And, feeding on disquiet thus disturb
> The calm of Nature with our restless thoughts?
> (ll. 192–98)

If these questions are merely rhetorical, then the charge of inhumanity leveled against Armytage is fair. But the poem, and Armytage's tale, have fed on disquiet, and thus his questions are to the point, especially given the eagerness with which the narrator then urges Armytage to resume his story, apparently ignoring the caution he has been given about the purposes served by listening to the tale. There is also a self-consciousness about how Armytage ignores his own lesson about the calm indifference of nature and tells a disturbing tale emphasizing that he was unable to help Margaret when she was alive. Armytage does insist before resuming that his tale should not serve as mere titillation. The story, Armytage claims, has a moral "power to virtue friendly" (l. 229), that is, there is potential virtue and power in rehearsing Margaret's loss, in revealing her and his own past impotence, and—by implication—even in giving rise to the poet-narrator's later disquiet and "impotence of grief." But the poem does not explicitly resolve the question of how disquieting, even sensationalist, stories yield to the calm seen in nature or in what way past impotence becomes present power.[92]

Having said this, I want to return to the question of what—if anything— the poem defines as poetic power. Looking at images of idleness and power in the poem is a good way to see that the questionable status of his view of nature does not wholly discredit Armytage, who does instruct the poet-narrator (and ultimately the reader) on how to avoid "the impotence of grief" (l. 500), although his final instructions are contained as much in the fact that he tells his tale as in what he says. Impotence is what distinguishes Margaret from Armytage: Margaret's futile attempt to recapture the past is associated with idleness (ll. 383, 431, 451), while Armytage's claim to power in the present shows he is not an "idle dreamer" (l. 231), unlike the Thomsonian figure with which the poem opens.[93]

But what of the power Armytage claims? And in what way is Wordsworth's figure able to claim the authority Thomson's could not? After all, Armytage was impotent when face to face with Margaret and her grief: "I had little power/To give her comfort" (ll. 275–76). It seems the power the poem desires is in large part that of offering comfort. However, if the poem can lay claim to such power, it is not in the time about which we are told, but in the present act of storytelling. That is, the power Armytage can claim is in the narrative present, which includes the fictionalization of his otherwise powerless past self.[94] In short, the sources of power in *The Ruined Cottage* are finally to be seen not so much in nature as in narration. Thoughts of man cannot coexist with nature's image of tranquillity, but what replaces the idle or impotent dream of "what we feel of sorrow and despair" (l. 520) is "meditation" (l. 524), or the present narration of the past rather than nature or the powerless nostalgia for what is lost or irremediable. Armytage's exemplary lesson is finally in his use of his voice, not his eye.

By insisting upon the presence of narration, *The Ruined Cottage* claims the power that Thomson suggested was lost. At the same time, though, Wordsworth wanted to claim more for poetry than his narrative sustains: he insists that poetry has moral power, and yet Armytage, his poet-figure, is unable to help the woman whose story he tells; the comfort and human community projected are felt only as human history is told and retold, forging a bond between Armytage-as-poet, the narrator who retells Armytage's story, and the reader who is implicitly invited to make the story his or her own. The power Wordsworth claims is then, in a way, marked as a pure creation of words in the same world of words in which Thomson felt lost. Ironically, insofar as it successfully recasts and revitalizes the Thomsonian figure with which it opens, *The Ruined Cottage* reinscribes Thomson in a tradition and in so doing, perhaps, makes most convincing its claim for poetic power over the past even as it underlines the radical gap between what it *would* claim and what it *can* claim, thus tacitly testing the contemporary ideologies that yoked sensibility, compassion, and commonweal.

These unreconciled tensions between literary historical power and the power to affect the present in *The Ruined Cottage* are also related to a feature of "The Female Vagrant," namely, the problematic aspects of the vagrant's "artless" story. Like the vagrant's insistence that she could not become a beggar (despite her relationship to the beggar in *An Evening Walk*), the narrator's emphasis in "The Female Vagrant" on the woman's artlessness is presumably meant to exonerate her from charges of having designs on her listeners—that is, to mark her as one of the virtuous poor—even as her testimony is intended to provoke social change (at least the awareness of the need for change, if not specific reforms). On the one hand, the insistence that the vagrant has no designs on her audience is meant to dignify the character as well as to invoke sympathy from the reader. On the other hand, the didactic intent requires Wordsworth to distance himself from his character and so foreshadows the active role granted narrator and listener at the expense of the displaced woman, Margaret, in *The Ruined Cottage*.[95] Like the artlessness of the vagrant's tale, the silencing of Margaret raises the specter of voyeurism or sensationalism, placing the listener in the position against which Armytage explicitly protests: "It were a wantoness, and would demand/Severe reproof, if we were men whose hearts/Could hold vain dalliance with the misery/ . . . , contented thence to draw/A momentary pleasure never marked/By reason, barren of all future good."[96] While Armytage's language recalls common eighteenth-century speculations over why representations of misery have moral uses (the usual answer being that they promote sympathy), the issue is particularly pointed for Wordsworth, in part because he acknowledges that *his* tales cannot be "artless" (that is, without some useful design on their readers) without also being morally suspect (that is, "wanton" or sensationalist).[97] At the same time, Armytage's cautions acknowledge that by giving voice to speakers such as the female vagrant (whose direct speech, by 1798–1799, is clearly marked as a form of empowerment) while insisting on his own distance from his speaker's artlessness, Wordsworth took away from the dignity he wished to grant such characters.

If I am right that questions about how to represent others' stories are thus central to the poem, it follows that while *Armytage's* story may trade "political for personal comfort," it is not clear that *Wordsworth's* story "is a capitalization upon inhumanity."[98] Wordsworth was not overtly worried about charges of ventriloquism or condescension and certainly not in those terms.[99] However, he did express anxiety about sensationalism or writing that promoted a taste for "sentimental common-places . . . [with] an imposing air of novelty."[100] The preceding quote, in fact, is taken from Wordsworth's discussion of how only the "vicious" parts of Thomson—his *stories*—were popularly acclaimed. In this context, *The Ruined Cottage* can be read as part of the series of Wordsworthian questions begun at least as early as the Salisbury Plain poems. These questions are not only about literary power but also about the effective power of narrative (based in part on Wordsworth's readings of Thomsonian narrative), specifically about whether or not poetry might testify to social or political realities. The poem, then, is self-consciously raising questions about whether stories like Margaret's can be told at all without being "untoward," or sensationalist.[101] Moreover, to question sensationalist exploitation is not simply to express dismay at literary taste or at the literary marketplace, although this is certainly involved.[102] It is also to question the very act of representation and, in the 1790s, to ask how poetry might testify to social and political ills without exploitation. In part, then, Wordsworth's drama is a projection of his writerly anxieties in the late nineties as he tried to revise or reimagine a role for poetry in his day; as importantly, it is testimony to his recognition of his own place in and questioning of the larger culture he documented.

Wordsworth's long-standing anxiety over his own, and poetry's, impotence was personal, professional, and political; indeed, it is difficult to know how the three realms could have been separate for Wordsworth in a period that saw him facing the loss of the first home he had had since childhood (as he decided to go into what looked as if it might be permanent exile in Germany) and the loss of the family he had begun with Annette Vallon, both losses related to the failure of the Revolution's promise of social change and human community.[103] Wordsworth was also having difficulties supporting himself and his sister, and he aligned his own situation as a writer with that of other laborers, especially in the Lake District.[104] In *The Ruined Cottage*, Wordsworth's insistence on the present activity of storytelling is thus a provisional solution to the problems he faced, especially the problem of how to image an active, socially or politically useful poetry. Wordsworth's achievement was that he envisioned his storytelling as action and as labor within a world in which both individual action and labor had themselves been recast, and in *The Ruined Cottage* he did so without obscuring the limits of what such labor could effect.

Wordsworth's relative tough-mindedness becomes clearer if one compares him with others who considered the same issues. Within twenty years, two other nineteenth-century writers explicitly and implicitly tackled the same question of the efficacy and utility of literary labor. The better known passage is from Thomas De Quincey writing on Alexander Pope. De Quincey, in 1848, distinguishes literature from reading material that "applies only to a local, or professional, or merely personal interest," and he similarly draws distinctions between what he calls the literature of knowledge—associated with teaching and giving information—and the literature of power—associated with sympathy and uniqueness and characterized as writing that turns "arid notional forms" into "vital activities"; De Quincey concludes, the "commonest novel ... sustains and quickens [moral] affections. Calling them into *action* . . ." (emphasis added).[105] It is worth noting in passing how De Quincey grants primacy to the more narrative and popular genre of the novel. More generally, attempting to rescue the arts from increasing professionalism and an increasingly impersonal market economy, De Quincey's organic metaphors ("arid" ideas turn to "vernal" life and "germinate" into action) inadvertently leave poetry with a thoroughly idealized and ungrounded field of action.[106]

Literary labor is also implicitly defined in William Cobbett's earlier and more literal discussion of gardening. While De Quincey attempts to distinguish "cookery book[s]" from "Paradise Lost" by elevating the latter, Cobbett's 1833 *The English Gardener* reverses the process: "It is useless to know how to write, unless by the use of that talent we communicate something *useful* to others. . . . I . . . advise the reader to begin by reading [my book] all through. . . . If he were to do this three times over, it would only require the time frequently devoted to three or four volumes of a *miserable novel*" (emphasis added).[107] Cobbett, in short, wants nothing of De Quincey's metaphorical gardens; he is defiantly writing and defending a literature of knowledge; indeed, he opens his book by stating that his "business is *to teach*."[108]

Perhaps most interesting—aside from the fact that Cobbett's book concentrates on gentlemen's gardens rather than cottage gardens and that it contains some clear misinformation—is the epigraph from *Proverbs* Cobbett uses on the original title page: "I went by the field of the slothful . . . grown over with thorns, and nettles . . . I looked upon it, and received instruction."[109] Given Cobbett's clarity of purpose (to teach or communicate useful information), this negative parable about sloth and labor is surprising, especially when placed against Wordsworth's representation of his narrator looking upon Margaret's garden—where nettles also grow (and rot)—to receive instruction.[110] The nettles were not retained in *The Excursion,* so Cobbett could not have known how directly he echoed Wordsworth's 1797–1799 poems. However, the epigraph inadvertently sanctions Wordsworth's tale as potentially useful. It also reveals the distance between De Quincey's metaphorical action, Cobbett's literal-minded calls for useful labor (especially ironic given that anyone following Cobbett's advice to transplant in direct, hot sun would labor less than usefully), and Wordsworth's ability to express, and in that expression to suspend, his anxiety over the nature, the uses, and the limits of literary labor. Such comparisons lend weight to Wordsworth's middle position, evidenced in his ironic awareness of the complexities and difficulties of producing "[k]nowledge not purchased by the loss of power," or of representing his own field of action as other than the field of the slothful.[111]

Continuing Conversations:
Literary History and Historical Efficacy, 1799–1802

Wordsworth's representations of his own activity did shift between 1799 and 1815. After 1799, for instance, his letters are more comfortable designating writing as work, as in his 1804 letter characterizing work both in the visual and the literary arts as "unwearied labour and diligence" or his 1814 letter describing the most recent revision of *The Ruined Cottage* (published in much revised form in 1814 as "The Wanderer" or Book I of *The Excursion*) as "written with great labour."[112] Wordsworth, indeed, was still reworking or reenacting his story as late as 1844.[113] Before turning to a brief concluding discussion of *The Excursion* of 1814, it is worth sketching in more detail Wordsworth's shifting views of poetic labor during the decade and a half following his departure from Alfoxden and the few if fruitful years of community he found there, especially because of his friendship with Coleridge. I would like to focus on two poems, one from 1802 and one written slightly earlier, in the period when Wordsworth left Alfoxden (having been under government surveillance) and contemplated leaving England to dodge the draft through what he thought might be a lengthy exile in Germany.[114] "A Poet's Epitaph" was written in Germany during a harsh winter of social and linguistic isolation. The poem describes exile as a form of poetic death, which is not surprising given that Wordsworth was contemplating his own separation from the country in whose literary tradition and political reforms he wished to have a role.

"A Poet's Epitaph" most obviously draws on Robert Burns's 1786 "A Bard's Epitaph" in its title, in its formal organization as a series of questions, in its explicit challenge to the reader to mourn the loss of a poet, and in its implicit occasion: exile.[115] Wordsworth also, however, invokes Thomson, most significantly in his return to the image of the noontime idle dreamer from *The Ruined Cottage*. The figure of the dreamer is used partly in order to contrast the poet with those who have professional status.[116] Unlike Burns's bard, but like Thomson's, Wordsworth's poet is "clad in homely russet brown" (l. 38) and

> . . . retired as noontide dew,
> Or fountain in a noon-day grove;
>   * * *
> In common things that round us lie
> Some random truths he can impart,—
> The harvest of a quiet eye
> That broods and sleeps on his own heart.
>
> But he is weak; both Man and Boy,

Hath been an idler in the land;
Contented if he might enjoy
The things which others understand.
(ll. 41–42; 49–56)

It is easy to see how "A Poet's Epitaph" might be read at first as a moment of bitterness more than of doubt; the description again is of the poet in retirement at noon, with the "noontide dew" and grove clearly marking the trope as related to Thomson's reclining poet in *The Seasons,* while the poet's clothing borrows from another Thomsonian figure of idleness, the poet in *The Castle of Indolence.*[117] But here, as he *contrasts* poetic and civic labor, Wordsworth conflates his poetic figure in idle (and traditional) retreat with what in *The Ruined Cottage* was the more active figure of Armytage "harvesting" images with "a quiet eye" from "common things." *The Ruined Cottage* attempted to find an argument for the power of poetry not so much by proposing specific programs to promote "virtue" but in the very activity of rehearsing and refashioning the tale of the tribe.[118] "A Poet's Epitaph," which was written between drafts of *The Ruined Cottage,* reveals the precariousness of the stance taken in *The Ruined Cottage;* "A Poet's Epitaph" replaces power or action with weakness and replaces the potent, if unstable, meditation of *The Ruined Cottage* with enjoyment and "random" truths.

Yet "A Poet's Epitaph" does not conclusively revise Wordsworth's representation of writing poetry. The poem explicitly celebrates dead poets over living professionals in a defiant, even bathetic, vein as an imagined farewell to poetry—a self-conscious *trial* epitaph on Wordsworth's hope that poetry might not be an "idle" dream. As such, it does not foreclose the possibility of an engaged poetry but is part of his continuing dialogue with poetic commonplace and with himself. This can be seen even more clearly by examining Wordsworth's similar return to the figure of the reclining poet, found in a slightly later poem that explicitly takes a leaf from Thomson's book: "Stanzas Written in My Pocket-Copy of Thomson's *Castle of Indolence.*"[119] "Stanzas" entertains a position opposed to that found in "A Poet's Epitaph." The latter ironically tries on the idea that poetry is ineffective idleness in the present. "Stanzas," by contrast, satirizes the idea that poets are idle dreamers. Between them, the two poems keep open the questions raised in *The Ruined Cottage* about the present efficacy of poetic labor.

In November of 1801, Mary Hutchinson (staying with the Wordsworths, but not yet married to William) was reading Thomson, while Wordsworth, and eventually the entire household, was reading Spenser; Wordsworth may also already have begun the work that would inform his late revisions of *The Ruined Cottage* (that is, *The Excursion*) in the same month.[120] Within six months, in May of 1802, Wordsworth drew on both Thomson and Spenser to write "Stanzas," with its portraits of two poets. One is a man "retired in . . . sunshiny shade" who "slept himself away" and was "wedded to" verse; the second is a man of play and invention: "To cheat away the hours that silent were:/He would have taught you how you might employ/Yourself."[121] The figure of Coleridge in the poem teaches the figure of Wordsworth (related to the earlier Thomsonian idle dreamer with his "sunshiny shade") to "employ" himself—not, as in *The Ruined Cottage* or the quotation from Burns, by using his own historically located position to construct a poetic self, but rather by retreating into mere play and fairy tale: to "*cheat* away the hours," displaying "all the glorious sights which *fairies* do behold" (ll. 51, 63, emphasis added).

The lesson of the Coleridge figure is not to be taken straightforwardly, given Wordsworth's title as well as his reiteration of the reclining figure in noontime shade, the site of such an obviously self-conscious struggle less than five years earlier. There is also an obvious edge to Wordsworth's use of a Spenserian vocabulary for delusion in his description of Coleridge "*entic[ing]*" Wordsworth "to hear/His music, and to view his imagery" (ll. 64–65, emphasis added), especially when the imagery has just been identified as part of a fairy tale as well as set within Thomson's castle of delusion. Moreover, the poem questions turning the production of poetic music from the engaged voice of storytelling into something quite different when it describes Coleridge as follows: "Instruments had he, *playthings for the ear,*/Long blades of grass pluck'd round him as he lay;/These serv'd to catch the wind as it came near" (ll. 55–57, emphasis added). Wordsworth's blades of grass are a double-edged replacement of Thomson's harp with a more earthbound and natural instrument, as well as being a literalization of Coleridge's hypothetical statement in his 1795 "The Eolian Harp," "What if all of animated nature/Be but organic Harps?"[122]

For Thomson, the harp was a rejected, if attractive, emblem of an age in which higher voices informed poetry, and poetry did not require labor. Indeed, it is useful to contrast Wordsworth's anxiety over his own profession with Thomson's (ignoring for a moment the fact that Wordsworth seems not to have focused in detail upon the anxiety evident in Thomson's work). Thomson increasingly proposed poetic labor as civic labor, although he had difficulty imagining precisely how poets and traditional poetic language might be inserted within the contemporary urban world; by the time he wrote *The Castle of Indolence,* he insisted that contemporary poetic composition was a form of labor, placing his emblem of unlabored music, the Aeolian harp, within the realm of illusion and false pastoral. Coleridge's 1795 harp is also ultimately rejected within Coleridge's "The Eolian Harp," a poem that further proposes the image of an organic harp as the fantasy of a poet "*at noon*" viewing through "half-clos'd eye-lids . . . many *idle* flitting phantasies" (emphasis added), repeating the figure of the idle dreamer.[123] By further literalizing Coleridge's harp, itself already a naturalized if idealized transmutation of Thomson's instrument, Wordsworth tacitly defines the music heard in *his* version of Thomson's castle in opposition to Coleridge's "witchery of sound"; as anyone who has actually made sound by blowing across a blade of grass knows, the noise is less than entrancing. In short, the poetic ears and eyes of the two figures in "Stanzas" are harshly ironic rather than defensive, let alone self-justifying.[124]

Much later, in 1829, Wordsworth would instruct Catherine Grace Godwin on the difficulty of writing Spenserian stanzas, calling the verse form "ill adapted to conflicting passion" and claiming that even in Thomson's hands the stanzas became "merely descriptive and sentimental."[125] In the 1802 "Stanzas," Wordsworth echoes Spenser and Thomson satirically, using the form of the Salisbury Plain poems and "The Female Vagrant" to question the way he had first used the Spenserian stanza in the late nineties. Earlier, his use of the form was a display of his own artfulness as well as a testing of the capacity of literary discourse to resist both sensationalism and nostalgia. By 1802, he represents himself as literally written into the book of British literature ("Stanzas Written in My Pocket-Copy of Thomson's *Castle of Indolence*"), specifically into an inexpensive, widely available version of Thomson's delusive castle, yet without an effective present voice. The irony in the poem suggests that Wordsworth does not capitulate to but overtly acknowledges his fear that he cannot write a poetry that both places him within the British canon and has the power to affect the world in which it was written.

I suggested earlier that poems of the late nineties, such as "A Poet's Epitaph," might most sensibly be read in line with poems such as *The Ruined Cottage* as moments in Wordsworth's continual dialogues with literary tradition, with popular culture, and with the social scientific, or the political, discourse of his day. "Stanzas," from 1802, can be read as continuing such dialogues and so as a poem that shows Wordsworth continuing his earlier attempts to insert his work within both history and literary history. Indeed, speaking of his much later revisions in *The Excursion*, Wordsworth describes his poetry as "conversational."[126] Even as he increasingly came to envision poetic achievement retrospectively and proleptically, that is, as ineffective in the historical present, he still was thinking seriously about the wide, present appeal of popular literature ("half-penny Ballads, and penny and two-penny histories"), expressing his wish to produce similarly broad-based writing, although he framed his wish as a desire to produce "flowers and useful herbs to take [the] place of weeds."[127]

Revising One's Self: Public and Private Conversations, 1802–1814

Despite continuities in his conceptions of himself and his poetry, after 1802 Wordsworth's claims for poetry as a potentially active force for effective political change diminished as his hopes of claiming a place in literary history became stronger and more explicit. With this in mind, I want to continue sketching the continuities and changes in Wordsworth's representations of the uses of poetry from 1802 through 1814 when the first published version of Margaret's tale appeared in *The Excursion*. As I have argued, disillusionment is not the most appropriate description of Wordsworth's stance in 1802. Nor does the poetry written before 1806 substantiate the charge that he retreated to wholly internalized concerns.[128] Certainly, whatever feelings of loss Wordsworth experienced between 1798 and 1802 were not purely internalized or personal, but involved his assessment of the then current political situation. In his political sonnet, "London, 1802," for example, Wordsworth writes that England needs Milton because she has forfeited "inward happiness"—presumably the paradise within that Michael promises Adam—and become, as Wordsworth says echoing Milton's description of Hell, "a fen/Of stagnant waters."[129] However, England's hell-like condition is a reference to both an inner and an outer state; similarly, the freedom mentioned in the sonnet's list of England's needs is carefully placed between and thus connected with both the private and the public realms: "give us manners, virtue, freedom, power." Admittedly, Wordsworth's diagnosis ultimately concentrates on an internal condition rather than on larger social structures: "We are selfish men," Wordsworth concludes. But he adds that lack of selfishness is what allows social sympathy, as Milton is said to have traveled unselfishly "on life's common way," that is, as a man among other men, even as he also looked inward: "and yet thy heart/The lowliest duties on herself did lay." By implication, it is the minds of selfish men that have made England what it has become, as Wordsworth alludes to Satan's vaunt in *Paradise Lost* that the mind makes heavens and hells.[130] But there is also the added proviso that, unlike Satan, Milton served duty and God—that is, he yielded to external constraints.

This focus on the interrelations between the personal and public realms was already implicit in the way *The Ruined Cottage* appropriated Thomson's Miltonic and Satanic sublime in the description of currant bushes that "o'erleap/The broken wall."[131] More self-consciously than Thomson, Wordsworth reraised Miltonic questions about the autonomy of the self by his use of traditional figures and by his attribution of such descriptions to the particular situation of the narrator. Throughout, Wordsworth's focus on the relationship between the private and public spheres was itself both a private and a public gesture, part of two related conversations: the first involved the political questions, including the questions about the art of power and the power of art that I have been tracing; the second involved a series of exchanges with Coleridge about the origins and proper ends of poetic work.

These exchanges with Coleridge can be heard in Wordsworth's poems as early as 1798 when Wordsworth began "Peter Bell" as a response to Coleridge after his failed attempt to collaborate with Coleridge on "The Ancient Mariner." "Peter Bell" revisits a central theme of *The Ruined Cottage,* namely, the transforming power of storytelling, and again grounds such transformations in the realms of both the social and the psychological, taking issue with Coleridge's emphasis on the supernatural.[132] Specifically, Wordsworth responded to Coleridge's accusation (as reported by Hazlitt) that Wordsworth was too matter-of-fact.[133] This poetic conversation then continues in "Ode: Intimations of Immortality" and "Dejection: An Ode," as well as in "Stanzas Written in My Pocket-Copy of Thomson's *Castle of Indolence.*"

The conversation with Coleridge is perhaps most clearly visible in Wordsworth's "Ode: Intimations of Immortality." Wordsworth's "Ode" marks a slight shift in his earlier political "dream" of social change in which poets might participate (perhaps even in the more modest ambitions articulated in his letter to Fox one year earlier).[134] Wordsworth nonetheless retains his insistence on shared realities, or "the light of common day," which he sets against Coleridge's midnight dejection and dark fantasy.[135] The 1804 ending of Wordsworth's ode also continues the insistence on a sympathetic, outward focus, although the poem—even as reflected by its original epigraph, "Paulò majora canamus [Let us sing a little higher]"—does look up and out of time, generalizing and idealizing (or at least allegorizing) local "matters of fact." However, in context—that is, in light of the conversations in which the 1802 poems participate—the "Ode," like "Stanzas," most centrally takes issue with and resists the wholly internalized heaven (or hell) that Coleridge posited. In other words, even though Wordsworth's "Ode" reassesses his earlier hopes of politically effective poetry, reconceived in 1802 as having been visionary, he continues his insistence that poetry is part of a larger social world. Moreover, it is not until 1806 that Wordsworth dismisses even his political hopes as a product of delusion, or a vision of the "light that never was."[136]

The 1806 line is from "Elegiac Stanzas," and the dark tone is most obviously related to the elegy's overt subject, namely, the death of Wordsworth's brother John at sea in February 1805. In "Elegiac Stanzas," Wordsworth explicitly rejects what he calls his former "fond delusion . . . faith [and] trust" and, with a revisionary twist, dismisses his earlier engagement as having, in effect, placed him "in a dream, at distance from the Kind [i.e., humankind]." It is his new "distress," he writes, that "hath humaniz'd [his] Soul." The human condition in which Wordsworth now sees himself sharing is more generalized; particular stories such as that of Margaret and Robert are replaced with references to "the Kind." Human existence is also more insistently characterized as a condition of individual powerlessness, or so Wordsworth suggests in writing that he has "submitted to a new controul:/A power is gone, which nothing can restore." Of course, both "The Female Vagrant" and *The Ruined Cottage* questioned the use of particular narratives as potentially sensationalist in effect, if not in intent. The earlier poems were also already self-conscious about the limits of the politically or socially effective power storytellers or poets might claim. In *The Ruined Cottage*, Wordsworth implicitly identified poetic power as that provisional and performative power passed from storyteller to audience, although the poem also entertained Armytage's suggestion that it is the eye actively reading nature rather than the voice that counts. "Elegiac Stanzas" questions the reliability of the poetic eye more explicitly. In the past, Wordsworth writes, he would have painted pictures of "Elysian quiet": "Such, in the fond *delusion* of my heart,/Such *Picture* would I at that time have made:/And *seen* the soul of truth in every part" (ll. 26, 29–31, emphasis added). In 1806, the truth—or what can be known—and human comfort are both overtly connected with speech: "This, *which I know, I speak* with mind serene" (l. 40, emphasis added). In this sense, although "Elegiac Stanzas" more emphatically declares the importance of voice, it keeps open the same questions about the power and value of poetry found in the earlier poems. What is new in "Elegiac Stanzas" is the strength of the suggestion that poets may claim no privilege, not even the limited power of storytelling, over the world: "Such happiness, wherever it be known,/Is to be pitied; for 'tis surely blind" (ll. 55–56).

Letters from 1806 through 1815 similarly suggest a shift in Wordsworth's conception of what poetry could accomplish.[137] In 1808, for instance, Wordsworth wrote to Samuel Rogers that poet George Crabbe's "verses" about rural poverty were not poetry at all but "mere matters of fact; with which the Muses have just about as much to do as they have with a Collection of medical reports, or of Law cases."[138] In 1807, he asked what the subjects about which he wrote had to with "routs, dinners, morning calls, hurry from door to door . . . with [the statesmen] Mr. Pitt or Mr. Fox."[139] Although he always mistrusted the urban bustle and professional lives that these letters also dismiss, Wordsworth had earlier explored what the Muse might have to do with, or to say to, matters of fact, the law, *and* Mr. Fox.[140] Along with this diminished sense of how poetry might affect the matter-of-fact world of real bodies and the body politic, Wordsworth's sense of the audience for and the subjects of his human tales had shifted by 1815.

Dorothy Wordsworth's comments on Hazlitt's review of *The Excursion* must have made her brother uneasy. She wrote of Hazlitt, "He says that the *narratives* are a clog upon the poem. I was not sorry to hear that, for I am sure with *common* Readers those parts of the poem will be by far the most interesting" (emphasis added).[141] The letter, written in 1814, claims both storytelling and common readers while it disclaims Hazlitt. Wordsworth's use of narrative even in the middle to late nineties had betrayed his uneasy awareness that the testimonial or documentary aspects of "common tales" (on one hand) and appeals to those with political power (on the other hand) might have points of divergence. His earliest narratives also revealed his nervousness about "common" or sensationalist readings of his "common tales." By 1815, however, as evidenced in his comments on the sentimentality and popularity of Thomson's narratives, Wordsworth's ideas about the power of narrative were less exploratory and more negative.[142] Furthermore, his attitude toward common readers had also become far more mixed, as when he wrote of negative reactions "from that portion of my contemporaries who are called the Public," adding of the members of this public that they, "in the senseless hurry of their idle lives do not *read* books . . . my ears are stone-dead to this idle buzz."[143] The image recalls how the narrator of *The Ruined Cottage* learns from Armytage (a common peddler) to reject idleness and to turn the "tedious noise" of an "insect host" into the sound of a "multitude of flies/Fill[ing] all the air with happy melody."[144] In the late (1807) letter above, however, common lives have become both idle and senseless, while Wordsworth represents himself as having lost his sense of hearing, startlingly (given the emphasis placed on storytelling and listening in *The Ruined Cottage*) turning his ears into a kind of stone monument. By 1808 he also complained of the "sickly taste of the Public in verse," adding that the "*People* would love the Poem of Peter Bell, but the *Public* (a very different Being) will never love it."[145] The conditional is revealing: like the generic "Kind" of "Elegiac Stanzas," the "People" are imagined, while the public—arguably the very forum in which Wordsworth originally wished to have an active role—is dismissed.

By mid-career, then, Wordsworth had reimagined poetic power retrospectively and proleptically as more a matter of fitting into a poetic tradition and less as a "matter of fact." This self-revision was accompanied by an increasingly internalized sense of the power of speech. For example, in the same 1807 letter that described the idle buzz of the public Wordsworth wrote,

> It is an awful truth, that there neither is, *nor can be, any genuine enjoyment of Poetry* among nineteen out of twenty of those persons who live, or wish to live, *in the broad light of the world*[.]
>   . . . [But t]rouble not yourself upon [my poems'] *present* reception; of what moment is that compared with what I trust is their destiny, to console the afflicted, . . . to teach the young and the gracious of every age, to see, to think and feel, and therefore to become *more actively and securely virtuous*[.]

... I do not mean London wits ... but grave, kindly-natured, worthy persons, who would be pleased if they could. I hope that these Volumes are not without some recommendations, even for Readers of this class, but their imagination has slept; and the voice which is the voice of my Poetry without Imagination cannot be heard. (emphasis added)[146]

The indifferent public (both present and future) that Wordsworth here dismisses is most clearly an urban and urbane audience. Yet while Wordsworth's rhetoric is in this sense similar to that which informed poems like *The Ruined Cottage,* in 1807 those whom Wordsworth imagines will read or listen to his poetry—those formerly taught both to question and to give voice to poetry's "power to virtue friendly"—are now those who live in imagination, both their own (presumably in rural shaded groves rather than "the broad light of the world") and Wordsworth's. That is, the *best* reception Wordsworth can imagine in such prose statements is clearly no longer public or present. Finally, too, the uneasy but continuous construction and reconstruction of the poetic self enacted in *The Ruined Cottage* seems something Wordsworth wishfully reconceives as more settled and stable: virtue, by 1807, is to be active, but also secure.

Repetitions of the Past: *The Excursion*

In 1814 Wordsworth published Margaret's story, recast as "The Wanderer," or Book I of *The Excursion,* the poem for which he was best known in his lifetime.[147] Embedding "The Wanderer" in *The Excursion,* Wordsworth added eight more books and introduced a new cast of characters; readers met not only the early poem's narrator and Armytage (become The Wanderer), but also the Solitary, the Pastor, and others in a variety of interpolated narratives, including the story of Margaret and Robert. I will not here offer anything like a full reading of *The Excursion* as a whole, but to make my point about Wordsworth's self-revisions, especially as seen in "The Wanderer," it is necessary to mention how the preface and the eight added books recontextualize the story that began as the female beggar of *An Evening Walk,* the Salisbury Plain poems, and "The Female Vagrant," a story repeated in *The Excursion* with relatively few changes from *The Ruined Cottage* (although much is added).

Critical reactions to the poem, in general, have been negative, often echoing the opening of Francis Jeffrey's 1814 review from the *Edinburgh Review:* "This will never do."[148] Jeffrey attributed some of the poem's weakness to the fact that Wordsworth, unlike "all the greater poets" of the past, did not live "in the full current of society" and—in effect—did not write for the tastes of an educated audience.[149] More modern critics also have objected to what Jeffrey calls Wordsworth's "preachments" and to his apparently changed relationship to social issues (although not following Jeffrey's view of what has gone wrong), as well as wondered, to quote Geoffrey Hartman, if at very least Wordsworth suffered from an "indigestion of ideas."[150]

Yet Wordsworth's preface and prefatory stanzas return readers to familiar issues of poetic labor, the poetic self, and the relationship between private and public, the last now expressed in terms of "Nature and Education."[151] *The Excursion,* Wordsworth explains further, is only part of an even larger "long and laborious Work," *The Recluse,* which will be concerned with "passing events, and . . . an existing state of things" (specifically in *The Excursion*) as well as with "the origin and progress of his own powers" (specifically in the then unpublished *Prelude,* intended as part of *The Recluse*). The preface also states that the tales of "the tribes/And fellowships of men," including tales of war—implicitly all part of the historical present or "passing events" to be dealt with in *The Excursion*—will have "their authentic comment" even as Wordsworth hopes "these/Hearing, [he will] be not downcast or forlorn."[152]

Clearly, by the time Wordsworth published *The Excursion* his ideas about the public effectiveness of poetry and his strategies for addressing (and representing) his audience had shifted. Wordsworth's new thinking can be seen most clearly in three features of the revised poem: first, its emphasis on embedding the self within larger national institutions (parallel to Wordsworth's prose statements embedding his own poetry within the literary tradition); second, its related representations of education, especially of The Wanderer in Books I and II and of the Solitary's "Despondency" and "Despondency Corrected" in Books III and IV; and, third, what some critics have seen as its retreat from narrative and a return to an emphasis on what is variously characterized as pontificating, description, or reading, especially in the Pastor's speeches in Book IX.[153] Read in light of these features, *The Excursion* is an attempt to ground the power of the self in larger, preexisting structures. For example, Armytage (perhaps the speaking self as armature and hermitage) is remade as The Wanderer and given a personal history, particularly an early education not only in nature but also in the Scottish church. The making and correcting of the Solitary, central to Books II through VIII, also seems an attempt to replace the endless re-presentations of storytelling set in motion by *The Ruined Cottage* with more institutional and more stable instruction as poetry's proper province and defense.

At the same time, however, *The Excursion* continues to enact and underline the difficulties with its representations of poetic work.[154] For one, the reconceived and conservative social construction of The Wanderer, for example, is not something Wordsworth could claim for himself, since his own "excursive" powers were dependent on patronage (as the poem's dedicatory opening to the Earl of Lonsdale makes clear). Second, despite the poem's attempts to provide instruction that will not lead to despondency, *The Excursion* is finally scarcely less ironized than Wordsworth's earlier poems. Beginning once again with The Wanderer's "common tale"—"hardly clothed/In bodily form"—proceeding through the not obviously successful attempts to cure the Solitary of his untoward responses to analogous tales of suffering, the poem's conclusion moves from "The Parsonage" to the "*Discourse* of The Wanderer" (emphasis added).[155] In other words, the poem moves from narrative to (institutional) place, back to speech, and ends with the Pastor's promise that there remain stories his "future labours may not leave untold."[156] "[P]rogress is not progress in *The Excursion,* but a series of doublings or repetitions," William Galperin has argued, speaking of the poem's proliferation of characters.[157] I would add that narrative and performative repetitions are equally indicated by the compositional history of the poem (including Wordsworth's reworkings of *The Excursion* through 1844).

Wordsworth's early claims for poetic power were made in the face of his own and his contemporaries' growing disillusionment with the political situation in England in the late nineties, and yet Wordsworth maintained an implicit insistence on poetry's power in more than literary history in that poems such as *The Ruined Cottage* are texts against social and political ills, including war. Arguments such as E. P. Thompson's to the effect that later Wordsworth defaulted in rewriting his poem as "The Wanderer" have been countered most notably by Galperin's argument that revisions in "The Wanderer" mark Wordsworth's explicit and modern realization that the gap between self and community, inspiration and worldly power, is not easily bridged. However, this latter argument depends on reading *The Ruined Cottage* as more purely romantic and unproblematic than I have argued it is. If one sees the earlier poem as already underlining the provisional and performative nature of the power it claims, then "The Wanderer" is neither a new tough-mindedness nor a default, but Wordsworth's reiteration of his own past vision. True, "The Wanderer" is an attempt to foreclose further repetitions; however, an insistence on the adequacy—and a form of blindness to the provisionality—of the power of poetic speech already appears in *The Ruined Cottage.* As Thomson already illustrated, one cannot write with a clear-sighted foreknowledge of the limits of one's power. Indeed, as the next chapter will suggest, this is one of the lessons Shelley took from his reading of Wordsworth.

Chapter III ▧

These Common Woes: Repetition and Conversation in the Work of Percy Bysshe Shelley

Mesdames, one might believe that Shelley lies
Less in the stars than in their earthly wake.

—Stevens, "Mr. Burnshaw and the Statue"

Conversing with Wordsworth:
Changing Selves, Recording Things as They Are

If Wordsworth did not ultimately succeed in demonstrating to himself the present political efficacy of his poetry, he nonetheless did affect literary taste, including how later readers and writers of poetry understood the poetic strengths of those on whom Wordsworth drew, such as Milton and Thomson. One might say that, while early on aiming at a kind of political agency, Wordsworth's poems, like Thomson's, achieved in retrospect a kind of cultural efficacy. In the same way, Shelley may be said to have influenced how modern readers understand Wordsworth, not least because of the younger writer's reenactment of Wordsworth's attempts to reconcile his desire to place his work within a poetic tradition with his insistence on poetry's involvement in history.

In Shelley's work there is a reconfiguration of the double focus found in Wordsworth's and Thomson's writings—on what the past allowed them to hear as poetry and on poetry's role in an historical present. Living a century

later than Thomson, Shelley eventually crafted an analysis of the acculturat-
ing work of poetry, a conceptualization of poetry's public role quite differ-
ent from Thomson's, in his move from natural description to allegories on
public issues, or Wordsworth's, in his move to narrative in the nineties or his
later diminished faith in a public that might be affected by poetry. Shelley's
thinking was allowed in part by his reading of earlier poets who among other
things refigured what he could imagine counting as poetry. In part, too,
Shelley was formed by his own class background, which did not raise for
him quite the same problems Wordsworth or Thomson faced of defining
their own poetic endeavors as a publicly useful labor. Nonetheless, Shelley's
historical and political position still left him with the problem of how to
claim authority for his own literary production and at the same time to
claim that his work authorized readers as independent agents; he thus also
faced the related problem of how to mark his own participation in larger po-
etic and political communities while maintaining a kind of autonomy in the
face of apparently already written historical and poetic scripts.[1] Ultimately,
Shelley reconceived Thomson's and Wordsworth's questions about how to be
written into the book (of British literature or of history) without becoming
a dead letter as a series of questions about how poets might be said both to
have and to allow others cultural agency.

In his critique of Wordsworth, Shelley marks perhaps most explicitly the
tension between the sources, the claims for, and the practical ends of imag-
inative desire. As *The Ruined Cottage* replaces Thomson's dreaming swain
with Armytage, and *The Excursion* replaces Armytage with The Wanderer, so
"Alastor" opens with and revises Wordsworth's words: "The good die
first,/And those whose hearts are dry as summer dust,/Burn to the socket!"[2]
In 1815, this dryness is Shelley's diagnosis of Wordsworth's ailment, using
Wordsworth's own pronouncement on those "whose hearts are dry as sum-
mer dust" to condemn him as ungenerous, as having given up on changing
the world, and as poetically boring—"[d]ull—O, so dull—so very dull!"[3]

But Shelley's view of Wordsworth changed over the years, and the above
does not represent Shelley's first understanding of the older poet. Shelley was
exposed to Wordsworth's poetry by 1811, during his stay in the Lake
District.[4] On 2 January 1812, Shelley wrote out from memory
Wordsworth's poem "A Poet's Epitaph" to mail to Elizabeth Hitchener, ex-
plaining that he found the first stanzas "expressively keen" and describing his
hope that the poem would give "some idea of the Man."[5] Within the week,
Shelley wrote again to Elizabeth Hitchener. A January 7 letter suggests that
Shelley already suspected Wordsworth would fail to fill the exemplary role
in which the earlier letter tried to cast him. This second letter is most explicit
about Shelley's disappointment with another member of the Wordsworth
circle, Southey, whom he characterizes as a kindly man, but without "the

great character which once I linked him to. . . . *Once* he *was* this character, everything you can conceive of practised virtue. . . . Wordsworth & Coleridge I have yet to see."[6] The conclusion at very least sounds a challenge to the two poets whom Shelley was never, as it turned out, to meet in person, but in whom he maintained a lifelong interest.

It is difficult to deny that Shelley's letters reveal some anxiety about the influence of these older poets. At the same time, like Godwin to whom Shelley compared him,[7] Wordsworth and more generally the group of poets with whom Wordsworth was associated seem to have held out for Shelley the possibility of an ideal community of poets and men. As Shelley says later in a somewhat different context, "one is always in love with something or other; the error, and I confess it is not easy for spirits cased in flesh and blood to avoid it, consists in seeking in a mortal image the likeness of what is perhaps eternal."[8] Shelley, at least during one important period of his life, tried to see in Wordsworth what he calls a mortal likeness of what may not be mortal; indeed, the lesson was one Shelley learned in part from his dialogues with Wordsworth, Coleridge, and Southey, who presented images against which Shelley tested himself, seeing the older poets not so much as rivals but as idealized figures in whom he found his own impulses and beliefs embodied and who provided for him models of engaged poetry.

To trace this dialogue, I want to focus in particular on four moments in Shelley's life and writings: first, Shelley's early recorded imaginations of Wordsworth and a poetic community; second, his continuing refiguration of his relationship with that community in the 1816 *Alastor* poems. Third, I will return to early Shelley in order to trace his developing thought on the poetic and political implications of narrative and lyric as it informs his work through his repetitions of Wordsworth in the 1819 poem, "Peter Bell the Third"; and fourth, I will examine the implications of Shelley's rehearsal in "The Triumph of Life" of what he variously figured as the problematic relationship between the public work of poetry and the literary works of poets, or between community and self, practice and theory, consummation and desire, history and metaphysics (the last associated for Shelley with epistemology and human identity).[9]

Let me begin with Shelley's position in 1812 just after his visit to Southey. Immediately following his words of disappointment about Southey in his 7 January letter to Elizabeth Hitchener, Shelley copied out a poem of his own, which he described as follows: "the subject is not fictitious; it is the overflowings of the mind this morning"; he adds that it is to be thought of "as a picture of my feelings not a specimen of my art."[10] Shelley's appeal to truth, that is, to the reality of his narrative, combined with his appeal to his own intellectual and emotional processes, is worth considering in some detail. First, his description of poetry as revealing the mind sounds a note repeated again in slightly different form later the same month in a letter to Godwin: "If any man would determine sincerely and cautiously at *every* period of his life to publish books which should contain the real state of his feelings and opinions, I am willing to suppose that this portraiture of his mind would be worth many metaphysical disquisitions."[11] This same language is used in Shelley's descriptions of the poems from the Esdaile Notebook, many of which he had hoped to publish in an 1813 volume of poems just because the work gave a portrait of his mind and despite his knowledge that the work was uneven.[12] In all of these cases Shelley's point seems to be that poetry gives some idea of the man, and, implicitly, that the self to which poetry thus testifies will appear different at different times of life. Presumably this view of the self in flux also dictates Shelley's emphasis in his description of his early poem: it is the overflowings of the mind of a particular morning. Indeed, a closer look at Shelley's criticism of Southey reveals a similar emphasis. Southey's former character, Shelley writes, included "practised virtue," that is, virtue put into practice, or in motion. What corrupted him, as Shelley explains it, was "the world, [he was] contaminated by Custom," which I take to mean at least in part that, for Shelley, Southey's loss of a "power to virtue friendly" was occasioned by the repetition that characterizes the habitual or customary.[13]

The mind's freedom from custom would come to be one of Shelley's persistent themes, a theme presumably fed and complicated by the metaphysical disquisitions that Shelley ordered from his bookseller by December 1812.[14] In Hume, for example, he would have found the idea that the self is not one entity, but "a bundle or collection of different perceptions, which succeed each other with an inconceivable rapidity, and are in a perpetual flux and movement."[15] Shelley's own writings on epistemology and identity from the period between 1812 and 1815 draw heavily on Hume, as is indicated in his note that "beyond the limits of perception and thought nothing can exist."[16] Shelley's remarks on Southey as well as on his own poetic efforts in 1812 reveal already, on the one hand, a metaphysical understanding of the poetic self as Humean, figured only as a series of perceptions, and, on the other hand, a desire to link his poetry to the real or historical world.

Indeed, when Shelley writes that the world has corrupted Southey, he presumably has in mind most immediately the pressures of the external world that blasted Southey's (and his generation's) hopes for radical reform. The diagnosis is not completely unfair. In 1812, Shelley entered the political arena in Ireland, Wales, and England and wrote with admiration to the author of *Political Justice*,[17] while Southey, far from maintaining his opposition, became Poet Laureate the following year. Like Wordsworth, Southey was of the generation most deeply affected by the general retrenchment and disillusionment of the years from the late nineties through the teens, a period when—as E. P. Thompson has said—it was difficult "for men to hold on to aspirations long after there appear[ed] to be no hope of inserting them into 'the real world which is the world of all of us'."[18] The younger Shelley approached the question of how to affect "the real world" with images drawn from this older generation, but without their disillusioning experiences. Less generously than Thompson, in 1817 Shelley identified Wordsworth's dissent as "too easily reconcilable" with "servility, and dependence."[19] Two years later, in the "Dedication" to "Peter Bell the Third," Shelley damns Wordsworth for accepting "'the world of all of us, *and where/We find our happiness, or not at all'.*"[20]

In January of 1812, however, Shelley seems to have admired Wordsworth's ability to see historical reality *without* acquiescing to it. He singled out the first two stanzas of "A Poet's Epitaph" for praise, and these stanzas (as opposed to the poem as a whole) focus not so much on the solitary poet for whom the epitaph is written as on social and political realities. This recalls another point Shelley makes about his own poem—the poem he included in his 7 January letter to Hitchener—presented not only as a record of a mind in motion uncontaminated by custom, but also as a record wherein, as Shelley presents it, the "facts are real; . . . literally true."[21] This is, on one level, a curious statement from the author of "Alastor," a poem the *British Critic* in 1816 saw as "nonsense which . . . spurns the earth, and all its dull realities."[22] Despite this contemporary judgment, the preface to "Alastor" is intended to instruct "actual men," it may be said, because the literal reality depicted is one of the "situations of the human mind."[23] However, in the earlier poem—significantly entitled "a Tale of Society as it is from facts 1811" in the Esdaile Notebook—the literal reality to which Shelley appeals is not so easily reconciled with the mental reality he equally insists informs the poem.

The poem also contains a curious echo and revision of Wordsworth's tale of Margaret in *The Ruined Cottage,* curious in that Shelley insists less than Wordsworth does on the act of perception and more on the facts perceived.[24] Shelley did not of course read Wordsworth's revised version of Margaret's tale in *The Excursion* until 1814, at which point Mary Shelley recorded the family's judgment on its author: "He is a slave."[25] Nonetheless, Wordsworth's story is related to passages from Southey's *Joan of Arc* on Madelon and Arnaud or on the death of a common soldier who leaves behind a wife "tortur'd with vain hope" or perhaps to Coleridge's even earlier *Religious Musings,* in which Coleridge writes, "O thou poor widow, who in dreams dost view/Thy husband's mangled corse, and from short doze/Start'st with a shriek."[26] While Shelley could not have read *The Excursion* yet in 1812, these two earlier poems or perhaps Wordsworth's "The Female Vagrant," which was published by 1798, could easily have been in Shelley's mind.[27] He had, after all, just returned from visiting the author of *Joan of Arc* and still hoped to meet the authors of *Religious Musings* and "The Female Vagrant," whose works he presumably discussed with Southey in 1811. We know he discussed politics with Southey; this was the source of Shelley's disappointment. What likelier source, then, for "a Tale of Society as it is from facts 1811"?[28]

Shelley's aged woman, like Wordsworth's Margaret, the Soldier's Widow in "The Female Vagrant," or the other unnamed women mentioned by Southey and Coleridge, has a loved one (in Shelley's tale, a son) taken from her by war. She lives in solitude with the "proofs of an unspeaking sorrow . . . /Within her ghastly hollowness of eye."[29] Unlike the women in the other tales, however, Shelley's has her family restored to her, only to die with her son because they cannot support themselves and refuse the mercy of the parish: "*the insolent stare*/With which law loves to rend the poor mans [sic] soul." On "this scene of legal misery," Shelley's poem closes. Southey's, Wordsworth's, and Coleridge's poems are texts against war, but one can see how in 1811 Shelley might have thought such poems presented war as an impersonal, almost extra-human force. There is nothing to be done about war, a point emphasized in each poem, as Shelley might have read it, by the fact that hope or vision is seen as devastating. For example, Coleridge's widow is only tortured by her dream vision; Southey's woman has a "dim eye" and—as with the vagrant in Wordsworth's "The Female Vagrant"— what hope she has is called "vain."[30]

Shelley's poem, in apparent contrast to Coleridge's, Southey's or Wordsworth's, emphasizes the "tyrants" who draft common soldiers and the "Power"—that is, political power—that ruins common people. Further, the hopes of Shelley's aged woman are fulfilled with the return of her son, and the misfortunes that are visited on the reunited family are those of English law, as Shelley echoes the images of sight or vision from Southey, Coleridge and Wordsworth, while shifting the source of devastation from the deluded hopes of the sufferers to the "insolent stare" of the law. I have been rehearsing the relationship between Shelley's poem and poems by Southey, Coleridge, and Wordsworth because I want to pursue a further point, namely, that because of the exchange among the older poets, to respond to one poet would be (even if inadvertently) to enter into a conversation already in progress, indeed, into a conversation that, through Wordsworth at least, includes Thomson and concerns the issue of how to position poetic narratives in contemporary landscapes. Shelley's political position is in pointed contrast to the stance implicit in the poems just mentioned as possible sources, especially those by Coleridge and Southey, yet it also echoes the stanzas Shelley admired, and explicitly had in mind, from Wordsworth's "A Poet's Epitaph." Shelley's point is that there can and should be legal reform. Moreover, his poem does not view its subjects paternalistically. While the widows in Coleridge's and Southey's poems remain shadowy, anonymous figures, Shelley allows his family some autonomy; he emphasizes in his introductory remarks that he has not put words in their mouths and that he respects their desire for dignity and independence: "The facts are real; that recorded in the last fragment of a stanza is literally true.—The poor man said:—None of my family ever came *to parish,* and I wd. starve first. I am a poor man but I could never hold my head up after that."[31]

Ironically, by insisting on the historical particularity of his narrative and on the dignity of those whose story he represents, Shelley revises Wordsworth in just the same way in which E. P. Thompson argues that Wordsworth, in *The Ruined Cottage,* revised Coleridge's and Southey's poems.[32] Shelley also repeats Wordsworth's move to direct dramatic speech in "The Female Vagrant," a strategy Wordsworth then revised in *The Ruined Cottage* and was revising further for *The Excursion* even as Shelley wrote. In this way, if unknowingly, Shelley's comments on his poem reconfront the problem of voyeurism with which Wordsworth grappled in his rewriting of "The Female Vagrant." In other words, Shelley's poem sets itself in opposition not only to Coleridge's and Southey's poems and to Southey himself, the man Shelley saw as contaminated by custom, but also, proleptically, to the Wordsworth Shelley would see in Book I of *The Excursion* and would describe in comparable terms as slavish or allied with servitude. At the same time, far from revising Wordsworth, Shelley actually follows in the footsteps of the early Wordsworth by humanizing the narrator of the tale of woe recounted and setting his poetry against that of Coleridge and Southey. It is a further irony of history that it was Wordsworth, engaged in rewriting *The Ruined Cottage,* who was the first revisionist and opposer of his own earlier self, that self whose poetic stance Shelley mirrored and in effect reenacted in 1812.

By 1814 Shelley was far more aware of how much of early Wordsworth's mind he could see in himself, which must have caused him some dismay given his view of the later Wordsworth, especially if he recalled Southey's words in 1812—"Ah! when you are as old as I am you will think with me."[33] However, this was not so clearly the case for Shelley in 1812, although by then he had already found his two major thematic concerns—the self, including the poetic self, and politics, or social change—and he was self-consciously aware that his thoughts on these subjects were articulated through his exchanges with the circle of poets associated with Wordsworth. The language Shelley used in 1812 to describe Wordsworth, Southey, and his own enterprises also indicates Shelley's desire to connect his various concerns: the mind in flux and historical facts, the growth or habituation of men and poets, the moral and the political.

Shelley's interest in what might most generally be called the moral and the political, and his sense that they were not easily combined, are also shown in his letter to his bookseller toward the end of 1812; he writes, "I am determined to apply myself to a study that is hateful & disgusting to my very soul, but which is above all studies necessary for him who would be listened to as a mender of antiquated abuses.—I mean that record of crimes & miseries—History. You see that the metaphysical works to which my heart hankers, are not numerous in this list."[34] This uneasy mixture remained a constant in Shelley's life; by 1816 he was juxtaposing Gibbon and Rousseau; by 1818, Herodotus and Plato. Already in 1812, the study of history, linked with political activity, is juxtaposed to the study of metaphysics, linked in Shelley's earlier letter with more introspective study and in the letter just quoted with personal desire.

"the subject is not fictitious": Private Desire and Public Community

When Shelley insisted to Hitchener that in his "a Tale of Society as it is from facts 1811" "the subject is not fictitious," "subject" most obviously in context meant the self or his own subject position, while the subjects represented his poem, what he called the facts, are in the next breath called "real," "literally true." Shelley continued throughout his career to consider how he might reconcile these "subjects" and how he might theorize to which subject poetry could bear witness. With the portrait of Shelley's developing sense of such questions from 1812 in mind, I turn to a second moment in Shelley's life, in particular to three of the poems in his 1816 volume. The *Alastor* volume shows, first, Shelley's continued awareness of the so-called Lake Poets. Critics have commented at length about the allusions to Wordsworth found in "Alastor," while "To—" ("Oh! there are spirits of the air") is a poem Mary Shelley says was addressed to Coleridge.[35] Finally, "To Wordsworth" is explicit about its subject, and we know that four years earlier Shelley had ordered and probably read the 1800 edition of the *Lyrical Ballads* as well as Wordsworth's 1807 *Poems in Two Volumes,* while in 1814 he had brought home a copy of the *Excursion.*[36] Shelley also sent a copy of his *Alastor* volume to Southey.

By 1816, Shelley's view of Southey was more charitable than it had been in 1812. Shelley wrote to the older poet, saying he trusted both poets could forget "how widely in *moral and political* opinions [they] disagree[d]" and that both could "attribute that difference to better motives than the multitude are disposed to allege as the cause of dissent from their institutions" (emphasis added).[37] Shelley again identifies Southey's moral or political opinions with the inner state (or set of motives) from which they arise, but he suggests the difficulty of uncovering inner motives and, further, betrays an anxiety about how readers ("the multitude") might exercise the right to their own opinions and allegations. Shelley's recognition of the difficulty of reading others or, more to the point, of trusting others to read his own dissent as he would, may be due to the fact that, by the time of the 1816 letter to Southey, Shelley was personally and painfully aware of the way in which motives could be misread. The years between 1812 and 1816 had included Shelley's Irish activism, his move to and then retreat from Wales, his flight with Mary Wollstonecraft Godwin, surveillance by the government following his political activities in Devon, and constant financial worry. The generally negative public response to "Queen Mab" and "A Refutation of Deism" had clearly also affected Shelley.[38]

Other aspects of Shelley's concern with moral, political, and literary community (a central topic in his letter to Southey) inform "To Wordsworth." In ways, the sonnet seems to be Shelley's recast version of "A Poet's Epitaph" in that it reads as an elegy. The poem on which "To Wordsworth" most obviously draws, however, is Wordsworth's sonnet, "London, 1802," with Wordsworth's reading of Milton echoed in Shelley's reading of Wordsworth. Just as Wordsworth hails Milton as one whose "soul was like a Star, and dwelt apart," so Shelley describes Wordsworth as having been a star or refuge and as one whose poetry—"consecrate to truth and liberty"—like Milton's according to Wordsworth, was in the service of freedom.[39]

While the end of Shelley's elegiac poem finds that Wordsworth has deserted the cause and so ceased to be a guiding light, the beginning of the sonnet emphasizes a somewhat different Wordsworth—the poet of nature, the author of "Ode: Intimations of Immortality" more than the author of those tales of society that, like "A Poet's Epitaph," are most clearly characterized as songs of "truth and liberty."[40] Moreover, if Wordsworth follows Milton by suggesting that public good will rest on private conscience, which in turn is shaped by external constraints, Shelley's poem first seems to distinguish between the Wordsworth who deserted political causes and the more private poet who "wept to know/That things depart which never may return:/Childhood and youth, friendship and love's first glow." Interestingly, these concerns again have Shelley entering a dialogue already established between Coleridge and Wordsworth and again following in Wordsworth's footsteps. Furthermore, as in the letter to Southey, Shelley seems to be paying attention to the motives behind opinions and feelings, which becomes a way of viewing, though not of denying the problematic nature of, the relationship between morals and politics as well as between metaphysics and history.

Wordsworth wrote the first four stanzas of his "Ode: Intimations of Immortality" in 1802, the same year in which his sonnet "London, 1802" invoked Milton. The ode as it stood in late March ended with the fourth stanza, in which the poet views the natural world and proclaims, "I feel—I feel it all," while still reading out of nature what is lost: "the visionary gleam . . . the glory and the dream."[41] More precisely, the poem ended with a series of questions that together pose the problem: where have these things gone? As Coleridge's reply in his 1802 "Dejection: An Ode" helps us see, the beginning of Wordsworth's ode has no reference to the process of aging per se; it is simply about the loss of "a glory from the earth." The epigraph about the child being father to the man was not added until 1815.[42] In answer to the 1802 ode's question of where the lost glory has gone, Coleridge provides a half reply, namely, that an *inner* light has failed: "I may not hope from outward forms to win/The passion and the life, whose fountains are within"; Coleridge adds that "the soul itself must issue forth/A light, a glory."[43] The end of Wordsworth's poem continues this conversation with the response that the soul itself—"our life's Star"—is not our own; it comes "from afar," and as we age—significantly imaged as a process by which the soul finds that "custom lie[s] upon [her] with a weight"—vision fades "into the light of common day." The compensation, Wordsworth insists, is a "philosophic mind" and an abiding "primal sympathy."

Shelley, then, enters the exchange between Coleridge and Wordsworth in "To Wordsworth." He writes of Wordsworth's sense of loss ("These common woes I feel"), thus underlining his own act of sympathetic imagination and echoing Wordsworth's insistence on commonality both in the sonnet to Milton and in the ode's description of how vision fades into and informs "the light of common day." Shelley thus resists part of Coleridge's point of view, namely, that disillusionment closes people off from the world. For Wordsworth, the loss of vision is (by 1804) necessary, but this loss is not fatal to social sympathies; for Coleridge, since nature lives only in our vision of her, the loss of vision need not be a necessary part of the process of aging, although if experienced it will prevent the imagination from turning outward.

At the same time, Shelley borrows some of Coleridge's criticisms of Wordsworth. Echoing Wordsworth's claim to feel the joy of spring despite his loss of what the second part of the ode will identify as "our life's Star," Coleridge portrays himself looking at the stars as follows: "I see them all so excellently fair,/I see, not feel, how beautiful they are!" Shelley returns to this point in his statement that Wordsworth's loss of his former self is something the older poet "feels"—that is, experiences—but does not "feel" in the sense of having an emotional response, as Shelley in deploring the loss of Wordsworth does feel: "One loss is mine/Which thou too feel'st, yet I alone deplore." Sympathetic feeling is here linked with not acquiescing to loss (for Wordsworth, the loss of childhood and his youthful self; for Shelley, especially in 1814–1816, of human community and Wordsworth); thus, Shelley relates Wordsworth's acceptance of loss to Wordsworth's desertion of truth and liberty.

This explanation I have just offered, in any event, seems a promising way to understand the connection between the two apparently diverse images of Wordsworth (beloved nature poet and political defector) in Shelley's sonnet, as well as Shelley's reported comment that Wordsworth "always broke down when he attempted [an ode]."[44] For Shelley, Wordsworth's problem is that he has accepted the inevitability of imaginative failure; no longer weeping for what is lost, he sees in the world only thoughts "too deep for tears" and so ends with "pale despair and cold tranquillity."[45] By implication, Wordsworth also thus abandons all hope of changing the world.

There is also another way that Shelley seems to repeat Coleridge's criticism of Wordsworth in "To Wordsworth." Coleridge argues (taking a stand reminiscent of Shelley's response to Southey in 1812) that age does not necessitate a change in the sense of leading to a capitulation to custom and that the visionary gleam, which Wordsworth claims has set like a star, is in fact merely a projection of inner light. Shelley's image of Wordsworth as a star seems to make the same point, namely, that Wordsworth was himself a star; the light he shed was his own. The end of Shelley's poem similarly recasts Wordsworth's understanding of the loss of vision by seeming to suggest it is not that vision has deserted Wordsworth, but that Wordsworth is the deserter. Such a reading does not do justice to the turns in Shelley's deceptively straightforward-looking poem, however. If Shelley's charge were simply that the older poet should have known that his mind was the source of imaginative vision and should not have betrayed his inner light, we would have to accuse Shelley of repeating the error, since the poetic voice in "To Wordsworth" equally looks outside of the self, to Wordsworth, and equally claims that a guiding light *from outside* has departed. And Shelley's insistence on Wordsworth as a guiding light seems quite consciously to seek an externalized object for emulation in the figure of the earlier poet.[46]

Shelley often explored irreconcilable viewpoints by writing dialogues in the skeptical tradition.[47] The title of the poem "To——" not only mirrors the title of "To Wordsworth," but thematically the two poems again repeat the argument between Wordsworth's and Coleridge's odes. "Oh! there are spirits of the air" also echoes the imagery in Coleridge's ode, referring to thwarted love, to the image of the blank eye viewing the stars and the old moon, and to Coleridge's statement that his "spirits fail." Shelley writes of "spirits of the air" and of how the "glory of the moon is dead."[48] In "To Wordsworth," in part just because it is an attempt to correct Wordsworth, Shelley tacitly explores the need to keep one's eyes on some mortal embodiment of an ideal—Wordsworth as "a lone star"—and not to desert what nonetheless will depart. In contrast, "To——" seems to take Coleridge's point of view, imaging the earth, that which is external, as "faithless" and focusing, like Coleridge, on the imaginative self: "Did thine own mind afford no scope/Of love, or moving thoughts to thee?"

However, we cannot take Shelley's poem as wholly affirming Coleridge's understanding of the loss of vision, since "To—" points out that Coleridge's dejection is itself imaginatively coloring the world. If "dreams have now departed," says Shelley, "Thine own soul still is true to thee,/But changed to a foul fiend through misery." Like the visionary in "Alastor," the person addressed in "To—" finds the self still bound to the world it finds inadequate, but to a world now informed by a "ghastly presence" or sense of its inadequacy. Moreover, in his "Essay on Life," Shelley cautions that the source of life is probably not similar to mind, since mind can only perceive. Any internalized quest occasioned by the proposition that the object of imaginative desire lies within the self is doomed; thus, the Coleridgean figure in "To—" is told that to pursue his dream would be a "mad endeavour." Finally, and perhaps most critically, Shelley proposes that the view given voice in "Dejection: An Ode" entails reaching a dead end as surely as does frustration in the face of the earth's inconstancy; "To—" ends, "Be as thou art. Thy settled fate,/Dark as it is, all change would aggravate." It seems that Shelley wants, on the one hand, not to despair of either change or the mental activity by virtue of which change (including political change) is envisioned and, on the other hand, to remain constant in *not* yielding to change of the sort Wordsworth and Southey (one implicitly, one explicitly) accept. Put another way, Wordsworth and Coleridge pose for Shelley the problem of leaving open the gap between aspiration and disillusionment—a gap that is equally closed, as Shelley sees it, by Wordsworth's repudiation of politics or his fixation on the necessary losses involved in worldly existence and by Coleridge's fixation on the loss of inner light or on the self, which for Shelley may come to the same thing. Shelley's earlier questions about morals and politics, self and history, then resurface as questions about the nature and ends of imaginative activity. And it is just such questions that are addressed in the paired poems to Wordsworth and Coleridge. "To Wordsworth" insists on imaginative desire and its frustrations as the necessary basis of moral sympathies even as "To—" suggests that to seek to know the origins or true nature of the desiring self may be madness.

These positions are explored at greater length in the title poem of the volume in which these paired poems first appeared. In "Alastor," the narrator, who mediates between the two human categories mentioned in the preface of the poem, is a Wordsworthian poet invoking nature as his muse and serving as a norm against which a young visionary poet is defined. In contrast to the narrator, then, the visionary poet is one who yearns for a union of his finite self with his ideal, or divine, inner double. The narrator views the visionary from the outside, characterizing the youth's quest as ending in a tragic death. Yet the narrator undermines his own position by invoking nature to aid in his singing of one who finds her inadequate; by his obvious admiration for the visionary; and by the way in which the final lament for the visionary casts doubt upon the value of life in the natural world. In short, "Alastor" is a poem of controlled ambiguity in which Shelley is exploring, skeptically, the terms of his own ambivalence.

However, while the narrator of the poem is clearly identified with the Wordsworth who wrote about the natural world, the entire narrative structure of the poem equally strongly invokes Wordsworth's narrative experiments in "Salisbury Plain," "Adventures on Salisbury Plain," "The Female Vagrant," and, finally, *The Excursion,* the last poem quoted in Shelley's epigraph to "Alastor." Thus, Shelley not only tests a Wordsworthian position in the characterization of his narrator, but that testing itself can be seen as a Wordsworthian strategy. In a related vein, Shelley explores not only two equally doubtful (or equally probable and compelling) positions, but he also offers a self-conscious examination of his own skeptical stance, that stance with which the Wordsworthian structure of the poem can be identified. The position Shelley himself takes—that of the skeptic—is one of the stances explored. Finally, if "Alastor" indeed wavers between two ways of viewing poetry, then the entire poem is in a sense an inquiry about poetry, as a close look at the poem itself, beginning with the preface, demonstrates.

Mary Shelley's note to "Alastor" says that the "poem ought rather to be considered didactic than narrative."[49] The "Preface" also asks for a consideration of the poem as didactic. The story of the visionary, we are told, is "not barren of instruction to actual men."[50] The "Preface" then details the moral to be drawn from the picture of the young poet. The visionary's fault seems to be his seclusion, his attempt to exist without human sympathy, although his error is allowed to be "generous." There is something worse than to be like the young poet, and that is to be one of those who keep "aloof from sympathies with their kind" without having the visionary's noble excuse. The youth's search ends in death and ruin only because he pursues something he imagines to be better than human or earthly love. The "Preface" then prepares us for a story—a "picture"—with a moral about love. And the moral, we are warned, will be that neither the visionary nor those "morally dead" who have no excuse for their lack of love provide us with a positive model of how to love.

Readers have not been led to expect the appearance of the narrator, but he continues to raise the issues found in the "Preface" by speaking of love. In fact, he seems to embody love properly directed in that he begins by invoking a muse whom he calls "Mother of *this* unfathomable world" (1. 18, emphasis added), and by pledging his devotion to this muse, "I have loved/Thee ever, and thee only" (ll. 19–20). Evidently the narrator neither disdains love nor searches for it beyond this earth. Given the categories introduced in the "Preface," he appears to be the positive model of love not found there.

The narrator further assumes that he can produce poetry in keeping with his love: asking nature to help him with his song, he offers himself as a lyre and wishes his song to "modulate" (1. 46), or be in harmony, with the natural world in which he sets himself. Even his attempt to understand death as one of nature's "mysteries" (1. 23) focuses explicitly on the earthly or physical aspect of death involving "charnels" and "coffins" (1. 24). Similarly, he expects "the tale/Of what we are" (ll. 28–29) to be located in nature, although admittedly in her "inmost sanctuary" (1. 38). Finally, the narrator's intimations of this secret held by nature are described, significantly, in the context of the natural cycle of the day, in "twilight phantasms, and deep noonday thought" (1. 40). Such hints allow the narrator to wait "serenely now/And moveless" (ll. 41–42), apparently satisfied that nature will move him and will grant him a song in harmony with her world that will also include "the deep heart of man" (1. 49).

When the poem continues with a tale—"There was a Poet" (1. 50)—it seems that the narrator has been granted his song. But the story is of a poet who did not find nature adequate. The moral of the tale, or so readers have been told in the "Preface," is that the visionary's dissatisfaction with earthly love leads to his ruin and death. The narrator has just spent fifty lines claiming nature as his muse and identifying himself as a Wordsworthian poet of nature. Quite aside from the epigraph drawn from *The Excursion* and Shelley's engagement with questions set for him by Wordsworth, a significant number of echoes from Wordsworth's Intimations Ode and *The Excursion* appear in the first fifty lines of "Alastor."[51] Most obviously, Shelley repeats Wordsworth's Thomsonian figure of the poet as an idler dreaming in the shade at noon (ll. 40–42). This narrator then hopes for, and even expects, a tale that will reveal to him the things of this world and, especially, the secret of what or who man is. Why then does he tell a tale of a poet's dissatisfaction with nature? Are readers to conclude it is not nature that has inspired this tale? Perhaps the narrator's trust is unfounded, and he should ask, like Coleridge as pictured in "Oh! there are spirits of the air," "Ah! wherefore didst thou build thine hope/On the false earth's inconstancy?"[52] This would imply that the Wordsworthian (or what Shelley defines as a Wordsworthian) narrator is not the model of love properly directed, since he finds no real community within, or answers from, nature. Rather, it seems possible that the equivocal poem about the visionary comes from the narrator's own mind, in the same way that Coleridge in "Dejection: An Ode" says "the soul itself must issue forth/A light."

On the other hand, it is possible that nature has inspired a tale of her own inadequacy; a process curiously emblematized by the natural (if Gothic) setting the narrator describes where "night makes a weird sound of its own stillness" (1. 30).[53] Indeed, the moment recalls Wordsworth's image of Armytage viewing the waters of Margaret's spring, waters that tacitly offer a figure of how nature does not minister to human comfort and that set in motion Armytage's ambiguous tale as well as his attempt to deny the apparent meaning of such figures. In "Alastor," however, it is clear that if nature reveals only her own lack, readers must conclude again that the human heart (which is, after all, the central object of the narrator's search) is not contained in or satisfied by nature. In either case, whether it is nature or the narrator himself who inspires the tale about the young poet, the poem emphasizes that the relationship between "'the world of all of us'" and her self-proclaimed Wordsworthian poet, the narrator of "Alastor," is not straightforward.[54]

This is in part a continuation of Shelley's critique of what he saw as Wordsworth's acquiescence to loss. The narrator's relation to his tale may also be linked to Shelley's developing metaphysical views, as seen in Shelley's discussion of love and nature in his "Essay on Love," written within three years of the poems from the *Alastor* volume.[55] In that essay, Shelley begins by speaking of love as "that powerful attraction towards all that we conceive, or fear, or hope beyond ourselves, when we find within our own thoughts the chasm of an insufficient void and seek to awaken in all things that are a community with what we experience within ourselves."[56] The syntax of this sentence is difficult, but seems to define love as the desire for a relationship with something outside of ourselves that will reflect our inner experiences. Such desire arises when we feel an "insufficient void" in our thoughts. It is even possible that this void is the inner experience we will find mirrored, although not what we wish to find. The nature of the essential inner experience desired becomes clearer as Shelley continues. He explains that we "are born into the world, and there is something within us which, from the instant that we live, more and more thirsts after its likeness." It is this "something" that Shelley goes on to call "a miniature . . . of our entire self, yet deprived of all that we condemn or despise," and our "anti-type." This view seems to inform Shelley's 1814 portrait of the early Wordsworth as one whose own experience of loss in "Ode: Intimations of Immortality" led him to see images of that loss in the world and so to form a bond of sympathy with the world. For Shelley, too, it is within the gap between what people want and what they do not have that they experience love, which is thus a result of unfulfilled aspirations.

At the end of the "Essay on Love," Shelley speaks specifically of turning to nature to find a likeness of the "something within" mentioned in the essay:

> In the motion of the very leaves of spring, in the blue air, there is then found
> a secret correspondence with our heart. There is eloquence in the tongueless
> wind, and a melody in the flowing brooks and the rustling of the reeds beside
> them, which by their inconceivable relation to something within the soul,
> awaken the spirits to a dance of breathless rapture.

In other words, Shelley is proposing that love of the natural world springs
from an attempt to find in nature a likeness of an "ideal prototype." Fur-
thermore, the way in which nature "awaken[s] the spirits" is not easily de-
fined. Shelley calls the correspondence "secret"; the relationship,
"inconceivable." Returning to "Alastor," it is possible to view the activity of
the narrator in this context.

The narrator has turned to nature seeking "the tale/Of what we are" (ll.
28–29) and for a song that will include "the deep heart of man" (l. 49). His
search seems to be identified with the thirst for a likeness of something
within him. His description of himself waiting "serenely now/And moveless,
as a long-forgotten lyre" (ll. 41–42) also suggests the vacancy that the essay
says is a prerequisite for turning outward in order to seek an image of the
"soul within our soul." Furthermore, the image of the lyre recalls the essay's
image of meeting our anti-type as meeting "with a frame whose nerves, like
the chords of two exquisite lyres, strung to the accompaniment of one de-
lightful voice, vibrate with the vibrations of our own." While this descrip-
tion recalls most vividly the veiled maid of the youth's vision, it also fits the
narrator who waits for an image of something within himself from nature:
the narrator, as one lyre, awaits nature's breath in order to harmonize with
the rest of nature's world. The image in the poem is of nature's world pro-
viding the necessary harmonizing chord, an image resonant with Thomson's,
Coleridge's, and Wordsworth's icons of ease of composition, although Shel-
ley's use of the aeolian harp does not acknowledge that the image is already
contested in his predecessors' work. The way in which Shelley's narrator then
goes on to tell the tale about the visionary, a tale that at first does not seem
to be from nature, reflects the suggestion in the essay that nature's relation-
ship to our inner soul is "inconceivable." In other words, in "Alastor," the
entire story, the tale beginning on line fifty, may be that likeness of some-
thing within himself, found in nature, for which the narrator has been
searching. The uncertainty of the connection between nature and the tale is,
according to Shelley, typical of the connection between nature and what it
inspires.

In the preface to "Alastor," Shelley writes that the "poem entitled
'ALASTOR,' may be considered as allegorical of one of the most interesting
situations of the human mind. It represents a youth . . ." The story of the vi-
sionary poet then follows. But what in "Alastor" is allegorical of a situation

of the mind? The "Preface" implies that the entire poem may be taken as such an allegory. Certainly the story of the youth's wanderings and visions can easily be read as a representation of a restless state of mind: the state of mind introduced in the epigraph from St. Augustine, "loving to love" or being in love with love itself, aptly describes the young poet's situation. He is "insatiate" and "thirsts for intercourse with an intelligence similar to [his own]." His vision of the maid can be interpreted most simply as psychological allegory: the youth's desire for love has resulted in his picturing someone or something equal to that desire. The "Preface" has prepared readers for such an interpretation, saying that the poet "images *to himself* the Being whom he loves" (emphasis added). But the poem entitled "Alastor" does not begin with the visionary's tale. It begins with the narrator's plea to the elements and to nature. This suggests that the narrator, as well as the subject of his tale, is part of Shelley's allegory. The act of representing the youth, as well as the youth's story, may be considered as allegorical of a mental situation. In effect, the way in which the mind draws upon nature for a likeness of itself—one of the problems that occupied Shelley in his "Essay on Love"—is a problem also explored in "Alastor"; the narrator's relationship to his tale (and to the origin of his tale) is allegorical.

This suggestion is strengthened by recalling the earlier echoes of Wordsworth, not only in the narrator's opening lines and representation of himself as a dreaming figure in the noon shade, but also in the quotation that ends the "Preface." The quotation draws attention to the way "Alastor" takes issue with *The Excursion* in particular with what Shelley read as Wordsworth's use of narrative to counsel an acceptance of the world. Wordsworth has The Wanderer tell a "tale of silent suffering, hardly clothed/In bodily form," but The Wanderer reads or reconstructs Margaret's story from physical evidence such as the "useless fragment of a wooden bowl" or the bits of sheep's wool on the cornerstones of the house.[57] The narrator of "Alastor" also tells the tale of someone who, like Margaret, is unable to tell his own tale (the visionary is first introduced to us in his grave). However, nature does not provide the narrator of "Alastor" with tangible signs from which to reconstruct his story, in contrast to the way The Wanderer is said to read Margaret's story from natural signs. In fact, we are not sure where the story about the visionary originates. Furthermore, Wordsworth's narrator protests that it would be "a wantonness" to relate Margaret's story without finding a moral to be drawn from listening to it.[58] Similarly, the preface of "Alastor" prepares Shelley's readers for a moral; however, the introduction of the narrator serves to blunt the Wordsworthian moral of the tale: if the instruction to be drawn from the poem is that one should direct one's love to (that is, find oneself in) things of this world, why is the narrator inspired to sing of the visionary? Again,

Shelley is reinterpreting Wordsworth's version of narrative, showing that the relationship between nature and what it inspires, as well as the relationship between a narrator and the subject of his tale (or between the perceiving subject and "the facts") is not fixed.

If "Alastor" is in part about the uncertainty of the narrator's connection with his tale, the origin and moral of which are problematic, the entire tale is also presented as the narrator's "likeness" of something internal, as described in the "Essay on Love." The story is called "a picture," or likeness, in the "Preface." Thus, the narrator feels an inner vacancy, turns outward, and finds himself in the story or image of the visionary. He is bound to his tale by an act of love (as Shelley describes love). It is necessary, then, to look more closely at the story of the visionary and to notice how his early history resembles the narrator's. Shelley writes of the visionary: "Nature's most secret steps/He like her shadow has pursued" (ll. 81–82). The visionary, like the narrator, seeks some disclosure from nature. Both also wait passively to be granted this disclosure. The youthful poet's first vision comes as he gazes on some ruins "till meaning on his *vacant* mind/Flashed like strong inspiration" (ll. 126–27, emphasis added), as earlier the narrator waits "serenely . . . /And moveless" (ll. 41–42).

The object of the visionary's quest recalls that of the narrator's quest as well: the young poet's second vision—that of the veiled maid—seems to represent something within the youth in the same way that the tale of the youth represents something within the narrator. The maid's "voice [is] like the voice of [the young poet's] own soul" (l. 153), and she clearly resembles the goal of love described in Shelley's essay as "the invisible and unattainable point to which Love tends."[59] The maid, then, is the externalization of the youth's desire to find his anti-type. Both the narrator and the youth suspect that what they are seeking might only be obtained in death, or in the realm beyond. The narrator spends his time in "charnels and on coffins" (1. 24) hoping to have some secret revealed to him. The young poet sees the maid "lost, for ever lost,/In the wide pathless desert of dim sleep" (ll. 209–10), and he wonders, "Does the dark gate of death/Conduct to thy mysterious paradise,/O Sleep?" (ll. 211–13). He assumes that the maid is unattainable in life (in the same way that the anti-type of which Shelley speaks in his essay is unattainable). Pursuing nature's secrets, as he has done up until this second vision, will not recapture the maid.

Here, however, the parallel between the narrator's relationship to the visionary and the visionary's relationship to the maid seems to end. The narrator seeks only for a tale, which is also called a likeness or image, that will reveal something to him, whereas the visionary seeks the original of such images. The poem does pursue the visionary up to the point of death, but the "Preface" calls the visionary's death an "untimely" tragedy, and his decision actively to seek death is censured. The narrator suggests that the quest beyond life distinguishes the visionary and constitutes his transgression: "He eagerly pursues/Beyond the realms of dream that fleeting shade [i.e., the maid of his vision];/He overleaps the bounds. Alas! alas!" (ll. 205–7).

The visionary is unwilling to settle for an (already faded) image of the maid. He seeks—eventually beyond the bounds of life—the veiled maid herself. The "Preface" speaks of the image conjured by the poet and says that he "seeks in vain for a prototype of his conception." The image of the swan further reinforces the suggestion that the poet wants to find and unite with the source of his vision. It is the swan's physical flight to his home and to his mate—who will "welcome [his] return with eyes/Bright in the lustre of their own fond joy" (ll. 283–84)—that leads to the youth's resolve to try the realm of death and beyond in his search. It is the eyes of the swan's waiting mate that are stressed, and it is eyes—presumably those of the veiled maid—that draw the poet onward in his quest to death and beyond. Both the eyes and the image of returning home indicate that the youth's desire is for a presence, an embodied and permanent reality with which he can join. He will not settle for an image of that reality. The central portion of the visionary's tale is, then, his quest after embarking in the shallop. It is from this moment that he knows that he is seeking the reality beyond his vision and that his only hope of finding that reality must lie outside of "the world of all of us."[60]

It is from this point in the narrative, as well, that the visionary presents the most unlikely subject for the narrator's tale. Before I can discuss why the poem gives an account of the youth's quest beyond life, however, I need first to examine the nature of that quest. The boat journey proceeds through a series of sublime, imaginatively charged landscapes that seem to present an allegory within the larger allegory of the poem. If the veiled maid represents something within the visionary, his soul within a soul, then the search for her must be an inner search. Shelley thus implicitly returns to the image of woman and swan from *An Evening Walk,* the Salisbury Plain poems, and "The Female Vagrant" and uncovers the bodies Wordsworth (and, before him, Thomson) buried in their landscapes; the status and content of the visionary's story unmasks such bodies as externalized figures of desire; similarly, the visionary's overleaping of bounds comments on the psychological source of Wordsworth's overleaping currants (and Thomson's similarly Satanic horse). In Shelley's poem, even death, insofar as it seems to offer some hope of finding the maid, is described as mirroring the internal state of the visionary. The poet stands with a "gloomy smile/Of desperate hope" (ll. 290–91) contemplating death, which is pictured with its own "doubtful smile" (l. 295). That death, in this passage, is a projection of the poet's mind is emphasized further in the lines following the above confrontation: the poet "[s]tartled *by his own thoughts*" finds nothing "*but in his own deep mind*" (ll. 296, 298, emphasis added). Both death and the maid who may exist beyond it seem to originate within the visionary's mind. And the journey toward both is a descent into the mind.

The poet's descent follows a stream that becomes an image of thought or consciousness. We lose sight of the stream when the poet dies, and the narrator calls the poet-youth "a bright stream/Once fed with many-voiced waves" (ll. 668–69). The narrator seems able to follow—and give voice to—both stream and visionary only up to their deaths. Furthermore, the stream is addressed—presumably by the narrator speaking for the visionary—in the following passage:

> —"O Stream!
> Whose source is inaccessibly profound,
> Whither do thy mysterious waters tend?
> Thou imagest my life. Thy darksome stillness,
> Thy dazzling waves, thy loud and hollow gulphs,
> Thy searchless fountain, and invisible course
> Have each their type in me: and the wide sky,
> And measureless ocean may declare as soon
> What oozy cavern or what wandering cloud
> Contains thy waters, as the universe
> Tell where these living thoughts reside, when stretched
> Upon thy flowers my bloodless limbs shall waste
> I' the passing wind!"
> (ll. 502–14)

The stream here explicitly represents the poet's life. The poem says that to ask where the waters of the stream will end is to ask where (and perhaps in what state) the poet's "living thoughts" will exist after his physical death. The aspect of life presented by the stream, then, is thought or consciousness, and the journey that follows the stream is again a descent into the mind.

To speak of a descent into the mind in search of the prototype of something within that thirsts after its own likeness—and it is that something with which the veiled maid has been identified—is to speak of an intense self-consciousness. The youth wishes to find the veiled maid (that is, that something within him) as a physical presence. But he can only experience her as a "fleeting shade" (1. 206), or as a pair of eyes luring him further and further into his own mind, for the visionary's journey (at least as far as the poem follows it) is an endless regress of consciousness.

The landscapes through which the visionary passes seem to represent just such a regress of consciousness. They provide increasingly involuted images of the visionary's mental situation. For example, the young poet is tempted to stop for some flowers that "[f]or ever gaze on their own drooping eyes,/Reflected in the crystal calm" (ll. 407–8). The poet's temptation is to place himself in some relationship to the flowers, or to be satisfied with the image of himself he finds in them. Recalling the "Essay on Love," love is the perception of a relationship between something outside of ourselves and our inner experience. The poet seems tempted, then, by the flowers' image of his own narcissistic activity. He is tempted by love. Such love, however, is not what the poet wants. He seeks that which desires such relationships, or the source of love.

The scene that follows in the journey then describes the poet's mistrust of love. Natural love is seen as something suspicious:

> . . . Like restless serpents, clothed
> In rainbow and in fire, the parasites,
> Starred with ten thousand blossoms, flow around
> The grey trunks, and, as gamesome infants' eyes,
> With gentle meanings, and most innocent wiles,
> Fold their beams round the hearts of those that love.
> (ll. 438–43)

There is a direct echo here of "Oh! there are spirits of the air," in which, advising his subject not to build false hopes on earth but to turn inward, the speaker expresses scorn that "natural scenes or human smiles/Could steal the power to wind thee in their wiles" (ll. 23–24). The vines and the seductive children in the passage above are similarly constraining: the image suggests that those who love within the context of nature are beguiled. Yet the poet's mistrust of the images he finds in nature has led only to a further image. Since the poet has just been tempted by the flowers to stop his quest, it is appropriate that nature should appear to be a deceiver. Moreover, this deception is itself presented in a tempting yet entangling image from nature, which (again) falls short of the reality the youth desires.

As the poet-youth is dying we are told that *his* blood has "ever beat in mystic sympathy/With nature's ebb and flow" (ll. 652–53). The landscapes that mirror the youth's inner experiences seem to exemplify this sympathy; it is just that the youth's quest is for something beyond. The landscapes not only represent the visionary's state of mind (including his suspicion of nature's images), but their progression represents a descent into his mind. In a regress of consciousness, for any image of a given mental activity there is always a further image to represent a consciousness of that activity, suggesting an endless succession.

The stage in the visionary's journey after the scene with the vines represents his awareness of such a succession. He sees a well that reflects whatever overhangs it. Bending over, he sees his own eyes "as the human heart,/

Gazing in dreams over the gloomy grave,/Sees its own treacherous likeness there" (ll. 472–74). The youth's consciousness, like the well, may keep yielding images of itself endlessly. He suspects that the death he seeks may also yield nothing more than his own image. It is at this point that a "Spirit seem[s]/To stand beside him" (ll. 479–80). This Spirit, unlike the veiled maid, is "clothed in no bright robes/Of shadowy silver or enshrining light" (ll. 480–81), and the visionary senses for a moment that the ultimate reality he seeks cannot be embodied, although he does not deny that there is some ultimate power behind the relationships he perceives. The Spirit is the vital force behind his sense of connection with the landscape around him: the wood, well, rivulet, and evening "for speech assuming/Held commune with him, *as if he and it* [presumably the Spirit]/*Were all that was*" (ll. 486–88, emphasis added). This mood is shattered "when his regard/[Is] raised by *intense pensiveness*" (ll. 488–89, emphasis added) and he sees "[t]wo starry eyes, hung in the gloom of thought" (1. 490), which lure him on. His own thoughts and his awareness of them distract him and then lure him on with an image, the eyes, of some living and available source of his self-consciousness.

The last scene before the poet's quest ends in death breaks the narrowing focus that otherwise characterizes the journey from ocean to stream to a final "spot" (l. 577). The landscape becomes increasingly barren, but the voices given to the "loud stream" (1. 550) being followed, those expressions of the poet's inner journey, become a babel. The poet's increasingly narrow descent leads to the final and most spectacular vision of his activity and of his relationship to nature. This vision is similar to Shelley's description in his "Essay on Life" of the state called reverie in which an individual dissolves into or absorbs the entire universe: such states, we are told, usually "precede, or accompany, or follow an unusually intense and vivid apprehension of life."[61] Yet at the same time that the entire universe has provided a mirror for (or been charged imaginatively by) the poet's life, he is seeking something beyond life. He is like the pine tree set against the panorama of the world: he stands "athwart the vacancy" (1. 562), barely rooted in the world. This vacancy recalls the inner void Shelley says leads to our search for an externalization of our inner soul and echoes the "vacant brain" (1. 191), vacant gaze (1. 201), and vacant scene (ll. 195, 201) that precede the poet's decision to search for the veiled maid. This inner void, then, leads to the visionary's "sympathy" with nature. Yet he finds within nature only that same void. The pine tree responds to the wind with "one only response, at each pause/In most familiar cadence" (ll. 564–65), in the same way as the poet responds to his relationships with nature: his search must be for something beyond a mere image of his situation. Furthermore, it may be that the visionary's search is doomed to fail.

Shelley will caution in the "Essay on Life" that the source of life is probably not similar to mind, since mind can only perceive. He adds that the mind cannot cause anything, in the usual sense of the word, since causation is only the perception of relationships. The young poet's quest seems to produce only such perceptions rather than the object of his quest. Shelley goes on in the "Essay on Life" to say that individual minds are actually "different modifications of the one mind."[62] As he tries to contemplate himself in this context—as a portion of the one mind—he finds himself "on that verge where words abandon us, and what wonder if we grow dizzy to look down the dark abyss of how little we know."[63] Shelley specifically equates this sort of speculative self-contemplation with abstraction and intellectual philosophy. Increased abstraction, particularly involving self-contemplation, is connected with reaching a dead end where words fail. Shelley must abandon reasoning and abstraction to offer an image. The image (here, of being on the edge of an abyss and growing dizzy) serves as an emblem of the mind's position upon reaching the end of knowledge. In other words, the end of such speculation can only be the mind offering an image of its own bafflement. This situation of the mind (with which Shelley was concerned at the time of writing "Alastor") is then portrayed in the tale about the visionary. This explains the images of narrowly escaped chasms—such as the image of the shallop skirting the edge of a whirlpool—that punctuate the young poet's mental journey. Finally, the visionary's descent into his own mind, like any self-conscious speculation, is destined to end in an image of the mind's frustration.

Let me recall here how the visionary represents the likeness of something internal sought by the narrator. Although seeking only a likeness of his antitype, the narrator finds in his tale an image of an apparently different sort, an image of his own search. The search ends for the narrator, as for the visionary, at the point at which the mind cannot pursue its speculations any further. The visionary's death occurs as he lies "on the smooth brink/Of that obscurest chasm" (ll. 636–37), so that his end echoes the end imaged as the edge of an abyss in the "Essay on Life." The physical death of the visionary serves as "[a]n image" (1. 661) for the narrator. That is, the narrator's tale, like the visionary's speculation, ends with an image of the point beyond which neither language nor thought can progress as such.

Yet in another sense, the story of the visionary does serve as a likeness of the imagination for the narrator. Imagination is shown as unconcerned with nature, self-seeking and, ultimately, self-destructive. As a restless mental activity that moves toward forming emblems of itself, and thus ending, imagination is identified with the "something within" that thirsts for its own likeness described in the "Essay on Love." Therefore there are traces of the imagination's activity in the tale of the young poet.[64] As Shelley will suggest most clearly in the later *A Defence of Poetry*, poems reveal an act of the mind. He speaks of

> the nature itself of language, which is a more direct representation of the actions and passions of our internal being and is susceptible of more various and delicate combinations than color, form, or motion, and is more plastic and obedient to the control of that faculty of which it is the creation. For language is arbitrarily produced by the imagination *and has relation to thoughts alone* . . . (emphasis added).[65]

In both the "Essay on Love" and the "Essay on Life" Shelley argues that a union with any ultimate reality behind this activity is unattainable in this world. No ultimate source of poetry or of thought can be embodied in language or in the flesh. But desire, if not the origin or object of desire, can be known. And it is desire that allows people to find images of themselves—if only of their feelings of vacancy—in nature.

Thus Shelley's tale is not only about the misguided or self-destructive imagination. The "Preface" leads readers to believe that the activity of the visionary cannot be ignored, and the presence of the narrator raises the possibility that there is a way of using the imagination's restlessness to claim the good, the light shed on the world, without ignoring (or being trapped by) the spiral of self-consciousness leading to the verge where words fail, which is the ultimate effect and image of imagination.

The luminaries mentioned in the "Preface," while struck with darkness and extinction, are nonetheless luminaries. The visionary also, while not seeking images of his own activity, leaves his impression on nature: "he did impress/On the green moss his tremulous step, that caught/Strong shuddering from his burning limbs" (ll. 515–17). The narrator similarly has failed to find a likeness of his ideal self and has produced a tale about the visionary's failure. Yet he has created his song, and this song, in following the footprints of the visionary and in revealing the narrator's desire, transforms the world. The gap between the narrator's success and his failure is a pervasive instance of a tension that informs the structure of the entire poem, the tension occasioned by the basic difference between the cause and effect of the imagination.[66]

These issues raised in "Alastor," and in the poems with which it was published, however, also show the difficulty of Shelley's attempts to imagine a poetic tradition or a human community in which he as a poet can place himself. Speaking of the desire for likenesses, the "Essay on Love" concludes that as "soon as this want or power is dead, man becomes the living sepulchre of himself, and what yet survives is the mere husk of what once he was," a more negative image surely also informed by Shelley's portraits of Wordsworth and Southey, who by 1816 Shelley says were not as they once had been.[67] But the essay and the poems from the *Alastor* volume thus also suggest the particular difficulties posed by Shelley's changed relationship to the earlier poets he admired. In "To Wordsworth," for example, the image of the early Wordsworth functions, in effect, as an ideal for Shelley, that is, to use Shelley's terms, as a mirrored reflection of Shelley's own anti-type or desires or, to use other terms, as a figure of the poetic self, of what might count as being a poet. Yet to see Wordsworth as a figure of imaginative desire is also a problem. Once having claimed the early Wordsworth as such a figure, Shelley cannot (as in "Alastor") easily dismiss the older poet, since to give up on Wordsworth is to some degree to risk becoming either like him a man who no longer aspires to change the world or like Coleridge a man whose aspirations are no longer directed toward the world and so equally a man without love, without community. In short, for Shelley to give up his earlier models of poetic achievement is to risk becoming "the mere husk of what once he was." The "Essay on Love," then, suggests what is at stake in Shelley's overdetermined insistence on maintaining the desire he describes so equivocally. The tone with which Shelley wrote to Peacock about Wordsworth in 1818—"That such a man should be such a poet!"—is not solely dismay that an admired poet had written the *Two Addresses to the Freeholders of Westmorland,* but also that imaginative desire could become so thoroughly divorced from a sympathetic imagining of historical and political good, or from the light shed on the world to which "Alastor" calls attention.[68]

"Slaves of Passion & Sickly Sensibility": Audiences, Narrative, and Lyric, 1812–1819

While it may be said that the protocols of reading Thomsonian description—used, among other things, to educate generations of readers—themselves describe a public facet of his early poetry, such cultural work was not part of what Thomson could imagine as part of poetry's public role. Indeed, Wordsworth's response to his contemporaries' criticisms of Thomsonian description as irrelevant informed his turn from a poetry of the eye to experiments with a more narrative and testimonial poetry. At the same time, even Wordsworth's earlier narratives betrayed a nervousness about "common" or sensationalist readings of his texts, and by 1815 he showed an increasingly internalized sense of the power of speech. Faced with what he understood as Wordsworth's (and Southey's) apparent defection, Shelley's desire to follow in their footsteps without ending (as Southey predicted he would end) by acquiescing to or despairing in the face of what he could not change becomes a poetic, a personal, and a political issue. The problem of narrative is especially fraught, insofar as Shelley repeats some of

Wordsworth's narrative strategies at the same time that he (as in "To Wordsworth") struggles with what Wordsworth seems to set as the "plot" or naturalized trajectory of a poetic career.

Shelley's confrontation with these issues was fed in part by his own later historical position. He not only inherited, primarily from Wordsworth, a re-figuring of the poet's engagement with history but also was born into a world in which the distribution of literature was increasingly mediated by impersonal, commercial transactions—a world in which the institution of paper money and a series of recessions suggested that commercial transactions did not guarantee value, or, more specifically, that the value of what was printed on paper was not guaranteed. As Shelley put it in "A Philosophical View of Reform," all of England's "great transactions . . . are managed by signs . . . expressed upon paper," but the government, having instituted paper money and public credit, no longer fulfills the promises on its "fabricated pieces of paper," thus "augment[ing] indefinitely the proportion of those who enjoy the profit of the labor of others as compared with those who exercise this labor."[69] Shelley's essay is intended as a political analysis, in line and sometimes in argument with the contemporary writings of Adam Smith (including Smith's labor theory of national economic wealth), Cobbett, and Malthus. But Shelley's rhetoric also has implications for those whose labor was the production of signs on paper, raising the question of how literary labor might be distinguished from what Shelley's tract identifies as fraud.

Moreover, Shelley was also aware of a new reading public—a public most often reading and buying novels—as a fact rather than as an anomaly. In other words, to imagine how a poet's work might make a difference within the public sphere—how to be, as Shelley put it, one "who would be listened to as a mender of . . . [historical] crimes & miseries"—required a consideration of how texts reached and were understood by early nineteenth-century readers.[70] And this involved the question of how his own pieces of paper might be stamped as genuine currency rather than a trick like that perpetuated by one of the newly wealthy whose mediocrity, Shelley wrote, "poison[s] the literature of the age."[71]

Shelley's awareness of the problematic relationship between writers, texts, readers, and politics, then, may be linked to a number of factors (including his readings of other poets, early nineteenth-century economic realities, and the reading habits of the contemporary public). Similarly, his interest in Gothic novels may be overdetermined, although one motive certainly was his interest in the numbers of people who were reached, moved, and even formed as readers by such novels. Shelley not only read Gothic novels but tried his hand at writing them, producing *Zastrozzi* and *St. Irvyne,* the last published in 1810. These volumes show his awareness of the seductions of narrative, a seductiveness that nineteenth-century reviewers attributed to Gothic and Gothic influenced novels.[72] For example, by 1794 Coleridge was criticizing Radcliffe's *Mysteries of Udolpho* because of its unnatural titillation of readers: "[C]uriosity is kept upon the stretch from page to page, and from volume to volume, and the secret, which the reader thinks himself every instant on the point of penetrating, flies like a phantom before him. . . . in the search of what is new, an author is apt to forget what is natural."[73] In 1825 Hazlitt more positively described *Caleb Williams* in much the same terms, saying "no one ever began Caleb Williams that did not read it through"; similarly, the *Quarterly Review*'s March 1818 review of *Frankenstein,* voicing a stock suspicion of Gothic images and plots—and inadvertently echoing Shelley's language about his goal of becoming one who would "mend" social ills—included the following sentence: "[this novel] cannot *mend* . . . its readers, . . . it fatigues the feelings without interesting the understanding; it gratuitously harasses the heart" (emphasis added).[74] Shelley's own 1817 anonymous review of the novel almost anticipates the *Quarterly*'s response, arguing more positively about the "harassment" the novel practices on readers: "We are led breathless . . . the head turns giddy, and the ground seems to fail under our feet."[75] His 1818 preface for the novel seems also to address the criticism: "The event on which the interest of the story depends is exempt from the disadvantages of a mere tale of spectres or enchantment."[76] Given Shelley's insistence on maintaining desire coupled with his analysis of the problematic status of nature in "Alastor," his defense of how narrative leads readers on and ungrounds them is not surprising.

Yet, Shelley's familiarity with more popular forms of fictional narratives as well as his discussions of how written signs might be manipulated and manipulative also forced him to recognize that narrative was not necessarily less suspect or less conventional, per se, than the pleasures of other forms of enchantment, such as those involving more visual or iconic images or signs. The distinction between narrative and other forms of representation is clearly made by the time Shelley wrote his 1820 *Defence of Poetry,* in which he explicitly addresses his suspicion that narrative ties people to the facts and facts have the potential to tie people to the customary: "There is this difference between a story and a poem, that a story is a catalogue of detached facts which have no other bond of connection than time, place, circumstance, cause, and effect."[77] To imply as Shelley does in this statement that the historical bonds of time, place, and circumstance are trivial betrays not only Shelley's skeptical views of causation but also his argument with his own early fascination with narrative seduction. Reading Shelley's statement about poems and stories, we might first take "story" to mean "tale," or "narrative," that which is driven by principles of succession. But in the course of defining the difference between story and poem, Shelley redefines narrative, even as he in effect argues that people are not bound to accept the historical circumstances, the plot or narrative, in which they find themselves and recognizes the potentially misleading nature or source and the mystified construction of such bonds. Like paper currency, he suggests, stories or detached facts are subject to manipulation.[78]

By 1820, however, Shelley distinguishes not only between poem and story but between story (detached facts, which we might call description) and plot (the mistaking of the contingent for the necessary), warning against confusing the former with the latter. In making these distinctions, he prefigures modern theories about narrative and description in the eighteenth- and nineteenth-century novel. I am thinking, for instance, of books such as Nancy Armstrong's *Desire and Domestic Fiction* on the novel "as the document and as the agency of cultural history" or Peter Brooks's somewhat different *Reading for the Plot,* especially his discussion of how narrative becomes "a dominant mode of representation and explanation" in the Romantic era, with plot defined as the "interpretative structuring operation elicited, and necessitated, by those texts that we identify as narrative."[79] I take it that "those texts we identify as narrative" tend to be those that present themselves as referential, located in time and place, expressive of temporality involving causation and transformation, and driven by principles of succession.[80] While we tend to contrast narrative texts in this last sense with lyric, driven by principles of repetition, recently William Ray has suggested associating repetition with description, which he argues functioned like plot to nurture in readers, of nineteenth-century novels, habits of organization and labeling, cognitive habits that promoted a cultural economy in which privilege and power were distributed on the basis of fluency in the conventions novels taught and required; that is, novels appealed not only to a contract with the reader of the sort Brooks describes narratives as invoking, but also to competence and knowledge of a different kind, namely, the ability to repeat and accumulate that description proposes.[81] In this sense, both plot and story (at least in the novels with which plot and story were most closely associated) become agents of control or of what Shelley called custom. And both involve interpretative structuring, or what texts do to or in readers.

If in 1812 Shelley's poetry focuses on the facts ("Society as it is from facts") to make a political point, "Alastor" employs a different strategy to suggest that poets need not accept the facts (the "story") as if facts necessarily form a plot; poets can reimagine the world as other than it is. "Alastor," as I have argued, specifically takes issue with Wordsworth's 1814 reinscription of the role of institutions (which is to say, cultural plots) in *The Excursion,* a poem that for Shelley made the older poet a "slave." The allegorical mode of Shelley's poem—the way in which it seems not to insert the subject into a temporal or historical world[82]—can thus be seen as an attempt to resist the acculturating operations of either description or plot, although this does not cut the *poem* loose from history.

Moreover, the way "Alastor" pointedly conflates the status of pictures, images, and tales (the visionary's tale is called a tale, a picture, and an image), and that it does so while distinguishing between the didactic and the "narrative," suggests a complicated theoretical account of story (or description), plot, lyric images, and the structuring operations both represented in and elicited by various kinds of texts. As I have already suggested, it is probable that Shelley's fascination with Gothic fiction as well as his readings of Wordsworth and Southey *in light* of his readings of fiction informed the development of his thoughts about the nature of narrative, description, and lyric. Shelley's awareness of the changed relationship between writers, especially of popular fiction, and readers also played a role in this thinking.

Shelley's critique of narrative, in fact, began well before "Alastor." Having laid out the issues involved in Shelley's questions about narrative, let me return to trace his developing thoughts about narrative in the early letters and in particular in the 1812 letter to Elizabeth Hitchener in which Shelley copied out the poem "*a Tale* of Society as it is from facts" (emphasis added). The letter at first seems to leap from topic to topic and begins by mentioning that Shelley is working on a novel: "a *tale* illustrative of the causes of the failure of the French Revolution to benefit human-kind" (emphasis added), suggesting that Shelley was still linking his insistence on the study of history with both facts and tales or what might commonly be called narrative features.[83] The letter then moves to an annotated itinerary of places Shelley had visited or intended to visit, including a note on how manufacturers were ruining nature in Cumberland, a note that then veers to take cognizance of how manufacturing exacted also a human cost and then as abruptly returns to natural description: "Children are frequently found in the River which the unfortunate women employed at the manufactory destroy. Wales is very different... the scenery quite as beautiful.—Southey says Expediency ought to [be] made the ground of politics but not of morals." The end of the paragraph then returns to Shelley's projected tale of the French Revolution, which he implicitly introduces as attempting to *connect* morals and politics. Shelley's discussion also disclaims another idea he attributes to Southey, namely, that reasonable explanations are beside the point in political discourse. A significant cause of vice, misery, and violence, Shelley proposes, has ever been "*expediency, insincerity,* [and] *mystery*"—by which Shelley seems to mean mystification. Concluding that custom has contaminated Southey, Shelley then offers his own "Tale of Society," presumably intended as one that does not mystify or inscribe a form of cultural control; after copying the poem he returns once more to his quarrel with Southey over ends and means—or, as it might be reframed, over morals and expedience, explanation and mystification.

I want to dwell on what seems at first a curious mixture of topics in this letter, with appeals to the beauty of nature (part of a plea that Elizabeth Hitchener come visit) interlaced with a perhaps more easily traced line of thought by which Shelley focuses on several series of events (his tale of the French Revolution, his report on lives in Keswick, his journalistic poem) that have bearing on his quarrel with Southey, a quarrel that on one level is about how to represent historical and political events. As Shelley's letter phrases it, "If a thing exists there can always be shewn [*sic*] reasons for its existence." Shelley insists he will not, in the interest of expediency—that is, to achieve his end (such as legal reform)—use mystification or lead his readers by the nose. His argument seems to be that it is just the sort of expediency and mystification he refuses to practice that causes or perpetuates vice, misery, and violence. Presumably, then, a desire to unmask or demystify the workings of history and to inform others about such workings informed Shelley's poetic tales and his projected novel, a suggestion reinforced by the rhetorical echoes in the title of his poem, which calls to mind Godwin's 1794 *Things As They Are Or The Adventures of Caleb Williams,* or perhaps even Richard Price's similarly titled Revolution Society sermon of 4 November 1789. In short, we should expect that in Shelley's poem the vagrants are vagrants for a reason; they are, among other things, not picturesque or sensationalist icons—Shelley's comments about expedience and mystification signal his interest in desensationalizing and defamiliarizing such icons.

Nonetheless, in his letter as a whole Shelley confusingly (and perhaps at this point in his thinking confusedly) mixes sensibility and natural description, storytelling, and political change. One might add psychology to this already unstable list, not only in the argument that individual and social morality should coincide,[84] but also in his description of his own poem as "a picture of [his] feelings," presumably feelings for those whose tale he tells, so that what counts as "real . . . literally true" are both the events and feelings represented *and* the authorial motive for telling such tales. This collage of contexts suggests that Shelley wants his motives to represent a kind of gold standard and to guarantee that his poem is moral rather than expedient. He certainly does not mean to emphasize the private and seductive nature of the self-revelation that informs his invitation to Elizabeth Hitchener to come visit—although Peter Brooks's proposals about narrative as "a form of human desire" and as involving a "need to tell as a primary human drive that seeks to seduce and to subjugate" may be relevant.[85] It is difficult not to take Shelley's deference to Hitchener in the closing of his letter as suggesting he was at some level aware of the potential of narratives for both seduction and subjugation. Shelley's letter ends insisting that "[y]our [Hitchener's] letters give me perpetual food for thought and discussion," a gesture that seeks to maintain the intellectual exchange (even flirtation) by suggesting that Shelley, perhaps like society and its narratives, is open to revision.

As early as 1811, in another letter to Hitchener also praising the beauty of Wales, Shelley reveals a clear talent for demystifying his own gestures. Talking about the way in which he is transported by the sublime landscapes, Shelley pauses to ask the following: "*why* do they enchant . . . it cannot be innate, is it acquired?—Thus does knowledge lose all the pleasure which invol[un]tarily [ari]ses, by attempting to arrest th[e] fleeting Phantom as it passes . . . it [presumably, pleasure] flies from all but the slaves of passion & sickly sensibility who will not analyse a feeling."[86] The transitions in this meditation are impressive, as Shelley records being as moved as a character in a novel of sensibility, then questioning this response, realizing that to question may be to lose the pleasure, nonetheless concluding that such pleasure may be illegitimate, a pleasure that stays only with "the slaves of passion." Strikingly, as in his report of his conversation with Southey, in which he also rejected as mystification that which was not explained, Shelley abruptly turns from landscape to "an anecdote," this time of a Welsh beggar who questions *Shelley's* intentions: Shelley reports the man as saying, "I see by your dress that you are a rich man— . . . You appear to be well intentioned but I have no security of it while you live in such a house as that, or wear such clothes as those."[87]

In one sense, both letters identify narrative as a demystifying gesture—similar to analysis or unfolding explanation—and set narrative against other forms of representation such as sublime landscapes and more descriptive or iconic images that elicit a pleasurable psychological response or what Shelley would come to call "passive perception."[88] Yet both letters also begin to question narrative, as well: in the first case, the covert recognition of how his reader might be silenced by his narrative; in the second case, the suspicions about intentions voiced by the beggar within the narrative. Moreover, these sorts of juxtapositions continue intermittently in the letters from 1812 through at least 1815. Another 1812 letter to Hitchener, for instance, discusses Shelley's plans to circulate his address to the Irish People, which he compares to the printing (and public circulation) of Paine's works.[89] The letter again mentions the planned political novel and then proposes settling in a Welsh castle, a Gothic set piece complete with moldering turrets and ghosts. Castles, he lightly says, are "fit *emblems* of decaying inequality and oppression," but the ghosts he will "welcome . . . [as] they would tell *tales* of old, and it would add to the picturesqueness of the scenery to see their thin forms flitting thro the vaulted charnels" (emphasis added).[90] Here it is emblems that speak of political injustice, tales that become picturesque. Despite this revaluation of terms, the letter repeats the

tacit but striking pattern in Shelley's thought about public action and po-
litical writing, which repeatedly in various forms tests narrative (and often
prose) against more visual or iconic images and signs (those of sensational-
ist, sublime, or Gothic fiction as well as of poetry). The letters also repeat-
edly set cultural plots such as historical wrongs against emotional plots, as
in the unanalyzed pleasures of "sickly sensibility," the power of which be-
longs to the realm of the psychological.

In the very early letters, narrative seems most often to be identified with the
record of history that Shelley set against the descriptive and psychologized
modes of sensibility or sublimity, although he also suggests that narrative may
itself have ways of awakening and directing desire that are open to question
(enacting a form of emotional enslavement to plot), while set pieces of Gothic,
sentimental, or sublime scenery (such as the crumbling castles in Wales) may
call attention to historical and political wrongs, or as Shelley says serve as em-
blems of "inequality and oppression." Such questions about the relationship
between the temporal, historical world and the enculturation of feelings sug-
gest why the phantoms dismissed by analysis and yet replanted in Shelley's
imagined castle in 1812 reappear not only in poems such as "Alastor" but also
in the following passage from an 1815 letter about a missionary—who seems
almost to have come from the stock of Gothic conventions—whom Hogg had
met on his travels: "It excites my wonder [Shelley writes] to consider the per-
verted energies of the human mind. . . . Yet who is there that will not pursue
phantoms, spend his choicest hours in hunting after dreams, and wake only to
perceive his error. . . . What [is] the power which awakens not in its progres-
sion more wants than it can supply?"[91] Earlier, simply to take pleasure in
ghosts rather than actively questioning such pleasure was to be a slave of pas-
sion and sickly sensibility. In this 1815 letter, to pursue phantoms is again part
of that which produces desire, not fulfillment, but the pursuit is marked as
"perverted." And, again, the letter turns abruptly from ghosts to politics, prob-
ably in response to an article from *The Examiner*.[92] Finally, specifically dis-
cussing contemporary political issues, the letter notes Shelley's "endeavour to
divest [his] mind of temporary sensations, to consider them as already histor-
ical. This is difficult. Spite of ourselves the human beings which surround us
infect us with their opinions."[93] The missionary's pursuit of phantoms and
Shelley's pursuit of history are not so far apart; moreover, sensation now is a
part (if an unwelcome part) of Shelley's engagement with current events,
which he is unable to reconceive outside of current public narratives. By 1815,
then, narratives and images are not so easily distinguished. Both are charac-
terized as subject to reification, potential blocks to the freedom "in which [the
mind] would have acted but for the misuse of words and signs, the instru-
ments of its own creation" (as Shelley would put the issue in the later "Essay
on Life").[94]

If all forms of representation are subject to mystification or (to use Shelley's vocabulary) may foster enslavement, then questions not just about his own use of narrative and lyric but about his readers needed to be addressed. In this vein, between 1812 and 1815 Shelley can also be seen shifting his sense of what might count as a political or public gesture, moving away from simply listing (or even explaining) things as they are for the record. He begins to question how such gestures might be received, that is, to focus on the more public distribution of text to reader. Here Shelley's questions about the relationship between the psychological and the historical begin to come together insofar as his insistence on historical explanation is clearly seen as subject to misappropriation (as when the beggar cannot read Shelley's motives).

Shelley was thus aware he wrote not simply for people, but for a public (to use Wordsworth's terms, if without Wordsworth's evaluation of the terms). Shelley worked out some of his thoughts in his letters; his reading and his knowledge of public reading habits further fed his analyses of the cultural work of literary forms. And the public, in Shelley's day, was increasingly reading novels. Shelley's own planned political novel is not mentioned again after the letters of 1812. But it seems that in these letters the idea of writing this novel galvanized Shelley's thinking on issues raised by much prose fiction, including novels of sensibility and sensationalist fiction, but above all Gothics, a form that explicitly raised questions about the relationship between writing, reading, and political action.

Both Mary Godwin and Shelley admired novels such as Matthew G. Lewis's 1794 *The Monk,* Charles Brockden Brown's 1798 *Wieland,* not to mention the 1794 *Caleb Williams,* by Godwin, whose work deeply influenced Brown. Between 1814 and 1816, Shelley reread *Caleb Williams;* Mary was reading *Wieland;* Shelley met "Monk" Lewis; and Mary Godwin Shelley began *Frankenstein.*[95] The seduction of reading figured prominently in contemporary criticism of these novels; the seduction of reading, and of eloquence, is also paramount in the texts themselves, as is a self-consciousness about the ends, sources, and repetitions inherent in their Gothic plots.[96] Certainly *Caleb Williams* is a novel driven by questions about the seductions of cultural narratives and in particular about how the truth must be "plausible," which in the novel is increasingly linked to the power not only of class and traditional institutions, but also of print circulation, as when Caleb Williams finds himself redefined by "the WONDERFUL AND SURPRISING HISTORY OF CALEB WILLIAMS," which has been anonymously circulated.[97] Throughout the novel, eloquence and the power to move others or to be believed are linked to mystification: just before his confrontation with the "wonderful and surprising" history, Caleb—sounding much like Shelley on the pernicious pleasures of passive perception—remarks on how "that which excites our wonder we scarcely suppose ourselves competent to analyse."[98] By the end of the novel—both the published conclusion and the first, unused manuscript ending in which Caleb Williams goes mad—Godwin has made clear that the self cannot be imagined, let alone become a public agent for change, outside of culturally plausible narratives.

Other Gothics similarly call attention to the gaps between authorial intention, linguistic expression, and public reception, if with less emphasis on print culture per se. For instance, the eponymous hero (or villain) of *The Monk* is introduced as follows: "all who have heard him are so delighted with his eloquence, that it is . . . difficult to obtain a place at church"; he is a man whose "eloquence [is] the most persuasive," a man whose speeches "irresistibly" attract attention.[99] Eloquence, or the ability to move one's audience, in short, is no guarantee of motive. Yet more strikingly, in Brown's *Wieland,* Carwin is a person with a seductive voice, "not only mellifluent and clear, but the emphasis was so just, and the modulation so impassioned . . . [i]t imparted . . . *an emotion altogether involuntary and incontroulable* [*sic*]" (emphasis added).[100] Even more interestingly, Brown's Carwin *throws* his voice—and, to do ill, he thereby constructs plots. In other words, he takes what is and through language makes his auditors the slaves of passion, subject to mystification.[101] Finally, Mary Shelley's *Frankenstein* self-consciously underlines such Gothic insistences on the seductions of voice and tale telling.[102] As in "Alastor," *Frankenstein*'s embedded narratives raise the question of whose voice is to be believed and point out how "falsehood can look so like the truth."[103]

Frankenstein as a whole relates this skepticism most clearly in the structure and internal commentary on telling tales. The monster first tracks down Victor in order to be allowed to narrate his own story; the center of that story is the overheard story of Safie, Felix's "Arabian" maid, who unlike the Arab maid in "Alastor" is given a name and taught English so that she may tell her own story: eavesdropping on and watching Safie's education, the monster learns to read and construct *his* own story, which, as he points out to Victor, consists of moving "representations"; Victor indeed tells Walton, "He [the monster] is eloquent and persuasive; and . . . his words [can have] power."[104] Further, the question of whether being moved by a narrative means being moved to act morally or alternately; whether it can mean being mystified and manipulated is posed even more pointedly by Victor, whose own desire to tell his tale is emphasized, and who, like Safie and the monster but more ambiguously, edits his own story, attempting to control its distribution and reception.[105] Moreover, he urges Walton's men to continue their quest "with a voice so modulated to the different feelings expressed in his speech . . . can you wonder that these men were moved"—a description that echoes the characterizations of the voices of both Lewis's Monk and

Brown's Carwin. While Walton mistrusts the monster, "call[ing] to mind what Frankenstein had said of his powers of eloquence and persuasion," we as readers are encouraged to call to mind what Walton has said of Victor Frankenstein's powers of eloquence and persuasion. Mary Shelley, in short, underlines the difficulty of judging and the perils of not judging the narratives as well as the representations in common circulation.[106] Of course Walton, too, has an audience, his sister, while we become eavesdroppers to the whole. The novel insists in its self-consciousness about narration that plot, like politics, is an arena in which morals should but by no means necessarily always do operate. The novel also (like the novels by Lewis, Godwin, and Brown) contains the warning that neither nature nor human nature are unambiguous texts.

Framed narratives and questions about "artful" speech were not the exclusive province of novels or Gothics, of course. *Caleb Williams* conspicuously first raises questions about the effects of eloquence on common readers and the unstable relationship between virtue and the command of language while presenting the character of Mr. Clare—a poet.[107] Wordsworth's *The Ruined Cottage* had already incorporated the use of framed narratives to question the power of plot (in two senses of the word—place and the operations of interpretation exacted from readers by narratives). The *Excursion* recast *The Ruined Cottage* to suggest the institutional and cultural limits of such operations just as Brown similarly recast Godwin's novel in *Wieland.* Here, it is useful to return to Mary Shelley's record of the Shelleys' response to Wordsworth's self-revision and its echo of Shelley on the pleasures of sensationalist or sublime icons as suited to the slaves of passion: "He is a slave."[108] This records an argument with Wordsworth on the confusion of plot and story (and unwittingly through Wordsworth again with the reading habits promoted by sensationalist literature). The argument also is part of both Shelleys' insistence that people are not bound to accept the plots or the historical narratives given them. The question, then, becomes how not to reinscribe such plots while still being a force for social action as a writer and in particular as a poet.

For Shelley, as I have tried to suggest, such recognitions preceded the reading of Wordsworth's *Excursion* in 1814, although readings of Wordsworth's poems about the social force of narrations and images—from "A Poet's Epitaph" through *The Excursion*—certainly informed Shelley's developing poetics. Shelley's thinking on such issues also continued, not only in the 1816 "Alastor" but also in the 1819 "A Philosophical View of Reform," in which those who place their bodies in the service of the state are called slaves. In the place of amoral public plots, especially those requiring blind obedience or engendered by passion, Shelley again, as in the early exchange with Southey on expedience, advocates full disclosure:

"It is better that [people] should be instructed in the whole truth; that they should see the clear grounds of their rights, the objects to which they ought to tend."[109]

The means of promoting such clarity of sight in "A Philosophical View of Reform" is not a matter of content (or as Shelley says "systems . . . professed") but, as one might put it, of redistributing the means and reconceiving the ends of cultural production. The question for Shelley becomes how to unsettle, or at least to resist settling for, Wordsworth's "world, which is the world/Of all of us." This, then, is to question how forms of literary representation work in readers and again how not to reify cultural stories (or, as Shelley put it in his 1815 letter to Hogg, how to escape the "infection" of public opinion) while still engaging in a public forum.

By 1816, Shelley also expressed his anxiety in other, related, ways about how to connect poetic activity with human society and with history. For instance, he wrote to Byron suggesting that negative worldly opinion ought not to prevent Byron from acting on the "pure, and simple" motive of wishing "to express [his] own thoughts; to address [him]self to the sympathy of those who might think with [him]"; Shelley also mentions that Byron might consider writing an epic poem on the French Revolution.[110] Finally, Shelley adds that Byron should not aspire to fame, although he assures his friend that fame follows "those whom it is unworthy to lead."[111] Wordsworth eventually represented his goal as securing a permanent station in Literature, a goal that to some extent displaced earlier hopes that poets might also be effective in their own lifetimes. Shelley, by contrast, suggests that only by aspiring to write effective poetry (with efficacy now a category distinct from "worldly opinion") can poets hope to acquire future fame: in essence, he redefines the canon of Literature as the record of those who so aspired (presumably including the early Wordsworth). Thus, while his references to both fame and epic certainly involve Shelley's thoughts on his own place in literary history, the letter to Byron may also be understood in relation to Shelley's concern about poetry's relationship to history more literally conceived, as in his 1817 preface to *The Revolt of Islam* in which he similarly refers to the French Revolution, addresses himself to those sympathetic to the reform movement, and attempts to place himself as a poet by claiming his writing as a form of present action.[112] Once again, motive (in the advice to Byron) is invoked as the private guarantee of public writing, although references to the need for an already sympathetic audience betray Shelley's awareness of how difficult it might be to read motives or to trust one's motives would be properly read.

Writing of *The Revolt of Islam,* Kenneth Neill Cameron points out that Shelley's belief in the possible efficacy of an epic on the French Revolution is ironically the same belief "Coleridge had urged upon Wordsworth some eighteen years before."[113] On Shelley's account of the spirit of the age, this irony is not mere coincidence. As he wrote, responding to an 1819 *Quarterly Review* article (which he thought Southey had written and in which Shelley was accused of imitating and perverting Wordsworth), there is a "certain similarity all the best writers of any particular age inevitably are marked with, from the spirit of that age acting on all."[114] In this way, Shelley rings changes on what Thomson and, in a different sense, Wordsworth struggled with, namely, the repetitions inherent in poetry. For Shelley, writing is not marked simply by its participation in what the culture counts as poetry, but by the ways in which literary culture engages and is engaged by the larger culture, the "spirit of the age acting on" literary producers. Thus a poet earns a place in literary history primarily by his or her engagement with actual history; to set out only to achieve literary fame is, as Shelley says to Byron, unworthy.

Shelley's appeal to the spirit of the age is most centrally a way of reaffirming his moral and political beliefs about commonality. At the same time, worldly opinion (those cultural plots Shelley sought to resist) and the spirit of the age (which Shelley says is "inevitably" rehearsed in the "best" writers) seem difficult to distinguish, even as both cultural plots and Shelley's pervasive "spirit" seem to leave motives to the side. In short, Shelley's political and literary analyses underline the difficulty of sustaining literary or political commonality without becoming enslaved to common narratives in the process.

There are further unsettling implications to Shelley's insistence that he and Wordsworth followed the same path because of the spirit of the age. In particular, Shelley could hardly have given assent to Wordsworth's account of the effects of aging on the poetic imagination, even as those effects were presented at the end of "Ode: Intimations of Immortality," let alone as evidenced in *The Excursion* as Shelley read it or as proclaimed by Southey when he told the young Shelley he would think differently when he was as old as Southey. To argue that poets of active imagination resembled one another by default, as it were, was not an argument Shelley could sustain given his judgment on Wordsworth and Southey as political defaulters and his discomfort with Wordsworth's views on poetic development or the "plot" of a poetic career, let alone his analysis of the perniciousness of cultural currency. Nor was it an argument he could avoid, and it seems that "Peter Bell the Third" is where Shelley most starkly records his recognition of this fact. If the poem reveals Shelley's ambivalence about Wordsworth,[115] it also records Shelley's suspicions of how cultural plots are played out in readers and writers as well as his self-doubts about his own endeavor and about his career as a reenactment of Wordsworth's.[116]

Wordsworth begins "Peter Bell" as early as 1798, in response to Coleridge's charge that he was too matter-of-fact. Reading Wordsworth's poem, as published in 1819, Shelley once again reopens the earlier exchange between the older poets and follows the earlier Wordsworth by rejecting Coleridge's retreat and by addressing himself to contemporary reality, transposing hell "into contemporary industrial society."[117] At the same time, Shelley proposes that Wordsworth fulfills Satan's prescription for the self as hell, having "sold himself to the devil in order to save himself from . . . uncertainties."[118] Shelley presumably introduces Wordsworth as Proteus to underscore how, like Proteus, Wordsworth changed to avoid facing questions. Specifically, "Peter Bell the Third" was written just following the (August) Manchester massacre and the (October) Yorkshire bread riots, which must have fueled Shelley's anger at Wordsworth's growing conservatism.[119] Finally, even as Shelley focuses on and deplores Wordsworth's resulting "loss of compassion," in "Peter Bell the Third," "the form of the poem itself—its genre, its methods, its tone—uncomfortably reflects the very vices Shelley would castigate. . . . There is 'Small justice shown, and still less pity'."[120]

That Shelley's poem should seem ungenerous is not surprising if we compare Shelley's earlier voiced admiration for the historical impact of epic poetry with his introductory statements, however satirically they are meant, on "Peter Bell the Third" as mock epic. Shelley enters his poem as the latest in a "series of cyclic poems which have already been candidates for bestowing immortality upon, at the same time that they receive it from, [Peter Bell's] character and adventures."[121] To deplore Wordsworth's insertion of himself within literary history by appeal to Southey's fame as Poet Laureate is one thing. But to describe his own highest aspirations by way of reaction, as an historian of Fudges, is potentially to doom himself to the cycle he deplores; if Shelley's satire does not accept what is, it still closes the gap between what is and what should be much as Shelley saw Wordsworth doing. The point is one Shelley himself made implicitly a few months later, by December 1819, when he wrote,

> Towards whatsoever we regard as perfect, undoubtedly it is no less our duty than it is our nature to press forward; this is the generous enthusiasm which accomplishes not indeed the consummation after which it aspires, but one which approaches it in a degree far nearer than if the whole powers had not been developed by a delusion. It is in politics rather than in religion that faith is meritorious.[122]

This is Shelley's reaffirmation of faith. As P. M. S. Dawson says, it "cannot be easy to maintain the necessary commitment when one knows that it is to a 'delusion'."[123] Shelley's and Dawson's remarks are about politics, specifically about resisting both expediency and utopian fantasy in the face of the political unrest of 1819. Yet the statements hold true of Shelley's view of the poetic as well as the political imagination, which, indeed, as Shelley argues, seem in this light inseparable. To avoid the error of demanding that one's ideals be embodied, without abandoning either the body of the world or ideals, is not easily accomplished either in poetry or politics. To succumb to such error, however, is to be caught in the very trap—the hell—in which "Peter Bell the Third" places Wordsworth.

It is in his 1819 encounter with Wordsworth that Shelley seems first fully to recognize the implications for himself of the fact that—to return to the 1822 letter about love—although "one is always in love with something or other[,] the error . . . consists in seeking in a mortal image the likeness of what is perhaps eternal."[124] In light of this explicit caution against seeking the likeness of one's ideals in a single image, it is not surprising to find Rousseau substituting for Wordsworth as Shelley's literary father in "The Triumph of Life." Moreover, the return to an allegorical mode—the refusal to consider "the human being in a point of view too detailed and circumscribed" (to quote from Shelley's prescription on how to analyze as opposed to simply "assum[ing] entire opinions")—may also be seen as Shelley's poetic answer to the problem of how to destabilize cultural economies.[125] That is, Shelley's style, far from marking his upper class affiliations, stems from his critique of the repetitions of "too detailed and circumscribed" views as rein-scribing cultural plots. Finally, the ways in which "The Triumph of Life" continues to open a space between heaven and hell and to figure readerly agency suggest Shelley's prefiguration of his own future readers (from the Chartists to Arnold);[126] his last poem also helps show what Shelley learned from his reading of Wordsworth and of novels.

Luminaries and Literary Fathers

There has been much debate over whether the movement of "The Triumph of Life" is toward celebration or defeat, a decision usually seen to depend on one's reading of Rousseau's story, which doubles (at least up to a point) the poet-narrator's.[127] Paul de Man, for instance, follows a series of turns in the poem by which, he says, "The Triumph of Life" is changed from a quest, like "Alastor," to a poem of motion whereby the veiling and unveiling of figures (or the glimmering suspension, which "may well be the mode of being of all figures") provide a caution about reading all texts.[128] According to de Man, "The Triumph of Life" identifies and thematizes the impossibility of defin-ing *or* abandoning the quest for a stable text. Further, he insists that Shelley's strategy cannot be designated a source of value and celebrated or denounced: it is simply Shelley's recognition of the problematic nature of reading.[129]

De Man's essay implicitly plays against readings such as Jerome McGann's, which proposes that by 1822 Shelley reassessed his impossible quest for an Absolute, accepted the "opposition[s that] rule our mortal day" (l. 229), and found that if "the world [was] not thereby redeemed, at least poetry and the creative act [were]," which is in a way to read Shelley as I have read both Thomson and the later Wordsworth.[130] More explicitly, de Man's reading calls into question Donald Reiman's conclusion that "[e]verywhere in 'The Triumph' the dark side of human experience is balanced by positive alternatives," a balance Reiman relates to Shelley's skeptical epistemology.[131]

McGann and de Man, though for different reasons, distinguish "The Triumph of Life"—especially in its self-conscious exploration of language—from earlier Shelleyan quests. Reiman's commentary, on the other hand, points out numerous parallels between the poet's last fragment and quite early texts, in particular, "Alastor."[132] My own desire is to skirt the controversy set in motion by de Man's resistance to the historicism of Reiman or McGann and to discuss the continuity of Shelley's poetic concerns and strategies from "Alastor" through the prose to "The Triumph of Life" in light of de Man's insights, although without abandoning my story of Shelley's historical embeddedness, especially in the case of his own developing analysis of the problematics of reading.

I have already argued that the overall structure of "Alastor" is that of the narrator's production of his tale, ending in a denial of the sufficiency of fictions, a denial that, with its accompanying lament, ends the poem. The figures that preside over the end of the visionary's tale in "Alastor"—the vertiginous chasm and the suspension of the "mighty horn" of the moon (l. 647)[133]—acknowledge the emptiness or circularity of the production of images whereby poetry provides only emblems of its own production (of the desire for likenesses but not the source of that desire). Still, the visionary's quest, while doomed to end without yielding what he wants, does cast light on the world and produce a series of likenesses. The narrator helps us see the visionary in mixed light: the poet is lost, but the narrator retraces his footprints (re-illuminating the trail), leaving us the poem.

The insistence on a double vision found in "Alastor" is repeated in both "The Triumph of Life" and *A Defence of Poetry.* In "The Triumph of Life," the poet-narrator again places himself in nature, only to distinguish himself from it and receive a vision of his double in the shape of Rousseau.[134] Rousseau's tale mirrors—at least up to a point—the narrator's: both have visions after they wake poised between heaven and hell, whether their situation is imaged spatially, like the narrator's (ll. 27–28), or temporally, like Rousseau's (ll. 332–34); both see shapes (ll. 87, 96, 352); and both ask questions.[135] Notably, too, both ask questions about their origins—Rousseau, directly; the narrator, in questioning Rousseau who, like the guitar in "With a Guitar. To Jane" talks only "according to the wit" of his companion, in any case.[136]

Not only does Rousseau, like the visionary in "Alastor," serve as a likeness of the narrator in search of the source and end of imaginative desire, but also Rousseau's "shape all light" closely resembles the visionary's apparition in "Alastor."[137] Rousseau, however, does not set out after the original or source of his vision. In light of Rousseau's *premature* acceptance of what "mere" images have to offer, it is not surprising that none of the chasms or whirlpools by which the visionary of "Alastor" dies reappear in "The Triumph of Life"; indeed, Rousseau turns his back on the cavern by which he awakens (l. 313ff.).[138] However, in allowing the shape to quench his thirst, he finds a new vision, which is introduced by an image of footprints like those found in "Alastor."

In the earlier poem, the narrator's projected image of his search for the origin of his desire for likenesses does produce likenesses for us, if not of origins, still of both the course and frustration of desire. The loss of the luminous visionary turns the light of "[a]rt and eloquence . . . to shade" (ll. 710–12) for the narrator; yet without the narrative of loss there would be no poem. Rousseau, in effect, cuts short his narrative: the "track" (l. 518) along which he moved no longer holds out any promises, nor is he thirsty any longer, having settled for the "presence of that shape" (l. 425), a presence that is compared to a "caress [that turns] . . . weary slumber to content" (ll. 422–23). If quests generate likenesses—and likenesses or similes are the major rhetorical figure of "The Triumph of Life"—then it is apt that the similes thin out as Rousseau ceases his questioning.[139]

In *A Defence of Poetry,* Shelley provides a difficult analysis of poetic language, part of which seems to illuminate the description of Rousseau's situation in "The Triumph of Life." Shelley notes that poets perceive orders "in the combinations of language" and "in the *series* of their imitations of natural objects" (emphasis added).[140] Presumably, these orders are associated with grammatical or rhetorical orders of words or with specifically ordered series of images ("imitations of natural objects"). He continues to say that there is one particular order or rhythm that is highest, and that gives most pleasure; this order is then identified as the one that most belongs (he does not say how) "to each . . . [class] of mimetic representation."[141] It is difficult to understand what Shelley means when he distinguishes classes of mimetic representation, each class having its own "best" order. However, we are given some clue as to the nature of these classes in the paragraph preceding Shelley's discussion of better and worse orders when he says that the order in men's "words and actions" is "distinct from that of objects and . . . impressions," expression having its own laws, which are those of "that from which it proceeds."[142] We may conclude that words or expression form a distinct class with its own intellectual and imaginative order. Moreover, if language "has relation to thoughts alone" and is "produced by the imagination," then we may conclude that the rule of order in expression will be derived from the rule or law of imagination.[143] Shelley proceeds to suggest that the particular virtue of poets—who presumably deal with expression—lies in their ability to approximate the beautiful, and he tentatively defines the beautiful as the relation between the "highest pleasure [that of approximating to the best order of whatever is being represented] and its cause."[144] What poets seek, then, is to relate the pleasure proper orders afford—in this case the order that belongs to expression—and the source or cause of that pleasure.

To relate a series of images, words, or tropes is to propose a relationship between elements of language—on one level, this is to produce similes or metaphors.[145] So poetry, in seeking to relate the pleasure of ordering and the source of that pleasure, seeks to provide a metaphor of the relationship between the cause and effect (or the source and end) of poetry and poetic language. Moreover, Shelley links imaginative ordering, if not the pleasure thereof, with the desire for likenesses, including thus the desire for metaphor and simile. It is not surprising, in light of this, that *A Defence of Poetry* concludes that poetic language is "vitally metaphorical," although it is worth noting that Shelley then glosses "vitally metaphorical" as meaning to mark "the before unapprehended relations of *things*" (emphasis added).[146] The point seems to be that metaphor uncovers relations, but of things. Rather than uncovering the source of our desire for likenesses—and the reason for the pleasure we take in likenesses—poetic language simply generates new likenesses (and new pleasure), leaving the relationship between these productions and their source mysterious.

However, poetry's quest for a meta-order is valorized: the "similitudes or relations" of poets, says Shelley, citing Bacon, are "footsteps"—albeit "footsteps of nature" rather than of that "which perceives them" or of that which generates them.[147] Footprints or likenesses are produced or noticed in the attempt to track down the relationship between the pleasure taken in perception and the cause of that pleasure. Although these footprints or relations are not the source or even the locus of such pleasure, nonetheless, in a curious twist, Shelley finally identifies the poet's use of language as the apprehension of "the beautiful—in a word, the good which exists in the relation . . . between existence and perception . . . perception and expression."[148]

Shelley's qualification of the status of the footprints or similitudes of poetry, in implying that nature's footprints are distinct from the mind perceiving and taking pleasure in them, seems to deny that the beautiful (i.e., the relation between the pleasure of poetry and its source) is what poetry yields. Yet if we recall that Shelley began by suggesting that poets approximate only the order or rhythm of the beautiful, it is possible to unravel this paradox, to an extent: poetry provides not simply individual similitudes—footprints—but an order or series of imitations. To expand Shelley's image, poetry yields not Crusoe's single footprint, leading to the companionship and servitude of some man Friday, but rather a likeness (another print) of how prints themselves afford pleasure to an observer and, more importantly, the question of why this is so. Thus, we are given a series of metaphors, a trail, suggestive of the pleasure of the chase. This series or trail is, of course, itself a metaphor and thus may properly be questioned in turn: what is *its* source? Why does *it* give pleasure? "Alastor" suggests that to raise such questions is to produce yet further metaphors, finally—and at best—ending with a figure of dizzyingly receding figures in a mise-en-abyme. Yet only by asking such questions does one produce the trail of footprints leading to this abyss. To do otherwise is, as Shelley explains it, to become a slave of passion and sickly sensibility.

We can now return to Rousseau to recall that in resigning himself to his "shape all light," he stops his own—and thus the narrator's and thus the poem's—production of similes; his *encounter* with an acceptable figure is itself a final figure. Moreover, Rousseau's last moment of introspection provides an emblem of this failure of desire: the trail of hunted deer—introduced in the poem only by their tracks—is obscured by a wave and replaced by a wolf who "[l]eaves his stamp visibly upon the shore" (l. 409), until the pursuer's track is itself washed away.

It is as if Rousseau had read the end of "Alastor," and, knowing that what he pursues will be replaced only by further images, and images only of his own thirst and frustration, he drinks, thus filling the vacancy that sets desire and language in motion. His "day's path" may well now "end as he began it" (l. 418), but in abandoning the quest to embody or externalize the source of his shape, in not questioning what it has to offer, he finds the world eclipsed by a "light from heaven" (l. 429), for which he seeks no further likenesses and thus in the pursuit of which he leaves no paths. Without the impossible attempt to embody this light and its source, the object of Rousseau's desire is sought and lost in one line—"forever sought, forever lost" (l. 431)—with no space left between his desire and its failure in which we might find luminous footprints. His days, then, are monochrome, "sick" (l. 430), and the end of his speech is a mere catalogue of the forms that follow the chariot of life without "the joy which waked like Heaven's glance" (l. 538). By contrast, the joy awakened by alluring and otherworldly looks is emphasized in "Alastor," in which the visionary is led on (even if misled) by a pair of eyes. Significantly, Rousseau's eyes are not only transformed or obscured, but his maiden is compared to daylight, which (when present) blots out "even the least/Of heaven's living eyes" (l. 391–92). Again, the image is of seeing so clearly that one's attempt at the stars is aborted; this settling for daylight, and so blazing no trails, is by implication a failure of vision. It is to settle for things as they are.

The effect of Rousseau's maiden is also related to a passage in *A Defence of Poetry,* in which Shelley images "the mind in creation . . . as a fading coal which some invisible influence . . . awakens to transitory brightness" and notes that "when composition begins, inspiration is already on the decline."[149] Rousseau's "shape all light," moving rapidly "between desire and shame" (l. 394) and foreshortening the path of Rousseau's desire, produces the following effect: "As if the gazer's mind was strewn beneath/Her feet like *embers,* and she, thought by thought,/Trampled its fires into the dust of death" (ll. 386–88, emphasis added). Again, it is as if Rousseau's premature knowledge that fading coals are all he will find results in the extinction of even those embers he once had, just as his acceptance of the shape or image, ironically, is the occasion of the loss even of the female shape that he accepts.

Like "Alastor," however, "The Triumph of Life" is not simply the story of a single visionary, Rousseau; it also questions the relationship between the narrative and the narrator. The narrator of "The Triumph of Life"—like the narrator of "Alastor"—is proposed first as a passive listener; as in "Alastor," too, his story parallels that of the subject of his vision, at least up to a point. Indeed, it has been suggested that Rousseau is a projection of the narrator's internal questionings, if not of the narrator's situation.[150] In light of this, it does not bode well for the narrator that *his* vision of "a Shape" (l. 87) bursts on him preceded by an image of the new moon holding the "ghost of her dead Mother" (l. 84), recalling both Rousseau's images of erased tracks or extinguished embers and the image of the horned moon, which presides over the end of the visionary's failed quest in "Alastor." The reappearance of this image at the *start* of the narrator's vision in "The Triumph of Life" suggests that, like Rousseau, the narrator may see too clearly and too soon the circular path and thus the futility of desire and creation.

However, the narrator of "The Triumph of Life" does not, as Rousseau does, cut short the poem (although, in a certain sense, *his* narrator—Shelley— did, if inadvertently). To see the distinction between Rousseau and the narrator, one might notice that Rousseau provides more than merely a figure of the narrator's plight. He is also invoked as the father of visions, despite Shelley's knowledge of the not-so-fatherly Rousseau of the *Confessions,* who abandoned his children.[151] In fact, Rousseau's failure as a father may be what qualifies him to join the visionary of "Alastor" in presenting the untoward effects of either accepting *or* rejecting impossible quests, as either case results in a denial of love (that is, of relations that are a "side effect" of the quest for origins and ends).[152] Thus, in ending his quest, Rousseau repeats in reverse the error of the visionary in "Alastor." The "Preface" to "Alastor" implies that the visionary keeps "aloof from sympathies with [his] own kind" and is one of those who are "neither friends, nor lovers, nor *fathers,*" although he is allowed to have been duped, "deluded by . . . generous error" (emphasis added). Neither is

Rousseau, for all his paternal failings, wholly condemned. Shelley also praises Rousseau, imaging him as one instructed by past luminaries as well as being a luminary in his own right, although the image is uneasily resonant of Wordsworth's reimagination of how poets are connected to luminaries of the past in a mighty chain, presumably something like the chains—or plots—Shelley hoped to break.[153]

Yet despite his failure as a father, Rousseau, like the luminaries of the world in "Alastor," may be said to provide "instruction to actual men." He does so by sounding a warning against yet another way of turning light to shade, of no longer loving "the shapes/Of this phantasmal scene" (ll. 696–97). If the visionary of "Alastor" seals his fate in refusing to settle for mere images, Rousseau accepts mere images too soon. In so doing he serves as a negative example in that he outwits himself, ending with "no sacred thirst of doubtful knowledge," no "illustrious superstition" (to quote again from the "Preface" to "Alastor"). Rousseau says that no external pressures, but rather his "own heart alone" (l. 241) overcame him. The strength of his own desires had him abandon a quest he too soon saw would not yield what he wanted: his complaint is that he would have triumphed had "the spark with which Heaven lit [his] spirit/ . . . [been] with purer nutriment supplied" (ll. 201–2). Rousseau implies both that he (unlike the visionary in "Alastor") accepted impure nutriment and that he did so because he saw there was nothing better supplied him.

To accept the validity of Rousseau's complaint that the world simply will never satisfy our highest desires is to accept the necessity of his early settlement for less. That is, to understand why Rousseau fails is to be doomed to the same clarity and fate. In short, the only way to learn from or to claim Rousseau as a past luminary—a literary father—is to refuse to understand him. In just this way, finally, the narrator refuses Rousseau's dismal insight and so learns from Rousseau; at least, having heard Rousseau's story, the narrator ends (as far as the poem goes) with a new question, a question Rousseau has implicitly answered in a way that (had it been understood) should have ended all questions. In this sense, the narrator serves as a figure of readerly agency. Similarly, the structure of the poem is simultaneously informed by Shelley's knowledge that readers and writers cannot step outside of ideological structures *and* by his resistance to reinscribing stories as plots.

In imaging the paradoxical relationship between the narrator and Rousseau, the entire fragment preserves a delicate balance like that of the narrator poised between heaven and hell. As Rousseau's shape is accepted, "veil by veil the silent splendour drops/From Lucifer" (ll. 413–14), an image first of the planet disappearing at daybreak, but also of Rousseau's too clear-sighted abandonment of imaginative quests and so of love as well. The narrator, however, confronts his vision through a veil-like shade, which keeps his vision glimmering without wholly obscuring the figure that he will confront, question, and continue to question. Similarly, throughout Shelley's career, his poetry confronts and reconfronts the double necessity and impossibility of embodying truth or effecting the worldly changes at which he aimed. Significantly, in "The Triumph of Life," unlike Rousseau's glimmering light of heaven (which he sees can never be attained or embodied, an understanding that leads him to abandon the attempt and the world), the scene the narrator sees is compared to the world, which glimmers as one attempts to see it in fading light. The very difficulty of the task, and even the very failure of sight, provide beauty. Between these two radically different yet parallel visions—of light that sets the viewer in darkness and of darkness that covers the world with light—the poem unfolds. Just as the fragment opens the space between heaven and hell, it preserves the narrator's simultaneous education by and mistrust of his vision, which allow him to continue.

As in "Alastor," the narrator's vision is both a projection of his desire to know what "life had been before" (l. 332), that is, to know his origins, and an image of the father of visions who tells him plainly that what is "forever sought [is] forever lost" (l. 431). Yet the father of visions also warns him that to know his desire is fruitless is to blot out Lucifer-Venus, the father of lies and love. If some pure source of pleasure and poetry cannot finally be known, neither can the impossibility of knowing be known or recognized if love and poetry are to continue. That is, love and poetry depend on self-deception of a sort. Throughout his career, Shelley maintains the delicate balance between the recognition of the true end of imaginative desire and the refusal of this recognition, a refusal that allows the production of poetry in the service of what "A Philosophical View of Reform" says may be a delusion. Thus "The Triumph of Life" refuses the recognition implicit in "Alastor," yet only in order to repeat the trajectory and structure of that poem.[154]

In a way, then, Shelley retraces in his last poem the lesson already figured in the delicately modulated rhetoric of commonality and separation found in the lines from "To Wordsworth": "These common woes I feel. One loss is mine/Which thou too feels't." It is in his repeated enactments of both commonality and separation Shelley writes cyclic poems that most seriously become "candidates for bestowing immortality upon, at the same time that they receive it from," his predecessors. Indeed, just as Shelley's last poem balances itself between heaven and hell, blinding itself to the true end of imaginative desire already traced in "Alastor," so too "Alastor" reenacts the uncertainties that already inform (and are already reenacted in) *The Excursion, The Ruined Cottage,* and *The Seasons.* In this process, Shelley provides the most self-conscious examination of the claims for poetic power, further suggesting the futility of inscribing anything that might reliably be termed a unique poetic self. "Alastor" already made explicit, however, that to reenact this futile quest, for Shelley—as for Wordsworth and Thomson—was to allow poetry. If Shelley does not solve the problems he raises about how poetry might do work within modern culture and its readers, his analyses pose questions that still haunt us today.

Chapter IV ❀

Par Nobile Fratrum:
The Earlier Work of
Ralph Waldo Emerson

Whoever sees my garden discovers that I must have some other garden

—Ralph Waldo Emerson, JMN, 7: 421

Emerson as Representative Man

I have been proposing that what Thomson, Wordsworth, and Shelley inherited (tropes, rhetorical strategies, and a sense of poetry's readers) did not always rest easily within their contemporary cultural situations. Their poetic production thus involved trying to refigure poetry and to give an account of poetry's power in their contemporary worlds without losing their bid to be poets, which is to say, in some way to have their writing resemble the work that defined poetry for them. At the same time, I have tried to show that the literary past was never in effect monolithic. What poetry was, or said, or what power poetry might be said to have, changed over time. On my account, this stems from cultural changes, including the changing cultural significance of poetic tropes and of literary strategies influenced by, among other things, other discourses in public circulation. Obviously, then, American poets inherited a different poetic tradition from that of their British contemporaries, if only because they understood the same poetry in a different cultural context.

Nonetheless, I believe the account of the various contexts in which poems live (in literary and historical contexts and in historically located readers) proposes a model useful for reading much poetry in English, even late-twentieth-century poetry written in the United States by those who define themselves against dominant literary and political cultures. The story one would tell about such poetry, however, would be infinitely more complex than the story I can tell here, given the multiple public discourses now in circulation and given that in the United States what "sounds like" poetry will vary, as there is less and less reason to assume that what forms poets' ears is in any way a common canon. This is, to my mind, no reason to mourn or despair. But it is my reason for concluding with a turn to a more contained field, namely the pre-Civil War work of a widely read nineteenth-century American poet, Ralph Waldo Emerson, born only eleven years later than Shelley.

I do not follow Emerson's career past 1847 and the publication of his first book of poems, in large part because to do justice to the events immediately leading to the Civil War (following the passage of the Fugitive Slave Law of 1850) would entail virtually another book, while to discuss later mid-century American public culture without addressing the Civil War would be unthinkable. My account of Emerson is intended to serve as a conclusion—a test case examining in particular what kind of sea change poetic tradition might undergo crossing the Atlantic. While the American context changed many of the details involved, Emerson's poetry shows how the attempt to reconcile inherited ideas about poetry with an historical present remains a defining feature of modern poetry, as does the attempt to defend poetry as a powerful form of productive labor to a world that was redefining the terms of power, productivity, and labor.

Emerson began with a composite image of poets and poetry: he had access to earlier American poetry, to an Americanized Thomson, to Wordsworth's response to Thomson, and eventually to Shelley's response to Wordsworth. Like the other poets on whom I have concentrated, Emerson's engagement with his predecessors helped to change the ears of a large audience, refiguring literary if not literal history. Yet, as with Shelley, Emerson's influence is not straightforwardly a result of his canonization or popularity as a poet.[1] In Emerson's case, his ideas about poetry (in essays and lectures) have proved at least as influential as the poems themselves. As he wrote to his future second wife, Lydia, his singing "is for the most part in prose."[2] In fact, there is little critical commentary on Emerson's poems per se, perhaps, as I will suggest, because Emerson's ear for poetry often rested uneasily with his prose redefinitions of poetry and the poet's role.[3]

Ultimately Emerson reveals how American poets shared with contemporary English poets the need to ground poetic vision in a larger authorizing structure, as well as the difficulty of finding without being subsumed by such a structure, and the obsession with the relationship between poetic and practical power. I do not want to deny that American writers faced some unique problems, however. Thus, before discussing Emerson's work, I want briefly to sketch the history of American print culture and poetry's place in that culture.

British poetry circulated widely in America in the early republic, but often as a sign of political or moral—not literary—virtue. Both public virtue and public authority were central topics of debate in the revolutionary period, which is not surprising given the need to justify the new nation and its rebellion against colonial rule. However, literary and especially poetic authority was not necessarily aligned with emerging redefinitions of political authority. Poets in particular inherited conflicting scenarios of rhetorical power. On the one hand, prose typically presented itself in the early republic as un-owned language circulating in the marketplace of ideas and authorized by appeal to some larger impersonal whole such as the progressive unfolding of history in virtuous, hardworking America. On the other hand, in America the props and set pieces of traditional poetry appeared to signal an attendant ideology of imported privilege, while the readership for poetry also aligned the genre with luxury. For earlier American poets, the rhetoric and readership of high poetry—which could figure an American production of civilized arts for skeptical foreign readers—appeared at home to claim what was most dangerous in the rhetoric of American politics, namely, personal exceptionalism, imported hierarchy, or decadence.

In the early United States, the rhetorics of political and poetic power were thus not easily reconciled. Nor could poets simply adopt the rhetoric of prose, although some tried. Among other things, there were long-standing suspicions even of the characteristic pose of public rhetoric. By the nineties, novelists like Charles Brockden Brown explicitly addressed suspicions of how personal narratives masked as public voices might be more demagogic than democratic. Other novelists like Hannah Foster self-consciously proposed novels as instruments for the construction (and policing) of a public imaginary. Brown and Foster both help illustrate debates over what and who constituted the American public as well as debates over the relationship between public action and private motives or private imagination. Foster also suggests how the contested vocabulary of "public" virtue was increasingly reconceptualized and privatized by the turn of the century.

In poetry, too, imaginations of a public role shifted, becoming more sentimental and elegiac even as earlier negative images of poetry persisted. By 1815, as the War of 1812 ended, American poetry's sense of powerlessness was at least three-fold: poetry and power often seemed associated in ways that could not be invoked in public discourse; the rhetoric of public power was in itself contested; and by 1815 the era of American revolutionary glory seemed closed, so that even the already problematic strategy of presenting poetry as the voice of unfolding national history was unavailable. In other words, by the time Emerson began writing, the heroic age of American history seemed closed; American literature seemed a blank page on which high poetry, given what Emerson inherited as the tropes and rhetoric of high poetry, could not easily be written. Since Emerson's first ambition was to be a poet, rehearsing this American background highlights the specific cultural constructions with which he struggled. Both the American context and his readings of British literature set the stage for Emerson's early rethinking of inherited figures—especially the figure of the solitary and apparently idle poet in rural retreat—and his obsession with the relationship between poetic retreat and engagement, private thought and public action.

Readership and Authorship in the American Marketplace of Ideas, 1770–1800

The writings examined in the previous chapters formed part of the American literary heritage, but it is also clear that they were read differently in an American context. For example, *Common Sense,* written in the United States and containing one of the first printed calls for independence from England, cites Milton's *Paradise Lost* in the course of an argument about how reconciliation between England and the colonies is no longer possible:

> Reconciliation is *now* a fallacious dream. Nature hath deserted the connexion, and art cannot supply her place. For, as Milton wisely expresses, 'never can true reconcilement grow, where wounds of deadly hate have pierced so deep'.[4]

There is no irony in Paine's suppression of the fact that Milton's rhetoric of political liberty was nationalistic—and specifically British—or that Paine borrowed from the older writer in order to argue that England must be cast off.[5] Milton serves Paine as both a moral authority and an authoritative source for revolting against misused political authority.

At the same time, Paine's quoted passage—from Satan's speech in Book IV of *Paradise Lost*—uses lines that in Milton follow shortly after the Satanic proclamation of autonomy ("myself am Hell") and that are in turn followed by a renewal of Satanic nay-saying: "Evil be thou my good." The same section of *Common Sense* strongly suggests Paine was well aware of the Miltonic distinction between proper and improper revolts; he writes about the just authority of a Congressional majority vote, "He that will promote discord, under a government so equally formed as this, would have joined Lucifer in his revolt."[6] Yet the Satanic echo in the passage against reconciliation with Britain was not intended to be read as impiety but as powerful language. Because for Paine Milton was a figure of political engagement and a source of English Country or Commonwealthman rhetoric, the lines from Satan appear—despite themselves—not so much as allusion but rather as a sign of rhetorical power linked with practical, political power. Milton's authority for Paine was thus not literary so much as moral and political.

At least in the early revolutionary period, the Declaration of Independence demonstrated the political and performative power of language, forming a nation that could represent itself as born of literary fiat and for which print and the public sphere were closely associated. But the authorship and readership of such language—Jefferson's language circulated over multiple signatures and was crafted for a specific occasion and an international audience—proposes no clear model for those whose ambitions were literary and personal.[7] Noah Webster could argue in 1783 that "America must be as independent in *literature* as she is in *politics*."[8] However, as Michael Warner has argued, it was often agreed that the production of great literature was, to quote Phillips Payson's 1778 Boston sermon, "the lot of but few."[9] And championing the few was not part of the political rhetoric of the revolutionary era; indeed, even the later Federalists, arguably supporters of government by the few, avoided the rhetoric of hierarchy.[10]

In short, in late colonial and early revolutionary America on the eastern seaboard, a gesture like Paine's use of Milton becomes politically efficacious insofar as his audience can recognize Milton's rhetorical authority *without* seeing it as related to any inherited class position, such as that of the British country gentry, and *without* connecting it to any bid for Milton's singular literary fame. The efficacy depends rather on what Michael Warner characterizes as "market-society negativity," wherein "the private subject finds his relation to both the public and the market only by negating the given reality of himself, thereby considering himself the abstract subject of the universal (political or economic) discourse."[11]

In new world writings, the use of the market as an image of political, social, and sometimes literary exchange was long-standing. For example, as early as 1758, Franklin's *The Way to Wealth* presents an overt anticommercial message, but Franklin uses the marketplace as an image for social and print-mediated relationships, replacing older metaphors of hierarchical authority and even of classical republicanism.[12] The image of the market served specifically to dismantle hierarchy and to deflect claims to inherited privilege. Yet the image posed its own problems, as Franklin's piece demonstrates. *The Way to Wealth* warns against manipulations of the market even as it depends on Warner's "market-society negativity," the rhetorical equivalent of the marketplace. The piece represents itself as language circulating without reference to its origins—its "original" meaning or its author. The issues such unauthored prose raises about appropriations of the past are thus more self-conscious than in most British writing.

Although Franklin's essay betrays deep uneasiness about the economy of public language and about who profits (practically or morally) from the manipulation and ownership of rhetoric, *The Way to Wealth* most clearly offers itself as a model of proto-American writing, championing the free circulation of ideas and the clever dismantling of any writerly hierarchy, as well as acknowledging the particular indeterminacy of the American "common reader."[13] Such is presumably part of Franklin's point, in line with the fact that even later, in his *Autobiography* written in the seventies and eighties, he implies he is not a believer in intellectual property.[14] Yet Franklin's portrait of the circulation of un-authorized print also already lays the groundwork for the more paranoid version of authorial powerlessness and the unreliability of common readers that appears in the nineties in novels like Brown's *Wieland* in which rhetorical power without some original authority is easily abused. In both cases, there is a clear sense that the American context might well offer political power to those who wrote and an equally clear sense of the political dangers *either* of speaking with or for inherited authority *or* of self-effacing ventriloquizing (like that of Paine; Brown's villain; and, in a different manner, Franklin and all of his characters). This was true well before the nineties, although it is worth noting that the nineties set a variety of distinctive and mixed tasks for its writers.

On the one hand, the nineties saw more newspapers founded than had been started in the previous century; printers and those who commented on print continued the republican rhetoric of print as linked to the public sphere and a readership of plain citizens. On the other hand, in the aftermath of the Federalist debates there was a rising undercurrent of anxiety about the ignorance of plain citizens,[15] an anxiety also fed by fears of international conspiracy stemming from the French Revolution (fears reflected in the 1798 Alien and Sedition Acts). Brown's 1798 *Wieland,* for instance, may be seen as the inverse of Godwin's *Caleb Williams.* As in Wordsworth's "Female Vagrant," *Wieland* raises questions about "artful" and "artless" tales; as in both Wordsworth and Godwin, Brown addresses questions of the relationship between cultural and personal narratives, but he raises the ante in questioning ventriloquism, which is literally represented in the text.[16] If Godwin suggests that cultural narratives necessarily infect how any individual can conceive of him or her self and his or her social and political position, Brown has a darker imagination of what would happen in a society with no secured narratives, no institutions, no paternal authority, no higher court of appeal that adjudicates cultural authority.

In *Wieland,* it is not simply that the source of language and speakers' motives are uncertain, but also that audiences in such a culture make what they will of eloquent language.[17] Although Brown most often mentions speech and oral performance, the novel presents itself as a series of written texts, letters, and diaries. *Wieland* is thus finally a cautionary tale for authors about their lack of control over whatever they set in motion, their lack of agency—the word is one Brown explicitly links with authorship[18]—and the general inability to control the individual passions that inform public decisions. At the same time, Brown tacitly recognizes his own act of ventriloquism and attempts to enter the very public debates he mistrusts; the advertisement for the novel insists it aspires to the condition of being useful, not frivolous, and ultimately, not to mention anonymously, defers to the public whose reception will determine whether a sequel "will be published or suppressed."

In the same period, best sellers such as Hannah Foster's 1797 *The Coquette* present a slightly different and more explicitly gendered version of the same debate over private and public uses of culturally circulating narratives. As Nancy Armstrong suggests about the sentimental novel in England, *The Coquette* enacts a domestication of public virtue.[19] In Foster's novel, the public sphere is recast as a public imaginary, and public rhetoric is shown to operate and circulate primarily in the private sphere, not in a public marketplace. Rather than serving the class issues Armstrong identifies as central to the sentimental novel in England, however, in postrevolutionary America the developing privatized discourse of sentiment served to defuse earlier ideals of civic action in the face of fears that revolution would be reenacted, reimported from France.[20]

One can see the domestication of earlier public rhetoric at work in Foster's uses of Commonwealth language borrowed from Thomson. When Paine appropriates Thomson, he turns to the public, Commonwealthman voice of "Liberty"; when Franklin cites Thomson repeatedly in both the Almanac and the *Autobiography*, he most often uses the poet of *The Seasons*, who serves as a model of education—neither the retiring observer in nature, nor the civic poet of the public sphere.[21] In *The Coquette*, Eliza's suitor quotes from Thomson's "Spring."[22] Foster's Thomson, like Franklin's, provides a model of an education in virtue, but in Foster virtue is specifically framed as virtuous retreat. Thus, marriage is recommended through Thomson's image of

> —"An elegant sufficiency,
> Content, retirement, rural quiet, friendship;
> Books, ease and alternate labor, useful life;
> Progressive virtue, and approving heaven;
> These are the matchless joys of virtuous love."

In *The Seasons*, the passage falls just after Thomson's aside to Lyttelton:

> . . . conducted by historic truth,
> You tread the long extent of backward time,

> Planning with warm benevolence of mind
> And honest zeal, unwarped by party-rage,
> Britannia's weal,—how from the venal gulf
> To raise her virtue and her arts revive.
> (926–31)

Thomson then moves to a warning against the deceptive "fervent tongue" (977) and "ensnaring love" (1102)—the characteristic passions of "barbarous nations" (1130). Foster, who explicitly makes republican womanhood a topic of the novel, thus draws on Thomson to make her own larger political point when her heroine is warned to weigh judgment against infatuation or "the delusions of fancy" (or to use Thomson's terms, deceptive fervor or passion).[23] She explicitly echoes a public concern of her era, which was anxious that the new nation not be cast as—or become through "party rage"—"barbarous." Foster also explicitly identifies fancy as dangerous because it makes people "too volatile for a confinement to domestic avocations."[24]

Thomson opposed "honest zeal" and rationality to divisive passion as part of his broader concern with enlightenment culture and consensus. In the American context, the vocabulary of "enlightened zeal" and energy, carefully distinguished from passionate violence, arose most clearly in public debates over Federalism and reappeared in the nineties in debates over whether the sedition act would give rise to party factions, as is reflected in *Wieland,* in which private zeal and private fires spell public disaster.[25] Adopting the vocabulary of public debates about private and public passion, Foster's novel then raises not only issues about women's place in the public sphere but also about all citizens' public participation. Implicitly, the novel advocates domesticating the fires and rhetoric of revolution when it warns against passion that results in public action.[26] Finally, Foster is also self-conscious about the novel's role in the transformations it both reflects and tries to fashion in its readers.

To describe the novel as participating in the transformations it also reflects is not simply to treat novels as operating in part as conduct books but also to comment on the very act of reading novels. As an epistolary novel, *The Coquette* sets in motion a community of voices, but despite the novel's subtitle—"A Novel; Founded on Fact"—readers clearly find a fictional community. Even in advertising itself as taken from an actual event, an event that was widely publicized in the newspapers, the novel reclaims narrative authority from the more usual forms of public print culture. Novels, after all, were read at the hearth, not circulated as public speech, even as the novel warns against fanciful or private imaginings and against the diversions of "fictitious" woes or the "representation" of death as a mere "pastime."[27] In this context, the disappearance of Eliza's voice at the end of the novel works as more than a sign of the silencing of a fallen woman (as it is usually taken to be and certainly in part is). Eliza's silencing also underlines Foster's protest against public spectacle generally, including the objectification, in the press, of Eliza Whitman, the original of Eliza Wharton, whose story was taken as a lesson about the dangers of strong-minded women. The novel explicitly analyzes the theater as a diversion from "true" feeling and the circus as indecorous, staged danger; it further recommends reading as a way to avoid both solitude and public display.[28] Foster's book thus tacitly offers itself as a kind of writing that will nurture publicly useful reason *and* private understanding, not serve voyeuristically to inflame passion. The epistolary form, more hopefully than in Brown, remodels the discursive community— thematically as a circle of friends and ultimately as an imaginary collective of private readers, neither a nation of citizens nor a number of unrelated private imaginations.

At least on the level of political commentary, Foster's novel is thus both subversive and conservative in its suggestion that Brown's worst fears can be allayed, that communities can negotiate how to "read" and how to shape individual character. Foster implies that freedom and independence are not forged in isolation (as both the fallen heroine and the villain suggest); they are negotiated within a kind of internalized neighborhood watch program, the imaginary "confederated whole."[29] The result is a transfigured image of the political powers of language and speech: the novel reinforces the very boundaries it tests and reinscribes more than women within community boundaries. At the same time, in moving to a public imaginary—one quite different from a sphere of civic action as the model of participation in the public order—the novel includes those who were not publicly enfranchised within the new symbolic order of citizenship.[30]

Whether subversive or conservative, *The Coquette* makes a bid for the importance of novels in forging and relocating the public sphere. As an object in public circulation, too, the book inadvertently raised questions about where and how the power of the printed word operated. Neither Brown's speaker Clara nor Foster's gradually silenced Eliza were intended to refashion women's place—if anything, both are emblems of the irrational, and both certainly warn of the need to police the private sphere within which they and the novels containing them circulate. Yet both novels, historically, called forth diverse audience reactions, especially reactions to the immediate success, primarily among women readers, of *The Coquette*.[31] One can speculate that the novel was seen as offering both a mind and a voice to Eliza Wharton in a way denied Eliza Whitman. Certainly, this sort of view seems to inform comments like William Cobbett's on Susanna Rowson's popularity. Rowson was the author of the first American best-selling sentimental novel, *Charlotte Temple,* which like *The Coquette* thematically circumscribes and silences its fallen heroine but at the same time confers authority on its readers and its author. Complaining of her popularity, Cobbett wrote, "I do not know how it is, but I have strange misgivings hanging about my mind, that the whole moral as well as political world is going to experience a revolution. Who knows but our present house of Representatives, for instance, may be succeeded by members of the other sex?"[32] In short, Cobbett saw Rowson's domestic and domesticating message as unleashing women in the public sphere. That novels were read so differently by different readers exemplifies just the uncontrolled circulation and use of language Brown addresses and fears.

Lastly, if the nineties presented writers with new concerns—over privatization, over public roles, and in particular over print's or reading's role in informing public action—it is nonetheless true that these are refigurations of concerns already present in Franklin's early writings, and that the period recast figures of writing and reading inherited not only from British texts but also from the writings and rhetoric of the revolutionary period.

The Poet's Work in the New World

In general, print culture throughout the eighteenth century on the eastern seaboard of America was associated with a republican public sphere and a public marketplace, although by the nineties novels vied with other forms of print culture and—in collaboration with national debates in the eighties and nineties—participated in redefinitions of the public sphere. Throughout, various forms of print bespoke anxieties about authorship and readership, even when what I have called un-authorized print, addressed to an abstract audience, claimed public presence by virtue of this very depersonalization. Moreover, to borrow from Michael Warner's astute analyses of print culture and mass culture in the United States, even in the earliest days of the republic there was not simply "a" public discourse and a "we" who apprehended it.[33] Not only did readers understand texts in various ways, but the account I have just rehearsed of Anglo-American print culture in the last three decades of the eighteenth century does not address the particular relationship of poets to public discourse or to print culture. While one might think that the American context would make the early national poet's task easier, this was not necessarily the case because the rhetoric of personhood for citizens (active or imaginary) was not always congruous with the ways in which poetic personhood was constructed.

Among other things, as William Charvat notes, poets and their readers were "thinking of the social status of literature and authorship in terms of British aristocratic tradition, . . . [wherein] imaginative literature was a class commodity, . . . a by-product of learning or *study*, which presupposed leisure."[34] Poetry was thus often a sign of "un-American" class pretensions. In the Adams-Jackson Presidential election, for example, the Republican General Committee of New York accused Adams of being "a philosopher, a lawyer, an elegant scholar, and a poet, too, forsooth," and as such too rarefied for the presidency.[35] Poets, the charge runs in effect, are unrepresentative in that they are part of an elite; as the archaic adverb "forsooth" suggests, they are also disqualified from public efficacy because they speak the wrong language.

While the issues abroad in Jacksonian America added a special edge to charges of elitism, the role of poet in the new world was fraught with related difficulties from at least the time of the founding of the nation. In the *Autobiography*, for instance, Franklin tells a similar if more ambivalent story about literary aspiration generally and poetry in particular. In line with his self-representation as a representative, civic-minded American, Franklin claims as his ancestry an "obscure Family," but one that traditionally served the public, read, even wrote poetry; not incidentally he misremembers an account of his maternal grandfather as a "*godly, learned* [the original read '*able*'] *Englishman*."[36] Franklin also notes his early ambitions to be a poet himself and then describes his father "ridiculing [his] Performances, . . . telling [him] Verse-makers were generally Beggars" (1318), advice Franklin passes on to James Ralph (1340–42).[37] In light of poetry's status both as luxury and as unprofitable, a tension between the common "obscurity" and the ambitions of poetry ripples through Franklin's text. The *Autobiography* most often treats writing as a form of apprenticeship and labor, as in Franklin's anecdote about learning how to write by rewriting and versifying pieces from the *Spectator* (1319–20). In such self-portraits Franklin makes writing a kind of useful commercial work that can help sell papers (1319–24) or be used for "improving [one's] Language" (1321); he becomes defensive when poetry is at issue: "I approv'd the amusing one's Self with Poetry now & then, so far as to improve one's Language, but no farther" (1341).

Even when he is describing reading rather than writing, Franklin shows the difficulties that faced genres such as poetry that might be considered marks of status. For example, Franklin often presents reading as part of what informs conversation and allows the negotiation of public identity in America; however, he also sees reading and writing as more blatant forms of cultural capital. It is not clear, for instance, if cultural capital inherited from his learned grandfather or the profit earned by his own labor is figured in anecdotes such as the one in which Franklin represents himself as transformed from "runaway Servant" to suitable social acquaintance when he meets and discusses literature with Dr. Browne of Burlington (1327–28).[38] Whether inherited or earned, his ownership of literary culture is a mark of social standing that Franklin's representative American speaker in the *Autobiography* and other writings will not usually claim.

Franklin's description of the uses of public libraries is similarly mixed in its approach to reading. At the end of part I of the *Autobiography*, we are told that libraries "have improv'd the general Conversation of the Americans, made the common Tradesmen & Farmers as intelligent as most Gentlemen from other Countries, and perhaps have contributed in some degree to the Stand so generally made throughout the Colonies in Defense of their Privileges" (1372). Literacy here is again tied to public virtue, specifically to liberty and the creation of the nation. This is also in part another portrait of contesting voices found (for instance) in the Federalist papers or in slightly different form in Crèvecoeur's attempt to imagine a polity of different cultures and geographies. However, Franklin also represents the literate American commoner using the figure of the Gentleman, certifying political worthiness by appeal to a social transformation of which an earlier Franklin, "Poor Richard," plain American, showed distrust. The reiteration of his account of founding a public library in part II, a sign of literacy's importance in Franklin's mind, refigures the uses of libraries, dropping the overt mention of gentlemen while reinscribing the association of education, intelligence, and (tacitly) *social* rank: "Reading became fashionable, and our People having no publick Amusements to divert their Attention from Study became better acquainted with Books, and in a few Years were observ'd by Strangers to be better instructed & more intelligent than People of the same Rank generally are in other Countries."[39]

Indeed, in part II (which was written later, in the early eighties), Franklin specifically privileges library books over "Almanacks, Ballads, and . . . common School Books" (1379) just in the period when fine arts or polite letters were first distinguished from writing generally and entered more clearly an economy of managed esteem.[40] Franklin defines founding libraries as public service (for the "common Benefit" [1379–80]). Yet his sentence is ambiguous: when he claims Americans read library books because they were not diverted by public amusements, is the claim that reading was a private rather than a public amusement? To define reading as *"fashionable"* suggests as much, while also implying that the public benefit of reading was actually a matter of public appearances. Or is reading offered in place of all amusement? The latter seems more in line with Franklin's usual work ethic and republican rhetoric. Yet Franklin's description of his own reading as "the only Amusement I allow'd my self" (1381) or his comment on how "a Book, indeed, sometimes debauch'd me from my Work" (1369) suggest his sense that reading books might be a mark of leisure, contradicting the more obvious figuration of reading, like writing, as a civic activity and so instrumental in public *work*.

Poetry was particularly vulnerable within such mixed representations of reading. Thomas Jefferson, for instance, voiced uneasiness about the young, and particularly women, reading poetry because he found it a decadent pursuit (echoing Franklin on reading as private distraction or idleness). Jefferson, again like Franklin, suggests that a product of leisure is hardly attractive within the rhetoric of the early republic, a rhetoric that stressed the absence of a leisure class and the virtue of a people who labored, in a language that confusingly mixed appeals to Lockean liberalism, classical republicanism, and a Protestant work-ethic.[41] In his most overt discussion of poetry's dangers, his letter on female education, Jefferson first rejects the time spent reading most novels as "time lost . . . which should be instructively employed. When this poison infects the mind," he continues, "it destroys its tone and revolts it against wholesome reading. Reason and fact . . . are rejected. Nothing can engage attention unless dressed in all the figments of fancy, and nothing so bedecked comes amiss. The result is a bloated imagination, sickly judgment, and disgust towards all the *real* businesses of life. . . . [Thus, imaginative literature should be avoided, except for] some few [novels] modelling their narratives . . . on the incidents of real life. . . . *For a like reason, too, much poetry should not be indulged*" (emphasis added).[42] Poetry— although Jefferson allows that some poets, including Thomson, may help form "style and taste"—is generally an indulgence; as in Foster's *The Coquette,* reading fanciful as opposed to factual literature separates readers from "the real" and encourages irrationality. Even more than Franklin's or Foster's, Jefferson's description of fanciful or imaginative reading suggests the problems of poetry in the republic, particularly in the last decades of the eighteenth century. Reading poetry was variously an idle luxury and a fashionable amusement, or likely to spread irrational fancy and imported hierarchy. At best, poetry was not found useful in "real life."

It is not that poets of the early republic lacked models for a civic poetry. Jefferson does not banish Thomson from his republic of letters, for example, although his comments single out Thomson's style, not his content. I have already mentioned the uses of Milton and Thomson within other forms of public discourse; both also provided models to which early republican poets could turn.[43] Take, for instance, Joel Barlow's *Columbiad,* an 1807 revision of his earlier (1787) *Vision of Columbus.* In *The Columbiad,* Barlow's Thomsonian surveying eye is itself a form of cultivation and domestication of the landscape that he presents as both original (Hesper's visionary instruction is represented as a kind of Adamic naming) and an opportunity for the authorless speaking of progressive history. As in prose of the period, Barlow's ideological authorization can be said to come from his mixed sense of speaking for a secularized version of providential history and progressive republicanism; his literary authorization and rhetoric, however, come by way of *Paradise*

Lost, The Seasons, and "Liberty." His endnotes, in fact, retrace epic gestures from the classical to the contemporary and openly confront the problem of transmitting pernicious cultural gestures; he writes that poets, among others, "have injured the cause of humanity almost in proportion to the fame they have acquired" by handing on pernicious ideas of epic heroism.[44]

Barlow's project is itself both Miltonic and Thomsonian in that he sets himself the task of transposing the epic and georgic gestures of his predecessors. For Barlow, such literary and political aims are finally intertwined insofar as the very "plot" of the poem, a self-conscious translation of the eighteenth-century British progress piece, positions the new American republic "as the latest development in a story known" first in Great Britain.[45] Thus, without any sense of contradiction, given his stated aim of refashioning, even perfecting, both literal and literary history, Barlow can write,

> Too much of Europe, here transplanted o'er,
> Nursed feudal feelings on your tented shore,
> Brought sable serfs from Afric, call'd it gain,
> And urged your sires to forge the fatal chain.
> (Book VIII, ll. 383–86)

In short, pernicious imports—hierarchy, slavery—will be identified and denounced; the larger universal forces for which the poem claims to be speaking and the poetic voice it appropriates, however, are not experienced as illicit transplants.[46] Nor does Barlow betray any anxiety over his use of anti-slavery rhetoric within a poem that often simply ignores the existence of native inhabitants in a land described as "vacant space" (Book I, l. 704) or as regions "[o]f man unseen" (Book I, l. 660). I will say more in a moment about this use of unreal native Americans and real slaves in other contemporary poetry. For the moment, I want to pursue some further implications of Barlow's traditional unmasking of traditions and his diatribes against greed coupled with celebrations of commerce (a coupling which echoes Franklin's earlier use of a metaphor of the marketplace within an essay against commercial profit).

First, in line with his choice of epic, Barlow's text proclaims his status as one who works poetically for the public good. He further suggests his public voice—notably presented as one of many, not as singular—will help construct a specifically American public; his preface and endnotes describe his ambition "to inculcate the love of rational liberty, and to discountenance the deleterious passion for violence and war," as well as to instruct: "why should we write at all, if not to benefit mankind? The public mind, as well as the individual mind, receives its propensities; . . . Nations are educated, like a single child. They only require a longer time and a greater number of teachers."[47] Taking his lead from those whose rhetoric informed the Revolution, then, Barlow's poem positions itself as civic and public, an attempt to enter the real businesses of life Jefferson mentions.

At the same time, the prose with which Barlow surrounds the poem (and his felt need for the prose) suggest more self-consciousness about the difficulty of "reconciling the nature of the subject with such a manner of treating it as should appear the most poetical," that is, reconciling his political and didactic with his poetic ambitions.[48] The inherited trope of the westward progress of civilization and the arts (making America from one perspective the obvious, even traditional, setting for the voice Thomson earlier adopted), and the apparent availability of the new world as setting for Barlow's visionary project, seem as if they should relieve him of anxiety over the joint public and poetic ambitions of his poem. Yet Barlow still confronted locally defined problems. On the one hand, Americans such as Noah Webster and Europeans such as Robert Southey were ready to complain that the new nation had not yet produced a literature of any merit.[49] On the other hand, there were perils to claiming exceptional merit within a republican context. Barlow's assumption of the voice of history and commerce strategically skirts both challenges to the would-be American epic poet.

However, although Barlow represents an epic landscape stripped of pernicious ideology, ripe for "the hand of culture," his project ultimately runs afoul of the already existing institutions fostered by just the invisible hand of commerce he uses to replace ideology.[50] That is, the history of the book as object and of the poem's readership—or lack of readership—tell a different story about Barlow's ability to offer poetry as a form of civic, public service. *The Columbiad* was issued as a luxury item (twenty dollars unbound); it was hailed as a triumph of fine bookmaking, but it was a financial disaster (despite the fact that Barlow also, in keeping with his radical republican views, issued two cheaper editions "in an effort to reach various levels of the public").[51] Barlow might insist that poetry was to be instruction, not property; civic and public, not luxury. Yet his attempt to reposition his poem did not effectively counter common assumptions that poetry was almost by definition a form of refinement.

While he had become a radical by the time *The Columbiad* was published, Barlow nonetheless first hoped to find a Baltimore publisher because "the wealthy in that country may think libraries an ornamental species of furniture."[52] In short, having declared himself a poet, Barlow knew his poems and their audience would participate in a culture of polite literature. Indeed, virtually all aspiring poets of the early republic were either from the wealthy classes or positioned as gentlemen by virtue of their education, mirroring their imagined, if not also their real, audiences—Barlow (like the more conservative circle from which he broke in 1788, including Timothy

Dwight and David Humphreys) attended Yale; Freneau, Princeton. Regard-
less of their didactic stance, poems and poets bespoke hierarchy and the ac-
complishment of someone of privilege.

A writer such as Phillis Wheatley, an African-American woman, could
in this context use heroic couplets to embody the position for which she
also argued; she would not be mistaken for someone attempting to
reestablish a traditional European hierarchy. While facing across the At-
lantic, that is, imagining their productions as displaying new world ac-
complishments to a skeptical older world, those attempting to craft a
national poetry might similarly highlight their command of traditional
poetic gestures. The penultimate stanza of Philip Freneau's 1786 "Literary
Importation," for instance, rails against England and the fact that book-
sellers would not count American writing as civilized literature: "Can we
never be thought to have learning or grace/Unless it be brought from that
damnable place." However, at home, as it were, the very marks of refine-
ment that defined poetry worked against most poets' claims to write a
publicly useful American poetry.[53]

The issue is even clearer in the work of Freneau. Like Barlow, Freneau
wrote and published civic poetry, as a survey of the titles he gave his poems
indicates: "American Liberty," "A Political Litany," "To the Americans,"
"America Independent," and "Sketches of American History," to list only a
few. Also like Barlow's, many of Freneau's political poems attempt to influ-
ence public policy by assuming the voice of history. For example, the 1795
"On Mr. Paine's Rights of Man," originally (in 1792) "To a Republican with
Mr. Paine's Rights of Man," responds to Paine's response to Burke. By the
nineties republicanism had entered a new set of debates, and Freneau's
championing of Paine—who has been called one of the ghosts haunting the
Constitutional debates of 1787–1791[54]—identifies his radical stance. Like
Barlow imagining the American landscape as a slate on which history might
be written anew within a kind of progress poem, Freneau rejects a hierarchy
of masters and slaves and predicts a future guided by Paine's writings. The
poem then invokes the future it has predicted:

> Roused by the REASON of his manly page,
> Once more shall PAINE a listening world engage:
> * * *
> —Advance, bright years, to work their ["systems formed by knaves"]
> final fall,
> And haste the period that shall crush them all.
> Who, that has read and scann'd the historic page
> But glows, at every line, with kindling rage[.]
> (ll. 11–12, 23–26)[55]

The final image above is of enlightenment written in and as progressive history across the continent, with the "bright years" as a future text set against older texts, which are represented as able to enkindle readers to righteous anger.

Freneau's emphasis on reading also marks his self-consciousness about his own audience. In "On Mr. Paine's Rights of Man," reading works in two ways. On the one hand, there is the reading of "manly" and reasoned texts (which are also transmuted to oratory with the world "listening"), a reading that among other things allows the poem to invoke on the page what has not yet arrived: a pure republic. On the other hand, there is a kind of republican zeal, a public fire, built on the reading of past injustices ("the historic page"), a fire by the light of which an enlightened future presumably unrolls. The images of light and fire are also those that circulate through more conservative texts of the mid to late nineties—such as Brown's *Wieland* or some of Hamilton's speeches—as signs of potential anarchy. Within Freneau's poem, these politically charged images of fire mark his ambition to be part of and affect the "real businesses of life," including the public business of the Constitutional debates. Yet how reading that inculcates reason and reading that inculcates passion are related—or how listening and reading might be related—is far less clear.

Indeed, within the reading and listening world of the nineties, the reasoned reading for which Freneau, like Barlow, calls was not a simple piety. There was widespread anxiety over the unleashing of private interest, on the one hand, or over the public's susceptibility to demagogues, on the other. Insofar as Freneau's reference is to the paralleled readings of history and of Paine, his poem both addresses and calls forth a newly cultivated, collective (the first person plural "we" is used throughout) national public. The poet's role, like the nation's, is said to be that of "guardian" of a larger trust; the poem does not claim to draft what it cultivates but simply "to see the end of time," or itself to read the natural culmination of history. This very position, however, is part of what made conservatives such as Dwight call Freneau "a mere incendiary, or rather . . . a despicable tool of bigger [French] incendiaries."[56] In other words, Dwight takes Freneau's light and fire as destructive forces and reviews the voice of Freneau's poem as that of foreign demagogues, not of reason or historical progress.

Freneau uses the rhetoric of a public, political debate in which images of fire and light were common. However, at the same time he deploys another rhetoric, that of poetry. The otherwise politicized images of fire mark (as for Thomson, in an earlier British context) Freneau's poetic ambitions by figuring the fires of imagination. Thus, the poem on Paine tacitly lays claim to a different kind of visionary power, both in its apostrophe to the bright years, which are instructed in a bardic voice to advance and hasten (as if the poet's words are not deferring to history but shaping it), and in its final vision of the Republic at the end of time as a kind of New Jerusalem the poem has the authority to prophesy if not bring into being.

For Freneau throughout the nineties, with his ties to Madison and Jefferson and his role as editor of several papers, the power of politics, of poetry, and of other forms of print may have seemed closely bound; when he collected his poems for publication in 1795, the majority of pieces he included were clearly on public matters. Moreover, his poem "To My Book," first published in the *National Gazette* in 1792, allies the "bard-baiting clime" for poetry with those opposed also to Freneau's politics, despite the fact that poetry was more likely written and read by the "well-born wights, that aim to mount and ride" rather than "the people" Freneau's poem sides with and celebrates.[57] Even in the early nineteenth century, putting together his two-volume 1809 collected poems, Freneau was still writing to both Madison and Jefferson (the former was then president) about the popular call for his poetic work, which suggests he saw his poetry as having some role in the public sphere (not least in his anti-Federalist suggestion that popular opinion mattered politically and literally).[58]

However, Freneau's work as a whole includes other pieces in which the tension between poetic and public power is closer to the surface. For example, his 1770 "The Power of Fancy," despite Freneau's political alliance with Jefferson, might well have been denied the women in Jefferson's later, imagined educational library simply by virtue of its title, not to mention its valorization of solitude and private fires. On one reading, "The Power of Fancy" simply rehearses familiar poetic gestures in a kind of post-Miltonic, Thomsonian visionary progress poem that includes some of the same gestures found in poems such as "On Mr. Paine's Rights of Man." The poem moves from heaven to hell, from ancient Greece and Rome to a fictional "now" in the third to the last verse paragraph, with passing references to world geography from India to California:

> Wake, vagrant, restless thing,
> Ever wandering on the wing,
> Who thy wondrous source can find,
> FANCY, regent of the mind;
> A spark from Jove's resplendent throne,
> But thy nature all unknown.
>   THIS spark of bright, celestial flame,
>   * * *
> Come, O come—perceiv'd by none,
> You and I will walk alone.
> (ll. 1–7, 153–54)[59]

Yet from his title through the final couplet, Freneau in effect presents an anthology of set pieces of *poetic* power, including also a Gothic vision of the "rattling of . . . chains" by fiends in hell and a small sentimental vignette of a lover's grave, as well as the poetic eye's bid for geographical and historical scope. The poem ends with the solitary poet and muse (in the final couplet's direct echo of Milton's "Il Penseroso"). In "The Power of Fancy," then, the poet whose republican verse uses the collective "we" and contains the refrain "without a king" claims descent from a "throne"—albeit a poetic throne— and tacitly claims to be the sole recipient of fancy's affections. The trope, of course, is traditional (found, for instance, in Thomson). Moreover, although Freneau reprinted it in 1786, the poem was written before the Declaration of Independence; its figure of the poet in retirement, associated with fancy, thus does not run afoul of later debates over fancy and reason or later calls for a national poet and poetry. Nonetheless, the power Freneau claims in poems like "The Power of Fancy" seems to have little to do with the power of history and of civic participation with which he later aligned his work.

"The Power of Fancy" thus finally helps uncover some of the ways that figures of poetic power were not so easily imported to Anglo-America where, if British poetry defined poetic standards, British country estates and country gentry were not so easily aligned with American agrarianism, especially not for a radical anti-British writer such as Freneau. Similarly, some of Freneau's other poems that imagine poetic power in rural settings also reveal how figures of the American landscape are especially vexed in their attempted translations of traditional figures of the site of poetic production.

Given the various ways in which poetry was associated with British leisured classes, with luxury, and with idleness, it is not surprising to find that American poets encounter difficulties with inherited tropes such as that filtered through Thomson, among others, of the poet lounging under the tree. The image appears, for example, in Freneau's 1788 "The Indian Burying Ground":

> Here still an aged elm aspires,
> Beneath whose far-projecting shade
> (And which the shepherd still admires)
> The children of the forest played![60]

Something peculiar has happened to the British country-party dream of leisure and power. The image is certainly still one of poetic power—the Indian's posture in death explicitly signals "the nature of the soul,/ACTIVITY, that knows no rest"—combined with a relative of British primitivism, figured in terms of ethnicity rather than class. The position from which the poem claims its vision is that of a native American; the poem's fancy is allied with the "fancies of a ruder race," a far cry from the sweep of historical progress that authorizes Freneau's political poems. In the final stanza—"And Reason's self shall bow the knee/To shadows and delusions here"—"here" is both the burial site described and, tacitly, the poem itself. Both strategies— a claim to a more original, precivilized imagination and the claim to classical Virgilian tropes of poets (like Collins's Milton) exercising their civic virtue from a rural retreat—are familiar from contemporary British poetry. The figure of the Indian is Freneau's added claim to Americanize the traditional trope. However, in America, leisure was not counted a virtue. Moreover, the culture of the original inhabitants was not so distanced from the historical present of the late eighties as to be easily appropriated as a site of imaginative possibility.

Freneau's figured site of poetic imagination implicitly acknowledges a contemporary foreign readership, as well, especially when the poem disclaims its reported fancies as "rude" and its setting as "delusion." If his trope of leisured or primitive retreat rested uneasily with American attitudes toward leisure (and with the reality of American Indian policies), it also faced contemporary European views of the new world. Indeed, the early republican vocabulary of a laboring people was often constructed against a prevailing skepticism about the barbaric climate and conditions of America, a skepticism perhaps best crystallized in Toqueville but also available early in works like George Louis Leclerc de Buffon's *Natural History* or the *Histoire des deux Indes,* whose authors suggest that because of its climate and its slave economy America "ha[d] not yet produced one good poet."[61] In short, the American context made some traditional tropes of poetic power suspect, but Europe was also a mirror in which Americans saw themselves reflected and which affected poets' ability to deploy traditional tropes. Specifically, the sense of a European audience affected how and how much of the American landscape could be claimed.

For instance, Jefferson's "Notes on the State of Virginia" was written in response to the Marquis de Barbé-Marbois's 1781 questionnaire. The questionnaire was specifically designed to test naturalists' notions that North American species were degenerate because of the barbaric climate. Jefferson's view of the Natural Bridge near Lexington, Virginia—included in his answer to the Marquis's question about waterfalls or cascades—is useful to examine in this light:

> The *Natural bridge,* the most sublime of Nature's works, though not comprehended under the present head, must not be pretermitted . . . It is about 45 feet wide at the bottom, and 90 feet at the top[.] . . . Though the sides of this bridge are provided in some parts with a parapet of fixed rocks, yet few men have resolution to walk to them and look over into the abyss. You involun-

tarily fall on your hands and feet, creep to the parapet and peep over it. Look-
ing down from this height about a minute, gave me a violent head ach [*sic*].
If the view from the top be painful and intolerable, that from below is de-
lightful in an equal extreme. It is impossible for the emotions arising from the
sublime, to be felt beyond what they are here: so beautiful an arch, so elevated,
so light, and springing as it were up to heaven, the rapture of the spectator is
really indescribable! The fissure continuing . . . opens a short but very pleas-
ing view of the North mountain on one side . . . This bridge is in the county
of Rock bridge, to which it has given name, and affords a public and com-
modious passage over a valley[.] . . . The stream passing under it is . . . suffi-
cient in the driest seasons to turn a grist-mill.[62]

The passage veers back and forth, surrounding the central set piece of the
sublime with Enlightenment catalogues and ending with a description of the
uses of the landscape for public purposes. The mixed rhetorics are particu-
larly puzzling if one tries to visualize how, exactly, those made dizzy by the
bridge find it also a "commodious passage." Jefferson's task seems to be
several-fold: to pose himself as a rational scientific speaker, to bespeak with
his sublime transport his participation in polite culture, and yet to avoid any
sense his transport is barbaric. After all, for a foreign readership, the natural
sublime might seem less an occasion for rhetorical or emotional display and
more a sign of a barbaric uncultivable landscape. Jefferson thus quickly de-
flects attention from the sublime landscape he presents. He defuses his de-
scription of "the abyss" by shifting perspective; we find an observer who can
control, by standing in, the so-called abyss, and who looks up instead of
down. The passage domesticates the landscape even before its display of the
usual rhetorical configuration of the sublime. Moreover, the rhetorical dis-
play itself—marked by fractured syntax with multiple clauses, adjectives,
and the use of the exclamation mark—is quickly replaced by a return to cat-
aloguing physical features. The passage ends with a final recuperation of the
bridge as what names a county and is in public use, that is, as already do-
mesticated.

The American insistence on public rather than private citizens may also
exert some pressure on Jefferson's language. But, given the impetus for his
writing—a series of queries from the secretary of the French legation at
Philadelphia—it seems his eye is at least as firmly on a European audience.
Indeed, Jefferson's invocation of the natural sublime is itself in part a gesture
of domestication; natural bridges are not part of the normal furniture of the
sublime, and as Jefferson himself points out they are not cascades, which
should be his subject. By categorizing his bridge with cascades, then, Jeffer-
son can be said to offer it a comfortable home within European thought.

Neil Hertz has characterized one version of the sublime, in which Jeffer-
son's list of dimensions also participates.[63] In Hertz's account, the mind,

overwhelmed by what it cannot domesticate, offers an image of its own baf-flement and in that figuration recoups itself. Jefferson's account also moves to a kind of sheer duality, but not of image so much as of rhetorical dis-courses: is this viewpoint dizzying (sublime) or picturesque, part of a named, delightful landscape; is it an occasion for indescribable (private) rapture or publicly claimed? On one hand, the rhetoric of the sublime itself inscribes the bridge in a recognizable discourse of refinement; on the other, what is indescribable may feed suspicions both of the degraded nature of the North American climate or landscape and of the degraded nature of the minds it nourishes. Jefferson thus alternately positions his prose as a sign of sublime transport, as a delightful picturesque travelogue, and as scientific description (the opposite of standing before the "indescribable").

The work of Jefferson and Freneau illustrates the difficulties of writing about the new world landscape. From abroad, the continent seemed unciv-ilized rather than a place of unlimited potential. Domestically, writing about American landscapes could be subject to the same suspicions of dema-goguery attached to other forms of language in public circulation, *or* it could be subject to charges of smuggling in foreign ideologies. What looked most civilized to a foreign readership was suspect at home. Freneau, Jefferson, and Barlow—all writing in the eighties—also set the stage for later literary treat-ments of nature and the American landscape, although their characteristic gestures are transmuted in later American writings to some degree. In par-ticular, after the War of 1812 there was a shift in poets' ability to draw on Freneau's and Barlow's representations of North America as a blank, undo-mesticated scroll on which history could be written.

The war ended in 1815, a year that most historians suggest was a water-mark in American history. Fewer mention that changes in the national his-torical landscape affected poetic treatments of the natural landscape. Historically, in 1815 Washington was in ashes; Andrew Jackson entered the public arena; and the end of the war began the opening and consolidation of American expansionism and commerce in what Charles Sellers calls a market revolution, or a turn from the culture of land to that of the market.[64] The most widely read poems of the period, including Bryant's "Thanatop-sis" and Lydia Sigourney's "The Mother of Washington," help suggest how public events affected poetic representations of the landscape, which was no longer figured as a blank scroll but as a tomb or a monument to *past* history. In particular, Sigourney's 1815 "The Mother of Washington," an amalga-mation of patriotism, monuments, and tears—the paraphernalia of senti-mental culture already in play in *The Coquette*—clearly addresses concerns generated by a changing economy and by a sense that the public heroism of the seventies was long gone (as Sigourney's subject, the death of Washing-ton's mother, signals).

On the face of it, "The Mother of Washington" recapitulates common-places about republican virtue, suggesting for example that women's civic duty is not "inglorious sloth" but educating children.[65] The didactic features of the poem, then, proclaim it a form of feminine civic labor, although it also includes a rhetorical sleight of hand whereby Sigourney spends three lines defining sloth—"to sport awhile/Amid the flowers, or on the summer wave,/then fleet, like the ephemeron, away"—which allows her readers the pleasures that are then dismissed. The poem thus reinscribes, even while it dismisses, earlier associations between poetry and idleness.

The popularity of Sigourney's work suggests that it was not simply defining a role for late republican womanhood. The poem casts its poetic voice as a reincarnation of something like Franklin's de-authorized, representative speaker, but the ways in which this poetic speech imagines itself circulating is not quite in Franklin's or Brown's or Freneau's public sphere. For Sigourney, history is not so much something for which she can speak, or in which her poem can participate, as something she imagines as a closed book. While some of Sigourney's writerly strategies surely arose from her position as a professional woman poet, the gesture and the popularity of the poem also resonate with current political events. It is as if, with the destruction of the city of Washington and the winning of the war, the country turned its past into a monument.

Written as if an inscription for the public monument erected to Washington's mother, "The Mother of Washington" ends with two apostrophes. First, the monument is instructed to rise and speak to mothers of their "kingly power [of] love"; the spectators are then instructed as follows:

> Ye, who stand,
>
>   * * *
>
> . . . though no high ambition prompts to rear
> A second Washington; or leave your name
> Wrought out in marble with a nation's tears
> Of deathless gratitude;—yet may you raise
> A monument above the stars—a soul[.]

There is an obvious domestication of ambition, both political—there will be no second Washington—and cultural, as the reader is put in the position of a woman told to emulate Washington's mother *without* hoping for her name in marble as an occasion for public displays of grief. In effect, Sigourney's readers are told not to imagine public ambitions for themselves.

Sigourney's poem thus represents a series of embedded gestures of dematerialization and internalization: the mother's true monument is no longer her children's bodies but their souls, and those souls will themselves not be figured in action (not even in publicly marked graves). Public action itself becomes that which gives rise to displays of affect (tears are what write names in marble), and even such display is marked as a form of high ambition not to be imagined. The poem, then, places itself in an odd position in several ways. Published the year that Washington (the city), like Washington (the man, who died in 1799), could be said to have no material existence except in memory, the injunction not to raise a second Washington rings with a slight doubleness. Unlike the civic gestures of Barlow or Freneau, Sigourney's poem recasts civic duty: one honors history by not attempting to translate it in the present; further, Sigourney tacitly recasts civic poetry as that which educates citizens not to make waves.

Yet Sigourney, sometimes known as "Mother Sigourney," was active in various public causes (abolition, American Indian causes) and was so well known that, within two decades of the appearance of "The Mother of Washington," *Godey's Lady's Book* was willing to pay handsomely simply for the right to list *her* name as an editor.[66] For all that it disclaims all forms of ambition as forms of notoriety, when Sigourney's poem represents republican virtue and labor it also succeeds in writing Sigourney's name on a different kind of monument, namely, the poem itself, raised by the tears of a privatized and sentimentalized "public." Still, even while making both her name and her writing financially profitable (and placing herself in a position quite different from that of the long "unnoted" subject of her poem), Sigourney images all profit as otherworldly. Again, some of Sigourney's strategies certainly stem from her place as a woman making her living with her writing; nonetheless, the poem also more generally reimagines a role for poetry: the private act of writing (and reading) can be the model of productive civic work, erasing any traces of imported hierarchy or decadent luxury. The passivity of the model, its kinship to pastoral elegy, is rewritten as virtue, not sloth.

The relationship between Sigourney's figured reader of her poetic monument and American citizenship generally is clear if one looks at other images in public circulation at the time. Sigourney's weeping and feminized mourner, for instance, is not unique; it echoes and is echoed in the iconography of middle-class ante-bellum mourning art, popular from at least 1780, which used the classical urn-and-willow design or, later, the female figure of Melancholia whose robes traced the draped lines of the willow.[67] The image of the weeping female mourner in fact originated in a more public image, the widely circulated memorial print of "America lamenting her Loss at the Tomb of General Washington," which shows a mourning woman in classical drapery leaning against Washington's tomb; the grieving woman is clearly identified iconographically and by title with the nation.[68] In short, individual middle-class mourning practices were allied with an appropriate posture for citizens; in Sigourney's poem in particular the nation and its figures of civic engagement are recast elegiacally: no longer a blank scroll on which history's last chapter may be written, the landscape has been refigured as a national monument to a past that has already been written.

William Cullen Bryant's work, especially "Thanatopsis," which was first drafted around 1815, can be read in the same context. Bryant's best-known poem, like Sigourney's (and Bryant borrows directly from Sigourney), also refigures the earth and the nation as monuments to a republic of the dead. Bryant was not able to turn his writing to financial gain until the forties, by which time he was earning far more as an editor and taste maker. His 1821 volume of *Poems,* however, sold only two hundred and seventy copies in five years.[69] Yet "Thanatopsis" was well known and praised even if it did not sell.

In Bryant's poem, readers are invited to imagine themselves as the figure to be mourned:

> . . . in the cold ground,
> Where thy pale form was laid, with many tears,
> * * *
> To be a brother to the insensible rock
> And to the sluggish clod, which the rude swain
> Turns with his share, and treads upon. The oak
> Shall send his roots abroad, and pierce thy mould.[70]

The landscape, thus, becomes "but the solemn decorations all/Of the great [and leveling] tomb of man."

Bryant later wrote many poems on public figures and against slavery in a more public mode. In "Thanatopsis," however, as in "To a Waterfowl"—the poems that captured his contemporary readership[71]—Bryant's poetic voice is one of fancy and solitude, and he imagines his own position by way of the Virgilian figure in retirement, filtered through the poetry of eighteenth-century Great Britain like Collins's Milton under his oak, although in "Thanatopsis" the figure is far further and more grotesquely under his tree. Bryant's critics often note that he was early impressed with the British graveyard poets, including Blair—from whose poem "The Grave" he borrowed directly—and Gray, and that by 1815 he had responded strongly to Wordsworth's *Lyrical Ballads.*[72] Yet even in "Thanatopsis," positioned as it is in the line of poems such as Sigourney's, Bryant shows his is not quite an English (still less a Roman) oak. If Freneau and Barlow imagined the continent as a blank unpopulated and undomesticated scroll on which history could be rewritten and wherein the poet could speak for history, Bryant suggests and speaks for "millions in those solitudes," all dead. Like Sigourney, he rereads the nation as a funeral monument, with reading figured less as that which arouses public passion or reason, and more as the reading of bodies and the display of sentiment. Unlike the sentimental novelist's voice such as Foster's in *The Coquette,* the poet's voice remains visionary and nationalistic, but it is also elegiac, speaking for what is past (indeed, from one perspective, burying the past in order to speak for it).

Early Emerson and The Monumental Past

It is in the setting just described that Emerson, age twelve in 1815, wrote to his brother William to celebrate the end of the war: "Fair Peace triumphant blooms on golden wings/And War no more of all his victory sings" (*L,* 1: 9). As Sigourney and Bryant were writing, Emerson—who had already attempted an epic ("Fortus") at age ten—dreamt of becoming a poet.[73] Despite Emerson's protest—"I do not wish to be shown early poems, or any steps of progress. I wish my poet born adult" (JMN, 7: 316)—I want here to use Emerson's early letters and journals, from 1815 through the early thirties, to explore his inheritance of commonplaces about poetry and the poet's role. Emerson's was a kind of stereoscopic vision, that is, a composite portrait formed by an education in the classics and in past British poetry; by less-formal readings of American writers of prose, including sermons, and poetry; and by his position in contemporary New England culture, by which I mean post-1815 social, economic, and political culture as well as literary culture.

More specifically, I will suggest that Emerson's first ambitions were poetic. An aspiring poet in a culture undergoing major changes, he internalized a dual literary past. As a youth Emerson struggled with conflicting ideas he inherited about poetry as a high calling, akin to secular grace, but also as an unprofitable, even embarrassing, object of personal ambition and a public sign of idleness or decadence. I then trace Emerson's developing defense of poetic labor and of the public value of poetry from 1815 through 1829, suggesting how American culture's constructions of poetic and public selves remained at odds. By the thirties and forties, Emerson developed rhetorical strategies in his lectures and prose for alternately testing and resisting or reconciling cultural commonplaces about poetry, civic action, and work. His prose thus was a form of cultural criticism; however, he also crafted it to construct a viable poetic persona for himself. His poetics of process and presence reopen both national history and transnational poetry. Yet, even as Emerson rethought the role of the poet in his prose, he found it difficult to embody his theories in actual poems, although he did turn to American and British contemporaries—especially Bryant and Wordsworth—for models. I finally concentrate on what Emerson's *poems* suggest about poetry's public role and note how his repetitions and translations of both the literary past and his own past self-representations most often provide him with a usable poetic voice.

Emerson's earliest journals and letters reveal he admired the work of Milton—a "grand man" and "great Epic poet," he wrote in 1820—and Thomson (though more the poet of *The Castle of Indolence* and *The Seasons* than of "Liberty").[74] He also had a good deal of Milton and Wordsworth by heart. Perhaps not surprisingly for someone raised in an early nineteenth-century Federalist Boston household, there is little mention of poets such as Barlow or Freneau. Yet while there are fewer early traces of the young Emerson's reading of American poets—though he listed the Federalist papers and Franklin's *Works* in his notebooks—by 1822 he was copying passages from Bryant; when he later daydreamed about establishing a college of "living learning," Bryant was one whom he imagined as a professor, despite reservations.[75] One can hear an echo of Bryant's influence as well as Emerson's reservations in an 1818 letter to his brother in which Emerson discusses his writerly ambitions: "I am going some night to the top of Parnassus . . . & there I will bid them [in context, either the muses or the feasts of polite literature] farewell in some tender elegiac stanza and so pathetick that I shall hear some voice issuing out of a blasted oak" (*L*, 1: 63–64).

Already, then, in early adolescence, Emerson idealized poetry—a stance he never entirely abandoned; he would without irony call his 1874 anthology of his favorite poems *Parnassus*. He also, however, made fun of the pathos and sentiment of the solitary elegiac poet under his classic oak, made popular in poems like "Thanatopsis," although Emerson may well have had poets from Gray through Akenside, Warton, or Collins more consciously in mind. At the same time, there is already an interesting turn in Emerson's ironized self-image: his 1818 letter most literally suggests not only a yearning for some originary relationship with nature (or some Mosaic access to a higher voice) but also figures access to that originality as a function of lack, or passivity. That is, the image includes an odd view of cause and effect: only after the poet climbs Parnassus and writes failed elegiac verses saying goodbye to the muses (that is, only after the poet tries and gives up on poetic ambition) is real inspiration issued to him.

Emerson repeatedly returns to similarly mixed views of the solitary and inspired poet as both his highest ambition and as a slight embarrassment. His letters are full of mentions of his own "uncultivated Muse" (*L*, 1: 16) and diffident allusions to the fact that he "profess[es] to be [a] Poet" (*L*, 1: 18). In a humorous 1821 letter to his aunt, he proclaims himself solitude's "sworn defender, by my oath to the muses" (*L*, 1: 100). Also, as in the 1815 letter on the end of the War of 1812, many of Emerson's youthful letters contain (or are entirely composed of) rhymed couplets, which he frequently identifies as marks of his literary apprenticeship, even as the pose is again typically tongue-in-cheek. He speaks, for instance, of "interspersing [his prose] with poetry alias nonsense" (*L*, 1: 46) or of his "poetical bloterature" (*L*, 1: 56).

Despite the Pope-like couplets (by 1818, merged with Byron's influence), however, the pose Emerson continued sometimes incongruously to try on, even in his couplets, was that of the visionary writer. He presents himself in a "fine frenzy" (*L*, 1: 58) or speaks of his verses as the "ebullitions of the genius of Poetry [and] the exuberance of a fine imagination or to speak emphatically [they] indicate the writer to be a man of vast sense & greatness" (*L*, 1: 59). In 1819, he says he is writing for school on "fancy & fairy land & enthusiasm & the like—an eccentrick [*sic*] though *inspired* medley" (*L*, 1: 86); the verses seem to be the following:

> Oh there are times when the celestial muse
> Will bless the dull with inspiration's dews,—
> Will bid the clowns gross sluggish soul expand
> And catch one rapturous glimpse of Fairy Land
> Tis when descending fancy, from the bowers
> Of blest Elysium seeks this world of ours
> 　　　　* * *
> Th enthusiast pauses as he musing stalks
> In the far wild-wood's melancholy walks.
> (*L*, 1: 86)

Again, the pose is familiar, with the solitary poet-enthusiast (almost a gloss on Collins's version of poetical character) visited from above in some natural setting. Also, even in this juvenile exercise, Emerson again describes how inspiration strikes when the would-be poet is dull, clownish, and sluggish.

What I have just identified as diffidence or slight embarrassment is not a single tone in Emerson's earliest writings. He represents his poet-self as a solitary enthusiast most often mixing (first) genuine humility about his own ambitions with (second) traditional melancholy as a prerequisite for poetic inspiration with (finally) a recognition of the standing of poets in American culture. One can see the mixed tones at work in Emerson's pose as a "despised & ragged poet" (*L*, 1: 99) in an 1821 letter to his aunt, written when he was a senior at Harvard. The letter suggests his verse is still "ragged," even as it ironically claims a traditional poetic pose. Finally, in 1821, Emerson's sense of how highly poets might be regarded has a personal edge: that year he was named class poet, a post he acquired only because seven other students had turned it down. A similarly mixed tone still informs—if in a less naive formulation—Emerson's self-representation in his 1835 letter of courtship to Lydia Jackson: "I am born a poet, of a low class without doubt . . . in the sense of a perceiver & dear lover of the harmonies that are in the soul & in matter. . . . Wherever I go therefore I guard & study my rambling propensities with a care that is ridiculous to people, but to me is the care of my high calling" (*L,* 1: 435).

Critics often talk of Emerson's retreat from or rejection of history or society in his work.[76] Most recently, this retreat has been framed by discussions of the values of a rising middle class in a developing market economy, particularly given literary culture's commodification within that economy.[77] Without denying that such studies underline salient features of Emerson's thought and culture, it is worth noting that his first self-representations are explicitly linked to his "high calling" as poet; his representations of the solitary self are rooted in inherited ideas about the status and nature of poets and poetry. At the same time, his inherited sense of what poetic vocation might require or entail was framed within an equally strong sense that the contemporary world might find his preparation for such a calling "ridiculous." That is to say, first, that for all Emerson's public ambitions—which are also clear—his most consistent and frequently voiced ambitions in his early years were to be a poet, a role that was less clearly public, despite those civic couplets on the end of the war from his early adolescence or other occasional forays into public-spirited poetry such as the poem he wrote as class poet in 1821.

Moreover, Emerson's sense of poetry as part of elite culture and as a high moral calling or secularized grace, often visited upon the solitary poet in a pastoral setting, is clearly derived from both British and American cultural (as well as theological) commonplaces.[78] Certainly, his rhetoric (of poetry as high calling, linked with a pose of introspection and humility) eventually allies poetry with his declared public vocation as minister from 1825 through the early thirties. What I want to emphasize is that Emerson's embarrassed representations of his literary aspirations suggest that early in his life he was unable to easily conceive of poetry as public work or to reconcile inherited theological, class, and literary commonplaces. In short, although the rhetoric of public work clearly changed in America between the 1790s and the 1820s, Emerson's earliest representations of poets and poetry rehearse longer-standing commonplaces about poetry, not all of which fit readily with his sense of himself as a citizen, as a religious man, or as a future bread-winner.

One commonplace that Emerson clearly internalized was his culture's particular double vision of poetry as part of polite society, or elite culture, and at the same time as not lucrative. As he wrote to his brother Edward in 1818:

> Were it my fortune to be in a situation like Lord Byron & some other British
> Poets, I think I would cultivate Poetry & endeavour to propitiate the muses

> To have nothing to do but mount the heights of Parnassus & enjoy the feasts of polite literature must necessarily be a very pleasing employment But in this country where every one is obliged to study his profession for assistance in living & where so little encouragement is given to Poets &c it is a pretty poor trade. (*L*, 1: 63)

The point is not unique to the period following 1815, nor are Emerson's clearly mixed feelings about what form of "employment" or "trade" poetry might be said to be.

The suspicion that poetry might be a frivolous or decadent activity is yet another commonplace Emerson confronted. Emerson's attitude toward leisured activity is not constrained by political considerations in the way, say, Freneau's or Franklin's attitudes were; he seems in the above letter to regard profitable work as an unfortunate necessity or duty more than as a pose required of Americans. Yet at least through the mid-twenties Emerson nonetheless often sounds indistinguishable from Franklin in his alternation between, on the one hand, finding his cardinal sin (albeit a sign of moral rather than civic sin) to be idleness or sloth and, on the other hand, framing poetry as a product of what looked, to the world and to Emerson himself, very like sloth. The journals and letters use self-chastisement over "laziness & procrastination" (*L*, 1: 89), distraction by "endless, thankless, reveries" (JMN, 1: 41), as a virtual refrain; as Emerson writes, "All around me are industrious & will be great, I am indolent & shall be insignificant" (JMN, 1: 39). He notes also that the world sees poetry "as the spell or disease which palsies activity and enterprise in life (JMN, 1: 280).[79] Indeed, his mixed presentation of his juvenile poetry as ode-like enthusiasm in neoclassical meter tacitly seems designed to ward off charges of the sin of literary sloth, as when early on he approvingly cites Johnson on looseness of measure as "flatter[ing] the laziness of the idle" (*L*, 1: 11). Five passages from the journals and letters of 1822–1824 are especially useful in tracing Emerson's ambivalent stance toward poetry and labor, and in particular toward what kind of public work poets might perform.

The first passage I want to examine in detail comes from an early 1822 journal. Emerson wrote six paragraphs (some later crossed out) he titled "Of Poetry," identifying poetry as the language of passions and distinguishing poetry from poetical expression, which dresses objects in beautiful language: "Poetical expression serves to embellish dull thoughts but we love better to follow the poet when the muse is so ethereal and the thought so sublime that language sinks beneath it" (JMN, 1: 65). In what first seems an odd tangent to this description of the best poetic language as a mere trace of something higher—mind and inspiration—Emerson also addresses the relationship between nationalism and poetry:

There are few things which the wellwishers of American literature have . . . more at heart than our national poetry. For every thing else . . . they are willing to wait . . . but they are in haste to pluck the . . . blossoms from the fair tree which grows fast by the hill of Parnassus. For when a nation has found time for the luxury and refinement of poetry it takes off the reproach of a sluggish genius and of ignorant indifference. . . . When the heart is satisfied . . . man is apt to exclaim "Soul, . . . eat drink and be merry; . . . I will go to the fields to play."—I would remind him that far off stand the ruins of Palmyra and Persepolis; the hands that builded them are unknown, . . . —I would remind him of the vast cemetery of the dead. (JMN, 1: 64–65)

Emerson's point seems to be, first, a Thomsonian view of progress, with poetry marking the apex of a civilization *and* serving as its memorial. Second, the passage suggests poetry redeems "luxury" (which is otherwise closely allied with "sluggish[ness]"), a word Emerson is still using in this period to describe decadence (see, for example, JMN, 1: 88). In short, he argues that poetic retreat is refinement, not decadent idleness and certainly not useless; it is the fruit of long labor, not "play," by means of which nations are inscribed in the historical record. Finally, as in Sigourney and Bryant, the nation is envisioned proleptically as already past, even as it is warned that a national poetry to memorialize its passing cannot be rushed. There is a tension between a view of the nation as still unripe, still unfolding to its summit, which will be marked by poetry, and a view of the nation as always already gone (or in luxurious decline) by the time poetry—by implication, an elegiac gesture that compensates for loss—appears. There is also an odd tension between the "ethereal" muse and "sublime" thought (which cannot be captured in the material world of language), and the solidity of poetry that must evolve slowly and serve as a national inscription.

What informs both gestures, however, is Emerson's attempt to imagine poets mattering both on Parnassus and in history, specifically American history. Thus, he frames the poet's labor as valuable not only by describing it as labor (it is specifically not play and not a decadent pursuit of pleasure) but also by grounding it in a larger authorizing structure: it serves and marks larger or higher entities (mind, muse, or nation). Once again, too, Emerson's view of the poet's agency is mixed: poets must be visited by the muse or struck by thought or must await the ripening of history; that is, they are instruments more than agents, at the same time that they are framed, though defensively, as laborers.

There is a second, related, passage from later the same year. On 3 July 1822, anticipating Independence Day celebrations and speeches, Emerson wrote to John Boynton Hill, a former schoolmate, about his fears that the Yankees have "marched on since the Revolution, to strength, to honour, &

at last to ennui," and then, commenting on rumored political corruption, he added, "Will it not be dreadful to discover that this experiment made by America . . . does not succeed? . . . Still we . . . will seek to believe that its corruption & decay shall be splendid with literature & the arts, to the latest time—splendid as the late day of Athens & Rome. . . . & a century hence, if the orator lives too late to boast of liberty, he may drop our famed figure of *anticipation,* & yet brag of past renown & present muses" (*L,* 1: 120–21). Here again there is a sense that the heroic age of the nation is past and that national glory will ultimately rest on literary refinement. While again Emerson figures American history, certainly the Revolution, as a closed book with literary history interestingly more open, the irony in his description of the orator suggests he is still struggling to imagine less contrary links between literary and national history.

The mention of oration in the letter was most immediately occasioned by the next day's planned Independence Day speech, although it also underlines Emerson's self-consciousness about his own trope of anticipation mixed with nostalgia and about the odd mixture of engagement and retreat in his pose. Earlier Emerson imagined poetic engagement as similar to public oratory, functioning as exhortation. For example, one of Emerson's juvenile poetic efforts—"Poem on Eloquence," recited at the Boston Latin School in 1816—allies eloquence with public power and, again, with labor; eloquence in the poem has the power to move men to overcome even military strength, like the muse descending "from above" and waking mankind from "indolent repose."[80] By contrast, in 1822 historical glory and national power are seen as past, while the muse is imagined as present in some unspecified future. Moreover, in the 1822 letter the paragraph on Independence Day orations ends as follows: "I shall leave [the next day's speaker] to his eloquence, & retire to certain cherry trees of the country. . . . I shall expend my patriotism in banqueting upon Mother Nature" (*L,* 1: 121). By 1822, then, poetic retreat—and natural subjects—are not so much set against political oratory; they are relabeled *as* patriotism.

The letter to Hill was written the same year that, in his journals, Emerson cautioned against those who could say "Soul, . . . eat drink and be merry; . . . I will go to the fields to play" and warned that such banqueting did not justify the muse. The tensions I have been marking between Emerson's sense of public and poetic selves and between poetry and history—as well as the tacitly contradictory efforts to ground poetry as a civic memorial and yet also a private retreat—were thus certainly not resolved. However, in the 1822 letter Emerson in effect is working toward his later strategy of transfiguring public vocabularies (play as civic service; banqueting in nature as patriotism), a strategy that would come to mark his lectures and essays.

Between 1822 and his entry into Harvard Divinity School, where he hoped "to put on eloquence as a robe" (JMN, 2: 242) in a different capacity, Emerson was clearly still struggling both with how to reconcile his poetic and public personae and with how to conceptualize the work and worth of poetry. For example, within a year of the above letter, Emerson was again writing to Hill, distinguishing between private and public histories and complaining that working (as a teacher) seemed to preclude writing; he noted, too, "I am seeking to put myself on a footing of old acquaintance with Nature, as a *poet* should" (L, 1: 127, 133, emphasis added). The poet, in short, is still private and set in nature, although Emerson also worries that he is finding the natural muse reticent, "not half poetical, not half visionary enough. . . . No Greek or Roman or even English phantasy could decieve [*sic*] me one instant into the belief of more than met the eye" (L, 1: 133). The question then that is added to the problem of poetic idleness is what, precisely, the poet's solitary banquet might yield. What met the eye, alone, obviously would not suffice. It seems Emerson was still seeking "some voice issuing out of a blasted oak." Moreover, it seems the models on which Emerson earlier relied for evidence that poetry put nations on the map were not yielding any clues as to what an American oak might have to say, especially to "a hard handed American who reckons acquisitions by dollars & cents not by learning & skill" (L, 1: 152).

The last comment above comes from an 1824 letter Emerson wrote to his brother about his own efforts to enter Harvard Divinity School as a second-year student, in order to save money. Emerson's need for a profession—a way to make a living—further troubled his attempt to reconcile poetic and public roles. Emerson's clerical vocation—his "professional studies," which coincided with his becoming "*legally* a man"—is in his journals framed as a matter of claiming "the power to act," specifically to use the "powers which command the reason & passions of the multitudes," which is to say, public power or (perhaps) "public preaching & private influence" (JMN, 2: 237–40). The same journal entry cites his imagination and his love of poetry—as well as his "passionate love for the strains of eloquence"— as what qualify him for the church, but the decision is also cast as a matter of using these qualities for a professional end, not to be a poet; indeed, as he rehearses his other options, he lists law and medicine—public and lucrative and respectable middle-class professions—not poetry.

In the decades after the Revolution, the power of the New England clergy and the related moral authority of literary accomplishment had been gradually eroded, with law increasingly the career choice of those who might previously have become clergymen.[81] In this sense, Emerson's choice of profession suggests a kind of compromise, although certainly family history also played a role in determining his choice. In any event, he did need a profession, and poetry did not count as such; yet he represents his profession as combining those interests he already associated with poetry *and* public influence: moral authority, imagination, a love of language, and a way of envisioning some merger between private solitude and public service, not to mention a way of construing his own private virtues as public power.

I have framed a public sphere in various ways in these arguments about Emerson's early views: as literal public oratory, or writing on public subjects that might affect "multitudes," and as part of what print culture had begun (re)constructing as a public imaginary since the nineties, a process that was both figured and complicated by the elegiac figures of nationhood in circulation by 1815. While 1824 was not yet the Jacksonian era, many of the features of Jacksonian America were already in place, including a rising sense—in Emerson's case, fear—of factionalism. Moreover, the country had already seen the panic of 1819 (and the serious postwar depression that lasted through 1824, at its worst in 1821–1822) and debate over the Missouri Compromise as well as the Vesey slave rebellion, not to mention the uproar over establishing public schools, which came to a head in 1825. In short, just what might constitute the public, or who could or could not regulate, educate, or even imagine "a" public, were issues very much in the air as Emerson arranged to enter "public" life by choosing a profession.[82]

Urban unemployment and the resulting riots and soup kitchens especially in places like Baltimore that marked the 1819–1824 depression also affected what might be counted as the public, especially insofar as neither the early republican rhetoric of public virtue nor the increasingly internalized public imaginary encompassed the more literal public realities of the postwar era. By 1822 Emerson was writing to Hill about the rise of demagogues following Monroe's election, specifically those calling themselves "the Middling Interest" (*L*, 1: 111). When the "Middling Interest" first appeared in Boston, it was the transfer of the term "interest" from private vice to public party with which someone raised in the vocabulary of Federalist republicanism might take issue.[83] Moreover, widespread unrest due to the depression, at its worst as Emerson wrote to Hill, made interested public factions seem dangerous to the national health. When, in the same letter, Emerson protested that a "*mob* is a thing which could hardly take place here [Boston]" (*L*, 1: 112), the protest speaks less of disbelief that mobs might appear in Boston than acknowledgment that they had been appearing regularly elsewhere.

Yet if in 1822 the term "Middling Interest" is one that appalled Emerson, two years later, in a journal entry about public education, he appropriated the term to define the public he thought writers needed to reach. Even before his words were in public circulation, Emerson clearly saw print as part of public education and worried that such an education was not available in the novels, romances (fit only for "coxcombs & deficient persons"), or newspapers, all that he saw as available to "the great body of society who make up nations & conduct the business of the world," a group he dubbed the "Middling Interest of mankind [who] are immersed in daily labours for daily bread" (JMN, 2: 278–79). In other words, what bound public and private (terms Emerson used throughout his life), as well as how to define what might be public, were open, contemporary questions, and the blurring of contested categories and definitions was part of contemporary practice.[84] Emerson's 1824 reapplication of the Boston party's title to something like the idea of the general public thus is both part of contemporary practice and an omen of his own later and more deliberate oratorical strategy of redefining or transfiguring public rhetorical terms.

I am not, here, tracing Emerson's political thought per se, but I am suggesting that in his earliest work his public and his poetic ambitions were internally troubled as well as at odds with each other and that he proposed various figurations of how to reconcile these self-fashionings. To become a clergyman using the tools of the poet is such a figuration, adapting the necessity of earning a living to both public and poetic ambitions. Emerson wrote in his journal, also concerning his decision over a profession, "I am ambitious not to live in a corner" (JMN, 2: 246). But what it might mean not to be cornered was unclear, as is obvious in the series of consecutive 1824 journal entries that conclude with his stated desire not to live in a corner, which form the next passage I want to examine in detail.

Directly after his journal entry dedicating himself and his imagination to the church, Emerson wrote about studying the American Revolution, looked back on "in the language of posterity when we say that it bears the palm away from Greek & Roman achievement. . . . [in that it was] the victory of every American. There are three things chief which the human mind studies; itself, God, & the Universe . . . combined in that . . . branch of art which is called History. . . . In a vague sense, history may be said to comprise also all the store of Natural knowledge" (JMN, 2: 242–43). The entry is at once followed by a series of drafts of poems, the first of which is a fragment on fortune, conquest, glory, and empire; the next, a description of a "secret shrine in a pleasant land/Whose groves the frolic fairies planned . . . twilight shade . . . [without] vulgar crowds"; the next verses insist,

> O when I am safe in my sylvan home
> I tread on the pride of Greece & Rome
> And when I am stretched beneath the pines
> * * *
> . . . what are they all [sophists and the learned] in their high conceit

When Man in the bush with God may meet.

                            * * *

Late in the world too late perchance for fame
Just late enough to reap abundant blame
(JMN, 2: 243–44)[85]

This series of disjointed journal entries brings together in a few pages national history and poetic muses, private and public ambitions. Suggesting that he is going to talk of the founding fathers (although he does not), Emerson's view of the originating event of American history repeats the idea that the "palms," or historical importance, of the nation will be cemented retrospectively by the "language of posterity." National history, in short, may already be in decline, but the *writing* of that history might remain open. By 1834, Emerson would push this view further. Given contemporary politics and the "mob," Emerson suggests, traditional patriotic action is impossible, so much so one "congratulates Washington that he is long already wrapped in his shroud & forever safe"; noting the current need for "Moral Education" and citing literary figures from Channing to Wordsworth, Emerson then offers poetry as a form of moral action, and the form best able to serve the country (JMN, 4: 326). The 1824 journal is less certain how to connect history, contemporary American society, and poetry.

Having mentioned national history, Emerson's 1824 passage discusses how general rules of history, including cycles of striving and luxury as well as the unfolding "hand of Providence" (JMN, 2: 242), may be derived from considering the past, a proposition that makes his definition of history as the study of the human mind and of God unsurprising. More surprising, although characteristic, is Emerson's description of the study of the universe as involving, first, human relations (which he then concludes is just part of history's study of the human mind) and, second, natural knowledge, which again involves human intellect: "all the victories of human science over the inanimate Creation & the eras & degrees of intellectual greatness" (JMN, 2: 243). I want to underline how the study of the universe is here named as a form of history and subsumed under history's study of the human mind: "comprehended in the first office [the mind's study of itself] we ascribed to the historic Muse" (JMN, 2: 243). In the process, both nature and natural knowledge are recast, as is history. At the same time, however, when Emerson sets his own pen to paper as a poet, he not only veers away from what seem public topics (not to mention his stated topic, the rise and fall of nations with changing fortunes, conquest, glory, and so on), but he does not clearly sustain his proposed vision of natural knowledge as part of the history of men thinking and *as such* part of history proper.

In contrast to the prose construction of natural knowledge I have just considered, nature becomes a far more literary—specifically poetic—matter as Emerson turns to an image of pastoral retreat (the fairy shrine) sequestered from the mob or "vulgar crowd." This is the setting in which his pen can bear "the palm away from Greek & Roman achievement." In other words, Emerson's prose starts by imagining a public place for writing in America; writing will commemorate the Revolution that he calls the "victory of every American," which in context is clearly his way of including the great and the common man and of providing an occasion for his own original thought. His attempt to embody such thought in poetry per se, however, replaces crowds with fairies; only in such a romance setting can Emerson's poetry imagine outdoing Greece and Rome. The prose arguments about what it might mean to matter in history reconcile public and private by elevating a kind of privatized public; the way the argument moves already presages Emerson's mature essayistic practices. The early poetic fragments, however, do not perform the kind of transfigurations of public vocabularies that the prose begins to describe and enact. Eloquence, to which Emerson saw himself dedicating his life, even eloquence *about* poetry, does not seem to inform prose and poetry in the same way.

From one perspective the journalistic poetry fragments might appropriately be taken as a typical Emersonian literary declaration of independence —he says he casts off the yoke of past learning and literary founding fathers to claim an "unlaurelled," American muse; his pines replace the more traditional oak. However, from another perspective, the substance of the couplets cannot be taken at face value. Among other things, the way in which Emerson represents his bid for poetic fame is deeply traditional: poets sprawled under trees in summer shade with higher voices speaking from the local flora was by 1824 a widespread trope of original poetic power. Not only is the commonplace repeated here, it is in effect ironized in the couplet on disclaimed "fame" and harvested "blame" in which Emerson turns from his sylvan retreat to notice, however defiantly, the world. History may be reviewed as a matter of the mind studying itself and God, but to the contemporary world, the mind meeting God in the bush is either ridiculous or outmoded ("mouldy"), or both. As I have already shown, Emerson's juvenile descriptions of poetry include similar gestures of embarrassment, mixed gestures that are representative of humility and of the unself-consciousness prerequisite to poetic inspiration, but that also acknowledge the ways in which Emerson's world might dismiss poets.

Part of Emerson's difficulty in reconciling his sense of civic duty with his poetic ambitions involved his inability to describe what kind of authority poetry might claim, an authority that might render poetry less "ridiculous." While later he would describe the poet as "representative," through the twenties the question remained open on several fronts as to what or who the poet represented: insofar as poetry claimed a moral or civic authority, it was not clear how the poet under his tree could figure that authority, both because the characteristic pose of the poet seemed more emblematic of personal vice than of moral virtue and because the public import of the poet's projected subject matter, nature, was not easily described. Given both his politics and the period in which Emerson wrote, he could not easily claim the American landscape as a scroll on which history might write itself as Freneau or Barlow did; Emerson clearly required that nature speak of "more than met the eye," but again at least in his early attempts at poems he seems unable to find a poetic voice that might speak for some larger moral or historical whole.

This leads me to the final passage from the period between 1822 and 1824 on which I want to comment—a poem Emerson wrote in his journal. Facing his entry into the Harvard Divinity School in what his notebook records as December 1824, Emerson recirculated his earlier view that his chosen profession as a member of the clergy was incompatible with poetic solitude. He again figures solitude and song as sloth, mourning that he must leave a "woodland life" of "woods & streams & the sweet sloth/Of prayer & song," bidding farewell to "twilight walks and midnight solitude" as well as to the "[b]ooks, Muses, study, fireside, friends, & love" associated with his "boyhood" (*Poems,* 304; JMN, 2: 405). "Song," as opposed to eloquence, it seems, is still solitary and rural (though here as much domestic as pastoral); the muses, on this account, visit the slothful.

The tropes in the fragment repeat Emerson's central dilemma over the apparent idleness and private nature of poetry. However, the language and the sound of the lines (in rough blank verse, with a catalogue of losses) also enter Emerson into a transatlantic conversation. The most obvious echo is of the lines from Thomson's "Spring" earlier used by Franklin and by Foster:

> —"An elegant sufficiency,
> Content, retirement, rural quiet, friendship;
> Books, ease and alternate labor, useful life;
> Progressive virtue, and approving heaven;
> These are the matchless joys of virtuous love."

By the 1790s these lines (quoted by a clergyman in *The Coquette*) proposed an internalized, domesticated ideal of citizenship and virtue. Following the War of 1812, however, redefinitions of middle-class labor attended shifts in the economy. Increasingly, definitions of work excluded domestic work.[86] By Emerson's day, the trope of domesticated rural retirement (with books, friends, and love) did not image a useful civic life. Emerson pointedly uses the trope in his poetic fragment in opposition to the professional role of clergyman he was about to assume.

For Thomson, poetic retirement was already a problematic figure, a figure that was then reappropriated for public purposes in the early American republic. As the image reappears in Emerson's journals, it is again the home of the poetic muses, although Emerson's muse can no longer easily be imagined performing "alternate labor" rather than indulging in "sweet sloth." Emerson's conversation is not just with Thomson or with an Americanized Thomson, however. The poetic fragment from his 1824 journal also rehearses Wordsworth's conversation with Thomson, and further, marking a different kind of affiliation with Wordsworth, Emerson's form draws on Wordsworth's blank verse. Emerson was already reading Wordsworth by 1820 (JMN, 1: 29), the year he noted that in *The Excursion,* Wordsworth's "choice of persons lays him open to ridicule" (JMN, 1: 271). The comment echoes Emerson's own repeated fear of ridicule and anticipates his later suggestion—of the middle to late thirties—that poetry might have a "lowly" subject matter.[87] Emerson not only paid attention to Wordsworth's subject matter but also to the sound of Wordsworth's poetry. In an 1835 lecture on English literature, Emerson commented specifically on Wordsworth's form, noting that only six English poets had ever mastered blank verse: Milton, Shakespeare, Thomson, Young, Cowper—and Wordsworth (EL, 1: 308).

In 1834, Emerson would record his fear that Wordsworth's voice was too much in his ear. After delivering his Phi Beta Kappa poem, he worried that he might be "overawed by the popular voice or deferring to . . . Mr. Wordsworth's . . . tastes" (JMN, 4: 317). Throughout his life, Emerson's reactions to Wordsworth varied, from including him in a list of geniuses (JMN, 2: 380–81; JMN, 3: 148; EL, 1: 381) to finding his work petty or offensive (JMN, 1: 162, 281; JMN, 3: 39–41). An engagement with, and passages from, Wordsworth appear frequently throughout Emerson's journals. Emerson's reading of the British poet seems to have been one site of his struggle to sound like a poet, a struggle that included questions about how not to seem ridiculous (the word is one Emerson projects as Wordsworth's problem several times) and about how to include an untraditional (for Emerson, an American) landscape within poetry, as well as about how to write a poetry of retirement that could be seen by the reading public as serving a larger purpose.

The end of Emerson's 1824 dedication of his talents to the church and his farewell to childhood and to "[b]ooks, Muses, study, fireside, friends, & love" specifically echoes, in cadence and in its use of lists, Wordsworth's (Miltonic) lines to Milton—"give us manners, virtue, freedom, power" (in "London, 1802"), in which Wordsworth confronted the problem of how poetry might bind the private and public. Emerson also thus (inadvertently) rehearses Shelley's response that "things depart which never may return:/Childhood and youth, friendship and love's first glow" in "To Wordsworth," the poem in which Shelley accused Wordsworth of not holding firm to his political ideals. Reread in an American context, framed by very different political views, Shelley's Wordsworth was not Emerson's. Among other things, the fact that Wordsworth was an English rather than an American contemporary complicated Emerson's relationship to the older poet's work.[88] Indeed, although Wordsworth wrote with apparent pleasure of being told his poems were "in the hearts of the American people" by 1838, he would also dismissively say after reading Emerson's essays in 1841 that Emerson and Carlyle, "who have taken a language which they suppose to be English for their vehicle, are verily 'Par nobile Fratrum.'"[89]

Wordsworth nonetheless served as a model—if sometimes a negative model—for younger writers on both sides of the Atlantic, and he offered Emerson, like Shelley, a way to reimagine sounding like a poet—and to join a living community of poets—while still offering something that could be seen as valuable to a contemporary world.[90] Among other things, Wordsworth's poems suggest how poetry might be made out of a poet's questions rather than answers, and specifically out of questions about poetry's role in contemporary public culture. But before turning to Emerson's more mature poems and his continuing relationship with Wordsworth's work in them, I want to consider in more detail how Emerson's professional career and his life as a public figure also shaped his thoughts on poetry and public action.

Emerson's Work, 1830–1847: Figuring the Public and the Poet

Emerson might be said to have chosen, in one way or another, a public life since 1829, when he was ordained, but more notably after he resigned his ministry with the Second Church in Boston in 1832 and began his participation in the lyceum movement.[91] The years between 1829 and 1835 were even more eventful for Emerson personally than professionally. He did give sermons, and his letters indicate he spent most of his writing time in the late twenties on sermons. However, he was at least as preoccupied with worries about his declining health, spending time in St. Augustine for that reason in 1827. The same year he was ordained (1829), he also married; within three years he was widowed. Moreover, by 1836, two of his brothers had died. In 1832 he resigned from the Second Church and undertook a year of travel abroad, where he met some of the poets whose work he had admired, including Coleridge, Wordsworth, and Carlyle; Emerson would also help publish and circulate Carlyle's work in the United States. By 1835, he had remarried and begun public lecturing, "pour[ing] out . . . decanters or demijohns of popular wisdom" (*L,* 2: 109), as he later wrote his brother William; by the spring of 1838 he announced he would live entirely by lecturing, "which promises to be good bread" (*L,* 2: 120). Having resigned his church office over the issue of the communion ceremony, public speaking and prose became the bread and wine he offered. Thus, Emerson redefined his public calling by saying he would "not preach more except from the Lyceum" (*L,* 2: 120).

There is an irony in Emerson's changing descriptions of his professional work, in his turn from a New England preacher to someone whose livelihood depended on the public (and on newspaper advertisements of his lectures).[92] Many of the lectures and published prose works that followed—*Nature* in 1836, *Forest Essays* (later *Essays: First Series*) in 1841—voice dismay over the emerging urban culture on which the effectiveness of advertisements and newspapers in part depended. Emerson's public prose takes poets and poetry as its central trope, if not also its stated topic, and returns to precisely those issues that Emerson's early journals and letters associated with poetry: solitude, nature and the American landscape, the relationship between private (domestic or rural) retreat and public service, and the value of poetic work or idleness. At the same time, the success of Emerson's lectures depended on his not being solitary, rural, or private, even though in some sense the prose was designed to educate a public for his poetry and to work out for himself as well as for his audiences what the contemporary value of poetry might be.

From one perspective, it seems that Emerson's felt need to reconcile his private and public selves could have been met by his turn to the moral, nonsectarian pulpit of the lyceum, which drew one of the most heterogeneous audiences of the period and took on the task earlier associated with American print culture, namely, binding an increasingly fragmented community into a common, public endeavor.[93] Thus, Emerson's lectures and essays about poetry could be said to serve both a poetic and a public role; they also allowed him to use his self-proclaimed talents (for eloquence and imagination) within a professional role. Yet to propose this requires a mental sleight of hand, if one Emerson's language often encourages. That is, although the lectures and essays were seen as poetic by virtue of their perceived eloquence and their topics, they were not poems. Moreover, the lectures—and to a lesser extent the published essays—were public by virtue of their performance in public or their dissemination in print. It is true that the prose through at least 1841 shows Emerson's increasing mastery of strategies for redefining public vocabularies, calculated not so much to resolve the questions that confronted him as to make unresolved questions the tissue of his rhetorical power.[94] Yet what his prose works provided their actual audiences or readers—the nature or efficacy of their public engagement—is not so clear. Leaving aside for the moment some recent assessments of Emerson as the high priest of untrammeled capitalism—which grant Emerson's prose a great deal of public power—in his own day Emerson's language was, like Thomson's or Shelley's, deemed obscure, a source of compelling sound, not sense.[95] If Emerson's profession reconciled his poetic and public ambitions, it did so without yielding poems per se and without serving clear public ends.

In effect, Emerson's contemporary audience may have reinscribed the gap he found between "the sweet sloth" and "delight" of song and service to a larger public, often national, purpose, or as he wrote, "discuss[ing] in a popular manner, some of those . . . *practical* questions of daily recurrence[,] *moral, political, & literary, which best deserve the attention of my countrymen* (JMN, 2: 279, emphasis added). Those who admired his linguistic "spell that transcend[ed] their knowledge"—his "charm . . . like music"—were not necessarily finding his lectures powerful in any practical or political sense.[96] Finally, such reactions bespeak a growing cultural acceptance of the very gap Emerson wanted to close between literary or moral concerns on the one hand, and political or public concerns on the other.

In other words, there was a tension between what Emerson attempted in his lectures and what his audience took from him. Indeed, it is worth dwelling for a moment longer on how Emerson framed his ambitions for his lectures and essays. Emerson stated his aims as a lecturer and culture critic were national—for his "countrymen"—and "practical." At the same time, his prose was clearly designed to construct and defend a poetic persona for himself. Turning to the essays, one can see that his major topics—solitude, nature, the public and the private, work and idleness—are precisely those associated throughout his early life with his desire to be a poet. It is in pursuing these poetic issues that the essays become also an attempt to uncover or demystify shifting definitions of public work and of intellectual labor in his day.[97] Emerson may well have begun with a nostalgia for the status and moral authority of the literate and literary clerical class from which he came. However, throughout his youth his primary desire was to be a major poet, an ambition for which American history offered no models of success. To understand Emerson's prose fully requires seeing that his initial project was to construct a role for poets and poetry in America, a goal that involved challenging the cultural values that left no place for poetry. Even now, to take his invocations of poetry as a retreat from public issues is to accept the very commonplaces Emerson attempted to challenge, namely, that poetry is *a priori* irrelevant to the world.

Admittedly, on first reading Emerson's prose seems to founder on the question of how to define labor in a way that includes writing (or thinking).[98]

For example, in 1836, in "Spirit," Emerson noted that "you cannot freely admire a noble landscape, if laborers are digging in the field hard by. The poet finds something ridiculous in his delight, until he is out of the sight of men" (*CW/RWE*, 1: 39).[99] The passage repeats a commonplace of Emerson's earlier thoughts about poetry. That is, poetry may be labor, but it is not only private, it is not commensurate with actual labor, in the face of which it becomes ridiculous, as Emerson echoes his more private description to Lydia Jackson from the year before of poetry's "high calling." Again, in 1837, in a letter to Amos Bronson Alcott, Emerson wrote that he preferred the "silent" muse of writing to the more public lecturing he was doing and complained, "I should prefer some manual or quite mechanical labor as a means of living that should leave me a few sacred hours in the twenty four" (*L*, 2: 75), while he told his brother William, "a little business spoils a great deal of time for the Muses" (*L*, 2: 90). In such passages, poetic, manual, and professional labor seem quite distinct. In what again seems at first a contradictory move, the 1837 lecture "The American Scholar" suggests all labor is commensurate; even "creative reading" is characterized as an activity of the mind "braced by *labor* and invention" (*CW/RWE*, 1: 58, emphasis added). Yet at the same time, the speech characterizes the "dignity and necessity of labor" first as that of the "hoe and the spade" and confesses "books only copy the language which the field and the work-yard made" (*CW/RWE*, 1: 61–62).

By the time of "The American Scholar," however, Emerson had embarked on a more self-conscious testing and challenging of public discourse in his prose constructions of a public role for poetry. Emerson begins "The American Scholar" with the proposition that "the sluggard intellect of this continent will . . . fill the postponed expectation of the world with something better than the exertions of mechanical skill. Our day of dependence, our long apprenticeship to the learning of other lands, draws to a close. The millions that around us are rushing into life, cannot always be fed on the sere remains of foreign harvests. . . . Who can doubt that poetry will revive and lead in a new age" (*CW/RWE*, 1: 52). The proposal is that intellectual labor, headed by poetry, will not only fulfill America's promise but be a labor more valuable than trade, analogous to the agricultural work that a growing American market economy was beginning to replace. Ultimately, however, the speech as a whole argues against a double vision in an attempt to resist professional specialization and the commodification of labor. It tries to reenvision labor as unalienated and citizenship as a whole, a body politic. "The American Scholar" does not thus simply valorize intellectual work, certainly not by repressing its difference from other forms of labor. Rather, Emerson tests the relationship and differences between forms of labor especially as labor informs national identity. For example, Emerson denies the distinction between "'practical men'" and "speculative men," redefining thought as action and action as power when he describes "every opportunity of action past by, as a loss of power"; yet by the close of the piece thinking and action are distinguished: "The mind now thinks; now acts" (*CW/RWE,* 1: 59, 61). The essay, in effect, keeps returning to (while turning over) the distinctions its audience would have internalized between practical action and thought, manual and professional labor, poetry and the public sphere. Here, the specific audience for the lecture is worth recalling: the Phi Beta Kappa Society. The concluding exhortation to unmask the quest for "money or power" as a "false good" and to embrace "the topics of the time" including the "literature of the poor . . . the philosophy of the street, the meaning of household life" (*CW/RWE,* 1: 65, 67) was not the standard fare of Phi Beta Kappa orations.

As "The American Scholar" tries to unsettle definitions of work and workers and of public status as it rethinks the poet's role, so other lectures and essays revisit traditional ideas about poetic idleness and solitude. For example, in "Spiritual Laws" (repeating a passage from an 1840 lecture on "Reforms"), Emerson writes that we "call the poet inactive, because he is not a president, a merchant, or a porter. . . . [R]eal action is in silent moments" (*CW/RWE,* 2: 93; EL, 3: 266). Emerson then argues that to "think is to act" and concludes that poetic power is not simply comparable to but above "all that is reckoned solid and precious in the world,—palaces, gardens, money, navies, kingdoms" (*CW/RWE,* 2: 94–95). In short, again, public or political office and power, like economic or even domestic status, are discounted; apparent idleness is revalued. Specifically, the essay addresses those who believe that lack of success in the political and economic world marks *writing* as an idle or useless pastime. The argument is pointed because Emerson never forgets that writing, as opposed to lecturing, does not yield economic power: "There are not in the world at any one time more than a dozen persons who read and understand Plato:—never enough to pay for an edition of his works" (*CW/RWE,* 2: 89), he writes, echoing his own comment to his brother, on publishing *Nature,* "I shall expect no profit" (*L,* 2: 28). At the same time, as "The American Scholar" already suggested, Emerson would not necessarily accept the equation of profit or use with economic power.

The essays, thus, revalue and imagine as commensurate the private realm of thought and public work. They challenge public values to open a place for the qualities Emerson associated with poetry. In the process, Emerson tacitly constructs more than one model of the poet, whose activity is sometimes represented as writing, sometimes as commemorative, sometimes as thought or inspiration, sometimes as oral performance.[100] Take for example the following passage, in which Emerson writes, "The poet in utter solitude remembering his spontaneous thoughts and recording them, is found to have recorded that which men in crowded cities find true for them also. The orator . . . finds that he is the complement of his hearers;— . . . he fulfills for them their own nature; the deeper he dives into his privatest secretest presentiment,— . . . he finds, this is the most acceptable, most public and universally true" (*CW/RWE*, 1: 63). The prose here requires some verbal legerdemain to get from spontaneous thought or inspiration to memory to writing to reaching a public. In the above passage, the poet's insight—that universal truth he is said to record—is made acceptable instead of ridiculous, public instead of merely private, in a rhetorical gesture that suppresses the less visible parts of the poet's work, those activities that might look like idle pleasure. For example, the public's "finding" occurs only as the poet is relabeled an orator. The active verbs all belong to the orator and his audience, not to the solitary poet. The grammar of the first sentence avoids representing the actual work of writing when it suggests that urban crowds have access to what the poet "is found to have recorded."

In a lecture such as "The American Scholar," from which the passage above is taken, such shifts would work well in that there *was* a literal audience invited to take the thoughts presented as equivalent to the more literal, physical action of lecturing; even in prose, the verbs invite the individual reader to place himself or herself in the singular and active subject-position of poet-orator, as much as in the position of the solitary re-collector or of those represented or "fulfilled" by the orator. In other words, Emerson refigures the exemplary poet in something like his own position as lecturer. He thus imagines a present, performative power for poetry. Even though his letters are full of complaints that lecturing left him no time for writing poems, public lectures provided him with an image for poetry as public action. A related gesture appears in a later letter to his wife, written after Emerson attended a production by the Italian Opera Company. The opera serves as an emblem of poetry as musical language, public action, and sheer physical presence in the letter, which wistfully re-envisions a comparable power emanating from poetic solitude: "If I could once get away into that private nook that I have been seeking ever since I can remember, I would take the benefit of this opera and write such verses as would take arms & feet & head & body to express, as well as the tongue" (*L*, 3: 396).

Refiguring the poet as lecturer or performer serves Emerson's defense of poetry. Throughout, Emerson's earlier thinking about poetry sets the terms of his arguments, as he repeatedly confronts the question of how to characterize the labor or idleness—as well as the private or public nature—of poetry. The solitude that Emerson inherited as the site of poetic production is what he tries to transform from the ridiculous to the acceptable, the private to the public, the useless to the true. However, he never forgot that lectures could support a man and reach a popular audience in a way poetry could not. If "The American Scholar" begins proclaiming that the new American revolution will be a poetry, not a market, revolution, the poet's lot remains that of "poverty and solitude" (*CW/RWE*, 1: 62), while the poet offers a public service only when he is confused with the orator.

There is also another point to the way Emerson's prose refigures the present power of poetry and conflates those who write with those who perform in public. At times, the blurred image of the poet as solitary-thinker, as writer-scholar, and as orator works as part of Emerson's rhetorical unsettling of a cultural vocabulary. Using poetry and poets as figures for all intellectual work, the lectures and essays address broader issues about public culture in Emerson's recuperation of the public uses of private thought.[101] Thus, in "The American Scholar" poetry serves as a figure for the next wave of American public life, which in turn is refigured within an American landscape in a way that allows Emerson to claim a public place for the moral and literary as well as to present an American poet in the face of both foreign skepticism about American literary culture and domestic skepticism about the productive value of literary work. To give another example, in his 1838 lecture at Dartmouth College Emerson wrote of "Literary Ethics," "Do not believe the past. . . . By Latin and English poetry, we were born and bred in an oratorio of praises of nature,— . . . yet the naturalist of this hour finds that he knows nothing, by all their poems, of any of these fine things" (*CW/RWE*, 1: 106). The lecture then advocates seeing American nature—the "noonday darkness of the American forest, the deep, echoing, aboriginal woods"—and characterizes the true scholar as "a solitary, laborious, modest, and charitable soul": "Do not go into solitude only that you may presently come to the public. Such solitude denies itself; is public and stale" (*CW/RWE*, 1: 106–13). Exactly what would echo in the aboriginal woods—a problem that surfaces more prominently in the poems themselves—is not spelled out, but "Literary Ethics" does challenge its audience to rethink the public importance of private solitude, of labor that looks like idleness, and of what Emerson's prose gives us a vocabulary for, namely, self-reliance that does not pander to the public or the past.

In short, Emerson's unsettled redefinitions are part of his work as a culture critic. Most strikingly, in "Literary Ethics" Emerson warns against reification of the images he uses to unmask cultural commonplaces about the private and public spheres. For example, he cautions that one cannot simply take on the (public) appearance of solitary thought. Similarly, in his 1840 lecture on "Politics," his analysis sounds much like Shelley's in statements such as the following: "Let us not politely forget the fact that its [the state's] institutions are not aboriginal. . . . that they all are alterable; . . . institutions [seem] rooted like oak trees[.] . . . But the fact is Society is fluid" (*EL*, 3:

240). Such gestures suggest both Emerson's resistance to having his "Man Thinking" made into a source of public pieties and his self-consciousness about the tension between his public role as lecturer and his disclaimers about public experience. Furthermore, in 1853 Emerson wrote that his "quarrel with poets is that they do not believe in their own poetry," a recognition of the ways in which poets, too (Emerson was specifically thinking of later Wordsworth), could internalize cultural values, the very values Emerson's lectures and essays propose poetry should show others how to rethink (JMN, 13: 236). Yet although by the forties Emerson increasingly and self-consciously found strategies by which he might attempt both to recast inherited figures of poetic production and to resist the emergent culture of a market economy, the struggle was not without cost.

My point, most generally, is that the "poet" of the essays and Emerson as poet are different. The way *poems* can and cannot link private and public is more complicated than the lectures and essays suggest in the theories about poetry's role they construct using the shifting figure of "the poet."[102] Among other things, the audience for poetry and for essays or lectures (even those about poetry) were distinct. Lyceum audiences might well be imagined transmuting the wine and bread of Emerson's secular wisdom; poetry readers were more difficult to imagine, especially as a cross section of "the" American public. Moreover, to sound like a poet involved in some way deploying the cultural norms for poetry. Finally, although Emerson's prose served as a forum in which he could rethink the role of poetry in America, the time he spent writing the prose helped contribute to the fact that he wrote relatively few finished poems. The great commonplace is that Whitman and Dickinson, not Emerson, co-founded what we think of as modern American poetry, and that it was Whitman in particular who wrote the poetry Emerson's essays imagine. Even if this is true, the question I want to pose is what kind of poetry Emerson's *poems* imagine. And to pose this question, I want to examine several of the poems he wrote during the period in which the essays and lectures that I have been discussing were written.

Earlier, I noted that Emerson's ideas about poetry through the mid-twenties did not necessarily translate well when he turned his attention to actual poems. But it does seem his public prose from the thirties allowed him more easily to claim in poems the solitude and apparent idleness that he earlier treated with ambivalence and embarrassment. Thus, in the poetry notebooks that he began in 1826–1827, we find the following:

> . . . He must have
> Droll fancies . . .
> Who in my vagrant verse shall look to find
> *A holiday from study or from toil,*

* * *

> Such *idler* will not be a man of name,
> But must be, & therein resembles me,
> *A little liable to ridicule*
> (emphasis added)[103]

The fragment then details the poet's pleasures as "the glad sense of *solitude,* the sure/The absolute deliverance from the yoke/Of social forms" and ends with the figured poet turning to birds, flower, bees, and leaves before the poem trails off (PN, 5; *Poems,* 313; emphasis added).

The primary difficulty Emerson confronts is how to enact and make visible in poetic form the process by virtue of which idleness, solitude, and the elements of nature can resist public ridicule and, indeed, become signs of the public work of resisting cultural narratives. Emerson's letters from the period already sketch the strategy he would use in his prose; in a letter to his aunt from August 1827 (speaking negatively of a sermon he had heard), Emerson wrote that every man hides what is distinctive, so that "all his communications . . . are unskilful plagiarisms from the common stock of tho't & knowledge & he is, of course, flat and tiresome" (L, 1: 207). The letter continues, "To *ask* questions, is what this life is for" (L, 1: 208). The shifts of perspective and definition in the prose make asking, rather than answering, questions Emerson's characteristic pose so that he can, in the suggested *process,* represent his voice (or voices) as speaking for or as a higher force or energy. As he would write in his journals, "Man is great not in his goals but in his transition from state to state. Great in act . . ." (JMN, 4: 327).[104] In the prose, the enactment of thought that claims a high authorization is how passivity, solitude, and the observation of nature yield a power and agency that Emerson can also claim is not self-indulgent or, to use another of his terms, not egotism.[105]

The "common stock" of poetic poses in the 1826–1827 poetry fragment, however, do not so easily avoid ridicule. The natural description that ends the piece suggests that what the poet in retreat found was not so easily represented, and certainly not in catalogues of flowers, tuneful bird, and busy bee:

> . . . another year of flowers,
> Once more to be the food of tuneful bird
> Low stooping on swift wing, or busy bee,
> Or the small nameless eaters that can find
> A country in a leaf.—
> (PN, 6; *Poems,* 314)

Even his final image—of finding a "country in a leaf," a potential emblem of the divinity available in local detail and thus available to the would-be poet in an American landscape—ends the blank verse fragment abruptly, with the hexameter line. Neither the poem's images nor its movement, it seems, provided an adequate representation of what justifies the poetic "dreamer."

By 1834, in "The Rhodora," the justification for flowers, birds, and natural beauty is far more clearly articulated, drawing in part on arguments spelled out in lectures such as "The Naturalist" or the series on "English Literature," as well as prefiguring arguments spelled out in *Nature,* on which Emerson would begin work within nine months of completing "The Rhodora." Interestingly, the structure of the poem is still from "the common stock" of poetic tradition in that the poem is an extended, sixteen-line sonnet in pentameter quatrains.[106] Indeed, some of the power of the poem depends on Emerson's effective use of literary tradition and of the sonnet's conventions, especially the turn. "The Rhodora" begins with natural description in a solitary setting and shifts after what is in effect the octave to an apostrophe claiming presence and voice within that setting. The apostrophe also echoes and revises another traditional voice, that of Gray's "Elegy," when it asks whether the flower's "charm is wasted on the earth and sky." Unlike Gray's, Emerson's flower does not waste its sweetness on the desert air, although the counterargument of the poem on the uses of natural beauty is complicated.

Emerson's poetic voice takes command ("Tell them," the third quatrain instructs, and then speaks for, the flower). The expected sonnet turn, then, is doubled as the speaker claims both power and humility in the final three lines, where the poem's voice shifts again and insists the speaker "never thought to ask" but "suppose[d]" in "ignorance" that the answer to the question posed involves a higher power directing both poet and flower. The argument of the poem, paraphrased, is quite similar to Emerson's move from nature to beauty and eventually to spirit in the 1836 *Nature:* nature "always speaks of Spirit. It suggests the absolute" and becomes the occasion for "influx of the spirit" (*CW/RWE,* 1: 37, 45). Moreover, the end of the poem echoes both early figurations of the poet as passively awaiting an influx of power and the well-known moment of Emersonian sublimity from *Nature,* in which he writes of how, crossing the "bare common . . . without having in my thoughts any occurrence of special good fortune, I have enjoyed a perfect exhilaration. . . . Standing on the bare ground . . . —all mean egotism vanishes. I become a transparent eye-ball. I am nothing. I see all" (*CW/RWE,* 1: 10).

As critic Carolyn Porter has pointed out, *Nature* served Emerson's attempt to remove what he called "the yoke/Of social forms," to uncover an active reality, and to formulate a metaphysics on which he could stand, with these philosophical ends serving also to authorize and inaugurate his career outside of traditional institutions.[107] This strategy raises questions, not least because Emerson's metaphysics, as in his early journal entries about poetry and history, threaten to subsume nature under other categories such as idealism and so to erase what in one sense he was originally trying to justify. Further, spirit, as Porter also notes, becomes both *telos,* or nature's referent, and original energy source, which as energy renders all readings of nature provisional.[108] Finally, in *Nature,* the visionary, like the poet in "The Rhodora," is both power source (speaking for and commanding the flower; seeing all) and instrument (the voice answers questions by assuming a pose of unself-conscious humility; the "I" who sees all is also "nothing"). While critics such as Porter frame the contradictions in Emerson's thought in terms of his public career, it is worth pointing out how similar contradictions inform Emerson's poetic ambitions in "The Rhodora."

Unlike the essays, however, "The Rhodora" presents itself in part as a closed and traditional form, although a form that is used effectively. For example, the line break between lines fifteen and sixteen allows Emerson to have his cake and eat it too, as the penultimate two lines disclaim agency even while they are full of self-assertion. Lines fourteen and fifteen read as follows: "*I* never thought to ask, *I* never knew;/But, in *my* simple ignorance, suppose" (emphasis added). The line break after line fifteen as well as the internal repetition also make the final line—"The self-same Power that brought me there brought you"—read as unqualified assertion, despite the representation of the "I" as mere instrument. Similarly, the echo of the sonnet form allows the syntax of the last two lines to form a concluding couplet (given the semicolon that stops the poem after line fourteen and the strong enjambment in lines fifteen and sixteen). At the same time, the use of quatrains links the central question posed in line thirteen, which opens the last quatrain, with line sixteen, which concludes both poem and quatrain with the answer to that question. Thus, Emerson's characteristic prose stance, the disclaiming of answers, is complicated by the poetic form he uses. We are left with the impression that the speaker of this poem has wisdom and speaks with authority.

Or, rather, Emerson seems to have it both ways. In part because of the crafty uses of poetic conventions, the voice can authoritatively disclaim authority and offer a supposition that arrives, certainly to late-twentieth-century ears, almost as sentimental piety (although that was clearly not Emerson's intention). In his lectures on "English Literature" from the same period in which he wrote "The Rhodora," Emerson explicitly links the respect accorded a poet and the ability to see poetry as more than ornamental with the poet's ability to speak *not* for himself but for a higher power (EL, 1: 273). "The Rhodora" authorizes itself and its solitary poet idling in nature similarly, marking the humility of the speaker as a prerequisite for the influx of power. The poem is thus a poetic enactment of *Nature*'s "I am nothing. I see all." The manipulation of traditional form—and of the readerly expectations the form invokes—also allows the poetic speaker of "The Rhodora" to claim power under the guise of disclaiming egotism, to end with assertion while still proclaiming (to quote *Nature*) that "a guess is often more fruitful than an indisputable affirmation" (*CW/RWE*, 1: 39), and to move from an apparently ornamental landscape to the final, epiphanic line.

Six months after composing "The Rhodora," Emerson recorded his vow "not to utter any speech, poem, or book that is not entirely & peculiarly my work" and in particular not to attend to occasion, audience expectations, or the desire "to make a good appearance" (JMN, 4: 335). At the same time, his lectures on "English Literature"—in which his canon was culled in large part from Thomas Warton's *History of English Poetry*—announced, "The truth is all works of literature are Janus faced and look to the future and to the past. . . . There never was an original writer. Each is a link in an endless chain" (EL, 1: 284). So, too, "The Rhodora" is Janus faced and thus attentive to its imagined audience, to whom the poem offers a redefinition of the poet in nature—a redefinition called forth precisely by contemporary attitudes about the uselessness of poetry—by means of the poem's links to the sonnet tradition. At least in verse, it seems the mantle of eloquence was related to the yoke of poetic form, if not to the yoke of social forms Emerson said he wanted to throw off. Moreover, while "The Rhodora" justifies the higher calling of the poet in rural retreat, it does not represent any public role for itself. In any event, although "The Rhodora" does reposition poetic power, Emerson did not rest content with its strategy for assuming a bardic voice from a culturally suspect position.

On the few occasions when Emerson wrote verse specifically for a public forum he particularly worried his poems did not adequately represent poetry's public value to a contemporary American audience. Such occasions highlighted the differences between poetry and oratory. As a poet, Emerson felt that every "*public* work" he had written was "noted at the time as a failure" (JMN, 4: 316; emphasis added). The comment has a specific context. In the summer of 1834, Emerson was commissioned to write a poem for the Phi Beta Kappa Society, one of the few times in his adult life he wrote poetry for a particular occasion or for oral presentation (which allies the poem with the lectures he had been giving). This uniquely public poem drops most of the features of the poetry Emerson wrote in his journals or poetry notebooks or described in his lectures. While the *Boston Daily Advertiser* of August 29 found the piece "interesting, relating to topics of a general nature connected with our country" (*L*, 1: 417n), his brother Charles was critical; Emerson himself never reprinted the poem. The occasion and the expectation of a civic subject matter, combined with Emerson's earlier questions about what authorized poetry, seem to have prompted a self-consciousness about the ways past and present might conspire to make the public poet seem a mouthpiece for less than divine outside powers.

The Phi Beta Kappa poem awkwardly merges images of an American natural landscape with those of a heroic poet within a national progress poem that lists civic heroes such as Columbus, Lafayette, Washington, and Webster.[109] The poem also includes a contemporary public vocabulary (patriots, references to "the state" and "the law") and transmutes both "state" and "law" to inner qualities. However, unlike the poetic spirit of *Nature*—who builds a house, a world, a heaven and is instructed to "Build . . . your own world"—the "true man" in the final line of the Phi Beta Kappa poem is promised only that he shall "greet with joy sublime the Angel Death," hardly a figure of present power (*CW/RWE*, 1: 45; *Poems*, 356). Faced with a live audience for his poetry, Emerson shifts to a public vocabulary and imagines his private poet dead. While by 1839, in his second lecture on "Literature," Emerson would link elegy with discontent and so with a "prediction of . . . recovery" (EL, 3: 237), the elegiac ending of the Phi Beta Kappa poem seems more a failure of imagination than a call for recovery.

The journals link this failed poetic attempt with Emerson's growing awareness that it was not so easy in poems to write only one's own thoughts as opposed to "merely the tune of the time" or "the newspapers," on the one hand, or "the images of Byron, Shakespear," on the other (JMN, 4: 315). Both the contemporary public and the literary past, in other words, construct the self. In poems, being one's self is especially fraught. Turning to the past has its dangers: the endless chain of poets figured in books such as Warton's *History* and claimed in the lectures on "English Literature" may have allowed Emerson to hear himself as a poet, but it equally threatened to make poems into dead letters—"the sepulchres of the fathers," as he would put it in *Nature* (*CW/RWE*, 1: 7; see also JMN, 7: 276). Moreover, Emerson suggests that the written self is also always aware of an audience and so constantly shaped by its social position: "Be genuine. So wrote I for my own guidance months & years ago but how vainly! . . . The child is sincere, and the man when he is alone, *if he be not a writer,* but on the entrance of the second person hypocrisy begins" (JMN, 4: 314; emphasis added).

A month after the unsatisfactory Phi Beta Kappa poem, Emerson's journal returns to the question of how the poetic self and the public are related: "The poet writes for readers he little thinks of. Persons whom he could not bear, & who could not bear him, yet find passages in his works which are to them as their own thoughts" (JMN, 4: 323). The distinction between public oral performance and private composition to be read by unseen individuals again suggests the difficulties of writing poems rather than lecturing about poetry. Insofar as thinking of poems as *written* performances could help remove the poet from the cultural narratives of the day, it also removed him from the sense that he might matter in the present. The present power of poetry, then, remained a question apparently more readily talked *about* in the theory and rhetoric of the prose than embodied in actual poems. As Emerson wrote of the bard in "Woodnotes I," a poem composed in 1835–1836 and first published in *The Dial* in 1840, "For this *present,* hard/Is the fortune of the bard" (*Poems,* 35; emphasis added).

"Woodnotes I"—for which Emerson salvaged a few lines from the Phi Beta Kappa poem—returns as well to the problem of how to justify and make visible what the poet has to offer: "What he knows nobody wants" (*Poems,* 35; see PN, 973). The claim is one the poem's speaker tacitly challenges through the four sections of the poem, which nonetheless culminates in an elegiac gesture, also recalling the end of the Phi Beta Kappa poem. The bard's speech is reported in the final section of the poem. The bard claims a close relationship with nature, saying even in death flowers will not "scorn to cover/The clay of their departed lover" (*Poems,* 39). These lines conclude the poem. The move is not unlike Bryant's: the land is made into a monument, while the harmony between nature and the poet, who speaks for the land, is (proleptically) elegiac. The poem unfolds in part, then, like an ode, as Paul Fry has characterized odes in English.[110] It begins as invocation, seeking an originary voice, a presence or poetic voice in the present; the poem then attempts ironically or dialectically to defer the failure its opening (on the present lack of bards) already anticipates. In "Woodnotes I," the poem's attempt to imagine "what [the poet] is" (*Poems,* 36) unfolds as an exemplary biography of a life lived in nature, the voice of the biographer making the private poet into a "*public* child of earth and sky" (*Poems,* 38; emphasis added). However, the poem also encounters the drawback of all biographies: it can only conclude with the poet's imagined death. Despite the poem's attempt to reinscribe the value of its natural description— the poet becomes "Caesar of his leafy Rome" (*Poems,* 35) in another transvaluation of what might count as power—the poet's power is imagined as a function of his death.

"Woodnotes I" does not explicitly acknowledge its relationship to Bryant's "Thanatopsis," which Emerson's journals make clear he knew well. But it is useful to compare the elegiac gestures of "Thanatopsis" and "Woodnotes I." Juxtaposing Bryant *and* Wordsworth with Emerson further illuminates the multiple ways in which Emerson's Janus faced poetry positions itself. For writers such as Thomson, Wordsworth, or to a lesser extent Shelley, poetry might seem a closed canon. For Emerson, it was the heroic and revolutionary age of American history that seemed closed; American literature seemed more a blank page. While many of the essays turn to just this openness to call forth a new, literary revolution, blankness itself (especially given the not particularly American nature of traditional poetic tropes, which then seemed doubly irrelevant in Jacksonian America) posed difficulties for the would-be poet. Emerson could proclaim that the "greatness of Greece [is] that no Greece preceded it" (JMN, 7: 280), but he also struggled with the fact that he had no living American tradition in which he could imagine inserting himself. Or rather, more to the point, from the perspective of the English tradition he admired, American literature seemed unwritten. Thus, Wordsworth's unwillingness to accept Emerson's language as English, in the 1841 letter already cited, might be seen as a sign of the younger writer's success in forging a new voice; at the same time, it also is a sign of one element informing Emerson's doubled consciousness.

Like Jefferson in his attempt to write the American landscape, then, Emerson had several audiences. From the perspective of New England, he did have the tradition of poets such as Bryant and Sigourney, in whose work the public power of poetry was sublimated in the figure of the solitary elegiac and elegized poet under his classic oak. Emerson's essays refigure the relationship between private poetry and public work found in poems such as "Thanatopsis" or "The Mother of Washington," which monumentalize and bury rather than engage or resist public culture. Yet the Phi Beta Kappa poem and "Woodnotes I" reiterate the elegiac nature of poetry's engagement with American nature and nationhood. In 1844, when he negatively characterizes American poetry and Bryant's work in particular as "thin" (JMN, 9: 83), Emerson implies that there is no poetic tradition to give a local resonance to Bryant's recycled graveyard poem; the comment also suggests that Bryant offers no way to link the solitary poet in nature with a living purpose.

By the forties, Emerson in his essays had found strategies by which he might reanimate inherited figures of poetic production; indeed, part of what motivated the prose was his attempt to imagine how to matter as a poet. Although just before he published his essays in 1841 he described the book as a kind of "*apology* to my country for my apparent idleness," the essays placed in public circulation a complicated defense of such idleness.[111] Such thinking informed his poetic practice, as well, and the poems from the forties reflect a new confidence and lightness of touch. Thus, between 1841 and 1844, Emerson wrote "The Poet's Apology"—published as "The Apology" in 1847. He tells his readers: "Tax not my sloth that I/Fold my arms beside the brook," and he adds, "Chide me not, laborious band,/For the idle flowers I brought" (*Poems*, 90).[112] Emerson's confidence in the poem may not be derived simply from the defense of poetry launched in the essays. It is not accidental that the direct address to the reader, the tetrameter, and the tropes of misunderstood poetic idleness recall Wordsworth's "A Poet's Epitaph," the same poem that Shelley marked as one of the poems by Wordsworth that most appealed to him. By 1831, Emerson also singled out the poem, specifically citing the lines on how the poet is received ("You must love him ere to you/He will seem worthy of your love") and Wordsworth's stanza on the poet as an idler in the land, enjoying "things which others understand" (JMN, 3: 305).

Emerson also, like Shelley, protested that Wordsworth's last stanza was "miserable."[113] Wordsworth concludes his poem with an invitation for the reader to "build thy house upon this grave." For Shelley, it was Wordsworth's insistence on poetry's political engagement and its opposition to professional, and especially legal or military, power that was attractive. For Emerson, it seems, Wordsworth's elevated description of the value of poetic labor in rural solitude and his acknowledgment of how the public missed or misunderstood that value was paramount; however he rejected as "miserable" the elegiac view of public power and the idea that the poet's constructive legacy was not living. Indeed, one wonders if the instruction to readers with which *Nature* ends—to emulate poets and build their own houses in the *world*—is not in part a response to "A Poet's Epitaph." At the same time, Wordsworth apparently gave Emerson permission to write his own inscription poem, written on his imagined poet-self, not on an imagined grave.

Much later in his life Emerson suggested that the "vice of Wordsworth is that he is a lame poet: he can . . . rarely finish worthily a stanza begun well. He suffers from asthma . . . of the mind." (JMN, 16: 244). The criticism is not of "A Poet's Epitaph" in particular. However, it is related to the argument Emerson earlier voices both with Bryant's "thin-ness" and with the older English poet, from both of whom he also learned something about not monumentalizing poetry and about the ways in which he could and could not position himself as poet.

In sum, Emerson looked back to an American tradition, through Bryant, that represented the historical past as monumental and closed, while providing no sense of how poetry rather than other print forms might live and matter in an American present. While there was no American tradition closed to Emerson, poetic production was equally figured for him through the British tradition. Thus, he struggled with the same kinds of historical changes in the readership for poetry and the emerging separation between those who wrote poetry and those who exercised public power that affected British writers, as well as with the somewhat different question of whether his "endless chain" of poets—a closed book to Thomson or Wordsworth, for instance—had perhaps always been closed to American voices and landscapes.

The poetics of process and presence (not to mention the repeated suggestions that the new breed of American hero would be a poet) Emerson articulated in his prose attempt to reopen both national history and transnational poetry. The poems themselves, however, take longer to find a voice that sounds both engaged *and* like poetry. Typically, for all his calls for literary independence and ignoring the past, it is in his repetitions and translations of both the literary past and of his own past self-representations that Emerson finds the poetic voice he seems to have been seeking. Thus, for example, his earliest imagination of poetic power—hearing a voice issuing from an oak—which invokes both British and American tropes, is transposed in the 1840–1841 "Woodnotes II" in which he assumes the voice of a native Concord tree, the pine. The poem is one his letters call "The Pine-Tree" (or "Pinetree") before he published it as "Woodnotes II" (*L*, 2: 407, 442; see also *L*, 2: 409, 435). The poem not only becomes a gesture of *translatio,* adapting the classic oak; it also rewrites the elegiac "Woodnotes I." "Woodnotes II" figures the landscape and its transmitted power as pure voice with short, breathless, heavily enjambed lines, the chant-like use of anaphora, and the frequent use of questions; there is no grave of a past bard on which the voice rests its claim to power.

However interesting and confident as a poem, however, "Woodnotes II" is still not in any obvious way a poem that engages public issues. Moreover, whatever theories Emerson launched in his prose about how the private influx of spirit could be a form of public resistance, his world framed his poems somewhat differently. Pieces such as "The Poet's Apology" appeared in books such as *A Gift: A Christmas, New Year, and Birthday Present* (Philadelphia, 1845); they were packaged as sentimental (indeed, generic) gifts for any "special" occasion. Both of the "Woodnotes" poems, admittedly, appeared in *The Dial,* but by April 1844, *The Dial* had folded.

In the face of such events, Emerson in 1844–1845 wrote "Hamatreya," one of the poems in which he most successfully confronts the problem of how poetry might figure its claims to both poetic power and public relevance. Hafiz's poetry in particular, to which Emerson had turned with great interest in the mid-forties, offered Emerson a poetic voice that could (as his journal explained it) mix the "physical & metaphysical" (JMN, 9: 381) even as Hafiz's poetry still bespoke Horace and, later, Pindar and Burns (JMN, 9: 382), which is to say the odic voice of poetry in English that informed Emerson's ear for poetry need not be abandoned. Hafiz was probably also a vehicle for Emerson's often triangulated conversations with Fuller, whose 1844 review of Emerson's essays challenged him precisely to mix the physical and metaphysical. As Fuller wrote in the *New-York Daily Tribune:* "Here is . . . the man of ideas, but we want . . . the heart and genius of human life to interpret it. . . . We could wish he might be thrown by conflicts on the lap of mother earth, to see if he would not rise again with added powers."[114]

"Hamatreya" returns to the American landscape-as-grave but repositions its speaker, or rather speakers. The poem also attends to something like the sense of cultural particulars or of the local for which Fuller called.[115]

"Hamatreya" opens in blank verse, with images of Concord "landlords"; the tone at first is narrative, almost an historical chronicle in its lists of produce and landowners and images of farm labor. The tone, however, modulates by line six as the poem opens a dialogue between the narrator and the voice of the farmers, who claim almost a Lockean view of property—they have mixed their labor with the land—even as they voice a Wordsworthian appreciation of nature: "I fancy these pure waters and the flags/Know me, as does my dog: we sympathize."[116] With the entry of a third position, that of the earth beneath which the narrator has already positioned the farmers, the poetic voice and meter change: "'Mine and yours;/Mine, not yours./Earth endures;/Stars abide—.'" The earth mockingly (and punningly) suggests "'the lawyer's deed/Ran sure, In tail'" only to be interred along with the laws and heirs. The narrator returns in a final, rhymed, quatrain:

> When I heard the Earth-song,
> I was no longer brave;
> My avarice cooled
> Like lust in the chill of the grave.

The subject positions—and the poetic authorization—in "Hamatreya" unsettle many of Emerson's earlier representations of poetry. For one thing, the poetic speaker is not so much visited with an influx of spirit as deflated by the song, which at least tentatively equates commercial and personal possession with poetic ambition. In any event, the speaker initially distances himself ("the hot owner sees not Death") from the farmers' lists of crops *and* their love of place, including the flowers with which they, to some degree like the speaker in "The Rhodora," feel at one. Thus the only form of avarice or courage the speaker can be disclaiming in the last three lines seems to be his own as moderator, or as one who can speak for others. At the same time, of course, Emerson inserts the earth's chant-like song, subtitled, as if it is not the speaker's. Yet even this metanarration does not suggest a constructive so much as a deconstructive spirit or oneness. The poem from one perspective, then, again equates poetic, historical, and for that matter political or legal "deeds" by suggesting that all inheritances are nothing; it reverses the Emersonian sublime to propose "I see all. I am nothing."

"Hamatreya" thus is in part a reply to Fuller: touching the earth, Emerson arises with something quite other than the renewal of power Fuller predicted. The higher voice Emerson so often seeks does not so much affirm there is nothing *other* as negatively redefine the poetic self as *nothing*. The last line, indeed, has a chilling resonance coming as it does from a man who admitted he opened his wife's coffin a year after she died (JMN, 4: 7). On the other hand, out of this failure to become the kind of poetic vehicle or oracle he earlier imagined Emerson makes some of his most moving poetry. If physical possessiveness (avarice or lust) is set against a motion that overturns everything, the poem also counters any elegiac tendencies. In "Hamatreya," the land is no longer the grave of Sigourney, Bryant, or later Wordsworth in that it is not monumentalized or sealed-off but rather reanimated as odic voice. Moreover, despite the discredited personal pronouns that ring in the farmers' words, the blank verse of the farmers—"How sweet the west wind sounds in my own trees!/How graceful climb those shadows on my hill"—like the slight echo of Marvell's "To His Coy Mistress" (in which the anaphrodisiac tendencies of the grave become a call to seize the day) leaves the debate between the physical and the metaphysical (and between the historical and the universal) unsettled.

"Hamatreya" thus renegotiates the boundaries between high poetic power and public concerns, both in its series of voices in debate and in its content. Certainly the greed for land and land ownership were current political and public topics. They were also topics that concerned Emerson, as the "Ode, Inscribed to W. H. Channing," on the war against Mexico, or as Emerson's stands against the Cherokee Removal Act and against slavery make clear. (His 1840 lecture on "Reforms" ends a list of the issues of the day with "treatment of Indians" and "Boundary Wars" [EL, 3: 257].) But by Emerson's day, it was clear that no poem would do much to change public policy. Wordsworth may have mailed poems to Fox; Emerson's public stand on the Cherokee Removal Act came in the form of a public letter to the president (published in a Washington newspaper), just as his increasing involvement in antislavery and then abolitionist activities came primarily in the form of lectures.[117] "Hamatreya," then, does not so much set out to use poetry for a specific platform as to assume poetic power in a way that clearly invokes and tries to subsume public issues, even as the poem worries over the way poetic ambition may thus mimic the public vices it tries to counter. That "Hamatreya" succeeds more as poetry than as political action, thus, does not suggest the poem is apolitical, nor that Emerson's poet was disengaged. Rather, in the poem Emerson makes visible his attempts to claim multiple identities that his culture increasingly inscribed as mutually exclusive.

In particular, Emerson's repeated attempts to transvalue notions of private and public, and poetic and civic, selves bespeak his own growing awareness of the ways in which he would not settle such issues. Earlier, in 1827, he had written to his brother Charles that the self constructed in writing was more genuine than the self in performance: "Speak, that I may suspect thee; write, that I may *know* thee" (*L*, 1: 191). By the end of the same year, he had already revised the claim: "As you exist to yourself & as you exist to me, you are two persons" (*L*, 1: 214). Within a decade, Emerson was less certain people could exist in writing, even to themselves, in any way that sequestered them from public narratives. Having nonetheless in 1834 attempted to hold to his view that anything done to please others "is a parenthesis in your genuine life" (JMN, 4: 335), he returned in 1844 or 1845, the period in which "Hamatreya" was written, to suggest "how different is it to render account to ourselves of ourselves & to render account to the public of ourselves" (JMN, 9: 123). The comment is followed with a quotation from Wordsworth's *Excursion,* and the task, once again, seems how to present himself in poetry as poet and still body forth the active poet imagined and justified as public hero in the lectures and essays. The problem is especially complicated given Emerson's intimations of the multiplicity of selves positioned in public and in private, in writing and in performance, in thought and in action, in poetry and in prose. Although such intimations fuel some of Emerson's best poems, his own historical and biographical position may at the same time have made it—and may still make it—difficult for his readers to see him as an Emersonian "poet" in his poems.

Certainly by the time the 1847 *Poems* appeared, Emerson was known publicly because of his (by then) two published collections of essays and his brief editorial association with *The Dial* as well as because of his status as a public speaker and as Carlyle's American promoter, not to mention a growing reputation abroad. Indeed, this reputation may explain why his poems went through four printings in one year. Although the book yielded a profit of just under a hundred and fifty dollars in the first year, this was far less than his lectures earned. Moreover, although reviewers praised his imagination, they found Emerson's poetry obscure and uncanonical.[118] *The Boston Courier,* for instance, deemed the entire volume "most peculiar" (L, 3: 366). Despite the apparent success of *Poems,* then, Emerson still made his livelihood, his reputation, and his mark as a man of letters, not of verse.

The poems in the 1847 volume are still in mixed voices—from "The Rhodora," "Woodnotes I," and "Woodnotes II" to his uses and appropriations of Hafiz to the more politically engaged "Ode: Inscribed to W. H. Channing" or "Hamatreya." The volume that opens with "The Sphinx" tellingly ends with the Concord "Hymn," which may well be one of the most successful public poems of Emerson's era but also, like "The Mother of Washington," vests its authority in its elegiac, deferential celebration and reification of a monument to what is past. Emerson's motive for ending his book with the "Hymn" may well parallel his motive for first ending *Essays: Second Series* with the lecture "New England Reformers" so that the essays move from "The Poet" to reform, enacting a "transformation of genius into practical power" (*CW/RWE,* 3: 49). However, although to some degree like the act of concluding a volume of essays with a lecture, ending *Poems* with the public voice of "Hymn" changes the genre within which readers position and understand the speaking voice and so the kind of poet Emerson could represent himself as being. In his 1840 lecture on "Private Life," Emerson wrote, "What is our . . . literature . . . but endless reproduction of what was immortal in the past, that is, of what was truly alive before? Indeed what is our own being but a reproduction, a representation of all the past?" (EL, 3: 251). The problem he describes is what kind of self can write with the living presence imagined for the past and still be poetry in the present.

Continuing Conversations

Thomson, Wordsworth, and Shelley placed themselves within literary history even as they failed in their attempts to matter within history more literally conceived. On one reading, Emerson could be said to reverse this pattern, that is, to have attempted to matter in literary history only to find himself more often credited (or damned) for his historical importance: he is the first American professional intellectual; he may well have helped craft therapeutic culture; he certainly is remembered less as poet than as someone who talked about poetry; for those who have read his poems, Emerson is most often remembered as a phrase monger, for lines such as "the shot heard round the world," or for the ways his poems circulated in gift books, as they to this day can be found excerpted on sketch pads or sentimental gift items.

If Emerson became fashionable, however, one cannot conclude that this was either intended or inevitable; his own dismissive remarks about "fashionists" (for example, in *L*, 2: 48 and *L*, 2: 385) and his vexed attempts to position his work both in and against the public sphere of his day suggest rather someone caught in the bind of his era, namely, how to make visible what he explicitly defined as not for show.[119] *Poems* was the only one of Emerson's books to be bound in white boards, but, again, this suggests mostly that (as with Barlow) Emerson had not changed the vexed status of poems in American print culture. Admittedly, without the same self-consciousness he brought to the "peddling" of his lectures, Emerson wrote to the prospective publisher of his poems that he had heard "a large proportion of purchasers prefer in works of this kind a costlier style of book. Perhaps then it would be better for author & readers to print a costlier edition first" (*L*, 3: 88, 308). Such attention to the market for poetry again mirrors Barlow's at the turn of the century. Barlow's and Emerson's gestures suggest a realistic acceptance of market conditions. Yet neither writer thereby accepted that their poems would become class markers or instruments in an economy of managed esteem. On the contrary, both assumed the active agency of their readers; Emerson in particular, like Shelley, assumed his readers would take his work to authorize their own acts of creative reading, not to mark their good taste.

It is, I think, an aptly ironic later emblem of Emerson's identity as poet that what one might think should be his *vade mecum,* the poem entitled "The Poet," is actually a series of manuscript drafts, first collected together in print under one title well after Emerson's death. "The Poet" as a poem by Emerson is then less a poem than a fiction or a creation of his readers.[120] Yet the essay "The Poet" was, and is, widely influential. Moreover, one portion of what editors took for "The Poet," a manuscript poem entitled "The Discontented Poet: A Masque," composed between 1840 and 1842, suggests the savvy with which Emerson continued to think about and in poetry, whatever his readers might have done with the readerly agency he offered them in his "little white book . . . whose fate the readers may now settle" (*L,* 3: 366).

The genre of "The Discontented Poet," the masque, was inherited from the Renaissance (and Milton). In particular, it was understood through Ben Jonson as merging soul and body; it was traditionally a public performance, involving those in public power within a poetic role. If for Shelley poets were to be the unacknowledged legislators of the world, for Emerson poets "should be lawgivers; that is, the boldest lyric inspiration should not chide and insult, but should announce and lead the civil code, and the day's work" (*CW/RWE,* 2: 136). What better forum for embodying this prose insight than a democratized masque?

In "The Discontented Poet" a solitary poet is positioned between the ideal or the dream and the real or the physical:

> . . . by false usage pinned about
> No breath therein, no passage out,
> Cast wishful glances at the stars
> And wishful hailed the Ocean stream,
> "Merge me in the brute Universe
> Or lift to some diviner dream."
> (*Poems,* 372)

"The Discontented Poet" ends again enacting a dialogue between poet and inner chorus, law and spirit. If the chorus is allowed the final word—"Put the Spirit in the wrong,—/That were a deed to sing in Eden,/By the waters of life to Seraphs heeding" (*Poems,* 373)—the title and form (not to mention that the chorus is mocking the poet's desire for closure) clearly present a conversation that is not over.[121]

So, too, Emerson's success and failure, like those of Thomson, Wordsworth, and Shelley, present *us* with continuing conversations over the public value of poetry and, indeed, over what role poetry as such might play within a culture of mass media and mass marketing of a sort Emerson would only dimly have been able to imagine. The question is, and has been, double-edged. On the one hand, the question is how, even whether, poems can engage public issues or transform public culture. Is a poem by definition *not* a forum or vehicle for public action? On the other hand, the question is whether public success is *ipso facto* not poetic: is engagement, or even publicity, something other than poetry (that is, something other than an essential ingredient of poems, rather than of the idea of poetry)? I have been suggesting that at least since the beginning of the modern era, these questions—as well as the inability to answer them and the need to keep asking them—have become part of the very substance of poetry. In 1866, in a journal entry used also for the 1868 essay "Originality & Quotation," Emerson wrote accepting the relationship between repetition and the natural forces he repeatedly characterized as the source of poetic power: "The thought, the literature, comes again, not because the man is servile, but because Nature is a repeater, & suggests the like truth to the new comer as to the ancient" (JMN, 16: 27). I have also been suggesting that it may be cultural forms and structures, not Nature, that repeat, and therefore, as Wallace Stevens would say, it may be the poet "is not the exceptional . . . /But he that of repetition is most master."

Notes

Introduction

1. See, for example, M.H. Abrams, *Natural Supernaturalism: Tradition and Revolution in Romantic Literature* (New York: Norton, 1971) or, also by Abrams, *The Mirror and The Lamp: Romantic Theory and the Critical Tradition* (New York: Norton, 1953).

2. See Mary Jacobus, *Tradition and Experiment in Wordsworth's* Lyrical Ballads (Oxford: Clarendon Press, 1976) [hereafter, Jacobus] or Anne Williams, *Prophetic Strain: The Greater Lyric in the Eighteenth Century* (Chicago: University of Chicago Press, 1984) [hereafter, *Prophetic Strain*].

3. I refer most generally to Bloom's *The Anxiety of Influence* (Oxford: Oxford University Press, 1973). For texts on changes in the production and distribution of (as well as the readership for) poetry, see Bertrand Harris Bronson, *Facets of the Enlightenment: Studies in English Literature and Its Contexts* (Berkeley: University of California Press, 1968) [hereafter, Bronson]; Jon P. Klancher, *The Making of English Reading Audiences, 1790–1832* (Madison: University of Wisconsin Press, 1987) [hereafter, Klancher]; Richard D. Altick, *The English Common Reader: A Social History of the Mass Reading Public, 1800–1900* (Chicago: University of Chicago Press, 1957) [hereafter, Altick]; Deborah D. Rogers, *Bookseller as Rogue: John Alman and the Politics of Eighteenth-Century Publishing* (New York: Peter Lang, 1986); Kathryn Shevelow, *Women and Print Culture: The Construction of Femininity in the Early Periodical* (London: Routledge, 1989) [hereafter, Shevelow]; Stuart Curran, *Poetic Form and British Romanticism* (Oxford: Oxford University Press, 1986) [hereafter, *Form*]; and Marilyn Butler, "Repossessing the Past: the Case for an Open Literary History," in *Rethinking Historicism,* ed. Marjorie Levinson et al. (Oxford: Basil Blackwell Ltd., 1989) [hereafter, "Repossessing"].

4. *Poetical Works,* pp. 240, 73. Unless otherwise noted, all quotations from Thomson are from *The Complete Poetical Works of James Thomson,* ed. J. Logie Robertson (London: Oxford University Press, 1908).

5. Butler, p. 59. Unless otherwise noted, all quotations from *The Ruined Cottage* and *The Pedlar* can be found in William Wordsworth, *The Ruined Cottage and The Pedlar,* ed. James Butler (Ithaca: Cornell University Press, 1979) [hereafter, Butler].

6. *A Defence of Poetry, Shelley's Prose or the Trumpet of a Prophecy,* ed. David Lee Clark (Albuquerque: The University of New Mexico Press, 1954) [hereafter, Clark], p. 297.

7. Ralph Waldo Emerson, *The Journals and Miscellaneous Notebooks of Ralph Waldo Emerson,* ed. William H. Gilman et al. (Cambridge: The Belknap Press of Harvard University Press, 1960–1982) [hereafter, *JMN*], volume 13, p. 236.

8. John Berryman, *The Dream Songs* (New York: Farrar, Straus and Giroux, 1969), Dream Song 231, p. 250.

9. William Wordsworth, *The Prose Works of William Wordsworth,* ed. W. J. B. Owen and Jane Worthington Smyser (Oxford: Clarendon Press, 1974) [hereafter, *PrW*], volume III, p. 125. The open letter, which appeared in pamphlet form in 1816, is reprinted in *PrW,* volume III, pp. 117–29.

10. E. P. Thompson, "Disenchantment or Default? A Lay Sermon" in *Power and Consciousness,* ed. Conor Cruise O'Brien and William Dean Vanech (New York: New York University Press, 1969) [hereafter, Sermon], pp. 149–81.

11. William H. Galperin, *Revision and Authority in Wordsworth: The Interpretation of a Career* (Philadelphia: University of Pennsylvania Press, 1989) [hereafter, Galperin].

12. Quotations from Shelley's poetry can be found in Percy Bysshe Shelley, *Shelley's Poetry and Prose,* ed. Donald H. Reiman and Sharon B. Powers (New York: Norton, 1977) [hereafter, Shelley].

13. Wallace Stevens, *The Collected Poems of Wallace Stevens* (New York: Knopf, 1954), p. 406.

14. See, for instance, Quentin Anderson's "Practical and Visionary Americans," *The American Scholar,* 45 (1976): 405–18 and Larzer Ziff's *Literary Democracy* (New York: The Viking Press, 1981).

15. For example, in the 1836 version of "Nature" (chapter eight, "Prospects") Emerson argues that "a fact is true poetry" after suggesting that even scientific facts are best uncovered by poetic dreams: "a dream may let us deeper into the secret of nature than a hundred concerted experiments." Ralph Waldo Emerson, *The Collected Works of Ralph Waldo Emerson,* ed. Robert E. Spiller, Alfred R. Ferguson, et al. (Cambridge: The Belknap Press of Harvard University Press, 1971) [hereafter, *CW/RWE*], volume I, pp. 44, 39.

16. "Power," from Ralph Waldo Emerson, *The Conduct of Life* (1860).

17. John Jay Chapman, "Emerson, Sixty Years Later," *The Atlantic Monthly,* LXXIX (January-February 1897): 27–41; 222–40; selected and reprinted in Merton M. Sealts, Jr. and Alfred R. Ferguson, eds., *Emerson's 'Nature'* (Toronto: Dodd, Mead & Company, Inc., 1969), p. 123.

18. In particular, as I hope the following chapters will make clear, I do not mean to dismiss critical accounts of the narrowness of the canon, especially English Romanticism's "six male poets," as Anne K. Mellor describes it in "On Romanticism and Feminism," *Romanticism and Feminism,* ed. Anne K. Mellor (Bloomington: Indiana University Press, 1988), pp. 3–9.

Chapter I

1. *The Background of Thomson's* Seasons (Minneapolis: University of Minnesota Press, 1942) [hereafter, *Background*], p. vi.

2. Any in-depth examination of eighteenth-century poetics would need to begin with Ernest Lee Tuveson, *The Imagination as a Means of Grace: Locke and the Aesthetics of Romanticism* (Berkeley: University of California Press, 1960) [hereafter, *Grace*]; Marjorie Hope Nicolson, *Mountain Gloom and Mountain Glory: The Development of the Aesthetics of the Infinite* (Ithaca: Cornell University Press, 1959) [hereafter, Nicolson]; Samuel Holt Monk, *The Sublime: A Study of Critical Theories in XVIII-Century England* (New York: Modern Language Association of America, 1935); as well as with numerous books and articles by M. H. Abrams, Walter Jackson Bate, Martin Price, Pat Rogers, Geoffrey Tillotson, and Earl Wasserman, to name a few of the seminal writers on the period. I draw throughout on John Barrell's *English Literature in History, 1730–80: An Equal, Wide Survey* (New York: St. Martin's Press, 1983) [hereafter, Barrell].

3. For a contemporary view of Milton as a politically engaged writer, see Samuel Johnson, *Lives of The English Poets,* ed. George Birkbeck Hill (Oxford: Clarendon Press, 1905) [hereafter, *Lives*], volume I, pp. 116–19, 157. See also Douglas Grant, *James Thomson: Poet of "The Seasons"* (London: The Cresset Press, 1951) [hereafter, Grant], pp. 177–78 on Thomson's republication of two Miltonic tracts in opposition to Walpole's (1738) domestic and foreign policies.

4. On Thomson's use of earlier writers, see Martin Price, *To the Palace of Wisdom: Studies in Order and Energy from Dryden to Blake* (Garden City, N.Y.: Doubleday and Company, Inc., 1964) [hereafter, *Palace*], pp. 352–53; *Background,* pp. 7–9, 13–16, *et passim;* Ralph Cohen, *The Art of Discrimination: Thomson's* The Seasons *and the Language of Criticism* (Berkeley: University of California Press, 1964) [hereafter, *Art*], p. 21ff.; and Ralph Cohen, *The Unfolding of* The Seasons (Baltimore: The Johns Hopkins Press, 1970) [hereafter, *Unfolding*], p. 92. See also Peter Hughes, "Allusion and Expression in Eighteenth-Century Literature," in *The Author in His Work: Essays on a Problem in Criticism,* ed. Louis L. Martz and Aubrey Williams (New Haven and London: Yale University Press, 1978), pp. 297–317.

5. See, for example, *James Thomson (1700–1748): Letters and Documents,* ed. Alan Dugald McKillop (Lawrence: University of Kansas Press, 1958) [hereafter, *Documents*], p. 52, and *Lives,* volume III, pp. 298–99.

6. Joseph Warton, *The Works of Virgil* (London: R. Dodsley, 1753), volume I, p. iii.

7. John Aiken, "An Essay on the Plan and Character of Thomson's Seasons," p. xxx. I quote from the edition of *The Seasons* printed by Robert Carr and published by Benjamin and Jacob Johnson in Philadelphia in 1804 [hereafter, Aiken]. For a full discussion of Aiken's and others' contemporary critical responses to this poem, see *Art,* pp. 88–94, 175–81, 388–95, *et passim.*

8. See, for example, *Palace,* pp. 360–64. See also *Unfolding,* p. 154, on the association between "Summer" and sublimity, as well as Grant, p. 112, on Thomson's use of Miltonic syntax. Mary Jane W. Scott, *James Thomson, Anglo-Scot* (Athens: The University of Georgia Press, 1988) [hereafter, Scott], p. 26, notes that Thomson probably owned a copy of *Paradise Lost* by the time he was a schoolboy.

9. Aiken, p. xxxiv.

10. Neither "Summer" nor *The Seasons* present a narrative or narrative action as such, and Thomson's poem was not in its day read as an epic per se. Virgil's *Georgics,* as Thomson himself notes in his preface to the second edition of "Winter," were a more obvious model (see *Art,* p. 119). For Addison's definition of epic, in his discussion of *Paradise Lost,* see *Spectator* no. 267 (5 January 1712) in Donald F. Bond, ed., *The Spectator* (Oxford: Clarendon Press, 1965) [hereafter, *Spectator*], volume II, pp. 537–44. On critical descriptions of the poem's unity and on the contexts in which "Summer" was read, in particular as a "test-case for unity," see *Art,* pp. 73–130, especially p. 92, and *Background,* p. 16.

11. Johnson clearly did not see *The Seasons* as an epic and complained of Thomson's "want of method" even while praising his descriptive genius (*Lives,* volume III, pp. 299, 298).

12. Swift to Charles Wogan (July–2 August 1732) in *The Correspondence of Jonathan Swift,* ed. Harold Williams (Oxford: Clarendon Press, 1963–65), volume IV, p. 53. For other comparisons between Thomson and Milton, see the 4 June 1726 *London Journal* review of "Winter" and the March 1728 article on Thomson in *The Present State of the Republick of Letters* (cited in Grant, pp. 54, 76).

13. See *Form,* pp. 86, 158–59, 174, and 181.

14. The description of *The Seasons* as "displaced epic" comes from Martin Price (*Palace,* pp. 352–53).

15. *The Poems of Thomas Gray, William Collins, and Oliver Goldsmith,* ed. Roger Lonsdale (New York: Longman, 1969) [hereafter, Lonsdale]; line numbers are from the "Ode on the Poetical Character," pp. 427–35. All quotations from the poetry of Gray and Collins can be found in this edition.

16. The quotation is from "The Argument" with which Thomson prefaced the 1746 edition of the poem (p. 52).

17. On transitions in the poem, see *Background,* p. 89; *Unfolding,* pp. 92–93, 132; and, more generally, John Barrell and Harriet Guest, "On The Use of Contradictions: Economies and Morality in the Eighteenth-Century Long Poem," in *The New Eighteenth Century: Theory, Politics, English Literature,* ed. Felicity Nussbaum and Laura Brown (London: Methuen, 1987), pp. 121–43, especially pp. 135, 143.

18. Aiken, p. xxxix.

19. Aiken, pp. xlvi–xlviii.

20. The suggestion comes from both John Barrell and John Williams, *Wordsworth: romantic poetry and revolution politics* (Manchester: Manchester University Press, 1989) [hereafter, JWilliams], especially chapter one.

21. Ronald Paulson, *Breaking and Remaking: Aesthetic Practice in England,
1700–1820* (New Brunswick: Rutgers University Press, 1989) [hereafter,
Breaking], p. 33, notes the century's attempt "to reconstitute an English art
of the contemporary (by which was meant business, credit, and upward mo-
bility, among other things)." Paulson draws on Michael McKeon, *The Ori-
gins of the English Novel, 1600–1740* (Baltimore: The Johns Hopkins Press,
1987) in his account of shifting definitions of the contemporary. See also
John Bender, *Imagining the Penitentiary: Fiction and the Architecture of Mind
in Eighteenth-Century England* (Chicago: University of Chicago Press,
1987), pp. 108–10, 114.

22. *The Works of Cowper and Thomson* (Philadelphia: J. Grigg, 1832) [hereafter,
C&T], p. 214.

23. *Lives,* volume III, p. 300.

24. *Documents,* p. 212. The pun on muses and amusement is one Thomson uses
several times in *The Seasons;* see, for example, the 1746 edition of "Summer"
(l. 283).

25. *Documents,* p. 36.

26. *Documents,* pp. 44–45.

27. The reference is also pointed out in *Documents,* p. 46. See *Prophetic Strain,*
p. 70, on Thomson's use of "Il Penseroso" in *The Seasons.*

28. *Lives,* volume I, p. 165.

29. For some contemporary disagreement on eighteenth-century allegory and
personification, see Patricia Meyer Spacks, *The Insistence of Horror: Aspects of
the Supernatural in Eighteenth-Century Poetry* (Cambridge: Harvard Univer-
sity Press, 1962), pp. 134–87; Paul S. Sherwin, *Precious Bane: Collins and the
Miltonic Legacy* (Austin: University of Texas Press, 1977) [hereafter, Sher-
win], pp. 98–99; and Earl R. Wasserman, "The Inherent Values of
Eighteenth-Century Personifications," *PMLA,* 65 (1950): 435–63 [here-
after, "Inherent Values"].

30. *C&T,* p. 185; but see also p. 336 where Cowper speculates that Homer
wrote allegory, which Cowper understands as meaning that "under the ob-
vious import of his stories lay concealed a mystic sense."

31. The "Preface" is reprinted in Thomson's *Poetical Works,* pp. 239–42.

32. The reference to Moses, like the later reference in the "Preface" to Job, also
draws on the eighteenth-century view of the scriptures as containing sublime
poetry. See also *Art,* p. 21.

33. Earl R. Wasserman, *The Subtler Language: Critical Readings of Neoclassic and
Romantic Poems* (Baltimore: The Johns Hopkins Press, 1959), pp. 169–88
and especially pp. 178–85 discusses the bifurcation of the moral and natural
foundations of poetry later in the eighteenth century, a split already forecast
by Thomson's uneasiness with his natural muse versus the more sublime
voices of past poets.

34. See *Art,* pp. 256, 267, and figures 3, 41.

35. The insects were "hornets" in earlier versions; the shift to gad-flies again em-
phasizes that this is not a naturalistic description of insects.

36. *Documents,* p. 52.

37. Thomson's views on the harmony of blank verse are found in a 1728 letter to Sir John Clerk, *Documents,* p. 59; see Josephine Miles, *Eras & Modes in English Literature* (Berkeley: University of California Press, 1957), pp. 56–57, on the linguistic characteristics of the sublime. It has been argued that Milton was normally read by the earlier eighteenth century as a poet of control and harmony, but the responses to Thomson's Miltonic music mention not only the negative lack of meaning but also, more positively, the "Energy" that "scorns to be controul'd" (by rhyme) in the poet's "bold, unfetter'd Lay" (*Documents,* pp. 53, 115). Once again, the image is of the solitary poet not in harmonious retirement but in sublime flight; the images are, Ronald Paulson notes, antithetical, although both are common in eighteenth-century writings on aesthetics (*Breaking,* p. 2).

38. Addison, in fact, complains of Milton's language—specifically of the repetition of the word "bound"—in the *Spectator,* no. 297 (9 February 1712), *Spectator,* volume III, p. 63.

39. Thomas Warton, *The History of English Poetry from the Eleventh to the Seventeenth Century* (1778; rpt. London: Alex. Murray and Son, 1870) [hereafter, *The History of English Poetry*], p. 512.

40. 10 October 1784 letter to Rev. William Unwin, *C&T,* p. 265.

41. *The Tatler,* ed. Donald F. Bond (Oxford: Clarendon Press, 1987), volume I, p. 80 [No. 9; 30 April 1709].

42. "Z" [Joseph Warton], *The Adventurer,* no. 63 (12 June 1753), (London: Printed for J. Payne, at Pope's Head in Pater-Noster Row; facsimile edition rpt. New York: AMS Press, 1968) [hereafter, *The Adventurer*], volume I, p. 374.

43. *The Adventurer,* no. 89 (11 September 1753), *The Adventurer,* volume II, p. 110. Specifically, Warton is trying to account for the wonders of ancient poetry (which he opposes to ancient reasoning or philosophy).

44. Furthermore, "truth" itself was increasingly seen as what was empirically verifiable and commonly shared, which were not the traits attributed to the visions of earlier poets, and especially not to Milton's (see *Lives,* volume I, pp. 170, 177–78, and Barrell, especially chapter two on the developing insistence on a common, and uniform, national language that promoted, among other things, British unity). On the relationship between the century's increasing emphasis on originality or first-hand experience and other literary virtues such as sincerity and immediacy, see Wallace Jackson, *Immediacy: The Development of a Critical Concept from Addison to Coleridge* (Amsterdam: Rodopi NV, 1973) [hereafter, Jackson]; Leon Guilhamet, *The Sincere Ideal: Studies on Sincerity in Eighteenth-Century English Literature* (Montreal: McGill-Queen's University Press, 1974) [hereafter, Guilhamet]; and Stephen D. Cox, *"The Stranger Within Thee": Concepts of the Self in Late-Eighteenth-Century Literature* (Pittsburgh: University of Pittsburgh Press, 1980) [hereafter, Cox], chapter two ("Eighteenth-Century Philosophies of Self"), pp. 13–34.

45. *Poetical Works,* p. 240.

46. *Marxism and Literature* (Oxford: Oxford University Press, 1977), especially pp. 45–54.

47. See Altick, pp. 43, 46–49, on Addison's importance and on the effect in general of periodicals, magazines, and their new readership.

48. *The History of English Poetry,* p. 330.

49. Joseph Warton, *An Essay on the Genius and Writings of Pope* (1756; fourth edition, London: J. Dodsley, 1782; facsimile edition rpt. New York: Garland Publishing Inc., 1970), volume I, pp. 208–9.

50. See David Hume, "Of Eloquence," *The Philosophical Works,* ed. Thomas Hill Green and Thomas Hodge Grose (Darmstadt: Scientia Verlag Aalen, 1964) [hereafter, *Philosophical Works*], volume III, p. 169, and John Sitter, *Literary Loneliness in Mid-Eighteenth-Century England* (Ithaca: Cornell University Press, 1982) [hereafter, Sitter], p. 39.

51. See W. Jackson Bate, *The Burden of the Past and the English Poet* (New York: Norton, 1972), p. 49, for the suggestion that eighteenth-century primitivism is an attempt to escape the burden of the past; and Joan Pittock, *The Ascendancy of Taste: the achievement of Joseph and Thomas Warton* (London: Routledge and Kegan Paul, 1973) [hereafter, Pittock], p. 29, on the growth of comparative and historical studies.

52. The ode was first printed in the 1748 edition of *Dodsley's Collection of Poems* (p. 432 in the Robertson edition of Thomson).

53. *C&T,* p. 265.

54. See *Background* throughout, but especially pp. 6–7.

55. *Documents,* p. 62.

56. Aiken, p. xxxi, emphasis his. For an account of description and narrative as stylistic modes in prose of the later eighteenth century, see Barbara M. Benedict, "Pictures of Conformity: Sentiment and Structure in Ann Radcliffe's Style," *Philological Quarterly,* 68 (Summer 1989): 363–77.

57. McKillop argues that in the early part of the century there was no line between the descriptive and the didactic; however, Rundle's comment suggests that the difference between early and mid-century views is one more of degree than of kind (*Background,* p. 4). See also Gordon McKenzie, *Critical Responsiveness: A Study of the Psychological Current in Later Eighteenth-Century Criticism* (Berkeley: University of California Press, 1949).

58. *The History of English Poetry,* p. 386.

59. On the natural sublime, see *Grace,* especially chapter three; on the conflicting views Thomson inherited, see *Background,* pp. 18–42.

60. While Thomson's descriptions of the natural world in his first poem do not usually rise to the unabashed psychological or visionary intensity of later poems like Gray's "The Bard," they are not simply the objective painting of rural beauty that many critics have found (see Jacobus, p. 109; *Palace,* p. 358). Joseph Warton's *Essay on the Genius and Writings of Pope* is the *locus classicus* for later eighteenth-century references to Thomson as a painter of nature (*Background,* p. 5).

61. The passage is reprinted in *Background,* p. 178.

62. *Documents*, p. 49.

63. *Documents*, p. 166.

64. See "Inherent Values," pp. 435–63, and Martin Price, "The Sublime Poem: Pictures and Powers," *Yale Review*, 58 (December 1968): 194–213 [hereafter, "The Sublime Poem"]. The rising interest in individual psychology and energy in which Thomson participates is also linked with the ideology of sensibility and the realities of a shifting economy, as Mary Poovey has pointed out in "Ideology and 'The Mysteries of Udolpho,'" *Criticism*, 21 (Fall 1979): 307–30 [hereafter, Poovey].

65. Letters from 1746 and 1748 make it clear that Thomson was following the growing fad of landscape gardening in England (*Documents*, pp. 185–87, 195–96). On Thomson's poetic landscapes and the picturesque, see *Background*, 75. James Sambrook, *The Eighteenth Century: The Intellectual and Cultural Context of English Literature, 1700–1789* (London: Longman Group Ltd., 1986) [hereafter, Sambrook], pp. 104–6, and *Background*, pp. 3, 7, 13–16, mention the various relationships between Milton's "Il Penseroso," Virgil's *Georgics* (clear sources of Thomson's meditations-in-retirement), theories of the sublime, and Thomson's landscapes. On the relationship between description and meditation—both in Thomson's work and more generally—see *Background*, p. 41; Ralph Cohen, "Association of Ideas and Poetic Unity," *Philological Quarterly*, 36 (October 1957): 465–74; and *Art*, pp. 131–87.

66. *Documents*, p. 16.

67. The phrases quoted are found in the last two lines of the concluding hymn added to *The Seasons*. See also *Palace*, pp. 352–53.

68. *A Treatise of Human Nature, Being an Attempt to Introduce the Experimental Method of Reasoning into Moral Subjects*, Book I, part iv, section 6 ("Of Personal Identity"), *Philosophical Works*, volume I, p. 540.

69. See *Grace*, throughout, but especially pp. 26, 93; *Palace*, pp. 79ff.; Cox, especially pp. 13–25; and Sitter, pp. 170–71. See also Christopher Fox, *Locke and the Scriblerians: Identity and Consciousness in Early Eighteenth-Century Britain* (Berkeley: University of California Press, 1988).

70. As Wallace Jackson notes, "man's essential identity had shifted from the plane of the social, civil existence, to that of the psychological" (Jackson, p. 83; see also *Grace*, pp. 144–45).

71. See Sitter, p. 71; Guilhamet, pp. 70–71; Pittock, pp. 71–72; and Cox, pp. 3, 7, 12.

72. "The Sublime Poem," pp. 194–213.

73. On the relationship between the natural and the rhetorical sublimes, see Nicolson, pp. 30–33, 300–1, 358–59, and Ernest Tuveson, "Space, Deity, and the 'Natural Sublime'," *Modern Language Quarterly*, 12 (1951): 20–38.

74. See, for instance, Gray's 1756 comment about perching like his bard "on Snowdon," in Thomas Gray, *The Letters of Thomas Gray, Including the Correspondence of Gray and Mason*, ed. Duncan C. Tovey, second revised edition

(London: George Bell and Sons, 1909–1912), volume I, p. 300; Johnson's complaint is in *Lives,* volume III, p. 438. See also *Palace,* p. 386. At the same time, as Stephen Cox has pointed out, theories of the natural sublime often complicated attempts to define the poetic self and its power, as poets found it sufficient to place their speakers in a "sublime" situation and then to focus on stock responses to such settings without evoking any sense of a particular self (Cox, pp. 52–53).

75. Sitter, p. 178; Jackson, p. 113.

76. In *Miscellanies of the Philobiblon Society,* volume IV (London. Printed by Charles Whittingham, 1857–58), p. 13.

77. *Documents,* p. 195.

78. *Poetical Works,* p. 240.

79. "Winter" [1730 edition], ll. 601, 630, 632–34.

80. Cox, pp. 8–9, 27–33, *et passim.* But see also Poovey, pp. 307–8, 311–14.

81. *Beyond Formalism: Literary Essays, 1958–1970* (New Haven: Yale University Press, 1970), p. 204.

82. See Barrell, pp. 51–79.

83. See, for example, Sitter, p. 95.

84. *Documents,* p. 136.

85. All quotations from Finch can be found in Anne Finch, Countess of Winchilsea, *Selected Poems,* ed. Denys Thompson (Manchester: Carcanet, 1987).

86. But see John Sitter's argument that many poems of mid-century, in their retreat from public concerns, do explicitly place poetry—with its felt lack of power—in the realm and under the auspices of the feminine (pp. 131–36). On Finch's relationship to a male (Miltonic) tradition, see Shevelow, p. 193, and Leslie E. Moore, *Beautiful Sublime: The Making of* Paradise Lost, *1701–1731* (Stanford: Stanford University Press, 1990), pp. 94–97.

87. Aiken, p. xlv.

88. *The History of English Poetry,* p. 438.

89. *Documents,* p. 76.

90. John Sitter notes that many eighteenth-century poets seem confused over whether poetry should soothe or rouse the passions (Sitter, p. 118).

91. See Pittock, p. 3; *Palace,* p. 95; Cox, pp. 8–9, 27–33; and Ronald Arbuthnott Knox, *Enthusiasm: A Chapter in the History of Religion, with Special Reference to the XVIIth and XVIIIth Centuries* (Oxford: Clarendon Press, 1950).

92. *Palace,* pp. 361–62. Aiken, p. xlix, is specifically discussing lines from the 1730 "Hymn" in the passage quoted.

93. The invocation of Milton's Lycidas and the image of soaring poetic power as "lonely" mark such passages as sublime, especially given Milton's status by the forties as *the* poet of the sublime (Sherwin, p. 8).

94. *Documents,* pp. 49–50.

95. Sambrook, p. 69. See *Documents,* p. 48, where Thomson writes to David Mallet that the "English People are not a little vain. . . . Britannia too includes our native Country, Scotland."

96. *Documents,* pp. 78, 79.

97. In "Liberty" Thomson portrays the kind of society he is urging his readers to maintain as a place in which there is "cheerful hurry, commerce many-tongued,/And art mechanic at his various task/Fervent employed" ("Liberty," I. ll. 182–84).

98. *Documents,* p. 83. Thomson's perspective is also linked to his status as a Scot (he writes of England, not Britain).

99. See Pat Rogers, "Introduction: the writer and society," *The Eighteenth Century* [*The Context of English Literature*], ed. Pat Rogers (New York: Holmes & Meier Publishers, Inc., 1978), pp. 3–4.

100. On progressivism and primitivism in Thomson, see Barrell, pp. 54–56; *Background,* pp. 89ff., especially pp. 106, 130; and Sherwin, pp. 84–85.

101. See Sitter, pp. 182–85.

102. See C. A. Moore, "Whig Panegyric Verse, 1700–1760: A Phase of Sentimentalism," *PMLA,* 41 (1926): 362–401 on Thomson's poem as a "Whig panegyric." "Whiggish" gestures are not restricted to those who were of the Whig party (Sitter, p. 105); the factions in eighteenth-century England might in any case more usefully be designated court and country parties (Sambrook, p. 86). See also Richard Feingold, *Nature and Society: Later Eighteenth-Century Uses of the Pastoral and Georgic* (New Brunswick: Rutgers University Press, 1978), pp. 5–7; and John W. Derry, *Politics in the Age of Fox, Pitt, and Liverpool: Continuity and Transformation* (New York: St. Martin's Press, 1990).

103. Herbert E. Cory, "Spenser, Thomson, and Romanticism," *PMLA,* 26 (1911): 51–91; Sitter, for example, mentions Pope (p. 94).

104. John Milton, "The Verse," introduction to the second (1674) edition of *Paradise Lost.*

105. See also Sambrook, p. 184, on this as a common association.

106. Collins's poem can be found in Lonsdale, pp. 488–91.

107. *Biographia Britannica,* ed. Andrew Kippis (second edition; London: Rivington and Marshall, 1789; rpt. Hildesheim and New York: Georg Olms Verlag, 1974), volume IV, p. 236 ("James Cook"). Sambrook's suggestion (p. 198) is seconded by the fact that the *Biographia Britannica* devotes one hundred and forty-five pages to Cook's entry.

108. *The Castle of Indolence,* II. LIV. l. 7; see also II. LII.

109. *Documents,* p. 74.

110. Sambrook, p. 79. The expansion of credit, government debt, stock, and paper money following the foundation of the Bank of England created new kinds of dependence, which some saw as preconditions for corruption. Others from Andrew Fletcher to Adam Smith constructed defenses of commerce. I am grateful to John Marshall for pointing out to me how appropriate it is that Scotland was the site of such theorizing, since Scotland, having given up independence in 1707 in order to gain commercial advantages, especially needed an account of how commerce would facilitate liberty, virtue, and sociability.

111. Sitter, p. 217.

112. Pittock, pp. 10, 103. I use the term "mass culture" sparingly to describe an emerging sense of a large, anonymous reading public, aware that there are difficulties in describing what constitutes a "mass" and that most critics would argue mass reading publics do not appear until about 1830, after the technological advances in paper making and printing of the early nineteenth century (for a succinct overview of the issues, see Patricia Anderson, *The Printed Image and the Transformation of Popular Culture, 1790–1860* [Oxford: Clarendon Press, 1991], especially pp. 9–11). Robert D. Mayo, *The English Novel in the Magazines, 1740–1815* (London: Oxford University Press, 1962), p. 2, details how Grub Street catered to a new taste for the sensational. See also Bronson, chapter two ("Strange Relations: The Author and His Audience," pp. 298–325, especially pp. 302–3); and Altick, pp. 30–66.

113. *Documents,* p. 13.

114. *Documents,* p. 98.

115. See Pittock, pp. 5–6, on Johnson's analysis of the *Spectator.*

116. *Documents,* pp. 105–6.

117. See Bronson, pp. 298–302, and Terry Belanger, "Publishers and writers in eighteenth-century England" [hereafter, Belanger], in *Books and Their Readers in Eighteenth-Century England,* ed. Isabel Rivers (Leicester: Leicester University Press, 1982), pp. 5–25.

118. *Documents,* p. 105.

119. *Documents,* p. 106. Thomson did not live in real poverty, but like all writers without a private income he had to depend on patronage for support. Intermittently, he did receive sinecures (ranging from 100 to 300 pounds a year). He was also reportedly often in debt and in need of gifts or loans from friends. See Grant, pp. 139, 147–86, 228–73.

120. Reprinted in *Documents,* p. 52. For over a century, *The Seasons* was the most popular poem in the English language (*Art,* p. 381). See also Sitter, p. 185, and *Lives,* volume III, pp. 289, 301, on the poor sales "Liberty" enjoyed.

121. On shifts in taste and class affiliations, see Pittock, p. 2.

122. *Documents,* p. 204.

123. Scott, pp. 204–42, *et passim,* suggests that as a Scot in London Thomson might have expected special difficulties.

124. See Bronson, pp. 303–7; and Cox, pp. 36–37. John Sitter describes the new literary contract as instituting what he calls "literary loneliness" (see, for example, pp. 9, 83–84, 103).

125. Altick, pp. 53–54; Belanger, pp. 5–25.

126. See Bronson, p. 305, on writing as a profession in the early eighteenth century.

127. *Documents,* pp. 200–1, 149–50.

128. *Documents,* p. 208.

129. See Altick, pp. 46–47.

130. 20 September 1729 letter in *Documents,* p. 65; 7 August 1735 letter in *Documents,* p. 95. Addison's complaint is from the *Spectator* (no. 62 [11 May

1711]), volume I, pp. 268–69. Thomson thus is both participant and instrument in the cultivation (or indoctrination) of a new readership.

131. *Documents,* p. 53. See *Documents,* p. 52; and *Art,* pp. 15, 100, 218–19, 315–80, *et passim,* for a discussion of criticisms of Thomson's style.

132. *Documents,* pp. 49–50.

133. The Goths came to be associated with the Druids as positive emblems of political liberty and of a native British taste, both of which Thomson defended even as he used the word "Goth" to refer to those who did not share his literary tastes. See Sambrook, pp. 181–84; Sherwin, p. 90; and Cox, p. 94.

134. For readings of Collins's poem, see especially Thomas Weiskel, *The Romantic Sublime: Studies in the Structure and Psychology of Transcendence* (Baltimore: The Johns Hopkins Press, 1976), pp. 124–35; Sitter, pp. 137–41; Sherwin, pp. 15–36.

135. See Sherwin, pp. 105–9.

136. See *Art,* throughout, but especially pp. 119–20, 132, 174, 183.

137. *C&T,* p. 270.

Chapter II

1. JWilliams, p. 50; Mary Moorman, *William Wordsworth, A Biography: The Early Years, 1770–1803* (Oxford: Oxford University Press, 1968) [hereafter, Moorman], p. 51; and Jonathan Wordsworth, *The Music of Humanity: A Critical Study of Wordsworth's RUINED COTTAGE* (New York: Harper and Row, Publishers, 1969) [hereafter, *Music*], p. 50.

2. *The Letters of William and Dorothy Wordsworth,* ed. Ernest De Selincourt; second revised edition, ed. Chester L. Shaver (volume I); Mary Moorman (volume II); Mary Moorman and Alan G. Hill (volume III); Alan G. Hill (volumes IV, V, VI, VII) (Oxford: Clarendon Press, 1967–1979) [hereafter, *Letters*], volume V, p. 3.

3. *PrW,* volume III, p. 73; see also *Letters,* volume V, p. 157, on Wordsworth's admiration of Thomson and Anne Finch.

4. For particularly compelling accounts of Wordsworth's readings of Milton, see, for example, Neil H. Hertz, "Wordsworth and the Tears of Adam," *Studies in Romanticism,* 7 (1967): 15–33 [hereafter, Hertz]; or Stuart Peterfreund, "'In Free Homage and Generous Subjection': Miltonic Influence on *The Excursion,*" *The Wordsworth Circle,* 9 (1978): 173–77.

5. *Aspects of Rhetoric in Wordsworth's Poetry: Monumental Writing* (Lincoln: The University of Nebraska Press, 1988) [hereafter, Kneale], pp. xvii, 29–30.

6. *The Prelude, 1799, 1805, 1850,* ed. Jonathan Wordsworth, M. H. Abrams, and Stephen Gill (New York: Norton, 1979) [hereafter, Norton *Prelude*], Book 6 of 1805 text, ll. 69–71; see also *An Evening Walk,* ed. James Averill (Ithaca: Cornell University Press, 1984) [hereafter, *EW*], p. 8.

7. As John Williams points out, "for poets of Coleridge's and Wordsworth's generation, James Thomson's place as a great poet seemed as assured as that of Milton" (JWilliams, p. 49).

8. *The Collected Works of Samuel Taylor Coleridge* (Princeton: Princeton University Press, 1971) [hereafter, *CW/STC*], volume VII, "Biographia Literaria," part I, chapter one, p. 25.

9. William Hazlitt, *The Complete Works of William Hazlitt*, ed. P. P. Howe after the edition of A. R. Waller and Arnold Glover (London: J. M. Dent and Sons Ltd., 1930–34) [hereafter, Hazlitt], volume XVII, p. 120.

10. *The Poetical Works of William Wordsworth*, ed. Ernest de Selincourt and Helen Darbishire (Oxford: Clarendon Press, 1940–49) [hereafter, *PW*], volume II, p. 331.

11. Raymond Williams, *Culture and Society, 1780–1950* (1958; rpt. New York: Harper and Row, Publishers, 1966), pp. 30–48.

12. *Letters,* volume I, pp. 62, 112.

13. *Letters,* volume I, p. 120.

14. *Letters,* volume I, p. 52.

15. See, for instance, reviews of both volumes in *Analytic Review,* 15 (March 1793): 294–97; *Critical Review,* n.s., 8 (July 1793): 347–48; *Critical Review,* second series, 8 (August 1793): 472–74; *European Magazine,* 24 (September 1793): 192–93; *Monthly Review,* 12 (October 1793): 216–18; *Gentleman's Magazine,* 64 (March 1794): 252–53. Excerpts from these reviews are reprinted in both *EW,* pp. 303–6, and in *Descriptive Sketches,* ed. Eric Birdsall (Ithaca: Cornell University Press, 1984) [hereafter, *DS*], pp. 299–301. The reviewers for the *Critical Review, European Magazine,* and *Gentleman's Magazine* all comment on the beggar's story.

16. *EW,* p. 304.

17. *DS,* p. 300.

18. *DS,* p. 299.

19. *DS,* p. 301.

20. *Letters,* volume II, p. 154; Wordsworth used the phrase in reply to criticism from his friend Francis Wrangham, with Wordsworth arguing that words have "poetic authority" when sanctioned by past use—in this particular case, use by Milton. On Wordsworth's relationship to Thomson, Marilyn Butler, *Romantics, Rebels and Reactionaries: English Literature and its Background, 1760–1830* (Oxford: Oxford University Press, 1981) [hereafter, MButler], pp. 57–58, suggests that Wordsworth's juvenilia confirms his own retrospective placement of himself (in 1815) in the tradition of natural description associated with Thomson. Alternately, both James H. Averill, *Wordsworth and the Poetry of Human Suffering* (Ithaca: Cornell University Press, 1980) [hereafter, Averill], pp. 63–65, and Alan Liu, *Wordsworth: The Sense of History* (Stanford: Stanford University Press, 1989) [hereafter, Liu], pp. 119–26, point to the way that Thomson's narrative digressions are what Wordsworth's later (1815) "Essay, Supplementary to the Preface" singles out as the points of interest in *The Seasons:* "In any well-used copy of the Seasons the book generally opens of itself . . . with one of the stories" (*PrW,* volume III, p. 74).

21. Liu, pp. 120–23; Averill, pp. 63–65.

22. *EW,* p. 52. See *EW,* pp. 6–7, and Paul D. Sheats, *The Making of Wordsworth's Poetry, 1785–1798* (Cambridge: Harvard University Press, 1973) [hereafter, Sheats], pp. 53–54, 226.

23. Sheats, p. 56. See also Laurence Goldstein, *Ruins and Empire: The Evolution of a Theme in Augustan and Romantic Literature* (Pittsburgh: University of Pittsburgh Press, 1977) [hereafter, Goldstein], pp. 166–67.

24. See JWilliams, p. 39; Moorman, p. 128; William Wordsworth, *The Poems,* ed. John O. Hayden (New Haven and London: Yale University Press, 1981) [hereafter, Hayden], volume I, p. 961; and Liu, p. 332.

25. *PrW,* volume III, p. 75.

26. *PrW,* volume III, p. 75; *PW,* volume I, p. 41; see also Moorman, p. 369; Jacobus, pp. 88–89; and Sheats, p. 46. In *Wordsworth's Art of Allusion* (University Park: The Pennsylvania State University Press, 1988), pp. 15, 19–41, Edwin Stein discusses Wordsworth's "echoic" techniques in the poem.

27. *The Prelude, 1798–1799,* ed. Stephen Parrish (Ithaca: Cornell University Press, 1977) [hereafter, *Prelude*], pp. 5, 87. See Stephen J. Spector, "Wordsworth's Mirror Imagery and the Picturesque Tradition" *ELH,* 44 (1977): 85–107; Galperin, pp. 54–56; and Frances Ferguson, *Wordsworth: Language as Counter-Spirit* (New Haven and London: Yale University Press, 1977) [hereafter, Ferguson], pp. 248–50.

28. See the discussions of this passage in Kenneth R. Johnston, *Wordsworth and The Recluse* (New Haven and London: Yale University Press, 1984) [hereafter, Johnston], p. 141, or Charles J. Rzepka, *The Self As Mind: Vision and Identity in Wordsworth, Coleridge, and Keats* (Cambridge: Harvard University Press, 1986) [hereafter, Rzepka], p. 31.

29. *EW,* p. 66, ll. 301–2; Liu, p. 124–25.

30. Liu, pp. 120–21.

31. See also Johnston, pp. 338–39, on Wordsworth's inserting himself into posterity, and (for a dissenting view) Jacobus, p. 90, on Wordsworth's projecting himself within the literary tradition *until* 1798. For further discussion of Wordsworth's conception of the tradition in which he wrote, see also Geoffrey H. Hartman, *The Unremarkable Wordsworth* (Minneapolis: University of Minnesota Press, 1987), throughout; Peter J. Manning, "Cleansing the Images" (unpublished manuscript); and Hugh Sykes Davies, *Wordsworth and the Worth of Words,* ed. John Kerrigan and Jonathan Wordsworth (Cambridge: Cambridge University Press, 1986) [hereafter, Davies], pp. 101–2.

32. *Letters,* volume II, p. 266. Wordsworth's immediate concern in the letter to Sharp is copyright law, or assuring the future financial security of writers' families. On this topic, see Lee Erickson, *The Economy of Literary Form: English Literature and the Industrialization of Publishing, 1800–1850* (Baltimore: The Johns Hopkins University Press, 1996) [hereafter, Erickson], pp. 60–69.

33. *Letters,* volume II, p. 266.

34. *Letters,* volume I, p. 211.

35. *Letters,* volume I, pp. 267–68.

36. *Letters,* volume II, p. 174.

37. See Sheats, pp. 21, 44, 56.

38. The suggestion is made by James Averill, *EW,* p. 6.

39. *EW,* pp. 301–2. See also William H. Galperin, *The Return of the Visible in British Romanticism* (Baltimore: Johns Hopkins University Press, 1993) [hereafter, *The Return of the Visible*], on the tension between tradition and the eye.

40. Alan Liu points out that "the eye of the picturesque" was overshadowed by the "Eye of Reason," then by the Jacobin "oeil de la surveillance" by 1792–1793 (Liu, pp. 136–37). The latter two icons would both have been known to the youthful Wordsworth from his association with political figures of the day (not least his own publisher, Joseph Johnson, who also published Thomas Paine).

41. JWilliams, pp. 27, 34–35. An especially important political analysis of vagrancy (and of the poor laws) appeared in Joseph Townsend's 1786 *A Dissertation on the Poor Laws. By a Well-Wisher to Mankind* (rpt. Berkeley: University of California Press, 1971) [hereafter, Townsend].

42. The variety of position taken in this debate can be found by looking, for instance, at James K. Chandler, *Wordsworth's Second Nature: A Study of the Poetry and Politics* (Chicago: University of Chicago Press, 1984) [hereafter, Chandler]; Nicholas Roe, *Wordsworth and Coleridge: The Radical Years* (Oxford: Clarendon Press, 1988) [hereafter, Roe]; Jerome J. McGann, *The Romantic Ideology: A Critical Investigation* (Chicago: University of Chicago Press, 1983) [hereafter, McGann]; Michael H. Friedman, *The Making of a Tory Humanist: William Wordsworth and the Idea of Community* (New York: Columbia University Press, 1979); Alan Bewell, *Wordsworth and the Enlightenment: Nature, Man, and Society in the Experimental Poetry* (New Haven and London: Yale University Press, 1989) [hereafter, Bewell], as well as the works already cited by John Williams and Marilyn Butler.

43. *Letters,* volume I, p. 315. For a debate on one of the poems included with the letter, see Marjorie Levinson, "Spiritual Economics: A Reading of Wordsworth's 'Michael'," *ELH,* 52 (1985): 707–31; and W. Thomas Pepper, "The Ideology of Wordsworth's 'Michael: A Pastoral Poem'," *Criticism,* 31 (1989): 367–82.

44. *Letters,* volume I, p. 159.

45. On Wordsworth and contemporary journalism, see Johnston, p. 45; and Jacobus, pp. 160–65, 177, 185. Wordsworth's interest in narrative is also related to his interest in the novel (Jacobus, pp. 255–57) and to the novel's reliance on the links forged in eighteenth-century thought between humanitarianism, sensibility, and the sense of sight (see Ann Jessie Van Sant, *Eighteenth-Century Sensibility and the Novel* [Cambridge: Cambridge University Press, 1993], chapters one through four). For a compelling analysis of the letter to Fox, see John Lucas, *England and Englishness: Ideas of Nationhood in English Poetry, 1688–1900* (Iowa City: University of Iowa Press, 1990) [hereafter, Lucas], pp. 101–6.

46. See MButler, p. 49; Marjorie Levinson, *Wordsworth's Great Period Poems: Four Essays* (Cambridge: Cambridge University Press, 1986) [hereafter,

Levinson], p. 20. On the source of the vagrant's story, see Wordsworth's Fen-wick note (Butler, pp. 476, 478–79) and Jacobus, 155.

47. *Letters,* volume I, pp. 119, 123–24.

48. By "newly politicized," I mean to suggest that Wordsworth is more centrally concerned with the social and political uses of poetry, not that his earlier work does not show the seeds of these later concerns. See David Simpson, *Wordsworth's Historical Imagination: The Poetry of Displacement* (London: Methuen, 1987) [hereafter, Simpson], pp. 161, 191–93, for a description of *An Evening Walk* as "social Gothic" and on Wordsworth's early sense of the social determination of character.

49. All quotations from the Salisbury Plain poems can be found in *The Salisbury Plain Poems,* ed. Stephen Gill (Ithaca: Cornell University Press, 1975) [here-after, *SP*].

50. See Alan Liu's review of David Simpson's *Wordsworth's Historical Imagina-tion: The Poetry of Displacement* in *The Wordsworth Circle,* 19 (1988): 174–75.

51. *SP,* p. 34.

52. In the Fenwick note Wordsworth says that the poem's descriptions of the 1770s are based on the events of the 1790s (Butler, pp. 478–79). See Lucas, pp. 41–42.

53. *SP,* p. 133.

54. *SP,* p. 29.

55. *SP,* pp. 30–31, 135–36.

56. Roe, p. 126–35; V. G. Kiernan, *Poets, Politics and the People,* ed. Harvey J. Kaye (London: Verso, 1989), p. 99; see also Simpson, pp. 191–93, 166–74, on the relation of Wordsworth's ideas to arguments about the poor in the late eighteenth and early nineteenth centuries.

57. *Complete Works of Thomas Paine* (Chicago and New York: Belford, Clarke and Co., 1885) [hereafter, *Paine*], n.p. See also Gordon K. Thomas, "'Glo-rious Renovation': Wordsworth, Terror, and Paine," *The Wordsworth Circle,* 21 (Winter 1990): 3–9, on Paine's influence on Wordsworth. The psychol-ogy of the poor is portrayed quite differently in Townsend's *A Dissertation on the Poor Laws:* the "poor know little of the motives which stimulate the higher ranks to action. . . . In general it is only hunger which can spur and goad [the poor] on to labour" (Townsend, p. 23; see also p. 54). Wordsworth's characterization of the female vagrant mixes images used by Townsend of the idle and criminal poor who are vagrants (p. 18) and the less threatening, virtuous poor in their cottages, who are imagined as female: "the widow with her tender orphans" (p. 69).

58. "Liberty," IV, ll. 636–40.

59. Jonathan Wordsworth, Michael C. Jaye, and Robert Woolf, *William Wordsworth and the Age of English Romanticism* (New Brunswick: Rutgers University Press, 1987), pp. 3, 200, gives notes on Barry's etching and on Barry, a friend of William Godwin, Richard Price, and others. The original piece is in the Yale Center for British Art, Paul Mellon Collection.

60. *SP,* p. 38. See Averill, p. 77, on the image of Stonehenge and "reactionary forces"; and Goldstein, pp. 129–33, 136–37, on the Gothic and inversions of the eighteenth-century progress poem.

61. Alan Liu suggests that Wordsworth's Spenserian stanzas displace his contemporary message by turning to allegory, while Karen Swann has argued that the very act of distancing allowed Wordsworth in the 1790s to criticize sensationalist literature with its feminized characters, plots, and audience (Liu, pp. 574–75n31, 189–90; and Karen Swann, "Suffering and Sensation in *The Ruined Cottage,*" *PMLA,* 106 [1991]: 83–95, especially p. 84 [hereafter, Swann]). See also Robert Mayo, "The Contemporaneity of the *Lyrical Ballads,*" *PMLA,* 69 (1954): 486–522, especially p. 496 [hereafter, Mayo], on the prevalence of deserted females in 1790s magazine literature.

62. *Letters,* volume I, p. 137.

63. For slightly different views of what might be called Wordsworth's dialogic poems from this period, see Susan J. Wolfson, *The Questioning Presence: Wordsworth, Keats, and the Interrogative Mode in Romantic Poetry* (Ithaca: Cornell University Press, 1986), pp. 17–41; and Don H. Bialostosky, *Making Tales: The Poetics of Wordsworth's Narrative Experiments* (Chicago: The University of Chicago Press, 1984).

64. Bewell, p. 7, however, points out that critics called the progress poem a product of "the *Jacobin* muse" (citing the 20 November 1797 *Anti-Jacobin*). My analysis draws more on Laurence Goldstein's work (see note 60 above).

65. See *Letters,* volume I, p. 189, on Wordsworth reading *The Ruined Cottage* to Coleridge. On Wordsworth's turn to narrative by the time of *The Ruined Cottage* as an attempt to express his concern with society's victims, see Jacobus, p. 142–43; on such attempts as an appropriation of others for the purpose of self-representation, see Rzepka, pp. 54–71.

66. *EW,* p. 38.

67. Sheats, p. 51; Liu, pp. 62–84. See also *The Return of the Visible,* throughout.

68. The passage is introduced with echoes of Collins's explicitly Miltonic image of Edenic vision and sound: "with soft affection's *ear,/The history of a poet's ev'ning ear*" (*EW,* p. 34, ll. 51–52, emphasis added). Moreover, with echoes of Thomson's related image, Wordsworth's landscape includes a restless horse eyeing a flood as well as a heat-beset swain.

69. See, for instance, Sermon, p. 151; Butler, pp. 5–6; Sheats, pp. 143–46; *Music,* pp. 3–4; Johnston, p. 45.

70. Liu, p. 314; Basil Willey, "On Wordsworth and the Locke Tradition," *Discussions of William Wordsworth,* ed. Jack Davis (Boston: D. C. Heath and Company, 1964), p. 65; Reeve Parker, "'Finer Distance': The Narrative Art of Wordsworth's 'The Wanderer'," *ELH,* 39 (1972): 91–92 [hereafter, Parker]; Geoffrey H. Hartman, *Wordsworth's Poetry, 1787–1814* (New Haven and London: Yale University Press, 1964; rev. 1971) [hereafter, Hartman], pp. 296–98; Abbie Findlay Potts, *The Elegiac Mode: Poetic Form in Wordsworth and Other Elegists* (Ithaca: Cornell University Press, 1967) [hereafter, Potts], p. 135. Slightly more detail on Wordsworth and Thomson is

offered by Davies, pp. 196–202; and Jacobus, pp. 39–44, 105, 109; only Chandler, p. 142, notes specifically that Wordsworth is "cribbing" from Thomson in the opening of *The Ruined Cottage*.

71. Annabel Patterson, *Pastoral and Ideology: Virgil to Valéry* (Berkeley: University of California Press, 1987), pp. 277–78; the description of a "labor theory of poetic value" is from Kurt Heinzelman's discussion of "Michael" and of pastoral versus georgic in *The Economics of The Imagination* (Amherst: The University of Massachusetts Press, 1980), pp. 221–22. Geoffrey Hartman, too, connects the trope of "ignoble leisure" with Virgil's contrast between leisure *(otium)* and more honorable, engaged, civic work ("'*Was It for This . . . ?*': Wordsworth and the Birth of the Gods," in *Romantic Revolutions: Criticism and Theory,* ed. Kenneth R. Johnston, Gilbert Chaitin, Karen Hanson, and Herbert Marks [Bloomington: Indiana University Press, 1990], pp. 8–25, especially p. 21). See also Davies, 202, 248; JWilliams, pp. 181–82; and Simpson, p. 136.

72. *Letters,* volume IV, p. 250; see also JWilliams, p. 114, on the connection between blank verse and seventeenth-century culture and politics.

73. *Letters,* volume I, p. 400.

74. *Letters,* volume VII, p. 292.

75. *Letters,* volume I, p. 641.

76. *Letters,* volume II, p. 113.

77. *Letters,* volume I, p. 136.

78. Mark L. Reed, *Wordsworth: The Chronology of the Early Years, 1770–1799* (Cambridge: Harvard University Press, 1967), pp. 162–67. See also George McLean Harper, *William Wordsworth: His Life, Works, and Influence* (New York: Charles Scribner's Sons, 1916) [hereafter, Harper], volume I, pp. 251–72.

79. This is not to deny that Wordsworth's 1795–1798 country retirement placed him in a dynamic *poetic* community or that the Wordsworths entertained politically controversial figures such as John Thelwall, hospitality that eventually resulted in the loss of their lease in Alfoxden (Sermon, pp. 156–68).

80. But see *Music,* p. 100, on parallels between Armytage and the dreaming man.

81. Manuscript B; Butler, p. 42.

82. *PrW,* volume III, p. 125. The lines of poetry are from Burns's "Epistle to J. L. *****k, An Old Scotch Bard"; on both Burns's poem and Wordsworth's quotation from it as gestures toward a more colloquial, spoken idiom, see Jacobus, p. 91. On Wordsworth's awareness of Thomson as also part of the tradition of Scots poetry and his statement that he was "indebted to the North [i.e., Scotland]," see *Letters,* volume IV, p. 402.

83. See *Music,* pp. 87–153, and Averill, pp. 134–41.

84. Butler, p. 85.

85. Chandler, p. 124.

86. Parker, pp. 103, 109–10.

87. See Sheats, p. 157.

88. Sheats, pp. 206–7.

89. Geoffrey Hartman argues that, unlike Thomson, who would have nature point to God, Wordsworth usually insists that nature "suffices imagination," but in a peculiar way (Hartman, pp. 298, 140), informing people only that it will not sustain them.

90. De Quincey quite early pointed out Armytage's ineptness (*The Collected Writings of Thomas De Quincey,* ed. David Masson [Edinburgh: Adam and Charles Black, 1890], [hereafter, Masson], volume XI, p. 304–8); see also *Music,* pp. 85, 98–99.

91. Sheats, p. 138.

92. But see Sheats and Averill for more unified readings of the poem, or Galperin, pp. 71–75, who sees *The Ruined Cottage* as far more a poem of closure than the later *The Excursion.* For others who read both *The Excursion* and *The Ruined Cottage* as unsettled and unsettling poems, see Ferguson, pp. 216ff. and Simpson, pp. 201–2.

93. Parker, pp. 94–95.

94. I take the idea of "the narrative present" from Hertz, pp. 20–21.

95. In other words, if the poem is to represent the virtuous poor speaking, it must disclaim any purpose to its poetic display. If, however, the art and purpose are made the narrator's, the narrative power and virtuous purposes for which a poem such as *The Ruined Cottage* explicitly argues are not available to Margaret, although one might see the framing introduced in *The Ruined Cottage* as a way of confronting the above-mentioned problems, only to find new questions are raised. See also Jacobus, p. 159.

96. Butler, pp. 58–59, manuscripts B and D.

97. See Averill, pp. 134–41, on eighteenth-century theories about representations of misery.

98. Anne Janowitz, *England's Ruins: Poetic Purpose and the National Landscape* (Oxford: Basil Blackwell, 1990), p. 119; Liu, p. 325. See also McGann, p. 84; Roe, p. 132; *Form,* p. 104.

99. The first charges of ventriloquism made against Wordsworth were directed against the use (or misuse) of characters in "The Wanderer" (Book I of *The Excursion*) by Coleridge in *Table Talk* on 21 July 1832 (*CW/STC,* volume XIV, "Table Talk," part I, p. 307).

100. *PrW,* volume III, p. 74.

101. I draw here on Karen Swann's proposal that Wordsworth's engagement with sociopolitical issues in *The Ruined Cottage* has to do with his resistance to sensationalism (Swann, p. 84).

102. See Swann, p. 84; MButler, pp. 179, 184; Johnston, p. 45; Bewell, p. ix.

103. Sheats, pp. 138–39; Sermon, p.168; Levinson, p. 21. See also Dorothy Wordsworth's 1805 echo of *The Ruined Cottage* in her letter on having visited in May 1794 the house in which she and William had been born: "all . . . in ruin, the terrace-walk buried and choked up with the old privot hedge" (*Letters,* volume I, p. 616; see also Robert Gittings and Jo Manton, *Dorothy Wordsworth* [Oxford: Clarendon Press, 1985], p. 45).

104. Alan Liu has provided a compelling and detailed account of northern England's move to an economy of debt in the nineties, paralleling shifts in the marketing of literature, so that in *The Ruined Cottage* the portraits of Robert (as weaver), of Armytage (as peddler), and implicitly of Wordsworth (as writer) are comparable (Liu, pp. 326–47; Swann, p. 94, would add Margaret [as reader]).

105. Masson, volume XI, pp. 53–57.

106. Masson, volume XI, p. 57; see also his images of flight, p. 59. For a more detailed account of how and when novels displaced poetry in the literary marketplace, see Erickson, pp. 1–11, 19–69.

107. Masson, volume XI, pp. 55–56; William Cobbett, *The English Gardener* (1833; rpt. Oxford: Oxford University Press, 1980) [hereafter, Cobbett], pp. 4–5. I would like to thank the students in my seminar on "Unacknowledged Legislators," given in the summer of 1989, for bringing Cobbett's book not only to my attention, but to my library. See also Klancher, pp. 121–29, on Cobbett's audience; Kevin Gilmartin, "'Victims of Argument, Slaves of Fact': Hunt, Hazlitt, Cobbett and the Literature of Opposition," *The Wordsworth Circle,* 21 (Summer 1990): 90–96, on Cobbett's rhetoric; and E. P. Thomson, *The Making of the English Working Class* (1963; rpt. New York: Vintage, 1966), pp. 746–62, on Cobbett's better known political writings and on his awareness of Wordsworth's work.

108. Cobbett, p. 3, emphasis his.

109. Anthony Huxley's introduction points out the practical problems with Cobbett's gardening tips (Cobbett, pp. vii-viii, x).

110. Butler, pp. 50, 51, manuscripts B and D.

111. The quotation can be found in *The Prelude,* Norton *Prelude,* Book 5 ("Books"), l. 425, p. 175.

112. *Letters,* volume I, p. 491; volume III, p. 144.

113. See *Letters,* volume VII, p. 542.

114. Sermon, p. 170; Levinson, p. 21.

115. See *The Complete Works of Robert Burns* (New York: E. R. Dumont, Publisher, 1890), volume I, part II, pp. 319–20, for Burns's poem and his extempore verses written at the same time, which imagine death as a probable result of his intended expatriation.

116. On Wordsworth's antiprofessionalism in this poem, see Clifford Siskin, "Wordsworth's Prescriptions: Romanticism and Professional Power," *The Romantics and Us: Essays on Literature and Culture,* ed. Gene W. Ruoff (New Brunswick: Rutgers University Press, 1990), p. 304. Erickson, p. 68, specifically associates the poem with Wordsworth's battle over extending copyrights. The poem was first published in the 1800 edition of the *Lyrical Ballads;* I cite the version of the poem that can be found in *PW,* volume IV, pp. 65–67.

117. Hayden, volume I, p. 961; Potts, pp. 117–18.

118. See *PW,* volume V, p. 5, l. 73.

119. See Lucy Newlyn, *Coleridge, Wordsworth, and the Language of Allusion* (Oxford: Clarendon Press, 1986) [hereafter, *Language of Allusion*], pp. 109–16.

120. See Mark L. Reed, *Wordsworth: The Chronology of the Middle Years, 1800–1815* (Cambridge: Harvard University Press, 1975), pp. 128–29.

121. See *Poems, in Two Volumes, and Other Poems, 1800–1807*, ed. Jared Curtis (Ithaca: Cornell University Press, 1983) [hereafter, *PTV*], pp. 581–83. For other readings of the poem and of Wordsworth's position in 1802, see *Language of Allusion*, pp. 113–16; Galperin, pp. 139–42; and Lucas, p. 117.

122. *Samuel Taylor Coleridge, Poetical Works* (1912; rpt. Oxford: Oxford University Press, 1967) [hereafter, *Coleridge*], p. 102; see Jacobus, pp. 42, 54, 69–72.

123. All quotes from "The Eolian Harp" can be found in *Coleridge*, pp. 100–2.

124. Lucy Newlyn argues in "Wordsworth, Coleridge and The 'Castle of Indolence' Stanzas," *The Wordsworth Circle*, 12 (1981), pp. 108–9, that Wordsworth is here fending off vocational anxiety and *justifying* indolence.

125. *Letters*, volume V, p. 58.

126. *Letters*, volume III, p. 191.

127. *Letters*, volume II, p. 248; 5 June 1808 letter to Wrangham. See also Peter J. Manning, *Reading Romantics: Texts and Contexts* (Oxford: Oxford University Press, 1990), pp. 169–72, 180–91.

128. Questions about when Wordsworth's disillusionment and retreat from public or political views first inform (or deform) his poetry have long occupied Wordsworth critics (See, for instance, Levinson, pp. 80–100). My discussion of Wordsworth's poems from 1802 as evidence that Wordsworth had not yet abandoned (though he may have modified) his earlier political hopes for poetry places me closest to E. P. Thompson, who suggests that Wordsworth remained an "odious democrat" until after the (1802) Peace of Amiens ("Wordsworth's Crisis," *London Review of Books*, 10 [8 December 1988], p. 6).

129. *Paradise Lost* XII. l. 587; Wordsworth's sonnet can be found in *PW*, volume III, p. 116; see *Paradise Lost* II. l. 621.

130. See *Paradise Lost* I. ll. 249–55.

131. Butler, pp. 48, 49, echoing Thomson's horse in the noon passage from "Summer."

132. See Bewell, pp. 115, 137–39. As Jacobus concludes, "Peter Bell" questions "imaginative activity that is also a retreat from reality" and "restates the redemption-theme of 'The Ancient Mariner' in terms that are not merely anti-supernatural, but emphatically humane" (Jacobus, pp. 263–65).

133. I draw on the account found in Jacobus, pp. 262–63. For more on the relationship between Wordsworth's and Coleridge's writings, see Reeve Parker's "'Oh Could You Hear His Voice!': Wordsworth, Coleridge, and Ventriloquism," in *Romanticism and Language*, ed. Arden Reed (Ithaca: Cornell University Press, 1984), pp. 125–43.

134. All quotations from Wordsworth's "Ode" can be found in *PTV*, pp. 269–77.

135. All quotations from "Dejection: An Ode" can be found in *Coleridge*, pp. 362–68.

136. *PTV*, p. 267; all quotations from "Elegiac Stanzas" can be found in *PTV*, pp. 267–68.

137. See Johnston, pp. 140ff. on the changes in Wordsworth's poetic project in this period.

138. *Letters,* volume II, p. 268.

139. *Letters,* volume II, p. 145.

140. See also Wordsworth's 1817 letter to Daniel Stuart, which proposes the remedy for the modern marketplace is to have workers properly respect farmers; farmers, landlords (*Letters,* volume III, p. 375), a far cry from what he earlier thought the Muse might have to say to the modern world.

141. *Letters,* volume III, p. 165.

142. The remarks on Thomson are found in the 1815 "Essay, Supplementary to the Preface" written in anticipation of critical responses to *The Excursion* (Johnston, p. 334). See also Galperin, p. 37, on *The Excursion* as testimony "to the inadequacy of narratives."

143. *Letters,* volume II, p. 150.

144. Butler, pp. 45, 57; ll. 24–25, 190–91. In *The Ruined Cottage,* the trope echoed and recast the figure found in Thomson's lines in "Summer": "Nor undelightful is the ceaseless hum [of insects]/To him who muses through the woods at noon" (ll. 282–83). Especially given Wordsworth's other revisions of Thomson's noontime dreamer, it is significant that *The Ruined Cottage* changed Thomson's noise (or "hum") into more ordered sound ("melody") just as it changed Thomson's poetic dreamer into the active narrator of Margaret's story, a transformation that Wordsworth no longer claims the power to effect by 1806–1807.

145. *Letters,* volume II, p. 194.

146. *Letters,* volume II, p. 146.

147. On the popularity of *The Excursion,* see Mary Moorman, *William Wordsworth, A Biography: The Later Years, 1803–1850* (Oxford: Clarendon Press, 1965), p. 183; Kneale, p. 45.

148. In John O. Hayden, ed., *Romantic Bards and British Reviews: A Selected Edition of the Contemporary Reviews of the Works of Wordsworth, Coleridge, Byron, Keats, and Shelley* (Lincoln: University of Nebraska Press, 1976) [hereafter, *Bards*], p. 39. John Merivale in the *Monthly Review* and Hazlitt in the *Examiner* were also harsh in their judgments on the poem, while Charles Lamb (and William Gifford) in the *Quarterly* praised it (see also John O. Hayden, ed., *The Romantic Reviewers, 1802–1824* [Chicago: University of Chicago Press, 1968], pp. 36, 41, 67, 86).

149. *Bards,* pp. 41–42.

150. *Bards,* p. 42; Hartman, p. 316. See also Liu, pp. 320–23; Averill, pp. 280, 283; Cleanth Brooks, "Wordsworth and Human Suffering: Notes on Two Early Poems," *From Sensibility to Romanticism: Essays Presented to Frederick A. Pottle,* ed. Frederick W. Hilles and Harold Bloom (Oxford: Oxford University Press, 1965), especially pp. 385–87; and Jean-Pierre Mileur, *The Critical Response: The Critic as Reader, Writer, Hero* (Madison: University of Wisconsin Press, 1990), pp. 44–52.

151. Quotation from *The Excursion* in this paragraph can be found in *PW,* volume V, pp. 1–2, 5.

152. Thus, as David Simpson suggests, in 1814 the poem "was intended as a major public statement . . . addressing topics of great public concern" (Simpson, p. 8).

153. Variously, critics describe Wordsworth's "oblique and self-conscious voice" (Hartman, p. 293); his use of exempla or "pontificating" (Averill, pp. 280, 283); his move to description or "reading" (Galperin, pp. 50–56); his "epitaphic lyric" (Liu, p. 365); even his "tissue of . . . devotional ravings" (*Bard*, p. 42).

154. If, as Ronald Paulson argues, *The Excursion* shows Wordsworth's "*earlier* self critiqued by a later," then (as Paulson also implies) the poem in some sense simply continues the activity of the earlier poems (*Breaking*, p. 142). For discussion of Wordsworth's politics in *The Excursion*, see also Levinson, p. 133, Hartman, p. 301, and Simpson, pp. 136–37, 206–7.

155. *PW*, volume V, pp. 29, 265, 286.

156. *PW*, volume V, p. 312.

157. Galperin, p. 45.

Chapter III

1. See P. M. S. Dawson, "Shelley and Class," in *The New Shelley*, ed. G. Kim Blank (London: Macmillan, 1991) [hereafter, *The New Shelley*], pp. 34–41.

2. Shelley, p. 70; See "The Wanderer," ll. 500–2: "the good die first,/And they whose hearts are dry as summer dust/Burn to the socket!" (*PW*, volume V, p. 25).

3. Shelley, p. 345; "Peter Bell the Third," l. 704.

4. G. Kim Blank, *Wordsworth's Influence on Shelley: A Study of Poetic Authority* (New York: St. Martin's Press, 1988) [hereafter, Blank], p. 26. There is little evidence that Wordsworth at this time paid much attention to Shelley (Harper, volume II, pp. 198–99). Some ten years later Wordsworth wrote to Henry Crabb Robinson, "What avails it to hunt down Shelley? (*Letters*, volume III, p. 579). The context of the letter indicates that Wordsworth—despite his reported (1827) admiration for Shelley's artistry (William Keach, *Shelley's Style* [London: Methuen, 1984], [hereafter, Keach], pp. xi, 235)—dismissed the younger poet, although he also thought it of little use to make public his dislike of Shelley (among other things, as the letter notes, Byron seemed to him worse).

5. *The Letters of Percy Bysshe Shelley*, ed. Frederick L. Jones (Oxford: Clarendon Press, 1964) [hereafter, Jones], volume I, p. 218.

6. Jones, volume 1, p. 223.

7. Clark, p. 309.

8. Jones, volume II, p. 434.

9. Clark, p. 185.

10. Jones, volume I, pp. 223, 226.

11. Jones, volume I, p. 242.

12. Kenneth Neill Cameron, *The Esdaile Notebook: A Volume of Early Poems by Percy Bysshe Shelley* (New York: Alfred A. Knopf, 1964), p. 4.

13. Jones, volume I, p. 223.
14. Jones, volume I, p. 342.
15. "A Treatise of Human Nature," *Philosophical Works*, volume I, p. 534.
16. "A Treatise On Morals," Clark, p. 183.
17. For book-length studies of Shelley's politics, see Gerald McNiece, *Shelley and the Revolutionary Idea* (Cambridge: Harvard University Press, 1969) and P. M. S. Dawson, *The Unacknowledged Legislator: Shelly and Politics* (Oxford: Clarendon Press, 1980) [hereafter, Dawson].
18. Sermon, p. 174.
19. Clark, p. 309.
20. Shelley, p. 324. The quotation is adapted from Wordsworth's late 1804 passage, published 26 October 1809 in Coleridge's *The Friend.*
21. Jones, volume I, pp. 223–24.
22. *Bards,* p. 379.
23. Shelley, p. 69.
24. See Blank, pp. 30–32.
25. September 1814, *The Journals of Mary Shelley, 1814–1844,* ed. Paula R. Feldman and Diana Scott-Kilvert (Oxford: The Clarendon Press, 1987) [hereafter, *JMS*], volume I, p. 25. Specifically, Shelley's attention was drawn to "the history of Margaret" in 1814 (*JMS,* volume I, p. 26).
26. Sermon, p. 151; Robert Southey, *Joan of Arc, Ballads, Lyrics, and Minor Poems* (London: George Routledge and Sons, 1894) [hereafter, Southey], pp. 8, 84; *Coleridge,* p. 120. The central image of the poor widow was also in common circulation (see, for example, Townsend, p. 69).
27. See Kenneth Neill Cameron, *Shelley: The Golden Years* (Cambridge: Harvard University Press, 1974) [hereafter, Cameron], p. 208.
28. Shelley's title, like his political thinking, may also owe a debt to Godwin's 1794 *Things As They Are; or the Adventures of Caleb Williams.* See as well William St. Clair, *The Godwins and the Shelleys: The biography of a family* (New York: Norton, 1989), p. 119, on the link between the phrase "Things As They Are" and the tradition of protest.
29. All quotations from this poem can be found in Jones, volume I, pp. 224–26.
30. *Coleridge,* p. 120; Southey, p. 84; PW ("Guilt And Sorrow"), volume I, p. 110. Wordsworth (although Shelley would not yet have read *The Excursion*) similarly describes Margaret's eye as "busy in the distance, shaping things," feeding a hope that is only "torturing" (*PW,* volume V, pp. 37–38).
31. Jones, volume I, pp. 223–24.
32. Sermon, pp. 151–52.
33. Jones, volume I, p. 223.
34. Jones, volume I, p. 340.
35. See, for example, Paul Mueschke and Earl L. Griggs's early article, "Wordsworth as the Prototype of the Poet in Shelley's *Alastor,*" *PMLA,* 49 (1934): 229–45 [hereafter, Mueschke and Griggs], as well as Earl R. Wasserman, *Shelley: A Critical Reading* (Baltimore: The Johns Hopkins University Press, 1971) [hereafter, Wasserman], p. 16. See also Cameron's

suggestion about Coleridge's "pervasive" influence on Shelley (Cameron, p. 208).

36. Blank, pp. 40–42, discusses in detail Shelley's developing interest in Wordsworth between 1812 and 1816.

37. Jones, volume I, p. 462.

38. For a description of the social forces and marketing strategies that furthered Shelley's relative success after 1817, see Charles E. Robinson, "Percy Bysshe Shelley, Charles Ollier, and William Blackwood: The Contexts of Early Nineteenth-Century Publishing," in *Shelley Revalued: Essays From the Gregynog Conference,* ed. Kelvin Everest (Totowa, New Jersey: Barnes & Noble, 1983), pp. 183–213.

39. Wordsworth's sonnet can be found in *PW,* volume III, p. 116; Shelley's poem, in Shelley, p. 88.

40. Shelley's admiration for Wordsworth's poetry (especially "Lines Composed a Few Miles above Tintern Abbey . . .") is reported by Thomas Medwin, *The Life of Percy Bysshe Shelley* (rpt. Oxford: Oxford University Press, 1913) [hereafter, Medwin], p. 251.

41. All quotations from "Ode: Intimations of Immortality" can be found in *PTV,* pp. 271–77.

42. See Levinson, pp. 87, 154n20.

43. All quotations from "Dejection: An Ode" can be found in *Coleridge,* pp. 362–68. I am grateful to Vernon Shetley for conversations on the relationship between Coleridge and Wordsworth. For a different reading of Coleridge's poem (and of Shelley's understanding of the poem), see Jerrold E. Hogle, *Shelley's Process: Radical Transference and the Development of His Major Works* (Oxford: Oxford University Press, 1988) [hereafter, Hogle], pp. 39–43.

44. Medwin, p. 251.

45. *PTV,* p. 277; Shelley, p. 87.

46. I take seriously Mary Shelley's opinion that "To—" was addressed to Coleridge, despite suggestions from Blank (p. 49) and Wasserman (p. 8) that the poem addresses Wordsworth.

47. The following argument is indebted to Wasserman, especially pp. 3–56.

48. "To—" ("Oh! there are spirits of the air") as well as Mary Shelley's comment on the poem can be found in Percy Bysshe Shelley, *Poetical Works,* ed. Thomas Hutchinson (London: Oxford University Press, 1970) [hereafter, Hutchinson], p. 525–26.

49. Hutchinson, p. 31.

50. Quotations from the preface to "Alastor" can be found in Shelley, pp. 69–70; the text of "Alastor," in Shelley, pp. 70–87.

51. See Mueschke and Griggs, pp. 235–39; Wasserman, p. 16.

52. Hutchinson, p. 525.

53. Nature's revelation of her own lack here also parallels the way the "spirit of sweet human love" (1. 203) later sends the youth an image of a very different sort of love.

54. The narrator begins by calling upon a brotherhood consisting of earth, ocean, and air. By implication, the narrator is connected with the missing element of fire. Spirit, passion, imagination—linked with fire by Romantic commonplace—are as much descriptions of the visionary as they are of the narrator and so undermine the narrator's stance as a poet of nature.

55. On the date of the essay, see *Shelley and his Circle, 1773–1822,* ed. Kenneth Neill Cameron (volumes I-IV) and Donald H. Reiman (volumes V-VIII) (Cambridge: Harvard University Press, 1961–85) [hereafter, *SAHC*], volume VI, pp. 638–39.

56. All quotations from the "Essay on Love" in the following three paragraphs can be found in Clark, p. 170.

57. *PW,* volume V, p. 29, ll. 638–39 and p. 25, l. 493.

58. *PW,* volume V, p. 29, l. 626.

59. Clark, p. 170.

60. Marilyn Butler ("Repossessing," pp. 76–80) notes that the journey by boat owes a debt to Southey's *Thalaba,* itself a response to Coleridge's "The Ancient Mariner." Thus Shelley again enters an already established dialogue.

61. Clark, p. 174.

62. Ibid.

63. Ibid.

64. For a broader argument on language and traces of the imagination in Shelley's poetics, see Jerome J. McGann, "Shelley's Veils: A Thousand Images of Loveliness," *Romantic and Victorian,* ed. W. Paul Elledge and Richard L. Hoffman (Cranbury, New Jersey: Fairleigh Dickinson University Press, 1971) [hereafter, Veils], pp. 198–218.

65. Clark, p. 279.

66. The sources of Shelley's skeptical theory of causality are traced by C. E. Pulos, *The Deep Truth: A Study of Shelley's Skepticism* (Lincoln: The University of Nebraska Press, 1954) and, more recently, Terence Allan Hoagwood, *Skepticism & Ideology: Shelley's Political Prose and Its Philosophical Context From Bacon to Marx* (Iowa City: University of Iowa Press, 1988).

67. Clark, p. 171.

68. Jones, volume II, p. 26.

69. Clark, p. 244. See also Klancher, pp. 129–34, to whom the following argument is indebted.

70. Jones, volume I, p. 340. Between 1780 and 1792 the number of English publications doubled; however, after 1815 the market began to favor serialized novels and essays in periodicals, books of essays, and popular novels over poetry, which by 1825 no longer sold well in the literary marketplace (Erickson, pp. 7, 28–40).

71. Clark, p. 245. Shelley is not specifically alluding to novels in this passage, but he is discussing what reading material appealed to a new class of readers, the middle class, with which the rise of the novel is associated.

72. What counts as "Gothic" is under debate these days. Along with Robert Miles, *Gothic Writing, 1750–1820: A Genealogy* (London: Routledge, 1993),

I take Gothic to entail an aesthetic (one associated with the reading public that both dismayed and made the reputation of someone like Thomson) as well as a collection of novels that delineate and deploy a set of generic conventions. Shelley's awareness of how well Gothic novels in particular fared in the marketplace is clear from his letter to his bookseller about marketing his own Gothic, *St. Irvyne*: "it is a thing which almost *mechanically* sells to circulating libraries" (Jones, volume I, p. 20). He was not, however, correct in assuming his contribution to the genre would fare well; the book lost money (Erickson, pp. 144–45).

73. Cited by Branford K. Mudge, "The Man with Two Brains: Gothic Novels, Popular Culture, Literary History," *PMLA*, 107 (1992): 97.

74. Hazlitt, volume XI, p. 24; The *Quarterly Review*'s piece is cited in Christopher Small, *Mary Shelley's* Frankenstein: *Tracing the Myth* (Pittsburgh: University of Pittsburgh Press, 1973) [hereafter, Small], p. 21–22.

75. Clark, p. 307.

76. Clark, p. 306.

77. Clark, p. 281.

78. See also Klancher, pp. 129–34, on Shelley's response to Cobbett on the "politics of the sign."

79. Nancy Armstrong, *Desire and Domestic Fiction: A Political History of the Novel* (Oxford: Oxford University Press, 1987) [hereafter, Armstrong, *Desire and Domestic Fiction*], p. 23; Peter Brooks, *Reading for the Plot: Design and Intention in Narrative* (New York: Alfred A. Knopf, 1984) [hereafter, Brooks], pp. xii and 19, paraphrasing Barthes.

80. I take this thumbnail sketch of what narrative is from Bonnie Costello, "Narrative Secrets, Lyric Openings: Stevens and Bishop," *The Wallace Stevens Journal*, 19 (Fall 1995): 180; Costello goes on to describe lyric as tending "toward the intransitive and subjective, and away from temporal expression, evoking instead a present that has no temporal referent. Lyric is marked more by repetition than by sequence."

81. I am drawing on "Ekphrasis, Fiction and Ideology in the French Novel: Remarks Preliminary to an Investigation of Description," unpublished paper for the Conference on Ekphrasis (New York: 27 May 1992).

82. See Tilottama Rajan, "The Web of Human Things: Narrative and Identity in *Alastor*," from *The New Shelley*, pp. 85–107; and *The Supplement of Reading: Figures of Understanding in Romantic Theory and Practice* (Ithaca: Cornell University Press, 1990).

83. Quotations from Shelley's letter are drawn from Jones, volume I, pp. 223–26; the novel—never completed—was to be called *Hubert Cauvin*.

84. Shelley writes that "a right criterion of action for an individual must be so for a society" (Jones, volume I, p. 223).

85. Brooks, p. 61.

86. Jones, volume I, pp. 119–20. See also Jones, volume I, pp. 126–28.

87. Jones, volume I, p. 120.

88. In *A Treatise on Morals* (probably from 1818–1819), Shelley distinguishes "sensation" from "reflection," associating the former with "passive

perception" and the latter with "voluntary contemplation," which is to say
with an exercise of the will (Clark, p. 186).

89. Jones, volume I, p. 239.

90. Ibid.

91. Jones, volume I, pp. 429–30.

92. The letter may also be an oblique gloss on a number of more personal cycles
of desire and error in which Shelley had by then been involved. The *Examiner* article, on how the Allies treated Napoleon's brothers and other family
members, was dated 27 August, though it may have appeared earlier. See
SAHC, volume III, p. 484.

93. Jones, volume I, p. 430.

94. Clark, p. 173; the passage reappears in *A Defence of Poetry.*

95. Emily W. Sunstein, *Mary Shelley: Romance and Reality* (Boston: Little,
Brown and Company, 1989) [hereafter, Sunstein], pp. 121–31; Small, 97;
SAHC, volume III, p. 409n.

96. The last is what Eve Sedgwick has called "metonymic contagion" in *The Coherence of Gothic Conventions* (rpt. London: Methuen, 1986), p. 149.

97. See William Godwin, *Things As They Are Or The Adventures of Caleb
Williams,* ed. Maurice Hindle (1794; rpt. London: Penguin Books, 1988)
[hereafter, Godwin], pp. 311ff.

98. Godwin, p. 307.

99. Matthew G. Lewis, *The Monk* (1796; rpt. New York: Grove Press, Inc.,
1952), pp. 43–45.

100. Charles Brockden Brown, *Wieland and Memoirs of Carwin The Biloquist*
(New York: Penguin, 1991) [hereafter, Brown], p. 59.

101. On *Wieland,* see Jane Tompkins, *Sensational Designs: The Cultural Work of
American Fiction, 1790–1860* (Oxford: Oxford University Press, 1985), pp.
40–61.

102. The novel is also clearly informed by a variety of other sources, from Coleridge to Rousseau to Richardson (see Sunstein, pp. 106, 126).

103. Mary Shelley, *Frankenstein, or, the Modern Prometheus: The 1818 Text,* ed.
James Rieger (1974; rpt. Chicago: University of Chicago Press, 1982), p. 88.
All further quotations from the novel are from this edition. On the connection between "Alastor" and *Frankenstein,* see L. G. Swingle, "Frankenstein's
Monster and Its Romantic Relatives: Problems of Knowledge in English Romanticism," *Texas Studies in Literature and Language,* 15 (1973): 51–56, 62;
and Small, pp. 141–45.

104. *Frankenstein,* pp. 96–97; 112–22; 143; 206. See Peter Brooks, "'Godlike
Science/Unhallowed Arts': Language, Nature, and Monstrosity," in *The Endurance of Frankenstein: Essays on Mary Shelley's Novel,* ed. George Levine and
U. C. Knoepflmacher (Berkeley: University of California Press, 1979) [hereafter, "'Godlike Science'"], pp. 210–11.

105. *Frankenstein,* p. 182; Frankenstein also says to Walton, "Since you have preserved my narration . . . I would not that a mutilated one should go down
to posterity" (207). The quoted passages in the following two sentences are
from *Frankenstein,* pp. 213 and 218.

106. See "'Godlike Science'," p. 220, and MButler, pp. 158–61.

107. Godwin, pp. 28–30. As with Wordsworth's attention to "artful" speech, Godwin thus also echoes the rhetoric of political treatises such as Townsend's.

108. September, 1814, *JMS,* volume I, p. 25.

109. The quote continues, "and be impressed with the just persuasion that patience and reason and endurance [are the means of] a calm yet irresistible progress. A civil war, which might be engendered by the passions . . . would confirm . . . those military habits . . . with which liberty is incompatible. From the moment that a man is a soldier, he becomes a slave. He is taught obedience . . ." (Clark, p. 253).

110. Jones, volume I, pp. 507–8.

111. Jones, volume I, p. 507.

112. Hutchinson, pp. 32–37.

113. Cameron, p. 315.

114. Jones, volume II, p. 127.

115. Blank, pp. 63–71.

116. See Keach, pp. 94–97.

117. See Stuart Curran, *Shelley's Annus Mirabilis: The Maturing of an Epic Vision* (San Marino: The Huntington Library, 1975) [hereafter, Curran], pp. 148, 143.

118. *Paradise Lost* IV. l. 75; Curran, p. 145.

119. Harper, volume II, p. 307.

120. I take this argument from Curran, pp. 150–51; see also Hogle, pp. 138–47.

121. Shelley, p. 325. Shelley also proposes himself as an historian of fudges, echoing the (1818) satire of Thomas Moore, which Hazlitt reviewed by 25 April 1818 (Hazlitt, volume VII, pp. 287–97); Hazlitt's first pages concentrate on Southey, Coleridge, and Wordsworth.

122. Clark, p. 256.

123. Dawson, p. 5.

124. Jones, volume II, p. 434. By 1822, Shelley's recognition is also linked with his 1821–1822 affair with Jane Williams. For an account of the principles that must have been entailed by Shelley's personal difficulties at this time, see G. M. Matthews, "On Shelley's 'The Triumph of Life,'" *Studia Neophilologica,* 34 (1962): 128–33 [hereafter, Matthews].

125. Clark, pp. 184–86, from "A Treatise On Morals." I am indebted here to Klancher, pp. 129–34, 171.

126. Ironically, in light of the poem's history as "the Chartist's Bible" in the late 1840s and early 1850s and later as a touchstone for the Fabians, *Queen Mab,* on Shelley's instructions, was first printed for an aristocratic audience who would not, Shelley thought, read it themselves but whose sons and daughters he hoped might (see Robert Woof's Exhibition Catalogue, *Shelley: an ineffectual angel?* [Kendal: Wordsworth Trust, 1992], p. 29).

127. See Paul de Man, "Shelley Disfigured," *Deconstruction and Criticism,* ed. Geoffrey H. Hartman (New York: The Seabury Press, 1979) [hereafter, de Man], pp. 42–43; and Donald H. Reiman, *Shelley's "The Triumph of Life," A*

Critical Study (Urbana: University of Illinois Press, 1965) [hereafter, Reiman]. Finally, see Lloyd Abbey, *Destroyer and Preserver: Shelley's Poetic Skepticism* (Lincoln: University of Nebraska, 1979) [hereafter, Abbey], p. 106.

128. De Man, pp. 55; 51–53.

129. De Man, pp. 67–69.

130. Jerome J. McGann, "The Secrets of an Elder Day: Shelley after *Hellas*," in *Shelley: Modern Judgements,* ed. R. B. Woodings (London: Macmillan, 1969) [hereafter, Secrets], p. 262. All quotations from "The Triumph of Life" can be found in Shelley, pp. 455–70.

131. Reiman, pp. 84; 69.

132. Reiman, pp. 48–49, 69. See also Abbey, pp. 8–9, 128; and Edward Duffy, *Rousseau in England: The Context for Shelley's Critique of the Enlightenment* (Berkeley: University of California Press, 1979) [hereafter, Duffy], p. 105.

133. The horned moon fades to "two lessening points of light" (l. 654), which recall the two "starry eyes hung in the gloom of thought" (l. 490), imaging the desire that lures the poet toward his death. The fading moon also serves as a synecdoche for natural flux; thus, what first appears to be an image of transcendence presiding over the visionary's end is on closer inspection rather more ambiguous. See Abbey, p. 137, for a discussion of similar images in "The Triumph of Life."

134. See Donald L. Maddox, "Shelley's *Alastor* and the Legacy of Rousseau," *Studies in Romanticism,* 9 (1970): 82–98; and Duffy, pp. 93–95, 105, for some mixed views of Rousseau's influence on "Alastor."

135. De Man, pp. 43–44; Reiman, p. 41; Abbey, p. 134; Matthews, p. 106.

136. Shelley, p. 451.

137. Reiman, p. 62.

138. See also Duffy, pp. 121–32 on Rousseau's role in the poem.

139. Reiman, p. 101.

140. Clark, p. 278.

141. Ibid.

142. Ibid.

143. Clark, p. 279.

144. Clark, p. 278.

145. Such ordering may, of course, also be syntactical. Structurally, it may be signaled in the movement from trope to trope, a movement to which Shelley calls attention in what Jerome J. McGann dubs "image anthologies" (Veils, p. 206). Alternatively, ordering may be emphasized by the proposed relation between tales embedded within tales.

146. Clark, p. 278.

147. Ibid.

148. Clark, p. 279.

149. Clark, p. 294.

150. See, for example, Reiman, p. 41.

151. See *SAHC,* volume VI, p. 568.

152. See *Secrets,* pp. 267–69, and John A. Hodgson, "The World's Mysterious Doom: Shelley's *The Triumph of Life,*" *ELH,* 42 (1975): 595–622, on love and Rousseau in the poem.
153. In "A Philosophical View of Reform," Shelley writes specifically of Rousseau as a luminary (Clark, p. 233).
154. But see J. Hillis Miller, *The Linguistic Moment: From Wordsworth to Stevens* (Princeton: Princeton University Press, 1985), pp. 114–79, and Hogle, pp. viii, 319–42.

Chapter IV

1. Shelley's poems were first mentioned in print in America in the 1818 edition of Leigh Hunt's *Foliage.* Relatively expensive imported editions of Shelley's poetry as well as some pirated collections that included his poems were available by 1821, although the first full American edition of Shelley's poems did not appear until 1845 (See Julia Power, *Shelley in America in the Nineteenth Century: His Relation to American Critical Thought and His Influence* [Lincoln: University of Nebraska Press, 1940], pp. 4, 9, 23, 196, 211). Emerson included two of Shelley's poems—"The Cloud" and "The Skylark"—in his late anthology, *Parnassus.* See also Emerson's comments on Shelley in his lectures on "The Present Age," *The Early Lectures of Ralph Waldo Emerson,* eds. Robert E. Spiller et al. (Cambridge: The Belknap Press of Harvard University Press, 1966-) [hereafter, *EL*], volume III, pp. 217–18; and *JMN,* 7: 316.
2. *The Letters of Ralph Waldo Emerson,* ed. Ralph L. Rusk (New York: Columbia University Press, 1939) [hereafter, *L*], volume 1, p. 435.
3. This recognition may inform Emerson's comment that it is the heart, *not* the ear, that writers should follow (*EL,* 1: 381–82); more often, Emerson speaks of wanting an eloquence that could "startle and melt & exalt the ear" (*L,* 2: 460).
4. Section III, "Thoughts of the Present State of American Affairs," *Paine,* p. 26. The quote is from *Paradise Lost* IV. ll. 98–99.
5. On the mixed rhetoric and reasoning mustered in support of the Revolution, see Joyce Appleby, *Capitalism and a New Social Order: The Republican Vision of the 1790s* (New York: New York University Press, 1984) [hereafter, Appleby]; on the use of Milton's language in this context, see K. P. Van Anglen, *The New England Milton: Literary Reception and Cultural Authority in the Early Republic* (University Park: Pennsylvania State University, 1993) [hereafter, Van Anglen], pp. 28–65; and Jay Fliegelman, *Prodigals and Pilgrims: The American Revolution Against Patriarchal Authority, 1750–1800* (Cambridge: Cambridge University Press, 1982), especially p. 174.
6. *Paine,* p. 32.
7. John Adams and Timothy Pickering, among others, would accuse Jefferson of plagiarism by the nineties, a mark of shifting (and contested) notions of authority and originality in the Federalist period. For a succinct description

of changing notions of originality in the nineties, see Jay Fliegelman's introduction to *Wieland* (Brown, pp. xxxvii-xl).

8. Noah Webster, *Grammatical Institute* (1783); cited in Michael Warner, *The Letters of the Republic: Publication and the Public Sphere in Eighteenth-Century America* (Cambridge: Harvard University Press, 1990) [hereafter, Warner], p. 122.

9. Phillips Payson, *A Sermon* (Boston, 1778; rpt. in Charles Hyneman and Donald Lutz, eds., *American Political Writing during the Founding Era* [Indianapolis: Liberty Press, 1983]: volume I, pp. 526–28); cited in Warner, p. 123. See also Warner, pp. 1–33, 63–64.

10. See Richard Buel, Jr., *Securing the Revolution: Ideology in American Politics, 1789–1815* (Ithaca: Cornell University Press, 1972) [hereafter, Buel], pp. 93–112.

11. Warner, pp. 67; 63.

12. The piece is variously reprinted as *The Way to Wealth* and as *Father Abraham's Speech*. I draw on Mark R. Patterson, *Paine, Authority, Autonomy and Representation in American Literature, 1776–1865* (Princeton: Princeton University Press, 1988) [hereafter, Patterson], pp. xvi–xxiv; and Warner, chapter three, especially p. 96. See also A. Owen Aldridge, *Early American Literature: A Comparatist Approach* (Princeton: Princeton University Press, 1982) [hereafter, Aldridge], p. 98, on how Franklin's piece was well known but itself circulated anonymously; it was not known to be by his hand until the late seventies.

13. See Larzer Ziff, *Writing in the New World: Prose, Print, and Politics in the Early United States* (New Haven and London: Yale University Press, 1991) [hereafter, Ziff], p. 93. Ziff's indeterminate readership I take to be another characterization (from the perspective of the writer this time) of Warner's abstract subject.

14. See his defense of Samuel Hemphill's 1734 plagiarized sermons (Benjamin Franklin, *Writings,* ed. J. A. Leo Lemay [New York: Library of America, 1987], [hereafter, Franklin], p. 1400) or his refusal of a patent for his stove (Franklin, pp. 1417–18). See Ziff, pp. 103–4.

15. Warner, pp. 125–26.

16. The echoes of Wordsworth's female speaker may come from cultural commonplaces; see Brown, pp. 145, 219, in which Brown seems to dismantle Wordsworth's association of artless sincerity, sympathy, and class; see also Clara's echo of Wordsworth's vagrant: "I will die, but then only when my tale is at an end" (p. 260). For a different reading of Brown's project, see Kenneth Dauber, *The Idea of Authorship in America: Democratic Poetics from Franklin to Melville* (Madison: The University of Wisconsin Press, 1990), chapter two.

17. See, for instance, Brown, p. 26. Even in the 1790s, the decade in which the first national copyright law was enacted, *Wieland* was published anonymously; the title page of *Wieland* simply read: "Copyright Secured," although Brown's authorship was no secret and his prefatory advertisement was signed with his initials (Brown, pp. xxxix, 4).

18. Brown, p. 183; see also, for example, Brown, pp. 150, 206, 246, 249, 266, 269, 272. On Brown's concern with agency and with theatricality, see Fliegelman in Brown, pp. xvii, xxx–xxxvi; Warner, p. 136–38, further discusses longer-standing American suspicions of politeness, which was equated with theatricality as opposed to true virtue. Some of Brown's paranoia over unseen, deadly, and agentless infections presumably also reflects the yellow fever epidemic of the period.

19. Armstrong, *Desire and Domestic Fiction.* See also Isaac Kramnick, "The 'Great National Discussion': The Discourse of Politics in 1787," *The William and Mary Quarterly,* 3d ser. 45 (1988): 3–32 [hereafter, Kramnick], on American debates over "virtue" in the decade preceding, specifically in the Federalist debates.

20. See Warner, pp. 173–75.

21. See Franklin, pp. 252–53, 326, 1246, 1249, 1250, 1252, 1388, in which Thomson is quoted on Newton, Locke, Boyle, and Bacon as well as on education of the young, on love as providing education, and, finally, in a prayer that the soul be filled with knowledge and virtue. See also Art, pp. 414ff. and Appendix I, on audiences for *The Seasons.* While the text was not institutionalized for use in schools in America until 1852, it was widely circulated; in the forty years between 1777 and 1817, thirty American editions were issued.

22. The quotation is from Boyer, here quoted from Hannah Foster, *The Coquette* (Oxford: Oxford University Press, 1986) [hereafter, *The Coquette*], p. 42. Boyer is quoting lines 1161–75 of "Spring."

23. *The Coquette,* p. 57. In *The Coquette* fancy and judgment are repeatedly contrasted; the former is explicitly aligned with infatuation, sensuality, and delusion (see pp. 26, 28, 51, 60, 88, 103).

24. *The Coquette,* p. 53.

25. Significantly, in *Wieland* the father of the family dies by spontaneous combustion. The phrase "enlightened zeal" appears in Hamilton's first Federalist paper; for a discussion of the renewed debates over energy and violence in the late nineties, see Buel, pp. 182–83.

26. On how Thomson's passage on marriage and an education in virtue might serve political ends, see Ruth H. Block, "The Gendered Meanings of Virtue in Revolutionary America," *Signs,* 13 (1987): 37–58; and Linda K. Kerber, *Women of the Republic: Intellect and Ideology in Revolutionary America* (Chapel Hill: University of North Carolina Press, 1980). Finally, see Nancy Armstrong and Leonard Tennenhouse, *The Imaginary Puritan: Literature, Intellectual Labor, and the Origins of Personal Life* (Berkeley: University of California Press, 1992), especially pp. 202–16, on the continuity between captivity narratives and the investment of national identity in the image of the isolated female body.

27. *The Coquette,* pp. 112–13.

28. Ibid; I am grateful to Elizabeth Hudon Canning for this suggestion.

29. *The Coquette,* p. 41.

30. Warner, p. 173.

31. While the usual view of appropriate reading for republican women was more limited—Milton, Shakespeare, *The Spectator,* sometimes Thomson, and Defoe, among secular works—sentimental novels were in circulation. On women's reading, see Richard D. Brown, *Knowledge is Power: The Diffusion of Information in Early America, 1700–1865* (Oxford: Oxford University Press, 1989), chapter seven. On the numbers of editions of Foster's novel printed, see *The Coquette,* p. xxii. On audience reactions to the novel, see Cathy N. Davidson, *Revolution and the Word: The Rise of the Novel in America* (Oxford: Oxford University Press, 1986), pp. 110–35, 140–50. On sentimental fiction and reading habits more generally, see Cathy N. Davidson, "The Life and Times of *Charlotte Temple:* The Biography of a Book," in *Reading in America: Literature & Social History,* ed. Cathy N. Davidson (Baltimore: The Johns Hopkins University Press, 1989), pp. 157–79.

32. Peter Porcupine [William Cobbett], *A Kick for a Bite; or, Review upon Review; with a Critical Essay, on the Works of Mrs. S. Rowson; in A Letter to the Editor, or Editors, of the American Monthly Review* (Philadelphia: Thomas Bradford, 1795), p. 24. Cobbett is specifically writing about a play by Rowson in this passage, the public aspect of which may affect his view.

33. Michael Warner, "The Mass Public and the Mass Subject," in *The Phantom Public Sphere,* ed. Bruce Robbins (Minneapolis: University of Minnesota Press, 1993), especially p. 236.

34. William Charvat, *The Profession of Authorship in America, 1800–1870* (1968; rpt. New York: Columbia University Press, 1992) [hereafter, Charvat], p. 6.

35. Quoted in John William Ward, *Andrew Jackson: Symbol for an Age* (Oxford: Oxford University Press, 1955), p. 65.

36. Franklin, pp. 1311–12; the original account is from Cotton Mather, *The Wonderful Work of Christ in America* (London, 1702), as pointed out by J. A. Leo Lemay and P. M. Zall in the 1986 Norton critical edition of the *Autobiography* (p. 5).

37. Charvat, p. 11, argues that although from 1780–1810 the status of poetry was high, it was "used universally in newspapers and magazines—not only as filler but as primary material. Editors never paid for it because the supply was unlimited: everybody wrote it."

38. See Ziff, pp. 88–89.

39. Franklin, p. 1380. This analysis of Franklin's position on libraries is indebted to Ziff, pp. 88–90.

40. Warner, pp. 132–38, points out that the tension between politeness and virtue was not usually a conscious tension.

41. See Appleby, chapter one, and Kramnick, pp. 3–32.

42. Letter to Nathaniel Butwell, Esq., 14 March 1818 from *The Writings of Thomas Jefferson,* ed. A. A. Lipscomb and A. E. Bergh (Washington, D.C.: The Thomas Jefferson Memorial Association, 1905), volume XV, p. 166.

43. William C. Dowling, *Poetry & Ideology in Revolutionary Connecticut* (Athens: University of Georgia Press, 1990) [hereafter, Dowling], pp. xiv–xv, calls Thomson and Pope the moving spirits of the Revolution.

44. *The Columbiad*, p. 847. All quotes are from Joel Barlow, *The Columbiad* (Washington City: Joseph Milligan, 1825), reprinted in *The Works of Joel Barlow*, ed. William K. Bottorff and Arthur L. Ford (Gainesville, Fla.: Scholars' Facsimiles and Reprints, 1970), volume II: *Poetry.*

45. I take this argument from Dowling, pp. 56–58. See also Aldridge, pp. 158–85, on the pervasiveness of the *translatio* theme in the Federal period.

46. However, see William C. Spengemann's *A New World of Words: Redefining Early American Literature* (New Haven and London: Yale University Press, 1994) [hereafter, Spengemann], pp. 166–70, on Barlow's difficulties with his genre, plot, and hero in the earlier *The Vision of Columbus.*

47. *The Columbiad*, pp. 382, 850.

48. *The Columbiad*, p. 375; see also p. 377.

49. Spengemann, pp. 2–7.

50. The quotation is from *The Columbiad*, Book I, l. 529; the argument about Barlow's use of commerce to replace ideology is from Dowling, pp. 101–26.

51. Cited in Charvat, p. 8. See Warner, p. 121; Charvat, pp. 7–10.

52. Cited in Charvat, p. 12.

53. *The Poems of Philip Freneau, Poet of the American Revolution,* ed. Fred Lewis Pattee (Princeton: The University Library, 1903) [hereafter, *Freneau*], volume II, p. 304.

54. The phrase comes from Alfred F. Young, "The Framers of the Constitution and the 'Genius' of the People," *Radical History Review,* 42 (1988): 11, 14.

55. *Poems of Freneau,* ed. Harry Hayden Clark (New York: Harcourt, Brace and Company, 1929) [hereafter, Freneau, *Poems*], pp. 124–25. All quotes from "On Mr. Paine's Rights of Man" are from this text.

56. Cited in Freneau, *Poems,* xxxii. Similarly, as cited in *Freneau,* volume I, p. 142, an earlier (1775) poem, which Freneau never reprinted, was first advertised in Holt's *New York Journal* of 6 July as blending "Ciceronian eloquence and patriotic fire." By 1798 both images—of Ciceronian eloquence and of fire—become signals of danger as in, for example, Brown's *Wieland.*

57. Freneau, *Poems,* p. 117.

58. Freneau, *Poems,* pp. xxiii–xxiv.

59. Freneau, *Poems,* pp. 207, 211. All quotations from "The Power of Fancy" are from this text.

60. Freneau, *Poems,* pp. 355–56; all quotations from "The Indian Burying Ground" are taken from this text.

61. Cited in Grantland S. Rice, "Crèvecoeur and the Politics of Authorship in Republican America," *Early American Literature,* 28 (Fall 1993): 97. See also Barlow's endnotes to *The Columbiad,* which address similar theories about climates and civilizations.

62. Thomas Jefferson, *Writings,* ed. Merrill D. Peterson (New York: The Library of America, 1984), pp. 148–49, from "Notes on the State of Virginia," Query V.

63. Neil Hertz, *The End of the Line: Essays on Psychoanalysis and the Sublime* (New York: Columbia University Press, 1985), pp. 40–60. While Hertz's discussion of "blockage," aligned with the mathematical sublime, obviously draws on psychoanalysis, I am taking the rhetorical features Hertz describes primarily as culturally disseminated and culturally legible.

64. Charles Sellers, *The Market Revolution: Jacksonian America, 1815–1846* (Oxford: Oxford University Press, 1991) [hereafter, Sellers], pp. 3–5; see also Sellers, chapter twelve, on the rise of bourgeois sentimental culture.

65. "The Mother of Washington" can be found in *American Women Poets of the Nineteenth Century,* ed. Cheryl Walker (New Brunswick: Rutgers University Press, 1992) [hereafter, Walker], pp. 5–7.

66. Walker, pp. 1–2.

67. See Karen Halttunen, *Confidence Men and Painted Women: A Study of Middle-class Culture in America, 1830–1879* (New Haven and London: Yale University Press, 1982) [hereafter, Halttunen], chapter five, on middle-class mourning practices.

68. The 1800 etching and engraving by James Akin and William Harrison, Jr. was issued within seven weeks of Washington's death and widely advertised as "admirably calculated to ornament the parlour, or hang as a centre-piece . . . it will also suit to enrich the labours of the needle upon white sattin, and will be found an agreeable pastime for the Ladies" (*Philadelphia Gazette,* 23, 25, 28, 30 January; 4, 6, 8, 11 February 1800). The piece is the prototype for the iconography of later American mourning art. See Wendy C. Wick, *George Washington: An American Icon; The Eighteenth-Century Graphic Portraits* (Washington, D.C.: The Smithsonian Institute Traveling Exhibition Service and the National Portrait Gallery Smithsonian Institution and the Barra Foundation, 1982), pp. 138–42.

69. See Charvat, pp. 105, 109ff.

70. Albert McLean, Jr. *William Cullen Bryant* (Twayne's United States Authors Series) (New Haven: College and University Press, 1964) [hereafter, *Bryant*], pp. 142–44, reproduces both the 1817 and the 1821 versions of the poem.

71. It was "To a Waterfowl" that Emerson, for instance, copied very early (1822) into his journals (*JMN,* 1: 392–93) and also returned to when thinking about what to include in his anthology, *Parnassus,* in the journals of the early seventies (*JMN,* 16: 224).

72. Parke Godwin, ed., *A Biography of William Cullen Bryant, with Extracts from His Private Correspondence* (1883; rpt. New York: Russell & Russell, 1967), volume I, p. 37; see also *Bryant,* pp. 29, 65–84, 119–20, for the suggestions about Bryant's uses of Blair, Gray, Thomson, Wordsworth, and Sigourney.

73. On "Fortus" and Emerson's knowledge of Milton and Wordsworth, see Robert D. Richardson, Jr., *Emerson: The Mind on Fire* (Berkeley: University of California Press, 1995) [hereafter, Richardson], p. 176. Where not otherwise identified, the primary source for facts about Emerson's life is Richardson.

74. See *JMN*, 1: 41, 379, 380. Also in 1815, the same year he wrote his poem on the end of the War of 1812, Emerson was excitedly reading Johnson's *Lives of the Poets,* including the life of Milton (*L,* 1: 10).

75. On Franklin and the *Federalist* papers, see *JMN*, 1: 399, 397; on Bryant, *JMN*, 1: 353, 392–93; and Richardson, p. 316.

76. Critical views of Emerson are nicely summarized in Eric Cheyfitz's introduction to the English translation of Maurice Gonnaud's *An Uneasy Solitude: Individual and Society in the Work of Ralph Waldo Emerson,* trans. Lawrence Rosenwald (Princeton: Princeton University Press, 1987); and in Michael Lopez, *Emerson and Power: Creative Antagonism in the Nineteenth Century* (DeKalb: Northern Illinois University Press, 1996). In one form or another, views of Emerson's solitary (and ethereal) ideal have been emphasized at least since Stephen E. Whicher's 1953 *Freedom and Fate: An Inner Life of Ralph Waldo Emerson.* More recently, Len Gougeon, in *Virtue's Hero: Emerson, Anti-Slavery, and Reform* (Athens: University of Georgia Press, 1990) [hereafter, Gougeon] and David M. Robinson, in *Emerson and the Conduct of Life: Pragmatism and Ethical Purpose in The Later Work* (Cambridge: Cambridge University Press, 1993) [hereafter, Robinson] have persuasively argued that Emerson was increasingly engaged in social and political issues by the late thirties.

77. See especially Sellers, chapter twelve; Michael T. Gilmore, *American Romanticism and the Marketplace* (Chicago: University of Chicago Press, 1985), pp. 1–34; and Mary Kupiec Cayton, *Emerson's Emergence: Self and Society in the Transformation of New England, 1800–1845* (Chapel Hill: University of North Carolina Press, 1989) [hereafter, Cayton].

78. See Robinson, pp. 12–29, for a synopsis of how what I have been calling "work" and one strand of idleness or passivity engages theological questions of works and grace current in the American Protestant circles of Emerson's day.

79. See also Cayton, p. 46; and, for example, *L,* 2: 242, 245. As Susan L. Roberson points out in *Emerson in His Sermons: A Man-made Self* (Columbia: University of Missouri Press, 1995), especially pp. 113–19, some of Emerson's anxiety about sloth can be linked with advice books and set pieces of theological sermonizing.

80. *Emerson: Collected Poems & Translations,* ed. Harold Bloom and Paul Kane (New York: The Library of America, 1994) [hereafter, *Poems*], pp. 287–88.

81. See Robert A. Ferguson, *Law and Letters in American Culture* (Cambridge: Harvard University Press, 1984), especially pp. 11–16, 87–88, 178–82; and Van Anglen, pp. 34–35.

82. On how the period between 1815 and 1848 may be characterized as Jacksonian, see Harry L. Watson, *Liberty and Power: The Politics of Jacksonian America* (New York: Hill and Wang, 1990) [hereafter, Watson]. Admittedly, unlike the 1819 panic, the 1837 panic was more a purely financial than a business affair: the economy continued to grow, although prices dropped; employment grew, although there were business failures; the east coast in

particular did not see what economists would call a real depression. Nonetheless, at the time both panics probably seemed related to banking (the panic of 1819 was related to the Second National Bank's attempt to raise bank reserves and curtail loose credit practices, while the 1837 panic coincided with Jackson's refusal to renew The Second National Bank charter). Emerson felt the 1837–1843 depression most, in that his money was tied up in bank stock: his letters from the period often read more like account books than personal communications. I would like to thank Michael Foley for offering me an economist's view.

83. See Cayton, pp. 36–49.

84. For Emerson's views on public spaces, crowds, and associations, see Gougeon, pp. 41–85, especially p. 47; and Christopher Newfield, *The Emerson Effect: Individualism and Submission in America* (Chicago: University of Chicago Press, 1996), especially pp. 97–105, 117–25.

85. I have silently omitted some of the revisions marked in the journal.

86. See Jeanne Boydston, *Home and Work: Housework, Wages, and the Ideology of Labor in the Early Republic* (Oxford: Oxford University Press, 1990), chapter seven.

87. Wordsworth's attention to "lowly" people is explicitly contrasted with what is "vicious" in Milton's "royal imagery" in an 1834 journal entry (*JMN*, 4: 312–13). On Emerson's uses of Wordsworth by the thirties, see B. L. Packer, *Emerson's Fall: A New Interpretation of the Major Essays* (New York: Continuum, 1982) [hereafter, Packer], pp. 105–9.

88. For a more general account of transatlantic literary exchange, see Robert Weisbuch, *Atlantic Double-Cross: American Literature and British Influence in the Age of Emerson* (Chicago: University of Chicago Press, 1986).

89. *Letters,* volume VI, part III, p. 519; *Letters,* volume VII, part IV, p. 231. "Par nobile Fratrum" can mean "a noble or a famous pair of brothers" or "a notorious or infamous pair of brothers." Wordsworth clearly intended the less positive meaning; he is quoting Horace's *Satires* (II.3, l. 243). Wordsworth's letter is echoed in the anonymous review of Carlyle in *Brother Jonathan* (27 May 1843): 109–10, describing Emerson and Carlyle as part of a new breed that "do not know there is any such language as English" (cited in Richard F. Teichgraeber III, *Sublime Thoughts/Penny Wisdom: Situating Emerson and Thoreau in the American Market* [Baltimore: The Johns Hopkins University Press, 1995], [hereafter, Teichgraeber], p. 203).

90. On Wordsworth's importance to Emerson, see Frank T. Thompson, "Emerson's Theory and Practice of Poetry," *PMLA,* 43 (1928): 1170–84; and Carl F. Strauch, "The Mind's Voice: Emerson's Poetic Styles," *ESQ,* 60 (1970): 43–59 [hereafter, Strauch]. My reading most closely accords with the conclusions offered by Packer, pp. 105–9.

91. See Cayton, pp. 149–60; Richardson, p. 153.

92. On the lyceum movement, see Cayton, pp. 140–41, 150–51; on the role of newspapers and periodicals in forging Emerson's reputation, see Teichgraeber, pp. 187–221; on Emerson's own awareness of the way ticket

sales depended on newspaper advertisements, see *L,* 2: 9, 99; *L,* 3: 127, 134, 148.

93. Cayton, p. 141.

94. In this, I closely follow the structural analyses offered in Julie Ellison's *Emerson's Romantic Style* (Princeton: Princeton University Press, 1984), especially chapter five; I draw also on the understandings offered in Packer, and in John Michael's *Emerson and Skepticism: The Cipher of the World* (Baltimore: The Johns Hopkins University Press, 1988). Such verbal manipulation was rooted in the political climate and political debates of the era of Jacksonian "persuasion" (see Watson and Marvin Meyers, *The Jacksonian Persuasion: Politics and Belief* [Stanford: Stanford University Press, 1960] and Patterson, pp. 142–43).

95. Charles Sellers, for example, writes, "In bourgeois culture, validating authority was passing from priesthoods to secular intellectuals; . . . their institutional locus from church through printed page and lecture platform to the modern university. A capitalist order requiring broad assent conferred bourgeois status on validating intellectuals, thereby disarming even the radical[.] . . . The pivotal exemplar was Ralph Waldo Emerson" (Sellers, pp. 375–76; see also pp. 375–80). Contemporary reactions to Emerson's prose are cited and summarized in Teichgraeber, pp. 184–86, 203, 208–9.

96. "A Disciple," "Emerson's Essays," *United States Magazine and Democratic Review,* 16 (June 1845): 590.

97. In *Seeing and Being: The Plight of the Participant Observer in Emerson, James, Adams, and Faulkner* (Middletown, Ct.: Wesleyan University Press, 1981) [hereafter, Porter], p. 93, Carolyn Porter describes "The American Scholar" as an attempt to demystify shifting cultural definitions.

98. For a view of shifting definitions of labor including literary labor, see Michael Newbury, "Healthful Employment: Hawthorne, Thoreau, and Middle-Class Fitness," *American Quarterly,* 47 (December 1995): 681–714. Emerson does not entirely fit Newbury's paradigm, in part because poetry was not professionalized in the way prose writing was (Joshua L. Rosenbloom, "Economics and the Emergence of Modern Publishing in the United States," *Publishing History,* 29 [Spring 1991]: 47–68).

99. On Emerson's gendered pronouns, see David Leverenz, "The Politics of Emerson's Man-Making Words," *PMLA,* 101 (January 1986): 38–56. Through his conversations with Margaret Fuller, Emerson became conscious of his uses of gendered language. See Christina Zwarg, *Feminist Conversations: Fuller, Emerson, and the Play of Reading* (Ithaca: Cornell University Press, 1995) [hereafter, Zwarg], p. 177.

100. See Hyatt H. Waggoner, *Emerson as Poet* (Princeton: Princeton University Press, 1974), p. 78; and David Van Leer, *Emerson's Epistemology: The Argument of the Essays* (Cambridge: Cambridge University Press, 1986), pp. 147–50, especially p. 149.

101. See also *Nature* and the 1834 journal entry from *JMN,* 4: 323, for other examples of how private thought is refigured as publicly useful. On the poet

and the political resonance of the figure as "representative," see Patterson, pp. 156–68.

102. See David Porter, *Emerson and Literary Change* (Cambridge: Harvard University Press, 1978) [hereafter, DPorter], pp. 2–3. On Emerson's figures of the poet (or masks) in the poems and essays, see DPorter, pp. 90–94, and Strauch, pp. 52–53.

103. *The Poetry Notebooks of Ralph Waldo Emerson,* ed. Ralph H. Orth, Albert J. Von Frank, Linda Allardt, and David W. Hill (Columbia: University of Missouri Press, 1986) [hereafter, *PN*], p. 4; *Poems,* p. 312.

104. The full sentence in the journal reads, "Great in act but instantly dwarfed by self-indulgence," an acknowledged self-consciousness the essays also represent in their shifts of perspective.

105. Individual agency—the term is also Emerson's—is clearly an issue over which his letters from the late twenties express concern; see *L,* 1: 188, 207. On how later Emerson responded to Fuller in readdressing the question of agency, see Zwarg, especially pp. 221–37. On how Emerson's sense of the "constructed nature of the self as a series of subject positions in debate" was related to his sense of Fuller's nascent feminist critique, see Zwarg, pp. 16–17, 177.

106. On the composition of the poem, see Richardson, p. 177. For a different characterization of the poem, see R. A. Yoder, *Emerson and the Orphic Poet in America* (Berkeley: University of California Press, 1978) [hereafter, Yoder], pp. 82–84. "The Rhodora" can be found in *Poems,* p. 31.

107. Porter, p. 95.

108. Porter, pp. 105–7.

109. See *Poems,* pp. 348–56.

110. See Paul H. Fry, *The Poet's Calling in the English Ode* (New Haven and London: Yale University Press, 1980), especially pp. 1–14.

111. Cited, *Poems,* p. 560; emphasis added.

112. The dating comes from *PN,* p. 733.

113. *JMN,* 3: 305. However, Emerson's distaste did not stem from the same source as Shelley's, even as both misread Wordsworth's irony in the poem.

114. From the *New-York Daily Tribune,* 7 December 1844, p. 1. Reprinted in *Margaret Fuller: Essays on American Life and Letters,* ed. Joel Myerson (Schenectady, N.Y.: College & University Press, 1978), p. 245.

115. This can be seen not only in Fuller's review of Emerson, but also in her *Summer on the Lakes, in 1843* (1844; rpt. Urbana: University of Illinois Press, 1991), for example, pp. 42 or 76. See also Zwarg, pp. 97–124.

116. "Hamatreya" can be found in *Poems,* pp. 28–29.

117. For an account of Emerson's engagement with and his letter on the Cherokees, see Gougeon, pp. 57–59.

118. Emerson himself described his poetry—which he was at first reluctant to collect for publication—as "rough & most uncanonical" (*L,* 3: 350; see also *L,* 3: 227, 234).

119. This is, in essence, Karen Halttunen's argument about attitudes toward hypocrisy in Victorian America generally.

120. "The Poet" (poem) appears in *PN,* pp. 63–65.

121. Both Yoder, p. 117, and David Porter single out "The Discontented Poet" for special notice; the latter offers a somewhat different reading than I offer here (DPorter, pp. 115–23).

Selected Bibliography

Altick, Richard D. *The English Common Reader: A Social History of the Mass Reading Public, 1800–1900.* Chicago: University of Chicago Press, 1957.

Appleby, Joyce. *Capitalism and a New Social Order: The Republican Vision of the 1790s.* New York: New York University Press, 1984.

Armstrong, Nancy and Leonard Tennenhouse. *The Imaginary Puritan: Literature, Intellectual Labor, and the Origins of Personal Life.* Berkeley: University of California Press, 1992.

Barrell, John. *English Literature in History, 1730–80: An Equal, Wide Survey.* New York: St. Martin's Press, 1983.

Bewell, Alan. *Wordsworth and the Enlightenment: Nature, Man, and Society in the Experimental Poetry.* New Haven: Yale University Press, 1989.

Boydston, Jeanne. *Home and Work: Housework, Wages, and the Ideology of Labor in the Early Republic.* Oxford: Oxford University Press, 1990.

Buel, Richard, Jr. *Securing the Revolution: Ideology in American Politics, 1789–1815.* Ithaca: Cornell University Press, 1972.

Cameron, Kenneth Neill. *Shelley: The Golden Years.* Cambridge: Harvard University Press, 1974.

Cayton, Mary Kupiec. *Emerson's Emergence: Self and Society in the Transformation of New England, 1800–1845.* Chapel Hill: University of North Carolina Press, 1989.

Chandler, James K. *Wordsworth's Second Nature: A Study of the Poetry and Politics.* Chicago: University of Chicago Press, 1984.

Charvat, William. *The Profession of Authorship in America, 1800–1870.* 1968; rpt. New York: Columbia University Press, 1992.

Cohen, Ralph. *The Art of Discrimination: Thomson's* The Seasons *and the Language of Criticism.* Berkeley: University of California Press, 1964.

———. *The Unfolding of* The Seasons. Baltimore: The Johns Hopkins Press, 1970.

Curran, Stuart. *Poetic Form and British Romanticism.* Oxford: Oxford University Press, 1986.

———. *Shelley's Annus Mirabilis: The Maturing of an Epic Vision.* San Marino: The Huntington Library, 1975.

Davidson, Cathy N. *Revolution and the Word: The Rise of the Novel in America.* Oxford: Oxford University Press, 1986.

Dawson, P. M. S. *The Unacknowledged Legislator: Shelly and Politics.* Oxford: Clarendon Press, 1980.

De Man, Paul. "Shelley Disfigured." In *Deconstruction and Criticism.* Ed. Geoffrey H. Hartman. New York: The Seabury Press, 1979, pp. 39–73.

Dowling, William C. *Poetry & Ideology in Revolutionary Connecticut.* Athens: University of Georgia Press, 1990.

Ellison, Julie. *Emerson's Romantic Style.* Princeton: Princeton University Press, 1984.

Emerson, Ralph Waldo. *The Collected Works of Ralph Waldo Emerson.* Volumes I-VII. Ed. Robert E. Spiller, Alfred R. Ferguson, et al. Cambridge: The Belknap Press of Harvard University Press, 1971.

———. *The Early Lectures of Ralph Waldo Emerson.* Volumes I-III. Ed. Robert E. Spiller et al. Cambridge: The Belknap Press of Harvard University Press, 1959–1972.

———. *Emerson: Collected Poems & Translations.* Ed. Harold Bloom and Paul Kane. New York: The Library of America, 1994.

———. *The Journals and Miscellaneous Notebooks of Ralph Waldo Emerson.* Volumes I-XVI. Ed. William H. Gilman et al. Cambridge: The Belknap Press of Harvard University Press, 1960–1982.

———. *The Letters of Ralph Waldo Emerson.* Volumes I-III. Ed. Ralph L. Rusk. New York: Columbia University Press, 1939.

———. *The Poetry Notebooks of Ralph Waldo Emerson.* Ed. Ralph H. Orth, Albert J. Von Frank, Linda Allardt, and David W. Hill. Columbia: University of Missouri Press, 1986.

Erickson, Lee. *The Economy of Literary Form: English Literature and the Industrialization of Publishing, 1800–1850.* Baltimore: The Johns Hopkins University Press, 1996.

Galperin, William H. *The Return of the Visible in British Romanticism.* Baltimore: The Johns Hopkins University Press, 1993.

———. *Revision and Authority in Wordsworth: The Interpretation of a Career.* Philadelphia: University of Pennsylvania Press, 1989.

Gougeon, Len. *Virtue's Hero: Emerson, Anti-Slavery, and Reform.* Athens: University of Georgia Press, 1990.

Hartman, Geoffrey. "'*Was It for This* . . . ?': Wordsworth and the Birth of the Gods." In *Romantic Revolutions: Criticism and Theory.* Ed. Kenneth R. Johnston, Gilbert Chaitin, Karen Hanson, and Herbert Marks. Bloomington: Indiana University Press, 1990, pp. 8–25.

———. *Wordsworth's Poetry, 1787–1814.* 1971; rev. ed. New Haven: Yale University Press, 1964.

Hoagwood, Terence Allan. *Skepticism and Ideology: Shelley's Political Prose and Its Philosophical Context from Bacon to Marx.* Iowa City: University of Iowa Press, 1988.

Hogle, Jerrold E. *Shelley's Process: Radical Transference and the Development of His Major Works.* Oxford: Oxford University Press, 1988.

Jacobus, Mary. *Tradition and Experiment in Wordsworth's* Lyrical Ballads. Oxford: Clarendon Press, 1976.

Janowitz, Anne. *England's Ruins: Poetic Purpose and the National Landscape.* Oxford: Basil Blackwell, 1990.

Keach, William. *Shelley's Style.* London: Methuen, 1984.

Klancher, Jon P. *The Making of English Reading Audiences, 1790–1832.* Madison: University of Wisconsin Press, 1987.

Kramnick, Isaac. "The 'Great National Discussion': The Discourse of Politics in 1787." *The William and Mary Quarterly,* 3d ser. 45 (1988): 3–32.

Liu, Alan. *Wordsworth: The Sense of History.* Stanford: Stanford University Press, 1989.

McGann, Jerome J. *The Romantic Ideology: A Critical Investigation.* Chicago: University of Chicago Press, 1983.

———. "The Secrets of an Elder Day: Shelley after *Hellas.*" In *Shelley: Modern Judgements.* Ed. R. B. Woodings. London: Macmillan, 1969, pp. 253–71.

———. "Shelley's Veils: A Thousand Images of Loveliness." In *Romantic and Victorian.* Ed. W. Paul Elledge and Richard L. Hoffman. Cranbury, N.J.: Fairleigh Dickinson University Press, 1971, pp. 198–218.

McKillop, Alan Dugald. *The Background of Thomson's Seasons.* Minneapolis: University of Minnesota Press, 1942.

Manning, Peter J. *Reading Romantics: Texts and Contexts.* Oxford: Oxford University Press, 1990.

Mayo, Robert D. *The English Novel in the Magazines, 1740–1815.* London: Oxford University Press, 1962.

Michael, John. *Emerson and Skepticism: The Cipher of the World.* Baltimore: The Johns Hopkins University Press, 1988.

Miles, Robert. *Gothic Writing, 1750–1820: A Genealogy.* London: Routledge, 1993.

Mudge, Branford K. "The Man with Two Brains: Gothic Novels, Popular Culture, Literary History." *PMLA,* 107 (1992): 92–104.

The New Eighteenth Century: Theory, Politics, English Literature. Ed. Felicity Nussbaum and Laura Brown. London: Methuen, 1987.

Newlyn, Lucy. *Coleridge, Wordsworth, and the Language of Allusion.* Oxford: Clarendon Press, 1986.

Packer, B. L. *Emerson's Fall: A New Interpretation of the Major Essays.* New York: Continuum, 1982.

Parker, Reeve. "'Finer Distance': The Narrative Art of Wordsworth's 'The Wanderer'." *ELH,* 39 (1972): 87–111.

———. "'Oh Could You Hear His Voice!': Wordsworth, Coleridge, and Ventriloquism." In *Romanticism and Language.* Ed. Arden Reed. Ithaca: Cornell University Press, 1984, pp. 125–43.

Patterson, Mark R. *Paine, Authority, Autonomy and Representation in American Literature, 1776–1865.* Princeton: Princeton University Press, 1988.

Paulson, Ronald. *Breaking and Remaking: Aesthetic Practice in England, 1700–1820.* New Brunswick: Rutgers University Press, 1989.

Porter, Carolyn. *Seeing and Being: The Plight of the Participant Observer in Emerson, James, Adams, and Faulkner.* Middletown: Wesleyan University Press, 1981.

Porter, David. *Emerson and Literary Change.* Cambridge: Harvard University Press, 1978.

Price, Martin. *To the Palace of Wisdom: Studies in Order and Energy from Dryden to Blake.* Garden City, N.Y.: Doubleday and Company, Inc., 1964.

Reiman, Donald H. *Shelley's "The Triumph of Life," A Critical Study.* Urbana: University of Illinois Press, 1965.

Rice, Grantland S. "Crèvecoeur and the Politics of Authorship in Republican America." *Early American Literature,* 28 (Fall 1993): 91–119.

Richardson, Robert D., Jr. *Emerson: The Mind on Fire.* Berkeley: University of California Press, 1995.

Robinson, David M. *Emerson and the Conduct of Life: Pragmatism and Ethical Purpose in The Later Work.* Cambridge: Cambridge University Press, 1993.

Roe, Nicholas. *Wordsworth and Coleridge: The Radical Years.* Oxford: Clarendon Press, 1988.

Rosenbloom, Joshua L. "Economics and the Emergence of Modern Publishing in the United States." *Publishing History,* 29 (Spring 1991): 47–68.

Ruoff, Gene W., Ed. *The Romantics and Us: Essays on Literature and Culture.* New Brunswick: Rutgers University Press, 1990.

Sellers, Charles. *The Market Revolution: Jacksonian America, 1815–1846.* Oxford: Oxford University Press, 1991.

Sheats, Paul D. *The Making of Wordsworth's Poetry, 1785–1798.* Cambridge: Harvard University Press, 1973.

Shelley, Percy Bysshe. *A Defence of Poetry, Shelley's Prose or the Trumpet of a Prophecy.* Ed. David Lee Clark. Albuquerque: The University of New Mexico Press, 1954.

———. *The Esdaile Notebook: A Volume of Early Poems by Percy Bysshe Shelley.* Ed. Kenneth Neill Cameron. New York: Alfred A. Knopf, 1964.

———. *The Letters of Percy Bysshe Shelley.* Ed. Frederick L. Jones. Oxford: Clarendon Press, 1964.

———. *Poetical Works.* Ed. Thomas Hutchinson. Oxford: Oxford University Press, 1970.

———. *Shelley's Poetry and Prose.* Ed. Donald H. Reiman and Sharon B. Powers. New York: W. W. Norton, 1977.

Simpson, David. *Wordsworth's Historical Imagination: The Poetry of Displacement.* London: Methuen, 1987.

Sitter, John. *Literary Loneliness in Mid-Eighteenth-Century England.* Ithaca: Cornell University Press, 1982.

Spengemann, William C. *A New World of Words: Redefining Early American Literature.* New Haven: Yale University Press, 1994.

Swann, Karen. "Suffering and Sensation in *The Ruined Cottage.*" *PMLA,* 106 (1991): 83–95.

Teichgraeber, Richard F., III. *Sublime Thoughts/Penny Wisdom: Situating Emerson and Thoreau in the American Market.* Baltimore: The Johns Hopkins University Press, 1995.

Thompson, E. P. "Disenchantment or Default? A Lay Sermon." In *Power and Consciousness.* Ed. Conor Cruise O'Brien and William Dean Vanech. New York: New York University Press, 1969, pp. 149–81.

Thomson, James. *The Complete Poetical Works of James Thomson.* Ed. J. Logie Robertson. London: Oxford University Press, 1908.

————. *James Thomson (1700–1748): Letters and Documents.* Ed. Alan Dugald McKillop. Lawrence: University of Kansas Press, 1958.

Waggoner, Hyatt H. *Emerson as Poet.* Princeton: Princeton University Press, 1974.

Warner, Michael. *The Letters of the Republic: Publication and the Public Sphere in Eighteenth-Century America.* Cambridge: Harvard University Press, 1990.

Wasserman, Earl R. *Shelley: A Critical Reading.* Baltimore: The Johns Hopkins University Press, 1971.

William Wordsworth and the Age of English Romanticism. Ed. Jonathan Wordsworth, Michael C. Jaye, and Robert Woolf. New Brunswick: Rutgers University Press, 1987.

Williams, Anne. *Prophetic Strain: The Greater Lyric in the Eighteenth Century.* Chicago: University of Chicago Press, 1984.

Williams, John. *Wordsworth: romantic poetry and revolution politics.* Manchester: Manchester University Press, 1989.

Williams, Raymond. *Culture and Society, 1780–1950.* 1958; rpt. New York: Harper and Row, Publishers, 1966.

Wordsworth, Jonathan. *The Music of Humanity: A Critical Study of Wordsworth's RUINED COTTAGE.* New York: Harper and Row, Publishers, 1969.

Wordsworth, William. *Descriptive Sketches.* Ed. Eric Birdsall. Ithaca: Cornell University Press, 1984.

————. *An Evening Walk.* Ed. James Averill. Ithaca: Cornell University Press, 1984.

————. *The Poems.* Ed. John O. Hayden. New Haven: Yale University Press, 1981.

————. *Poems, in Two Volumes, and Other Poems, 1800–1807.* Ed. Jared Curtis. Ithaca: Cornell University Press, 1983.

————. *The Poetical Works of William Wordsworth.* Volumes I-V. Ed. Ernest de Selincourt and Helen Darbishire. Oxford: Clarendon Press, 1940–49.

————. *The Prelude, 1798–1799.* Ed. Stephen Parrish. Ithaca: Cornell University Press, 1977.

————. *The Prose Works of William Wordsworth.* Ed. W. J. B. Owen and Jane Worthington Smyser. Oxford: Clarendon Press, 1974.

————. *The Ruined Cottage and The Pedlar.* Ed. James Butler. Ithaca: Cornell University Press, 1979.

————. *The Salisbury Plain Poems.* Ed. Stephen Gill. Ithaca: Cornell University Press, 1975.

Wordsworth, William and Dorothy. *The Letters of William and Dorothy Wordsworth.* Volumes I-VII. Ed. Ernest De Selincourt. Rev. Ed. Alan G. Hill. Second revised edition; Oxford: Clarendon Press, 1967–1988.

Ziff, Larzer. *Writing in the New World: Prose, Print, and Politics in the Early United States.* New Haven: Yale University Press, 1991.

Zwarg, Christina. *Feminist Conversations: Fuller, Emerson, and the Play of Reading.* Ithaca: Cornell University Press, 1995.

Index